BATTLEGROUND

THE MEDIA

BATTLEGROUND

THE MEDIA

VOLUME 2 (O–Z)

Edited by Robin Andersen and Jonathan Gray

GREENWOOD PRESS
Westport, Connecticut • London

Library of Congress Cataloging-in-Publication Data

Battleground: the media / edited by Robin Andersen and Jonathan Gray.
    p. cm. — (Battleground)
  Includes bibliographical references and index.
  ISBN 978–0–313–34167–0 (alk. paper)
  1. Mass media—Political aspects.   I. Andersen, Robin.   II. Gray, Jonathan (Jonathan Alan).
P95.8.B38 2008
302.23—dc22   2007032454

British Library Cataloguing in Publication Data is available.

Library of Congress Catalog Card Number: 2007032454
ISBN: 978–0–313–34167–0 (set)
      978–0–313–34168–79 (vol. 1)
      978–0–313–34169–4 (vol. 2)

First published in 2008

Greenwood Press, 88 Post Road West, Westport, CT 06881
An imprint of Greenwood Publishing Group, Inc.
www.greenwood.com

Printed in the United States of America

∞™

The paper used in this book complies with the
Permanent Paper Standard issued by the National
Information Standards Organization (Z39.48–1984).

10 9 8 7 6 5 4 3 2 1

CONTENTS

GUIDE TO RELATED TOPICS

OBSCENITY AND INDECENCY

Areas that have challenged the media's right to freedom of speech have long revolved around issues of human sexuality, and expressions and language that violate standards of taste and decency. The history of censoring sexually explicit scenes considered to violate standards of decency goes back to the early days of film. As social mores and community standards have evolved over the years, so too have legal protections and the definition of what is acceptable and what is not on television, radio, and film. The changes in Federal Communications Commission (FCC) policy brought about by the wardrobe malfunction that exposed Janet Jackson's breast during her halftime performance with Justine Timberlake illustrate that these topics remain battleground issues for the media.

OBSCENITY

Given our Puritan heritage, the long history of battles fought over the definition of obscenity, and the measures taken to stop it, should come as no surprise. Under British law in the time of the monarchies, sexually explicit writings and images were considered "obscene libel," and were outlawed. When the Puritans left Britain to pursue religious freedom, they brought their codes of sexual modesty and chastity with them. Hundreds of years later, despite the Sexual Revolution of the 1960s, America remains a country in which depictions of nudity and sexuality make many uncomfortable and are frequently met with calls for sanction or censorship. Despite the fact that the First Amendment provides for the separation of Church and State, this is one area in which religious beliefs about sexuality and sin have consistently spilled over into the realm of law.

Throughout the nineteenth and twentieth centuries, both the federal and state governments passed laws to stop the flow of material considered to be obscene or indecent. In 1842 Congress passed the first antiobscenity statutes, barring the "importation of all indecent and obscene prints, paintings, lithographs, engravings and transparencies." This statute was amended numerous times to include photographs, films, and phonograph records. The Comstock Act of 1873 made it illegal to use the U.S. postal system to distribute obscenity. At that time, "obscenity" was defined as material that has a "tendency to deprave and corrupt those whose minds are open to such immoral influences." This broad definition was used by both the U.S. Customs office and U.S. Postal Service to ban such works as Walt Whitman's *Leaves of Grass*, James Joyce's *Ulysses*, and Ernest Hemingway's *For Whom the Bell Tolls*.

With the arrival of cinema in the early twentieth century, efforts to stop the flow of erotic imagery in this country intensified. City and state censorship boards sprung up around the country to prohibit the exhibition of films containing sexually explicit scenes. In 1915, the Supreme Court upheld the practice of these censorship boards, arguing that film was not covered under the First Amendment. This gave the green light to film censorship all over America. In response, the movie studios banded together in the 1930s to adopt the Hays Code, a set of self-imposed decency standards designed to "clean up" Hollywood and protect the studios from the loss of revenue caused by local censorship. These standards were later abandoned when the Supreme Court reversed its original position on cinema, granting the medium First Amendment protection in 1952.

By the middle of the twentieth century, as sexual mores began to change, an increasing number of court cases began to challenge the various antiobscenity statutes around the country. Finally, in a series of rulings, the Supreme Court developed a legal definition for the obscenity (see "Defining Obscenity" sidebar). Once they had defined this category of speech, they ruled that any form of communication meeting the criteria of obscenity is *not* protected by the First Amendment. This means that federal or state laws banning obscenity do not violate the First Amendment. Because of the great variety of sexual and moral standards throughout our country, the Supreme Court left it up to the states to determine if, and to what extent, they would ban obscene communication.

Ironically, the issue of obscenity is one of those rare topics that has the power to unite political activists from both ends of the political spectrum. Conservative voters often express concern about obscenity on the basis of the threat that they feel it poses to the family. On the other hand, some liberals are also concerned about obscenity, arguing that pornography contributes to violence against women. Here we see that calls for censorship can come from both the right and the left, sometimes on the very same issue, even if for very different reasons.

The development of new communication technologies has greatly complicated the issue of obscenity in our country. In 1957, when first defining obscenity, the Supreme Court included the "contemporary community standards" clause into the definition in an attempt to take into consideration the reality that

DEFINING OBSCENITY

The legal definition of obscenity was developed in a series of Supreme Court cases, most notably *Roth v. U.S.*, 1957, and *Miller v. California*, 1974. Currently, in order for a piece of mediated communication to be considered obscene—and therefore lacking First Amendment protection—the following conditions must be met:

1. An average person, applying contemporary local community standards, finds that the work, taken as a whole, appeals to prurient interest. (The legal definition of "prurient interest" is as follows: a morbid, degrading, and unhealthy interest in sex, as distinguished from a mere candid interest in sex.)
2. The work depicts in a patently offensive way sexual conduct specifically defined by applicable state law.
3. The work in question lacks serious literary, artistic, political, or scientific value.

American sexual and moral standards vary widely by locale. Yet, new means of transmitting sexual imagery have rendered this standard difficult to apply. When a small town decides that they don't want pornographic magazines in their local bookstore, residents seeking such material have the option of buying it in a larger city, where fewer restrictions exist. But whose values should determine the national standards regarding "taboo" material for electronic media? The Internet allows for the transmission of explicit imagery to anyone with a computer, regardless of where they live, making it very difficult to set or enforce obscenity or indecency laws governing computer communication. Each time a new communication technology is invented, providing new ways to disseminate controversial content, our national commitment to freedom of speech is tested once again. Given the political and religious diversity of our country, the continuing development of communication technologies, and the ever-popular nature of sexually explicit media content, the issue of free speech and obscenity is sure to continue challenging future generations of Americans.

INDECENCY

In addition to American concerns about sexually explicit media content, our nation also has a long history of identifying certain words and images as taboo, and therefore off-limits in "polite society." At one time in our nation's history, social convention served as an effective censor of "vulgar" language or gestures, and most people were willing to abide by the unwritten rules of convention. With the many social changes of the late twentieth century, these rules, like so many others, were gradually tested. Because both radio and television are regulated by the U.S. government, these channels of communication have been the terrain on which the debate about the boundaries of propriety has taken place.

The FCC, which sets the rules governing our broadcasting system, has defined indecency as "language or material that, in context, depicts or describes, in terms patently offensive as measured by contemporary community standards for the broadcast medium, sexual or excretory organs or activities." Indecent programming contains patently offensive sexual or excretory material that does not rise to the level of obscenity. Since obscenity lacks First Amendment protection, it cannot be broadcast on the public airwaves. Indecent speech, on the other hand, is covered by the First Amendment, and thus cannot be barred from the airwaves entirely. This poses a dilemma: how can a free society balance the rights of adults to consume adult-oriented material with the goal of shielding children from language or imagery that some feel is inappropriate for young audiences?

The solution, as devised by the FCC, in response to several key Supreme Court rulings, is known as the "safe harbor" provision, which prohibits the broadcasting of indecent material between the hours of 6:00 A.M. and 10:00 P.M. Broadcast companies, stations, and on-air personalities violating this rule are subject to fines. Like the laws prohibiting obscenity, rules restricting indecency are inconsistently enforced, with great fluctuations depending upon the political/religious climate predominating in the nation at any particular time. When our nation is in a more conservative period, greater concern is expressed about the transmission of such material.

The fines imposed on broadcasters by the FCC for indecency violations were, at one time, set at a relatively low rate of several thousand dollars per incident, and only rarely enforced. This changed significantly following an incident involving singers Janet Jackson and Justin Timberlake, in which Ms. Jackson's breast was inadvertently exposed to a national audience watching the CBS television coverage of the half-time performance of the 2004 Super Bowl. In response to the tremendous public outcry about the event, particularly from conservative viewers, Congress and the FCC raised the indecency fines to over 20 times their original level. Viacom, then owners of the CBS network, were fined a record-breaking $550,000 for airing the incident, despite the fact that all parties involved claimed that the "wardrobe malfunction" had been an accident.

During the same period, "shock-jock" radio personality Howard Stern, long famous for his "off-color" language and humor, became a target for public concerns about indecency on the airwaves. Clear Channel Communications, the national radio chain that had carried Stern's syndicated program, dropped him from their program line-up after being charged heavy fines for airing his material. In a move clearly designed to send a strong message, the FCC also issued fines of over half a million dollars to Stern himself for violating restrictions on broadcasting indecency. Some critics at the time argued that the real reason for the strong stand taken against Stern was that the radio personality had begun to use his airtime to criticize President Bush.

Whether it was indecency or politics that turned Stern into a target, it was a new communication technology that provided the "solution." In a development that illustrates the power of new media to allow "taboo" messages to bypass existing restrictions on controversial speech, Howard Stern moved from broadcast to satellite radio, which, at the time of this writing, is not governed by content restrictions on indecency.

THE COMMUNICATIONS DECENCY ACT

The Communications Decency Act attempted to introduce a wide range of broadcasting-type controls on the Internet. When the act passed into law on February 1, 1996, as part of the Telecommunications Reform Act, it met with protest from a broad range of groups promoting freedom of speech, from the American Civil Liberties Union to the Electronic Frontier Foundation (EFF). The EFF launched a blue ribbon campaign calling for Internet users to protest the legislation by displaying the anticensorship blue ribbon on their Web pages.

Critics charged that the Communications Decency Act was one of the most restrictive forms of censorship applied in the United States and that it turned the Internet from one of the most free forums for speech to one of the most tightly regulated. The Act made it a crime to knowingly transmit any communication accessible to minors that could be considered "obscene, lewd, lascivious, filthy, or indecent." It also prevented any publicity of abortion services. Publishers of offending material could be prosecuted, but also those who distribute it—Internet service providers. In an attempt to avoid prosecution, they may have had to act as private censors. The penalty was a sentence of up to two years in prison and a $100,000 fine.

By June 1996, a three-judge panel in Philadelphia ruled that the Act was unnecessarily broad in its scope, violating constitutional guarantees to freedom of speech. The Act also infringed on privacy rights by empowering federal agencies to intervene in, for example, the sending of private e-mail between individuals.

On June 26, 1997, the U.S. Supreme Court agreed with the district court judges that the Act was unconstitutional. The judges pointed out, in part, that TV and radio were originally regulated because of the scarcity of room in the airwaves, which is not true of the Internet. The judges stated that the concern to protect children "does not justify an unnecessarily broad suppression of speech addressed to adults. As we have explained, the Government may not 'reduc[e] the adult population...to...only what is fit for children.'"

After the Communications Decency Act was struck down, new legislation was passed, the Children's Internet Protection Act (CIPA). The federal statute requires Internet blocking of speech that is obscene, or "harmful to minors," in all schools and libraries receiving certain federal funding. CIPA, also known as the Internet Blocking Law, was also challenged. The EFF charged that the law damages the free speech rights of library patrons and Web publishers.

On June 23, 2003, the Supreme Court upheld CIPA. The court found that the use of Internet blocking, also known as filtering, is constitutional because the need for libraries to prevent minors from accessing obscene materials outweighs the free speech rights of library patrons and Web site publishers. However, many independent research studies show that Internet blocking software is incapable of blocking only the materials required by CIPA. The CIPA law is problematic because speech that is harmful to minors is still legal for adults, and not all library patrons are minors.

CONCLUSION

Debates regarding obscenity and indecency are so heavily charged because they speak to core values and behavioral norms by which various groups and individuals expect or demand others to live. Thus, for instance, gay and lesbian literature, film, and television have often been coded as obscene or indecent when judged from a conservatively heteronormative value system, resulting in parental warnings being attached to programs that in any way mention, much less depict, gay or lesbian sexuality. Even medical terminology remains obscene and/or indecent to some, especially in media that is available to children. This poses the significant problem to regulators and producers of determining a standard definition of "obscenity" and "indecency," and predictably entails outrage and activism on behalf of those who disagree with the standard of the moment.

As the reactions to obscenity and indecency change with varying levels of severity, as rules and conventions ebb and flow, and as ever-developing media technologies introduce new battlegrounds, so too will our definitions of what should and should not be said or shown change in the future. Obscenity and indecency are likely to form the substance of many a debate long into the future, as we use media depictions and imagery as the fodder for vigorous discussion over what constitutes appropriate behavior both inside and outside of the media.

See also Gay, Lesbian, Bisexual, Transgendered, and Queer Representations on TV; Government Censorship and Freedom of Speech; Media and the Crisis of Values; Media Reform; Pornography; Regulating the Airwaves; Representations of Women; Shock Jocks; Youth and Media.

Further Reading: Bernstein, Matthew. *Controlling Hollywood: Censorship and Regulation in the Studio Era*. New Brunswick, NJ: Rutgers University Press, 1999; Heins, Marjorie. *Not in Front of the Children: "Indecency," Censorship, and the Innocence of Youth*. New York: Hill and Wang, 2001; Hilliard, Robert L., and Michael C. Keith. *Dirty Discourse: Sex and Indecency in Broadcasting*, 2nd ed. Malden, MA: Blackwell, 2007; Leff, Leonard J. *The Dame in the Kimono: Hollywood, Censorship, and the Production Code*. Lexington: University Press of Kentucky, 2001; Lipshultz, Jeremy H. *Broadcast Indecency: FCC Regulation and the First Amendment*. Newton, MA: Focus Press, 1997; Sandler, Kevin. *The Naked Truth: Why Hollywood Does Not Make NC-17 Films*. New Brunswick, NJ: Rutgers University Press, 2006; Sova, Dawn B. *Forbidden Films: Censorship Histories of 125 Motion Pictures*. New York: Facts on File, 2001.

Gwenyth Jackaway

ONLINE DIGITAL FILM AND TELEVISION

As the distribution of film and television becomes increasingly available through the Internet in digital form, it continues to influence the modes of production, business models, marketing, cultural practices, and meaning creation that surround the consumption of the new products. The current conflicts that are being negotiated between public and private space, programming and on-demand consumption, sharing and piracy, and corporate control and publicity are also part of a much longer history of film and television distribution of the postwar era.

Online video, both downloaded or streaming, has become a widely practiced form of film and television consumption. The term "online video" generally refers to video received over an Internet connection through the use of a browser or other video application. The relatively new method of distribution and exhibition, in conjunction with the increasing affordability of digital video for production, also has changed the definition of what constitutes film, television, or entertainment online. Consumers of online visual media watch a range that includes pirated movies, professional or home-recorded television shows, home movies, music videos, amateur or "independent" films, and so on. Because of the broad, growing, and free (with an Internet connection) selection of "shows," various media corporations assess whether to fight the new modes of production to consumption (in the form of lawsuits) or embrace them (as opportunities for publicity).

QUALITY ENTERTAINMENT

The battles currently being fought often reiterate the history of film against television, quality versus content, and public space versus private. From the mid-1950s to 1960s, primarily in the United States and parts of Europe, television overtook film as the primary vehicle for visual entertainment. Although viewers had to watch small, black-and-white screens, they enjoyed the free entertainment brought to their homes (once they invested in the set). As Hollywood saw its viewership and revenue drop, many of the major studios invested in productions that would be differentiated from television's low quality: widescreen color spectaculars such as *Ben-Hur* (1959). Similar to early television, online video continue to be a low-resolution and small-screen medium, a quality still necessary to make download times invisible to the viewer. One of the first applications for streaming video was RealVideo, first released in 1997 as part of a media player application, RealPlayer. Upgraded from an earlier audio-only product, the new RealPlayer provided low-grade video during a time when most Internet consumers were using telephone modems with low bandwidth connections of 14.4 or 28.8 kilobytes per second. By the early 2000s, streaming video has been taken over by the dominant PC penetration of Flash Player–based playback technology (started by San Francisco company Macromedia), which has had greater success at embedding video within a Web page and, consequently, has played a part in the explosively successful practice of online video sharing on Web sites such as YouTube.

Like the battle between the quality theater screen versus the black-and-white television (and quality Beta videotapes versus VHS during the video age), currently there is some division between the television screen and the computer monitor. On one end, some television set manufacturers create product differentiation by following the path of the home theater from the 1980s, emphasizing large screens, high-fidelity sound systems, and, in the 2000s, high-definition images. On the opposite end of the spectrum, manufacturers have taken notice

YOUTUBE

From 2005 to 2007, YouTube has become the most extensively used video sharing Web site for users to become both online media creators and consumers. YouTube's service is a Web site where visitors can upload and share their own digital video clips as well as watch others' contributions.

The company was founded and developed in 2005 in Menlo Park, California, by three friends who also found investments from a venture capital firm. In just over a year, YouTube's success made it a hot commodity that was eventually fetched by Internet search engine and advertising company, Google Inc., for $1.65 billion in Google's stock. The site's success can be attributed to various reasons such as the spreading availability of broadband by 2005, the founders' astute understanding of the emerging market of sites such as MySpace, and the existing penetration of Macromedia's Flash Player 7 in PCs.

It is YouTube's policy to forbid uploaded content that constitutes copyright infringement, but in practice this is not stringently policed. By late 2006 and into 2007, the company had taken measures to survey more closely and prohibit piracy. Once put into full effect, it remains to be seen how much this will influence traffic to the site, since a good portion of viewers visit the site to share user-recorded selections. Other than copyrighted materials, YouTube prohibits other content such as pornography or the glamorization of criminal conduct.

---

of the fact that there is a significant consumer base for low-grade media distribution given the wide popularity of Flash Player for online video and the relative success of portable media devices such as DVD players and video iPods. As of the publication of this entry, the gap between the TV set and computer monitor is nearly closed as LCD monitors and flat-panel television sets are designed to perform similar or the same functions. Cable providers work to control the broadband Internet market as well as offer Internet access through the cable TV user interface. Computer and operating system manufacturers are offering home theater or media PCs that come ready with TV tuner cards, personal video recorder (PVR) software, DVD drives, and remote controls. As a result, viewers often use one screen for many of the same purposes, such as browsing the Internet with their computers, watching DVDs off of a DVD player or a DVD drive on their computers, and watching streaming media through their browsers or through digital cable.

IN-HOME AND ON-DEMAND VIDEO

One quality of online video that differentiates it from television (both broadcast and general cable) is its availability at all times and in almost all locations. Viewers with broadband Internet access can visit a site such as YouTube and watch TV episodes when they want and as many times as they want. With the increasing use of high-speed connections and wireless routers in the home, viewers can also move about their houses with portable computers and not be tied down to the location where the larger and immobile TV set resides. In metropolitan areas, Wi-Fi connections are becoming increasingly available for free or for purchase in cafes, public areas, and trains, making it possible for users with laptops or other portable Wi-Fi devices to access online video in public locations as well. Steps also have been taken to make Wi-Fi access possible during air travel as well as make video viewable on mobile phones.

The success of on-demand video is part of a history of in-home visual media consumption marked first by the success of television over the movie theater and then by the mass-market spread of video rentals in the 1980s. Consumers responded positively to the opportunity to see a movie at home rather than see it on the big theater screen at a higher price. With the introduction of thinner and lighter DVD technology, by the late 1990s, it became possible to establish different business models such as that of Netflix, an online DVD rental service that sends discs to customers by mail. This business and cultural model further focused attention on the home because the spectator did not even need to leave the home to access a copy of a movie. This cultural practice, however, has been challenged by the other component of the on-demand concept—spontaneity— which is still an advantage of traditional video rental stores. Consumers who cannot wait for movies to arrive by mail or who prefer to decide on a movie on the spot will still choose to go to a rental shop rather than use an online DVD rental service.

Both qualities of delivering selection directly to the viewer and the spontaneity of on-demand service were part of a broader concept of video-on-demand (VOD) that has been in development since the 1990s and in wider practice in the 2000s. While media services such as YouTube and Movielink realize VOD online where media can be downloaded or streamed, cable television providers have been developing digital cable to realize the ability to offer movies and shows on demand. Comcast, the largest cable provider in the United States, began offering Digital Cable On-Demand in 2001, a service that allows subscribers to watch a selection of movies for free or for pay and to select, play, pause, rewind, and fast-forward the movie as if using a VCR or DVD player. Online, a similar viewer experience is available on sites such as archive.org for free and several other sites for pay. The initiative to create services such as this has come from the development of VOD, but also from the competitive success of TiVo, which since 1999 tapped into a user experience that viewers readily embraced with usage and subscriptions. TiVo offered a digital video recorder with an electronic programming guide and user interface that acclimated users to a VOD paradigm before broadband was developed in the early 2000s. With it, viewers could choose, record, and play back programs with ease. Online video consumption is also shifting as consumers increasingly are using video game consoles as digital video recorders and some are subscribing to services that allow viewers to access their recordings online from any Internet-connected computer or laptop.

KEY HISTORICAL DEVELOPMENTS

May 1975: Sony launches Betamax for home video in Japan.

October 1985: Blockbuster Video opens its first store and enters the existing video rental business. Within the next year, the company grows into a multibillion dollar international video rental chain.

January 1988: Sony concedes defeat of its Betamax line and begins production of VHS recorders.

December 1996: Macromedia releases Flash 1.0.

February 1997: RealVideo debuts as part of RealPlayer 4.0, the first streaming video application offered by the company, Progressive Networks.

August 1997: TiVo, Inc. is created and in a year releases its first trial boxes.

April 1998: Netflix begins operations.

January 2000: Homestar Runner debuts as an online Flash cartoon.

2001: Comcast launches its first rollout of Digital Cable On-Demand over the course of the year. The rollout continues across North America over the course of several years.

February 2005: YouTube is created.

July 2005: FCC reports that subscribership to high-speed services for Internet access increases by 34 percent in 2004 to 37.9 million lines in service.

December 2005: "Lazy Sunday" is aired and is spread virally through YouTube. Hits exceed 5 million by February 2006.

June 2006: "Lonelygirl15" debuts on YouTube.

November 2006: Google finalizes the purchase of YouTube for $1.65 billion of Google's stock.

December 2006: NBC releases "Dick in a Box" on YouTube. Hits exceed 20 million by spring 2007.

March 2007: Millward Brown survey reports Flash reaches 97.3 percent of Internet-connected PCs.

CULTURAL AND BUSINESS PRACTICES

The cultural practices that drive many of the above business models and technological innovations also mutate as services and restrictions are delineated by the various industries. Many user communities celebrate the opportunities to connect with media content and other users, opportunities that are not available in movie theaters or on television. For example, fans of old European movies can share their copies through peer-to-peer file sharing sites, diasporic Asian communities can watch the most recent television episodes from their homelands through bit torrent, and viewers from different countries can share international shows within a browser (from Turkish news on YouTube to *South Park* on Comedy Central.com). Many of these practices that have brought users together and communities closer to their homelands are opposed by media corporations because of the unmeasured or pirated nature of the shared media and consumption.

Some corporations not only battle the dissemination of copyrighted materials being distributed by users, but also oppose a type of user-created programming. In the same way that friends and communities shared mixed audio cassette tapes in the 1980s and 1990s (songs arranged and "programmed" for a target audience), online video sharing sites such as YouTube give users the chance to gather their own selection of clips on personal pages. The pages showcase their personal user-created content as well as videos collected from other sources with the intention often being, as with MySpace pages, to program media that defines the tastes and interests of the page owner. As a result, these user pages can be bookmarked to target their own audiences who migrate to their programming. For instance, users whose interests range as widely as political campaign materials, parkour demos, geriatric video blogs, and up-to-the-minute episodes of *American Idol* can go to their favorite sites to one-stop shop for the latest entries. Frequently, the amateur programmers who offer these video content sites edit out commercials or mix together free and copyrighted material, a characteristic that viewers usually enjoy and that concerns broadcasting companies. Activists such as Stanford Law Professor Lawrence Lessig and scholar/musician Paul Miller (aka DJ Spooky) speak out publicly in support of creative rights and against copyright legislation that they believe unconstitutionally inhibits the progress of science and useful arts.

Some independent online productions have found particular success from the cultural phenomenon of "viral video," which addresses the traffic that a particular video clip or video producer attracts through word of mouth, Internet sharing, and community-based popularity and aggregator sites such as Digg and Netvibes. Within weeks or just hours, a popular video on YouTube can spread internationally through the above "viral" networks of individual users and community sites sharing the video clip. Often the popularity of a video is a one-time sharing experience; in other cases, it can lead to the continued success of a strong fan base as has happened with, for instance, Flash-based online cartoon Homestar Runner and the fictional serial webcam video blog, Lonelygirl15.

These operations were started by individual or group artists who looked to the Internet as a positive outlet for distribution and attention. Many corporations, on the other hand, have been more wary and slower to catch on. One example of corporate reaction to viral videos is the explosive success of "Lazy Sunday," a comical music video that was featured on a December 2005 episode of NBC's *Saturday Night Live* (*SNL*). Fans downloaded and shared several copies of the video on YouTube until the number of hits exceeded 5 million by February 2006. NBC's response at that point was to demand the removal of all user-added copies of the video from YouTube. Since then, NBC has tried to find a balance and to use YouTube to attract and measure their viewership. The broadcasting company set up its own branded presence on YouTube and was more prepared for the success of its next *SNL* Christmas video, "Dick in a Box," which it not only posted on YouTube but also touted as the version that could not be aired on the FCC-controlled broadcast television. This move showed how corporations like NBC were attempting to capture the same sort of success realized by independent viral video producers and they were working within a rhetoric of "the director's cut."

More versatile media companies have made use of viral video to get in touch with their viewers and to gain attention for their products. For instance, cable stations such as Viacom-owned Comedy Central have taken opportunities to use the Internet to interact with viewers and to initiate culture-producing activities. Comedy Central (after having pulled most of its content from YouTube) offers almost all episodes of its popular *The Daily Show with Jon Stewart* and *The Colbert Report* on its Web site edited in much the way that fans edit clips for sharing on YouTube. Comedian Stephen Colbert has called upon his viewers to contribute erroneous information on the collaborative Web encyclopedia, Wikipedia, as well as offered a "green screen challenge," for which viewers could use green screen footage from his visit to Skywalker Ranch to contribute their own movies on YouTube. In a similar vein, the marketers of the 2006 movie *Snakes on a Plane* included an online contest to which groups could submit their own short movies based on the ad-lib, "[Animal] on a [mode of transportation]." Finally, some movie distributors have purposely fed corrupted versions of movies into bit torrent communities so that user-pirated movies, once shared and opened, do not show the expected movie. Porn video companies have made use of the model but to their advantage; they send out files mistitled as mainstream movies that, once downloaded and opened, show pornography and feature their Web site addresses to attract more traffic.

Online film and television has just started its first wave of popularity. It remains to be seen how the media and the online communities will continue to grow in the future and how corporations will shut down or work with pirated material that is shared between peers.

See also À La Carte Cable Pricing; Alternative Media in the United States; Digital Divide; The DVD; Internet and Its Radical Potential; News Satire; Online Publishing; Piracy and Intellectual Property; TiVo; Transmedia Storytelling and Media Franchises; User-Created Content and Audience Participation.

Further Reading: Davis, Joshua. "The Secret World of Lonelygirl15." *Wired* 14, no. 12 (December 2006): 232–39; Follansbee, Joe. *Get Streaming!: Quick Steps to Delivering Audio and Video Online*. Burlington, MA: Focal, 2004; Garfield, Bob. "The YouTube Effect." *Wired* 14, no. 12 (December 2006): 222–27; Jenkins, Henry. *Convergence Culture: When Old and New Media Collide*. New York: NYU Press, 2006; Keen, Andrew. *The Cult of the Amateur: How Today's Internet Is Killing Our Culture*. New York: Currency, 2007; Kharif, O. "Online Video: Next Stop, Nasdaq?" Business Week, September 27, 2006. http://www.businessweek.com/technology/content/sep2006/tc20060927_385661.htm; Lessig, Lawrence. *Free Culture: The Nature and Future of Creativity*. New York: Penguin, 2005; Levy, S. "Lawrence Lessig's Supreme Showdown." *Wired* 10, no. 10 (October 2002). http://www.wired.com/wired/archive/10.10/lessig.html; Mullaney, T. J. "Netflix: The Mail-Order Movie House that Clobbered Blockbuster." Business Week, May 25, 2006. http://www.businessweek.com/smallbiz/content/may2006/sb20060525_268860.htm; Rayburn, Dan, and Michael Hoch. *The Business of Streaming and Digital Media*. Burlington, MA: Focal, 2005; Shalat, Andrew. *How to Do Everything with Online Video*. New York: McGraw-Hill Osborne Media, 2007.

Tamao Nakahara

ONLINE PUBLISHING

The introduction of new do-it-yourself (DIY) digital publishing software and the emergence of online communities engaged in both creative and collective-intelligence endeavors have created new opportunities for—and raised new concerns about—public expression and the circulation of knowledge. Contemporary debates about online publishing raise important questions about who should have the right to determine/police access, accuracy, creativity, ownership, reliability, and value in a networked era and they point to the changing roles, standards, and styles of reading and writing in American society and around the globe.

THE DEBATES

On the one hand, there are those who see user-friendly online publishing tools—blogs, wikis, Web video—as contributing to the emergence of new modes of multimediated, nonlinear, and interactive writing that provide new creative freedoms and possibilities for artistic and public expression. These same tools and platforms also potentially provide opportunities for historically marginalized communities to gain voices by circumventing traditional publishing routes that had previously ignored or misrepresented them, or spoken on their behalf. All of these possibilities are championed as both challenging the status quo by redefining who has the right to publish and whose voices have the rights to be heard as well as contributing to new democratic possibilities for exchanging ideas. On the other hand, critiques of digital publishing have ranged from the reactionary to the critical. While some complain about a decline in standards for both writing and reading—of poor grammar, inaccurate and "undesirable" information, and an erosion of expertise—others point to the limitations imposed on true creative and public expression by transnational corporations threatening to prosecute perceived intellectual property and digital copyright infringements (more reactionary voices have pointed to the increased opportunities for intellectual property theft that accompany digital publishing endeavors). Additionally, critics have argued that the creators of Web 2.0 and other writer-friendly technologies continue to set the standards by which these technologies can be used and narrowly define modes of creative expression. Moreover, opportunities for participating in these new publishing worlds are still hampered by a digital divide that limits both access to technologies and knowledge of how to use them. In this regard, the Internet still remains largely a domain for middle-class white men.

CREATIVE FREEDOMS

One of the key debates concerning digital publishing has been the degree and types of new creative freedoms it affords both professional and nonprofessional writers (even as these same technologies blur distinctions between professional and nonprofessional writing). Arguably, free online software and services like Blogger, Drupal, and Wordpress allow users to easily create, customize, and manage their own Web sites, blogs, and other multimedia projects. Coupled with collaborative open-source code sharing initiatives and emerging DIY cultural attitudes, these technologies are imagined as encouraging experimentation with new forms of online publishing while also lowering the entry bar for technologically disinclined users by providing quick, easy, and affordable (in many instances, free) access to avenues of creative production for anybody with Internet access.

Digital editing software like Adobe Premiere, FinalCut Pro, or Windows Movie Maker make it easy to create original films without film processing costs or (much) technical know how. These same software programs also allow users to play with and rearrange existing media materials into parodies, thematic compilations, and mash-ups that combine distinct media sources—such as clips from the ABC series *Desperate Housewives* and Madonna's "Material Girl"—in order to generate something new, occasionally critical, but always meaning-altering. Video hosting sites like YouTube, Veoh, or Vimeo make such creations available to large numbers of online users, who are free to comment and must—consciously or not—incorporate these new possibilities into their lexicon of available meanings and understandings for existing media texts and how they are expected to engage with them.

Additionally, digital technologies and software open up new opportunities for online publishing that are at once multimediated and nonlinear. Online writing initiatives can easily combine text, video, audio, and animation fields in nonderivative ways that allow new types of stories to be told where each mode of writing adds something new to the overall meaning or means of engaging with the piece. Hyperlinks and trackbacks permit pieces to be written (and read) in nonlinear ways, much like a puzzle that has more than one way of being correctly assembled, offering multiple directions and interconnections, each producing new overall meanings that emerge based on the ways the different parts have been assembled.

The popularization of online blogs has redrawn the lines between public and private forms of writing, providing open forums for writers to share personal experiences and opinions, anecdotes and impressions, with the possibility of receiving feedback from readers they have never met about their innermost thoughts and feelings. These same spaces can also serve as sites of critical discourse and deliberation outside of officially sanctioned channels, offering original and filtered entertainment reviews and political commentary. In some instances, amateur critics like Harry Knowles at AintItCoolNews.com have gained semiprofessional recognition because of the popularity of their Web sites. Web sites like TelevisionWithoutPity.com have marketed themselves as offering snarky fan-written reviews of popular television series even though the majority of writers for the site are paid freelance journalists.

Online publishing endeavors also allow historically marginalized communities a public voice and community-building network that bypasses traditional publication and publicity channels that have previously either ignored or misrepresented them, or spoken on their behalf. While Web sites dedicated to creating works of fiction and reporting news that address gay, lesbian, bisexual, and transsexual (GLBT) communities (and offer new opportunities for the general public to engage and learn about issues that concern this community) provide positive outlets for expression, online publishing also offers the same expressive opportunities for those promoting hate speech and bigotry.

Meanwhile, fan fiction sites have emerged as consumers have claimed the rights to create original stories based on their favorite media texts and make them publicly available. Fans of the series *Lois & Clark: The New Adventures of Superman* wrote an entire fifth season for a series that ABC cancelled after four. Often, fan stories focus on character relationships, plot devices, or thematic concerns that are only tangentially addressed in the official text and are, therefore, not derivatives, but (unofficial) extensions of a story world originally created by others. These online publishing initiatives raise important questions about both who has the right to tell stories about popular but privately owned heroes and which stories count in terms of the overall meanings accrued by particular characters. Why does fiction about Batman written by GLBT fans not count as canonical even when it might be more innovative than the officially sanctioned stories commissioned by Time Warner Incorporated and DC Comics?

CREATIVE CONSTRAINTS

The creative freedoms potentially offered through online publishing possibilities must first overcome cultural, economic, and legal constraints in order to truly revolutionize how writing transpires. As the example of unsolicited fan fiction suggests, questions over ownership, fair use, and intellectual property violation pose real obstacles for creative engagement with popular culture. Fan sites face threats of legal action from intellectual property owners, particularly when fan art, fiction, and other community activities take the story in unapproved directions that challenge dominant cultural assumptions of good taste and morality as well as profits.

While fan art and fiction can be argued to constitute fair use of copyrighted materials, the uneven economic grounds upon which fans and owners do battle regularly favors the latter, who can—and have—dragged "violators" into court, forcing them to incur large legal expenses. These threats continue to deter creative expression even if they are legally permitted under fair-use statutes. Even when creators are willing to assert their fair-use rights, popular hosting sites typically espouse conservatism when it comes to threats of copyright violation. YouTube regularly yields to the demands of media owners to remove questionable materials, making it increasingly difficult for online publishing endeavors to find an audience or home in which to grow.

Creativity may also be constrained by the very tools provided for users to create online publications. Robert Schrag has argued that in assessing the creative opportunities generated by DIY technologies, it is necessary to consider the ways in which they already advantage certain modes of expression over others through the tool selection they provide and the tutorials they offer new users. Schrag suggests that these structures not only limit what counts as "allowable" creative expression, but also tend to "[nudge] the creative impulse toward the slippery slope of commodification," conflating creativity and consumerism. While user-generated Web content is largely believed to be noncommercial, the recent acquisition of YouTube by Google for $1.65 billion suggests that not-for-profit creative endeavors can be profitable for the corporations hosting such works.

Finally, creative freedom continues to be limited to those who have access to online publishing tools. According to the Pew Internet & American Life Project, as of June 2005, an estimated 65 million adult Americans, 32 percent of the U.S. population, do not have Internet access. These statistics are particularly revealing of discrepancies structured by age, class, race, disability, and education level. Thus, while online publishing offers possibilities for marginalized communities to express themselves, lack of access often reinforces existing publishing hierarchies that have traditionally limited their abilities to participate.

COLLECTIVE INTELLIGENCE

Another key debate about online publishing has focused on the emergence of collaborative communities working together to generate knowledge and information. Henry Jenkins has adapted Pierre Lévy's work on collective intelligence in describing how virtual communities "leverage the combined [individual] expertise of their members" toward a shared knowledge-building task. Online knowledge communities privilege aggregate knowledge production and evaluation through collective deliberation designed to reach democratic consensus on what should or should not count as valid and valued information. These processes are evident in how Wikipedia works, where an informal, voluntary community of thousands each put their individual knowledge to work in collaboratively building a public encyclopedia. In theory, anyone can add to, delete, correct, or update a Wikipedia entry—with all changes tracked and recorded for both historical documentation and collective deliberation. In this manner, the community works to self-correct and filter out inaccurate information (see "Wikipedia" sidebar).

Online publishing collaborations that seek to harness collective intelligence in building participatory knowledge communities challenge (or threaten, depending on who you ask) established models of expertise that sought to locate knowledge solely in the heads of individual credentialed masters. Knowledge communities not only potentially challenge hierarchies of who gets to claim expertise, but also what forms of knowledge ought to be prioritized. Thus, the collaborative online works generated through collective intelligence might be central to revitalizing democratic notions of participatory citizenship by offering alternate sources of information than those privileged by state, corporate, and other institutionally bound forms of knowledge built on the expert paradigm.

Of course, any claims that online publishing will restore the vitality of the American public sphere must take into account the continued digital divide that limits the number of participants—and therefore the number of subjects and approaches being articulated—within any collective knowledge formation. For

WIKIPEDIA

A wiki is a type of Web log (blog) that is collectively worked on by multiple authors. Created in 2001, Wikipedia is an online encyclopedia written and edited by thousands of volunteers spanning the globe. According to the Web site, as of March 2007, there were over 75,000 active contributors (though only about 1,000 or so regular ones) working on more than 5,300,000 articles in more than 100 languages (though English far eclipses any of the other languages represented with approximately 1,670,000 articles). Daily, an average of 4,000 new articles are added to the site, though nearly half of those are deleted that same day for lack of value, accuracy, or proper sourcing. There were over 38 million visitors to the site in December 2006 alone, making it the 13th most popular destination on the Internet and the third most popular news and information source, beating out CNN.com and Yahoo News.

Reading and Writing Wikipedia

Wikipedia's popularity has translated into the Web site's regular use by high school and college students researching term papers and even by the American judicial system. Over 100 judicial rulings—13 coming from the circuit court of appeals, one step below the Supreme Court—have relied on Wikipedia in reaching their verdicts. Such widespread use has also produced a backlash over concerns about the site's accuracy and verification standards. The site has been vandalized by intentional misinformation. An entry on John Seigenthaler, Sr. linked him to conspiracies about John F. Kennedy's assassination. Seigenthaler was the one to identify the hoax. The site faced further controversy when Wikipedia's founder, Jimmy Wales, violated the encyclopedia's ban on self-editing. Wales thrice removed information from his own entry concerning former partner Larry Sanger that played up the latter's role in founding Wikipedia.

In order to counter such problems, Wikipedia has recently adopted a more definitive editorial hierarchy, in which volunteer administrators have been given the authority to edit, remove, and prevent changes to particular articles. While the vast majority of articles remain open for anyone to edit, certain hotly contested or regularly hoaxed pieces are now protected or semiprotected (you must be a registered Wikipedia member for at least four days to edit a semiprotected piece) against changes. Amongst these entries are those on Albert Einstein, George W. Bush, Adolf Hitler, and Christina Aguilera. While implemented to ensure better quality control, protection practices reassert a hierarchy of expertise that Wikipedia's open-access structures supposedly challenge. Perhaps not surprisingly, many college professors refuse to let their students quote Wikipedia as a source. Others, however, see Wikipedia as an opportunity to get students involved in community-based knowledge-building initiatives.

---

example, the majority of Wikipedia's 1,025 entries in Swahili have been written by whites living in the United States because of a lack of access to computers in Africa. This raises important questions about who has the right to speak for whom and whether or not traditional power hierarchies structured along racial and geographical boundaries are being recreated online despite the community-generated ethos of collective intelligence endeavors.

Moreover, much online collective intelligence is not directed toward challenging the political or economic status quo, but in actively participating within consumer culture. Fan sites that seek to collectively decipher spoilers about their favorite media franchises or to map the complex continuity of comic book superheroes—though often critical of how fans or popular properties are being addressed/exploited by corporate ownership—rarely make the leap to demanding revolution. Still, such communities do require a reimagining of the historic relationship between producers and consumers where the latter are no longer passive recipients of cultural product but active participants in shaping the outcomes. As a result, many creators now see the cultivation of fan communities through online play (hinting at future directions) and conversation (usually through "informal" chats) and a demonstrated willingness to acknowledge fan desires and frustrations and occasionally act on them as strategic viral branding strategies for ensuring consumer loyalty.

Skeptics dismiss collective intelligence as producing inaccurate—even occasionally purposely misleading—information and lacking an organizational infrastructure that can properly guard against misinformation (hence the often dismissive stance taken by academics when students cite Wikipedia as a source). Greater concern, however, might be directed toward the ways online information is often passively consumed rather than collectively generated. Collective intelligence is premised on the notion of an active community that not only pools its resources, but works together to self-correct information. The extent to which visitors to Wikipedia (or even to fan spoiler sites) enter prepared to actively participate by questioning and debating the information provided or by bringing their own knowledge bases into conversation with what the site already provides is unclear.

See also Blogosphere; Digital Divide; Google Book Search; Internet and Its Radical Potential; Online Digital Film and Television; Piracy and Intellectual Property; Surveillance and Privacy; User-Created Content and Audience Participation.

Further Reading: Cohen, Noam. "African Languages Grow as a Wikipedia Presence." *New York Times,* August 26, 2006; Hafner, Katie. "Growing Wikipedia Revises 'Anyone Can Edit' Policy." *New York Times,* June 17, 2006; Hartley, John. "Laughs and Legends, or the Furniture that Glows? Television as History." *Flow: A Critical Forum on Television and Media Culture* 3, no. 5. http://jot.communication.utexas.edu/flow/?jot=view&id=1214; Jenkins, Henry. *Convergence Culture: Where Old and New Media Collide.* New York: New York University Press, 2006; Johnson, George. "The Nitpicking of the Masses vs. the Authority of the Experts." *New York Times,* January 3, 2006; Mitchell, Dan. "Insider Editing at Wikipedia." *New York Times,* January 24, 2005; Motoko, Rich. "Digital Publishing Scrambles the Rules." *New York Times,* June 5, 2006; Schrag, Robert. "Hegemony on a Hard Drive." *Flow: A Critical Forum on Television and Media Culture* 2, no. 1. http://jot.communication.utexas.edu/flow/?jot=view&id = 652.

Avi Santo

PAPARAZZI AND PHOTOGRAPHIC ETHICS

Visual imagery is a core component of communication media and stunning and controversial images circulate throughout the media spectrum. From advertisements to Internet sites, in newspapers and magazines, on billboards and television, photographs are used to create consumer desire, grab the attention of newsreaders, create fear and astonishment at disasters, and spark outrage for destruction, scandal, and abuse. We live surrounded in a spectacular visual geography, the world made visually available in ways unimagined in the past. From the macro-photography of insects that awe and excite, to a microscopic world that unfolds before our eyes, the earth and its wonders seemingly come to life through photographs. Yet even in this proliferation of imagery, certain pictures become emblems for social concerns and others circulate as the icons of global controversy.

New technologies have expanded the possibilities for documentation, and the ways photographs can be taken and disseminated. Digital cameras and computers made the images of torture at Abu Ghraib possible, and cell phones allowed the clandestine footage of the execution of Saddam Hussein. Imagery of war is central to the history of photojournalism, and the representation of suffering and death remains a highly contested topic. Humanitarian workers recognize that the public must see suffering to understand the need for resources and relief. Yet graphic imagery can also create "compassion fatigue" and voyeurism, responses that distance viewers from feelings of empathy for the people shown suffering in photographs.

In the midst of this visual representation are the camera operators and editors, photojournalists and tabloid paparazzi, graphic designers and composers, and the editors and news managers who decide what is welcome and culturally edifying, and what is outside the bounds of often nebulous ethical practices. Such practices are constantly in flux as ratings pressures and new media, bloggers, and the public challenge the constraints of traditional gatekeepers and expand the universe of image circulation.

A HISTORY OF THE PHOTOGRAPH

Since its invention in the mid 1800s with the first daguerreotype, photography has been appropriated for different scientific, cultural, artistic, and legal uses. In the age of.enlightenment and progress, the photograph was seen as an essential technical tool, one able to probe the world and create representations more revealing than what the human eye could see. The camera lens was considered more accurate than the human lens. A series of images demonstrated how horses actually ran and forever changed their depictions in painting. Colonial photographers circled the globe and used the camera to capture and quantify other peoples and cultures, often as objectified specimens for scientific data. And early psychologists catalogued everything from human emotions to abnormalities through photographs, often of the disabled. The photographic process ultimately advanced to the point where it could record what humans could not see, everything from x-rays to microscopic photography.

At the same time portraits, once only the domain of the wealthy that could afford paintings, became accessible to a more general public through early traveling photography studios. In addition, artists used the camera to create beautiful images in painterly traditions, many of which became significant cultural treasures. With the advent of mass media in the twentieth century, films, newspapers, and magazines became dominant visual media. These developments were not without controversy, especially the introduction of first graphics, then pictures into the pages of the press, which were often sensational images that boosted the sale of newspapers. When television added sound and movement to imagery, it brought visual story telling into American living rooms. By the 1950s, television became the dominant mass medium, utilizing as never before, first film cameras then video technologies for visual forms of entertainment, sales, and news. Yet the still photograph and the photomontage remained essential components of the mass media and with digital technology they have moved easily into new media formats, including the Internet. These new technologies allow images to circulate the globe with an immediacy that makes any event or crisis known to the world, especially through the most dramatic visual representations.

PAPARAZZI AND CELEBRITIES

One of the most popular and contested terrains of entertainment practice and sensationalized nonfiction culture is celebrity reporting, and the candid photograph frequently leads the prize story. Those considered the most valuable are images often captured by daring and intrusive photographers willing to do almost anything to get the shot. Paparazzi stake out events and locations for days at a time, they follow, and sometimes stalk, stars and celebrities to get the unusual picture able to command a high price. Those are the ones used to sell tabloid papers and tease TV audiences to stay tuned through the commercial break. Paparazzi bear an enormous cultural burden; they are under pressure to record the most sensational situations, the most private celebrity moments, and many times the most unflattering poses, for these are the ones that most interest the public and please the editors. Yet they are often reviled by the same culture they try to please by filling a quite evident demand. They are accused of violating the privacy of public figures and are sometime sued and even attacked by those they try to capture visually. An outraged Alec Baldwin approached the vehicle and started swinging at the photographer in front of his house trying to get pictures of his wife Kim Basinger and their newborn baby. Analysts attempt to account for this intrusive aspect of celebrity culture; some blame the sensational media, others the spoiled celebrities and ruthless photographers, while still other lay the ultimate blame at the feet of the public and its endless desire for titillating celebrity gossip.

It is most likely a combination of these factors, and most importantly the dynamics of the interaction between the culture of celebrity, and media practices. As the most profitable, least difficult entertainment content, mainstream media talk endlessly about the stars, who at the same time are promoting the movies, TV shows, albums, and products tied to cross-promotional deal and corporate synergy. In addition, psychologists of media culture have identified the "para-social interactions" that certain viewers experience with media celebrities.

CAMERON DIAZ AND THE PAPARAZZO

On November 10, 2004, the *New York Post* published a story about the actor Cameron Diaz titled, "Cameron 'Snaps.'" Most of the celebrity news piece consisted of two dramatic photos. The larger image, taking two-thirds of the page, show Diaz physically attacking a 21 year-old "paparazzo" named Saul Lazo. She is shown swinging and grabbing the photographer's camera in a scuffle that took place when Diaz and Justin Timberlake were leaving a Hollywood hotel. The smaller inset photo pictures a distressed-looking Lazo grabbing Diaz from behind in an attempt to retrieve his expensive camera. Readers are informed that Diaz, 5'9", 117 pounds, is a fitness freak who is trained in the martial arts. Timberlake also intervened, trying to stop the second photographer, Jose Gonzalez, from taking pictures of the "wild melee."

Timberlake evidentially failed, and the two photographs were published in the *Post* as "exclusive photos from U.S. Weekly" credited to Fame Pictures. Diaz and Timberlake reportedly kept the pricey gear. The incident illustrates the pressures for exclusive, exciting, and candid images, even as they are taken at increasing risk to photographers themselves for the commercial benefit of media owners. Such candid shots please readers eager to gaze into the private lives of celebrities, even as it angers those very "celebs" caught on camera.

Although they are seemingly larger than life, the familiar faces of those that entertain, advise, astonish, and annoy us can often seem like people we know personally. Folklorists understand that the stories and characters, the heroes and villains that populate fictional fare become the embodiment of our own deepest fears and greatest triumphs. As pivotal figures, celebrities themselves and their agents seek to control their own images and the range of information released to the public. The positive, hip personas created by a posse of promotional agents begin to seem stilted and commercial to fans and audiences, evoking the desire for more personal, unvarnished views. Celebrities complain that their personal lives should be off limits, yet paparazzi argue that they opened the door by working in the industry. These interconnected issues and practices have led to problems that revolve around questions of privacy, as opposed to spectacle, and voyeurism in contrast to participation and empathy. These same parameters frame debates about other uses of visual imagery.

SPECTATOR CULTURE

When viewers sit and watch, and look at magazines, images have been carefully arranged and presented for their fascination and pleasure. The world is set before their eyes, and the act of being a spectator feels natural, indeed comfortable. Such consuming visual choreography invites viewers to gaze at any aspect of the public or private world without feeling like they are violating the privacy of others. Learning to view the world in such a manner confers a sense possession and privilege, and some media scholars argue that it leads to a cultural and public attitude that promotes voyeurism. Ensconced as we are in an endlessly reproduced visual world, the constant waves of images give no order of priority, and as Susan Sontag noted, the result is a kind of leveling of meaning in a fast-moving confusing world of pictures. Nowhere are these issues more important than in evaluating the representational styles of global crisis and conflict.

WAR REPORTING

Many dedicated photojournalists have taken pictures of the victims of war and humanitarian crises in different places and at different times around the globe. Many of those images have been printed and distributed in the United States and in the international press, and viewed by millions. Journalists, especially freelance photographers, risk their lives to document wars, disasters, and suffering, and some die in the process. Many believe their work will make a difference. Such dedication to life and death issues forces us to consider carefully the meanings and actual social impact of the visual record of war and suffering.

Seeing and Believing

War photographers often consider themselves the eyes of the world's conscience. They hope that by capturing the most disturbing pictures they can arouse the attention of the public and political leaders. They seek to bring home the "truth" of war. Many assert that visual documentation carries authority and credibility; we believe what we see, and when real suffering is brought to our attention, we cannot ignore it and we will take action to stop it. These somewhat more sophisticated pronouncements are other ways of assigning truth to the old adages "the camera never lies" and "a picture is worth a thousand words." But if the camera never lies, we must ask what kind of truth it tells and what information is contained in its message.

The photograph is a powerful emotive, but as a single image, or even a collection, the information contained there is limited. We can feel shock or sorrow for those pictured as they lay dead or suffering, but the image cannot reveal what has happened to them. A graphic image of a dead body does not explain events that took place before or after the death, nor can it tell us who did the killing. It offers no political context, much less an analysis.

One example of this type of imagery is the news photographs of the civil war that took place during the 1980s in the Central American country of El Salvador. The United States supported the Salvadoran security forces, and the often-bloody conflict was depicted in the U.S. press. News photographs often showed gruesome piles of dead bodies and even severed heads in city morgues, individuals thrown along the side of the road, or being dug out of shallow graves. Most often such bodies were unable to be identified, and they remained anonymous with no personal history. When bodies are presented in this way, viewers cannot respond to the people they once were. There is little humanity left in a lifeless cadaver featured in a magazine layout.

Hopelessness

Both John Berger and Susan Sontag have written eloquently about what we can know from photographs of horror and what range of emotional response is possible. As a passive spectator looking at such pictures of the dead, the impression is one of finality, even disgust. The act exists in the past by the time it reaches the eyes of the magazine reader. There is nothing to be done at present. Such images proclaim forcefully that the worst has already happened. Such brutal images stand in contrast to another way of presenting the dead: showing them when they were alive. One example from that period of a more humane treatment was a picture on the June 6, 1983 cover of *Newsweek* magazine, which featured the first American adviser killed in El Salvador. It is altogether different from the Salvadoran cadavers. The *Newsweek* cover photo of Lt. Cmdr. Albert Schaufelberger, III, is very specific. His name is spelled out in full, and the photograph was taken when he was very much alive. Standing at a dignified three-quarter pose in uniform, the aura of his humanity and individuality is still present. The bold print announces, "Central America, The First Casualty." Identified as the first casualty, we can only assume that the pictures of corpses printed for three years before the one American's death seem not to have been considered with the same humanity.

Moral Engagement

The portrayal of human suffering without a rational explanation or cause poses another problem for photojournalism. When captions proclaim "victims of random violence," or "political violence," they elicit a particular response, one of bewilderment. Instead of being able to take action to alleviate the suffering, the viewer is frozen. Susan Sontag argued that the possibility of being "affected morally" by the photograph requires a relevant political consciousness. John Berger also pointed out that without a sociopolitical understanding, the viewer cannot act in a way that would prevent further suffering. Know the cases and sources of conflict is essential to understanding how it can be stopped. Chaotic violence in foreign countries becomes mystified without an explanation of its causes and possible solutions. Such mystification leads to vague assertions and a general sense of disgust. The countries become places "at war with themselves," of simply emblematic of violent cultures that do not value life. As Susan Moeller pointed out in *Compassion Fatigue*, viewers can only feel pity for so long without drawing the conclusion that the people are simply "pitiful."

Pictures that fail to explain violence accuses no one and everyone, the sense of moral obligation that would lead to a commitment is gone. The assumed effects of concerned photojournalism are nullified. As we lay the magazine down, the image has become a corruption, a distancing, an acceptance of the way things are. Each new photo layout positions the view now as a voyeur.

Photographs and Context

The visual image is a particular type of document. As time frozen, the photograph remains a moment yanked from the historical flow that produced it. The news photograph circulates through time and place, yet it is a moment frozen in temporal space. Time captured by the camera as a single image can then be placed into some other context: a news page, an art gallery, an anti-war pamphlet, or an assassin's hand for identification purposes. This quality of the photograph enables it to be used to make a number of abstract points and convey a variety of meanings. The news text can direct the photograph's meaning in ways that either evoke or block empathy for the dead.

Justifications

Pictures of dead bodies can be explained in numerous ways. Many news stories that contain images of suffering offer a variety of justifications for human loss. Victims of violence often lose their humanity and become pawns in a game of strategy of national interests; in whatever way those interests are articulated at the time. With regard to war and conflict in foreign countries, arguments include what would happen if the wrong people came to power, the overriding concern that the country would fall into the hands of the wrong people. Innocent victims caught in the cross fire become unfortunate but "necessary consequences" of fighting for abstract principles such as security or our way of life.

HIGH-TECH WEAPONS AND THE WAR ON TERROR

Over the years, media coverage of war has increasingly downplayed the death, pain, suffering and grief caused by war. During the first Gulf war, *collateral damage* became a common term for civilian casualties, and its cold, antiseptic sound helps distance the public from war's human costs. During the first Gulf War, *Time* magazine identified dead or wounded civilians "who should have picked a safer neighborhood." After 9/11 when the United States was criticized for killing civilians in Afghanistan, well-known *New York Times* commentator, Thomas Friedman, claimed that the people being bombed did not mind dying when he wrote, "It turns out many of those Afghan 'civilians' were praying for another dose of B-52's to liberate tem from the Taliban, casualties of not" (*New York Times*, November 23, 2001). Presently, in the midst of a continuing war, very few images of death or even wounded U.S. soldiers are published in the pages of the press or show on television. Instead, as the U.S. president called to expand the war on terror with the invasion of Iraq, television stories featured the power of the weaponry to be used; especially the high-tech bombs and aircraft, and those images became the visual icons of war. Imaging and emphasizing the drama, excitement and power of modern warfare represents conflict from a narrow perspective and allows the government, military, and the public to avoid debate about the deadly effects of war to noncombatants, as well as to those who fight.

Because photographs of suffering on their own cannot explain the causes of pain or suggest courses of action to alleviate suffering, such images should be presented with ethical parameters. Because death and suffering are often hidden aspects of our culture, images showing such taboo topics are often used as ratings-boosting fare. Only context that evokes empathy is able to prevent shocking images from becoming little more that titillating spectacles presented to an increasingly desensitized, voyeuristic public. With regard to the victims of war, both showing and not showing the death presents media dilemmas. Eliminating the images of war's human cost, allows the public as well as those who call for military actions, to forget the consequences of war, and the responsibility of human destruction in its wake. Yet a context and treatment that objectifies or justifies suffering and the death of civilians is equally irresponsible.

HUMANITARIAN WORK AND THE NEWS CONTEXT

Humanitarian aide workers are well aware of the complexities of visual representation of crisis, and understand the need for coverage, but coverage that promotes civic engagement instead of compassion fatigue. They understand that horrific images must be contextualized with narratives of inclusion, personal stories able to evoke public empathy for the victims they are trying to help. Viewers must be able to recognize their shared humanity, not view the victims of crisis as outside the bounds of our own sense of community. It must be understood that people in crisis have done nothing to deserve such horrific conditions. Above all, visual imagery must not exploit suffering for commercial purposes, but seek to maintain the dignity of those depicted.

CONCLUSION

Compelling visual imagery enriches the lives of the public in many ways. Significant issues are enhanced through photojournalism when they convey information and knowledge, and edify the public. They bring global communities together when disasters strikes and they can help mobilize international relief efforts. The best visual documentation is contextualized within a news frame that depicts and enhances working solutions and civic engagement.

See also Advertising and Persuasion; Alternative Media in the United States; Bias and Objectivity; Celebrity Worship and Fandom; Disabilities and the Media; Hypercommercialism; Journalists in Peril; Media and Electoral Campaigns; Media Literacy; Parachute Journalism; Presidential Stagecraft and Militainment; Propaganda Model; Sensationalism, Fear Mongering, and Tabloid Media; Tourism and the Selling of Cultures; World Cinema.

Further Reading: Berger, John. *About Looking.* New York: Pantheon Books, 1980; Berger, John, and John Mohr. *Another Way of Telling.* New York: Pantheon Books, 1982; Butler, Judith. *Precarious Life: The Powers of Mourning and Violence.* New York: Verso, 2004; Evans, Harold. *Eyewitness: 25 Years through World Press Photos.* New York: William Morrow, 1980; Marshall, David P. *Celebrity Culture Reader.* New York: Routledge, 2006; Messaris, Paul. *Visual Persuasion: The Role of Images in Advertising.* Thousand Oaks, CA: Sage Publications, 1997; Moeller, Susan. *Compassion Fatigue: How the Media Sell Disease Famine War and Death.* New York: Routledge, 1999; Newhall, Beaumont. *The History of Photography.* New York: Museum of Modern Art, 1982; Sontag, Susan. *On Photography.* New York: Farrar, Straus and Giroux, 1977; Sontag, Susan. *Regarding the Pain of Others.* New York: Farrar, Straus and Giroux, 2003.

Robin Andersen

PARACHUTE JOURNALISM: INTERNATIONAL NEWS REPORTING

As a term, "parachute journalism" invokes both the exciting image of the scribe coming to the rescue from the sky and the pejorative notion of the unprepared neophyte landing over his head in a big story abroad, but in fact it involves a broad assortment of practices that share the characteristic of a reporter covering news in a place other than the ones in which he or she has experience. That defines much of journalism, from high-profile coverage of major wars and events of global significance, to local reporters who drive from their usual beat to encounter regional events where little reportage normally occurs. To the extent that an increase in parachute journalism reflects a decreased commitment by even prestigious news operations to maintaining staff in foreign bureaus, the phenomenon deserves some of the opprobrium commonly directed its way. But compared with foregoing coverage altogether, or leaving it to wire services alone, there is something to recommend the practice, especially where it is done with care and forethought, and where it is properly supported with local resources.

ETHNOCENTRIC PARACHUTES?

A key byproduct of news organizations' reliance on parachute journalists is that we are often invited to see a distant world in chaos through ethnocentric perspectives. Foreign countries most frequently become news when they experience a coup, earthquake, or other such disaster. Amid such chaos, the highly paid, perfectly coifed network correspondent hits the ground and calmly explains the catastrophe. Thus, while war, political scandal, famine, and pestilence rage on with foreign-looking others populating the television screen, the white American reporter can become the lone point of identification, as the rational observer providing viewers with a stark visual contrast between (foreign) chaos, and (Western) rational order. Moreover, when parachute journalists are unfamiliar with local customs and culture, they may prove poor interpreters of what both they and the camera witness, hence further exacerbating notions of foreign irrationality, and continuing an age-old subjugation of foreign voices, whereby the West speaks for and on behalf of "the rest," and whereby the West is granted the power to make sense of and play cultural analyst to foreign nations and peoples. Travelers in a foreign land commonly focus on difference, strangeness, and peculiarity, as centuries of traveler's tales have shown us, and so a perpetual risk for parachute journalists is that they make foreign cultures seem yet more foreign. For example, in times of war, divisions of "us" and "them" can be made all the more prominent when as viewers, much of our only contact with "them" comes through reporters who have little cultural understanding of those featured with their cameras and interviews.

In a world in which news often develops where no journalists are present, parachute journalism is an inevitability. Its various iterations unfold from circumstances guided primarily by the economics of news organizations. Even where full-time correspondents are stationed, they cannot be everywhere at once. A reporter schooled in the ins and outs of Jerusalem will likely discover in Tyre a new situation for which previous reporting has provided little or no preparation. The circumstances drawing journalists to a given locale often rapidly transform the setting and its significance, exacerbating the difficulty of operating safely and knowledgeably.

FINDING ONE'S LOCAL LEGS

The problem, while made more prevalent by the diminution of the foreign staffing by news organizations in recent years, is as old as reporting itself. Reporters not based in a place have an increased likelihood of getting basic facts wrong, drawing conclusions from insufficient evidence, and lacking historical and cultural familiarity with the settings in which their stories are situated. At the same time, the greater experience and sophistication of many correspondents whose employers can afford to "parachute" them into a situation can mitigate against such problems to a substantial degree. Purveyors of news are likely to select their best-qualified reporters, often with previous foreign experience, to undertake the kind of spot reporting that market factors some-times dictate. Sometimes contract journalists who are based in the region or who have considerable experience in the type of story being covered can pro-vide a deeper level of background preparation, or better contacts on the ground; such stringers or freelancers typically come with references and a track record, yet they, too, may still be encountering a new situation, and can themselves be categorized as parachute journalists by dint of having sped to the scene from the nearest metropole. Whatever the degree of local knowledge the reporter brings to the situation, to those on the scene who have no experience with that reporter, the interloper might as well have dropped in from the sky.

Sometimes correspondents flown in from domestic or other foreign postings work together with such stringers or with local handlers (often called "fixers"). The image of the solo operator appearing on the scene with phrasebook, maps, and flak jacket fails to capture the more common reality of the parachute correspondent. The negative connotations of the term are not without founda-tion, however. From a local perspective, correspondents arriving from elsewhere often appear to lack proper contextual understanding and to rely disproportion-ately upon technology (which, in many instances, does not work properly away from communications centers; only the best-supported correspondents have satellite phones, for example).

STRUCTURAL DETERMINANTS AND RESPONSES

Like much of journalism itself, however, unfavorable views of parachute jour-nalism focus criticism disproportionately on the individual when it should be centered on structural factors generated by corporate profit incentives. Main-taining large—or any—numbers of foreign correspondents is an expensive venture. Thus some news organizations have found it more profitable to focus on local, often cheaper reporting: five minutes a day of celebrity gossip, for in-stance, will likely cost a small fraction of the price tag associated with keeping open a foreign news bureau. When news is a business, then, the high costs of international reporting often result in scaled-down coverage. At the same time, many news organizations regard the costs of high-quality international news reporting as simply not justified by matching levels of interest from readers or viewers, whose focus is most often local. Thus, when demand suddenly arises for coverage of one of the globe's myriad uncovered locales, some solution is demanded, and parachute correspondents are summoned to the task. Low in-terest in international news may, of course, be a function of poor reporting or a lack of commitment to making international news more interesting, but with price differentials playing a key role in dictating decisions about coverage, news organizations have little impetus to approach international news with greater resources.

Parachute correspondence lacks the organic connection to a story ideally provided by a journalist experienced in the milieu at the center of the story, but given the unlikelihood of such situated reportage taking place from many of the world's hot spots at a given moment, often the best that can be hoped for is a well-prepared professional landing with access to a network of information and assistance, or failing that, with the resources and resourcefulness needed to develop such a network quickly. Such goals are most likely to be met by larger news organizations with reservoirs of talent experienced in previous episodes of sudden need for news from places not ordinarily covered, often including former foreign correspondents. Independent reporters with such experience do exist, however, and their regional basing can often make them equal or superior to their better-financed peers in a given situation.

In some instances, news organizations rely upon roving reporters who may visit a series of capitals and the odd hinterland locale, rather than remaining based in an area on a full-time basis. While not as beneficial as having full-time correspondents stationed throughout Africa, for example, the practice at least allows for semiregular contact with sources and some semblance of ongoing coverage of the region. Far from ideal, the arrangement serves nonetheless to maintain institutional ties while doubtless giving short shrift to many stories that require closer and more sustained attention.

To fill such gaps, a variety of journalistic operators and support personnel may in turn serve as parachute correspondents in less-scrutinized realms while maintaining more regular surveillance of population centers in which they live. Several types of correspondents combine to provide coverage of the vast, generally under-covered realms beyond the metropolitan centers of primary interest to readers and journalists. In addition to the shrinking number of journalists in longer-term foreign postings for such newspapers as the industry-leading *New York Times*, the *Washington Post*, and the *Wall Street Journal*; chains such as McClatchy and Cox; and networks such as CNN; there are local journalists who string for foreign publications, freelancers who cover a region, and subject and area specialists who may travel or establish a domestic or foreign base from which they venture to cover stories as assigned, or on their own. Some will wear different hats over time. Virtually all will at some point share the designation parachute correspondent, and some will perform the variegated duties associated with such a catchall position much more effectively than others.

The question of quality of coverage will sometimes relate closely to the story being covered. A key distinguishing characteristic is often linguistic acumen: a journalist operating in a milieu where language differences preclude direct interviewing—a frequent occurrence, no matter how educated and skilled the reporter—is in need of an interpreter. The acquisition of cultural and historical background is of great importance, even if little such material makes its way into most reports: even the most up-to-date information is frequently misleading if presented absent adequate attention to context. Financial resources, such as the ability to hire the best fixers and interpreters, can make a large difference as well, casting a different light on the question, "What color is your parachute?" Indeed, those who have served in foreign-correspondent positions previously are the correspondents most likely to be called upon for future service, regardless of their experience in a given region. It is the skill set—the ability to operate efficiently in diverse foreign settings—that is most prized, and part of that skill set is working with others who can bridge gaps in knowledge, access, and language.

While not inexpensive, coverage by parachute correspondents is generally much less costly than maintaining full-time correspondents in many locations, where salary, lodging, transportation, and staff support frequently require supplementation with full-time security. Many locations are considered hardship postings, and elite journalists are less likely to wish to remain in them for extended periods, reintroducing the element of lack of familiarity with each successive replacement. There is justification for bringing in an experienced reporter from another location to provide either periodic or crisis reporting. Research can be quickly assembled to provide background for a given situation, but it takes significant climbing of learning curves to gain the hard-earned experience of choosing the right vehicle and driver; disassembling a telephone and

JOHN BARRETT: PARACHUTE JOURNALIST BEFORE THERE WERE PARACHUTES

The practice of stationing foreign correspondents anywhere but in a very few important European capitals did not exist before the twentieth century, but reportage from around the world found its way home on a regular basis. When journalist-turned-diplomat John Barrett passed through the Philippines aboard an American ship following the outbreak of Asia's first indigenous nationalist revolution against Spain in 1896, the archipelago and its nearly 8 million inhabitants were completely unfamiliar to U.S. readers. Barrett, addressing the relatively sophisticated readership of the North American Review, warned in 1897 against heeding advice from a breed of commentator increasingly ubiquitous amid the ever-growing news media: "Our commercial interests must not be kept from the conquest by the reports of retired manufacturers who have made their own fortunes at home and report impressions gained by superficial observations of leisurely travel; by correspondents who come in by one door, as it were, and go out by the next."

Praising the islands' "inexhaustible and varied resources, which at present are only partially developed," Barrett pronounced the Philippines "a fit land for rebellion and insurrection," claiming that "the spirits of air and earth alike nurture unrest." His list of first impressions, trade statistics, and generalizations about the "lazy" but "gentle, polite and hospitable" Filipinos pointed to a certain covetous embrace of the milieu's value. Noting that Manila's battlements would be no match for American naval weaponry, he dismissed the inconvenient fact of the revolt as an unthreatening trifle, claiming without the benefit of having encountered the rebels in person that "it would appear to be only a question of a few months before the flame of revolution is reduced to a spark." Within a year, U.S. troops would be on the ground on the main island of Luzon, and within two years they would be mired in a grisly guerrilla war that would in time bring thousands of U.S. casualties and uncounted hundreds of thousands of dead Filipinos. By then, Barrett had moved on to new adventures.

See John Barrett, "America's Interest in East Asia," North American Review, March 1896.

attaching alligator clips to a modem to transmit a story from the field; knowing when to hide, and how; how to detect surveillance, and how to escape it; how to arrange for travel documents, tickets, and lodging; and when to hit the dirt when certain sounds transmit the order to do so.

PROSPECTS FOR PARACHUTE JOURNALISM

Many reporters without such experience are thrust into situations calling for reportage from an unfamiliar locale, however, and the resourceful and experienced ones are able to operate effectively by remaining aware of their limitations and leveraging their strengths. A foundation in domestic coverage of a diasporic community can serve as excellent preparation for travel to the homeland of that population, especially if sources and references can be transmitted in the process. A specialist in a subject area—medicine or public health, for example—can tap into professional networks. A veteran war correspondent can forecast how weather, terrain, or other factors may influence the development of a situation.

Not all parachute correspondents are such experienced hands, however. The novelty of the embedded correspondents in the ongoing war in Iraq has brought undue confidence to many neophytes entering the war zone, and instances of touristic reportage divorced from balanced sourcing have increased. If such cases are taken as instances of parachute journalism, the bad odor associated with the term grows stronger. Such journalists might, however, be better classed under the new terminology, "embeds," in that while they may appear suddenly and soon enough disappear from the milieu, they are in most instances joining a pack of journalists focused on the same general story, as opposed to entering into the situation as solo interlocutors.

Parachute journalism, then, is subject to a broad range of definitions, and even within a defined niche, the qualities brought to the practice by individuals and organizations that may be sponsoring them vary considerably. The phenomenon, with its roots in the first foreign reportage, has grown with the ease and affordability of transportation, and is open to a broader range of participants than ever before, guaranteeing that its lowest common denominators will continue to place the term and those it describes in an unflattering light. At the same time, it remains likely that elite practitioners of the craft will be among the most skilled, most experienced, and best supported journalists working. Just as journalism reaches new heights and depths with its expanding permutations, so, too, will parachute journalism continue to place side by side, in the settings of some of the world's best stories, with adventurers, charlatans, and masters of the imperfect art of journalism.

See also Al-Jazeera; Embedding Journalists; Global Community Media; Hyper-commercialism; Journalists in Peril; Media Watch Groups; Paparazzi and Photographic Ethics; Sensationalism, Fear Mongering, and Tabloid Media; Tourism and the Selling of Cultures.

Further Reading: Bullard, Frederick L. *Famous War Correspondents.* New York: Beekman, 1974 [1914]; Emery, Michael. *On the Front Lines: Following America's Foreign Correspondents*

Across the Twentieth Century. Washington, DC: American University Press, 1995; Erickson, Emily, and John Maxwell Hamilton. "Foreign Reporting Enhanced by Parachute Journalism." *Newspaper Research Journal* (Winter 2006); Hamilton, John Maxwell, and Eric Jenner. "Redefining Foreign Correspondence." *Journalism* 5, no. 3 (August 2004): 301–21; Hess, Stephen. *International News and Foreign Correspondents.* Washington, DC: Brookings Institution Press, 1996; Knightley, Phillip. *The First Casualty.* 2nd ed. London: Prion Books, 2000; Lande, Nathaniel. *Dispatches from the Front: A History of the American War Correspondent.* New York: Oxford University Press, 1996; Lundstrom, Marjie, "Parachute Journalism: The Damage Wrought by Regional Stereotypes." *Poynter Online,* http://www.poynter.org/dg.lts/id.4682/content.content_view.htm; Moeller, Susan D. *Shooting War: Photography and the American Experience of Combat.* New York: Basic Books, 1989; Nossek, Hillel. "Our News and Their News: The Role of National Identity in the Coverage of Foreign News." *Journalism* 5, no. 3 (August 2004): 343–68; Vane, Sharyn, "Parachute Journalism," *American Journalism Review* (July/August 1997): http://www.ajr.org/Article.asp?id=659; Vaughan, Christopher A. "Reporting from Imperial Frontiers: The Making of Foreign Correspondents a Century Apart." *Asia Pacific Media Educator* 7 (July-December 1999); Willnat, Lars, and David Weaver. "Through Their Eyes: The Work of Foreign Correspondents in the United States." *Journalism: Theory, Practice and Criticism* 4, no. 4 (November 2003): 403–22.

Christopher A. Vaughan

PHARMACEUTICAL ADVERTISING

In recent years, the Food and Drug Administration (FDA) has allowed pharmaceutical companies to advertise prescription medications directly to consumers. That decision led to a precipitous rise in drug advertising and a corresponding rise in demand for advertised medications. Indeed, as demand for advertised pharmaceuticals has increased, the prices for these brand-name medications have also climbed. Supporters of direct-to-consumer advertising (DTCA) suggest that pharmaceutical advertising improves patient education, promotes active participation in personal health, and also helps to destigmatize certain medical conditions. Critics, however, warn that DTCA represents an intrusion into the realm of personal health by commercial interests, drives up the cost of prescription medications, and threatens the economic sustainability of the American health care system.

Media critics have long expressed concern at advertising's penchant for selling junk food, cars whose exhaust pollutes the air, cigarettes, alcohol, and other unhealthy or dangerous products. But what happens when advertising sells medicine and drugs? Beyond the prevalent, multimillion-dollar business in advertising directly to doctors, direct-to-consumer advertising through television, magazines, and other media has wedded the media, advertising, and health care in new and highly contentious ways. Balancing the pros and cons of DTCA regarding medicines and drugs forces one to consider whether the simultaneous capitalist and social motivations behind DTCA exist in a state of natural and inevitable conflict.

INCREASED EDUCATION, OR AN INFORMATION GAP?

Industry representatives and advocates suggest that consumer education—especially among some previously neglected minority communities—is a positive byproduct of DTCA. And FDA regulations seem to support this, with the law requiring any advertisement that gives information about a medication's benefits to also give information about its risks. Furthermore, DTCA also benefits patients in the following ways: consumers may not be aware that treatments exist for certain conditions; they may suffer from symptoms without realizing that they are part of a treatable disease; new treatments may become available for existing medical conditions; or a new remedy with fewer side effects or more effectiveness may become available. In any of these cases, DTCA campaigns that educate consumers can be seen as being positive.

This benefit is particularly notable in one minority population, but woefully lacking in another: racial minorities, and the elderly, respectively. Racial minorities, traditionally "underserved by lower quality health care," have seen a positive effect of DTCA in the promotion of dialogue between patients and their doctors. Conversely, the aging baby-boomer population in America is at particular risk for being overexposed to DTCA literature and underserved by its contents. The vast majority of advertised drugs are directed toward this population, and the demographic "accounts for $8.40 of every $10 of all prescription

---

REMOVING THE STIGMA OF DEPRESSION, BUT DOES *EVERYONE* HAVE IT?

Two separate DTCA campaigns for antidepressants highlight both sides of the debate as to whether DTCA destigmatizes difficult medical conditions or causes hyperawareness among consumers regarding otherwise "normal" symptoms.

"Depression Awareness Campaign," 2003

As Schulz explains, with no single word in the Japanese language to "properly capture the generally accepted medical definition of depression as a chemical imbalance," the campaign sought to generate public awareness of depression. The campaign communicated one consistent message: "Your suffering might be a sickness. Your leaky vital energy, like your runny nose, might respond to drugs." The campaign framed both the disease and its treatment in the culturally understandable terms of "energy" and "vitality," familiarizing consumers both with the symptoms and benefits of treatment.

Depression Campaign, 2001

Appearing on the heels of the September 11, 2001, terrorist attacks, a DTCA campaign for Paxil emphasized the drug's antianxiety benefits. The campaign listed symptoms indicative of chronic anxiety, including worry, anxiety, or irritability. This symptom list concerned some physicians: "At what point does an understandable response to distressing life events become an indication for drug treatment, and a market opportunity?" (Mintzes 2002, p. 908).

drugs sold in the United States" (Morgan and Levy 1998, p. 30). However, this is also the group at the highest risk for misunderstanding prescription drug ads, and for failing to clarify concerns with physicians. There is evidently an uneven distribution of benefits from DTCA education, with some populations benefiting and others at risk for serious side effects as a result of what Lisa Foley calls the "medication information gap."

DESTIGMATIZED BUT OVERMEDICATED?

While DTCA can help to "normalize" previously misunderstood or stigmatized medical conditions, the proliferation of advertising for medical conditions across a spectrum of seriousness can also lead to a tendency to diagnose even the most minor of medical ailments as being suitable for prescription treatment. DTCA has the potential to destigmatize certain conditions, encourage a visit to a physician, and let people know "they're not alone." Advertisements for antidepressants, for example, have helped to mitigate the stigma of depression as being a sign of mental or emotional weakness (Schulz 2004, p. 39) and have instead normalized the medically accepted definition of depression as a chemical imbalance (see "Removing the Stigma of Depression, But Does *Everyone* Have It?" sidebar).

While serious medical conditions such as depression are certainly alleviated by widespread knowledge of the causes and potential treatments, there is the potential for other normally occurring medical "conditions" to be overemphasized by DTCA, and to be overtreated as a result. Physiologically normal conditions such as baldness, shyness, or the occasional inability to perform sexually are framed as serious medical conditions by DTCA campaigns and are presented to consumers as jeopardizing the very enjoyment of life itself unless treated with a prescription medication. Some critics worry that this trend will promote the development of what Barbara Mintzes calls a "nation of healthy hypochondriacs," but not necessarily a healthier nation.

PATIENT, HEAL THYSELF ("ASK YOUR DOCTOR ABOUT…")

Just as in other forms of consumer advertising, DTCA taps into the deepest anxieties and worries of consumers about their health and well-being, and strikes an emotional chord in order to prompt patients to demand a specific medication. This is an anxiety that doctors traditionally would seek to alleviate through sound medical advice, rather than prey on. This forms the crux of the debate over the ways in which DTCA has profoundly altered the traditional doctor/patient relationship. In this traditional relationship, educated and specialized doctors dispensed advice and experience along with prescriptions. With the increase in DTCA, this relationship has morphed into a physician-patient-advertiser triad. In essence, there is now a third party looming large in the examining room: the pharmaceutical ad.

This emerging triad has prompted changes in both patient and physician behavior. Consumer surveys often show that consumers are more satisfied with the information provided by advertisements than by their physicians, and that consumer confidence in the advice of doctors has dropped substantially in recent years. Patients arrive at medical appointments knowing what type of health care they want and how their doctor should provide it, and they frequently request specific branded medications. Recent studies have revealed that nearly half of all patients would try to persuade their doctor to prescribe the specifically requested drug (A. Brown 2001, p. 22), sometimes even changing doctors to get the desired prescription. There is also troubling evidence that doctors are not only experiencing, but succumbing to, consumer pressure to prescribe the most heavily marketed drugs. In 2004, doctors wrote nearly 35 percent more prescriptions for the drugs promoted most heavily to consumers than for others (Charatan 2000, p. 783). Even more worrying is the revelation that almost half of all doctors surveyed in one study acknowledged they'd "prescribed medicines they knew were ineffective, simply because they were expected to" ("A Spoonful of Sugar," 2004).

By scientific rationale, prescription medications are chemical compounds designed to ameliorate a specific medical condition. Therefore, on a purely medical level, the choice of a prescription medication should be based on scientific efficacy and not on the strength of the related advertising campaign. By introducing branding practices and intensive advertising to the decision-making process, DTCA encourages consumers to pressure doctors for prescriptions based upon emotional appeal rather than on chemical/medical sensibility; contributes to the steady erosion of physician authority in the doctor-patient relationship; and leaves little room for truly private, privileged decisions based solely on medical authority.

THE RUNAWAY MONEY TRAIN

When examined from the perspective of the pharmaceutical industry, the DTCA trend has been phenomenally lucrative. When the same numbers are applied to the American health care system, however, it becomes apparent that the DTCA trend may be contributing to ever-escalating health care costs and may in fact threaten the long-term sustainability of the system.

There was a nearly 14,000 percent increase in DTCA spending between 1991 and 2005, and DTCA now ranks as the "fourth largest advertising category in the U.S. market, behind only cars and trucks, restaurants and movies" (Roth 2003, p. 180). The pharmaceutical industry's willingness to commit to such enormous budgets is predicated upon the return on investment in the form of drug sales and high-profit margins of both moderately advertised and so-called blockbuster medications.

The pharmaceutical industry focuses on a select group of "blockbuster" medications each year: those that receive both the bulk of ad spending and the majority of subsequent prescriptions. In 1999, for example, just 10 medications accounted for nearly half of all DTCA spending, the industry concentrating its efforts on a few "blockbuster" medicines. A solid return on investment from such targeted spending is clear: 65 percent of total prescription drug sales in 2000 were for the most heavily advertised drugs (Alleyne 2002, p. 107).

Evidence shows that DTCA is one of the most cost-effective marketing sectors in the U.S. economy. In 1999, Pfizer spent $57 million to promote its antihistamine, Zyrtec, and saw a 32 percent increase in sales over 1998 revenues. This increase boosted Zyrtec's drug-sales ranking by 23 spots, while a similar campaign increased Aventis's competing antihistamine, Allegra, by 34 spots. There was no sudden exponential growth in pollen output or sudden increase in the number of people suffering from allergies. There was, however, an increase in the sale of prescription allergy medications as a result of the Allegra DTCA campaign (Mullen and Fisher 2004, p. 185).

THE HEALTH CARE SYSTEM: COSTS AND PRIORITIES

Much of the blame for skyrocketing health care costs has been directed at the increase in prescriptions for expensive, highly advertised medications instead of cheaper generic or over-the-counter equivalents (see "Brand Names versus Generic/Over-the-Counter: The Economics"). The National Institute for Health Care Management, for example, suggests that consumer advertising may be responsible for 10 to 25 percent of the recent increase in prescription drug spending. The increase in spending is vast: it is estimated that in 2002, Americans "paid almost $208 billion for prescription drugs...almost double that spent in 1996" ("TV Ads Spur a Rise in Prescription Drug Sales," 2002, p. 998). As a percentage of total health care costs, prescription drug costs are the fastest growing, rising substantially each year. Growth of such speed and magnitude is exerting tremendous pressure on the budgets of individual consumers and on the financial viability of the health care system as a whole.

Just as it is critical to examine DTCA's role in the increasing costs of health care in America, it is also important to identify where the gap is occurring. If vast sums of money are committed to DTCA campaigns each year, which budgets are being depleted within the pharmaceutical/health care industry, and to what effect?

The enormous financial rewards enjoyed by pharmaceutical companies as a result of DTCA campaigns has prompted a structural shift in recent years; today an ever-greater percentage of drug budgets in particular, and industry resources in general, are earmarked for DTCA. In 2000, 15 to 20 percent of total drug marketing costs (Bell et al. 2000, p. 329) were devoted to DTCA. By 2003, it was estimated that as much as 90 percent of a brand's total promotional budget was earmarked for DTCA (Mehta and Purvis 2003, p. 194). The increase in advertising resources is mirrored by a shift in industry structure, as pharmaceutical companies downsize their research and development departments while bolstering marketing sectors.

Prompted by the earnings potential of DTCA, the shifting of both money and nonfiscal resources toward DTCA suggests the pharmaceutical industry is adjusting economically and structurally to enable a continuation and/or intensification of the DTCA trend. While this may make economic sense from the perspective of the pharmaceutical industry, it may leave a gap in the health care system in the context of research/development, and impede research progress on medical conditions that lack "blockbuster" treatments.

DOCTOR, THE CUSTOMER IS HERE TO SEE YOU

Just as medications are seen less as chemical compounds than as consumer products in the DTCA prism, patients are positioned as mass-market consumers instead of as medical subjects. Close analysis of the discourses of the pharmaceutical industry reveals a tendency to frame potential consumers as sources of profit, rather than as individuals. This tendency can dehumanize individual patients in favor of a more dispassionate economic discourse.

Internal industry publications and sources frequently refer to consumers in terms of economic benefit, failing to acknowledge that real human suffering and varied personal experiences underlie each prescription. Consumers are

---

BRAND NAMES VERSUS GENERIC/OVER-THE-COUNTER: THE ECONOMICS

One of the central debates in the study of DTCA is the promotion of brand-name medications that have equally effective, and, oftentimes, less expensive generic or over-the-counter equivalents.

Example 1

The acid-reflux/heartburn medication Nexium, and its over-the-counter counterpart, Prilosec, are virtually equal in terms of effectiveness. However, in the wake of a massive marketing campaign to promote Nexium, it has become one of the top-ten best-selling medications in the United States, garnering nearly $3 billion in yearly sales.

Example 2

A 1999 medical study revealed that neither heavily advertised Vioxx nor Celebrex "alleviated pain any better than the older medicines" (Berensen et al. 2004). Despite this finding, Vioxx's 2003 sales topped $2.5 billion and comprised 11 percent of Merck's total revenue that year ("Costs of Recall Hurt Merck's Results; Lilly's Profit Is Up," 2004). In contrast, the over-the-counter pain relievers referenced in the study cost pennies a dose.

Example 3

The allergy market has been fundamentally transformed by DTCA campaigns for prescription antihistamines. Formerly dominated by over-the-counter remedies, now 53 percent of allergy sufferers buy prescription products (Aitken and Holt 2000, p. 82). One large health management organization (HMO) estimated that it spent "$20 million dollars paying for costly, heavily advertised, non-sedating antihistamines when generics would have sufficed" (West 1999).

classified according to measurements of "highest potential lifetime value," "appropriate performance metrics," and "value per patient (return per script multiplied by duration of use)." Just as the weakening of physician authority in the patient relationship can cause an imbalance in quality of care, the inflation of the patient's economic value over his or her physiological health is a real and important byproduct of the DTCA trend.

There is evidence that even physicians have begun to refer to patients from within an economic framework. Surveys have found that many doctors have prescribed medications in order to satisfy patient demands and not to meet the specific physiological demands of the medical condition. In part, this acquiescence on the part of physicians can be attributed to the desire to maintain a positive working physician-patient relationship. Doctors do not wish to alienate patients or to lose business, and emphasize that there is a desire, as "with anyone else who provides service, to keep the customer happy" (D. Brown 2004). The designation of patients as "customers" is indicative of the ways in which the physician-patient relationship has adapted to the discourse of the DTCA trend. In this sense, the evolution—or degradation—of the relationship can be seen as: doctor-patient, to doctor-patient-advertiser, and finally to doctor-consumer-advertiser.

CORNFLAKES, ACUPUNCTURE, AND ALTERNATIVE VIEWPOINTS

With advertising budgets for DTCA campaigns approaching or surpassing those for other categories such as consumer goods and food products, it is useful to compare both the type of advertising and its potential effects on consumers. It can be asked of DTCA, "If we start advertising [prescription medications] like corn flakes, does it trivialize medicine?" (Elliott 1998). Consumer products are generally harmless—the choice of one breakfast cereal or wrinkle-reducing cream over another isn't likely to cause physiological harm to the consumer—while medications can seriously harm or kill patients if not prescribed or taken properly. Indeed, there is a substantial gap in the magnitude of the decisions involved in assessing risk and reward of, for example, a breakfast cereal, as compared with a prescription medication.

This serious difference raises legitimate and important concerns about the advisability of treating prescription medications as if they were general, casual, and benign consumer products, and promoting them as such. Furthermore, a sense of "needing" a specific consumer product can be inspired by creative advertising, while "needing" prescription medications should ideally be based on physiological factors and physician recommendations. The similar advertising methods between prescription medications and general consumer goods encourage the stimulation of popular demand for products whose use should be based solely on medical need.

It is also worth noting that, as a product of the pharmaceutical industry with financial interests in the return on investment of DTCA campaigns, prescription medications tend to be favored in the media over other health alternatives.

The prevalence of DTCA and the cultural authority it holds as a mode of consumption effectively precludes alternative treatments, such as homeopathic or natural remedies, as well as unbranded generic or over-the-counter medications. In the context of the prevailing social order, DTCA privileges heavily advertised, expensive medications over all other possibilities. This is evident both at the micro-level, in the changing physician-patient relationship, and at the macro-level, with the increasing costs of health care in America.

The World Health Organization itself debates the merits of DTCA, arguing that it represents an "inherent conflict of interest between the legitimate business goals of manufacturers and the social, medical and economic needs of providers and the public to select and use drugs in the most rational way" (Mintzes 2002, p. 908). However, there is also indisputable proof that DTCA facilitates education and dialogue, as well as normalizes serious and previously stigmatized medical conditions. Presently, advertising's persuasive modes remain the primary source of public knowledge about certain medical issues and medications. In the absence of effective alternatives such as public education campaigns at both national and global levels, critics can only hope that the profit motives of the pharmaceutical industry can be reconciled with the serendipitous byproducts of education and personal health empowerment.

See also Advertising and Persuasion; Body Image; Disabilities and Media; Hypercommercialism; Media and Citizenship; Product Placement; Video News Releases; Women's Magazines.

Further Reading: Aitken, Murray, and Frazier Holt. "A Prescription for Direct Drug Marketing." *The McKinsey Quarterly* (Spring 2000); Alleyne, Sonia. "Commercial Medicine: Black Doctors Say Drug Ads May Not Be a Bad Thing." *Black Enterprise* 22, no. 1 (August 2002). http://findarticles.com/p/articles/mi_m1365/is_1_33/ai_89648495; Angell, Marcia. *The Truth About the Drug Companies: How they Deceive Us and What to Do About It.* New York: Random House, 2004; "A Spoonful of Sugar: Pharmaceutical Companies Are Finding Sneaky—But Effective—Ways of Getting Around Laws that Prevent Direct Advertising of Prescription Medicines to the Public. Should We Be Worried?" *Choice: Australian Consumers' Association* (June 2004). http://choice.com.au/goArticle. aspx?id=104325; Avorn, Jerry. *Powerful Medicines: The Benefits, Risks and Costs of Prescription Drugs.* New York: Knopf, 2004; Bell, Robert A., Michael S. Wilkes, and Richard L. Kravitz. "Direct-to-Consumer Prescription Drug Advertising, 1989–1998." *Journal of Family Practice* 49, no. 4 (April 2000); Berensen, Alex, Gardiner Harris, Barry Meier, and Andrew Pollack. "Despite Warnings, Drug Giant Took Long Path to Vioxx Recall." *New York Times,* November 14, 2004, A1; Brown, Anne B. "The Direct-to-Consumer Advertising Dilemma." *Patient Care* 35, no. 6 (March 30, 2001): 22–33; Brown, David. "Promise and Peril of Vioxx Cast Harsher Light on New Drugs." *Washington Post,* October 4, 2004, A14; Charatan, Fred. "US Prescription Drug Sales Boosted by Advertising." *The British Medical Journal* 321, no.7264 (September 30, 2000): 783; "Costs of Recall Hurt Merck's Results; Lilly's Profit is Up" *New York Times,* October 22, 2004, C3; Elliott, Stuart. "Take Two Direct Sales Pitches for Prescription Drugs and Call Your Pollster in the Morning," *New York Times,* July 29, 1998, D5; Foley, Lisa. "The Medication Information Gap: Older Consumers in the Void Between Direct-to-Consumer Advertising and Professional Care." *Generations* 24, no. 4 (Winter 2000–01): 49; Higgs, Robert. *Hazardous to Our Health? FDA Regulation of Health Care Products.*

Oakland, CA: The Independent Institute, 1995; Jhally, Sut. "Advertising As Religion: The Dialectic of Technology and Magic." *Cultural Politics in Contemporary America,* ed. Ian Angus and Sut Jhally. New York: Routledge, 1989; Jhally, Sut. *The Codes of Advertising: Fetishism and the Political Economy of Meaning in the Consumer Society.* London: Frances Pinter Publishers, 1987; Kassirer, Jerome. *On the Take: How Medicine's Complicity With Big Business Can Endanger Your Health.* New York: Oxford University Press, 2005; Klein, Naomi. *No Space. No Choice. No Jobs. No Logo.* New York: Picador, 2002; Mehta, Abhilasha, and Scott C. Purvis. "Consumer Response to Print Prescription Drug Advertising." *Journal of Advertising Research* 43, no. 2 (June 2003): 194–206; Mintzes, Barbara. "Direct to Consumer Advertising is Medicalising Normal Human Experience." *The British Medical Journal* 324, no. 7342 (April 13, 2002): 908–11; Morgan, Carol, and Doron Levy. "To Their Health: RX Companies Are Trying to Figure Out the Best Method for Reaching Aging Boomers." *Brandweek* 39, no. 3 (January 19, 1998). http://calbears.findarticles.com/p/articles/mi_m0BDW/is_n3_v39/ai_20165080; Mullen, Lawrence J., and Julie D. Fisher. "A Visual Analysis of Prescription Drug Advertising Imagery: Elaborating Foss's Rhetorical Techniques." *Communication Studies* 55, no. 1 (Spring 2004): 185–96; Roth, Martin S. "Media and Message Effects on DTC Prescription Drug Print Advertising Awareness." *Journal of Advertising Research* 43, no. 2 (June 2003): 180–93; Schulz, Kathryn. "Did Antidepressants Depress Japan?" *New York Times Magazine* 22, August 2004; "TV Ads Spur a Rise in Prescription Drug Sales." *Pediatrics* 109, no. 6 (June 2002); West, Diane. "The War on Drugs." *Pharmaceutical Executive* 19, no. 4 (April 1999): S5.

Tissa Richards

PIRACY AND INTELLECTUAL PROPERTY

Do you own a computer or a cell phone? Do you download music, cut and paste text, stream movies or television shows, or "grab" pictures to post on your MySpace or blog? Do you always pay for using these media? If not, you may be a pirate! Your right to access and use cultural content on the Internet, radio, TV, CDs, and DVDs is threatened by a growing body of laws that privatize ideas and creative expressions and make criminals out of those who participate in the production and circulation of our common culture. Media industries say they need copyright protections to remain competitive. But many artists, academics, and public-interest groups suggest that some acts of piracy may be a justifiable response to this expanding legal framework.

Intellectual property (IP) refers to a set of legal rights granting exclusive use of particular immaterial products to an individual or institution. These rights recognize certain creative expressions—or ideas, such as a song, the design of a desk chair, a company logo or name (like Levi's), a story, or a movie—as property that can be owned or exchanged. "Piracy" is the term widely used to describe the "theft" of IP; but given the intangible nature of what is "stolen," the act of piracy is better described as an infringement on legal rights.

The rationale behind the protection of IP is that granting exclusive rights to economically exploit one's creative work encourages innovation, which benefits society as a whole. But expansion of IP protections is encroaching on individuals' ability to access and use shared cultural resources. This blocks the social circulation of ideas, which stifles creativity, thwarts innovation, and creates or perpetuates social and economic inequalities by establishing a market in privatized information. Is piracy—the infringement on IP rights—a justified response to this expanding legal framework that criminalizes participation and creative engagement with the production and circulation of cultural expressions common to a society?

TIMELINE

1709—Britain's Statute of Anne is the first copyright law enacted.

1790—The Copyright Act of 1790 is the first U.S. federal copyright law, offering protection for a 14-year term with the option of one 14-year term extension.

1883—The Paris Convention for the Protection of Industrial Property is one of the first international IP treaties, requiring contracting states to recognize each other's IP protection laws.

1887—The Berne Convention for the Protection of Literary and Artistic Works requires contracting states to recognize the copyrights of authors from other contracting states as they would their own.

1893—The United International Bureaux for the Protection of Intellectual Property (BIRPI), formed from the merger of two smaller bureaus established by the Paris and Berne Conventions, becomes the administrative body for the international protection of IP.

1909—The U.S. Copyright Act of 1909 extends the term of copyright to 28 years, with the option of renewing for another 28-year term.

1967—The World Intellectual Property Organization (WIPO) is formed as a replacement for BIRPI.

1974—WIPO becomes an organization of the United Nations.

1976—The U.S. Copyright Act of 1976 extends the term of copyright to life of the author plus 50 years, or 75 years for works of corporate authorship.

1994—The Agreement on Trade Related Aspects of Intellectual Property (TRIPS) shifts the protection and enforcement of IP onto the international trading system, requiring members of the World Trade Organization (WTO) to adopt standardized IP laws or face trade and economic sanctions.

1998—The U.S. Copyright Term Extension Act (also known as the Sonny Bono Copyright Term Extension Act or the Mickey Mouse Protection Act) extends copyright protection to life of the author plus 70 years, or 95 years for works of corporate authorship.

1998—The U.S. Digital Millennium Copyright Act (DMCA) criminalizes circumvention of—and the production or distribution of devices or services for the circumvention of—systems that control access to copyrighted works, commonly known as Digital Right Management (DRM) systems.

2001—The European Union Copyright Directive (EUCD) criminalizes DRM circumvention in the European Union.

PRIVATIZING IDEAS

There are five basic types of IP that fall into two categories. Industrial property rights are established through laws governing patents, trademarks, trade secrets, and industrial designs, while copyright laws govern the ownership and exchange of creative and artistic expressions that circulate more broadly in a society. There are also other forms of IP protection that do not fit into these categories, such as the registration of Internet domain names, geographical indications such as Kona coffee and Bordeaux wine, the layout of integrated circuits, and plant breeders' rights. Though the duration of legal protection varies by type and by country, minimum international standards have been established for members of the World Trade Organization (WTO).

Patents are granted to the inventor of a new product or process deemed to be practical and novel. When a patent expires, the invention enters the public domain and can be freely used and commercially exploited by anyone. Companies often attempt to extend legal protection by altering a product or offering it for a "novel" purpose. For example, in 2001 pharmaceutical giant Eli Lilly lost a protracted legal battle to maintain exclusive rights to their most valuable product—Prozac—by repatenting it for a new use.

TRADEMARKS

Trademarks are distinctive signs—ranging from combinations of letters, numbers, and words, to visual symbols, sounds, shapes, colors, and fragrances—that link a particular product or service to a specific business. McDonald's Golden Arches are a trademark, the word "Kleenex" is trademarked by the Kimberley-Clark company, and UPS holds a trademark on a particular shade of brown.

INDUSTRIAL DESIGN RIGHTS

Industrial design rights protect the aesthetic value of nonutilitarian designs with original and unique visual appeal. Shapes, patterns, ornaments, and configurations can be considered IP as they are applied to clothes, fashion accessories, jewelry, cars, furniture, appliances, packaging—just about any manufactured good. The shape and layout of cell phones such as Motorola's RAZR and Apple's iPhone are examples of protected industrial design rights.

TRADE SECRETS

Trade secrets are forms of information that have economic value only if they remain secret. The recipe for Coca-Cola is a trade secret, as is the secret sauce in Big Macs. But the range of protections is vast: formulas, compounds, prototypes, processes, calculations, analytical data, sales and marketing information, customer lists, financial information, and business plans are only some of the possible forms of information that can be protected as trade secrets.

COPYRIGHT

Copyright is actually a bundle of rights that protects literary or artistic expressions by defining the conditions for their reproduction, distribution, importation, sale, derivative works, adaptation, translation, broadcast, exhibition, and public performance. Copyright encompasses, but is not limited to, books, plays, newspapers, computer programs, films, databases, musical compositions, paintings, photographs, maps, sculpture, architecture, and advertisements. "Fair use"—a legal concept specific to the United States—and the related "fair dealing" found in the common law of some other countries protect limited use of copyrighted materials for academic and research purposes.

PROTECTING MICKEY MOUSE

These categories of rights overlap in their protection of certain ideas. For example, Mickey Mouse is covered by both copyright and trademark. When the copyright on Mickey expires—which would have been in 2000, if not for a 20-year extension of copyright protection enacted by the 1998 Copyright Term Extension Act (sometimes called the Mickey Mouse Protection Act due to the extensive lobbying by Disney that aided passage of the law)—use of his image will still be protected as a trademark of Disney.

This wide range of IP protections attempts to remove from the public domain a vast quantity of ideas and expressions. Such privatization makes it difficult to create new ideas and expressions without infringing on those already protected. Is an act of piracy "theft" if it draws on the same common cultural resources from which the idea infringed upon was developed? Understanding both the emergence of IP rights and the current context in which they operate allows us to question the criminality of some acts labeled as piracy.

"CRACKING DOWN" ON PIRACY

On April 14, 2007, following a string of raids on illegal manufacturers, shops, street vendors, and homes spanning 31 provinces in China, authorities destroyed approximately 42 million pirated copies of CDs, DVDs, and print materials by bulldozer, bonfire, and shredding machine. These public spectacles were reminiscent of a similar media conflagration staged in Bangkok's Pantip Plaza—which had been a veritable shopping mall of pirated goods—on the eve of China's entry into the WTO in 2001. The bright glare of these public performances, designed to showcase China's commitment to protecting IP, illuminates some key questions in the debate over the limits of IP protection, especially as it is globally propagated through international trade deals under pressure from private industries.

Public bonfires make for a good show but do little to staunch the flow of pirated media goods. The intangible digital data that comprise the copyrighted material on music CDs, DVD movies, computer software, and text files can be infinitely duplicated, and the availability and affordability of technology used to do so has made pirated media cheap and widely available. China is criticized for not doing enough to protect IP rights, but given the indestructible and reproducible nature of information and media, what can really be done to protect it as property?

While the United States has focused on preventative measures, instigating youth education programs to publicize the criminality of IP rights infringement and relying on the "chilling effect" of threatened lawsuits, China has resorted to global displays of violent force that distract from their tacit policy of mostly looking the other way. Neither country has succeeded in deterring piracy, and increasingly, media industries are turning to DRM systems—copy restrictions encoded into the media materials themselves. But these are often "cracked" soon after they are implemented, opening them up to duplication and distribution in black markets, while limiting how legitimate consumers can use the media for which they have paid.

Though the film industry measures losses to piracy in the profit they might have made from legal sales, there is no reason to expect that those who buy a DVD for $2 would pay $30 if the pirated copy were not available. In China, the pirated copies are often all that is available, and the black markets in pirated goods may actually serve to introduce people in China to the Western culture of consumption, engendering demand for more products and opening new channels of distribution for legitimate markets.

CAN WE SHARE? THE COMMONS AND THE CREATION OF THE AUTHOR

The concept of granting and protecting rights that establish ideas or their expressions as property developed within a Western European philosophical and legal framework. Resources are seen as part of a "commons" shared by society, from which anything can only be "fenced off" by exclusive use rights—and thus become property—through the application of labor. Because we have a right to the work we do, we are able to claim rights over that which we work on.

FOLKLORE AND FAIRY TALES

But IP is not easy to separate from the commons. Unlike material property, IP is not "scarce"—it can be used without being used up. The almost infinite reproducibility of music, stories, images, and ideas allows them to circulate within a society as "public goods," where they can be enjoyed and even used as the basis of new forms of expression without detracting from the "commons." What amount of work does an individual have to do to modify an idea or expression common to society to be able to claim exclusive rights to it? What allowed the Brothers Grimm to claim authorship of fairy tales that had been circulating for centuries? How was Nirvana able to record and sell the traditional American folk song "Where Did You Sleep Last Night?" How can the ideas and cultural expressions we all share—public goods—be privatized?

THE PRINTING PRESS

While we have been creating, expressing, and inventing for millennia, legal protection of exclusive use rights to ideas and their representations only developed as a response to changes in the notion of authorship brought about by the rise of liberal individualism and the invention of technologies for mass reproduction such as the Gutenberg printing press.

THE AUTHOR

By making reproduction more time and cost efficient, the printing press greatly increased the distribution of texts, creating legal problems in publishers' competing claims to the rights to copy remarkably similar manuscripts acquired from different "authors." In response, Britain's 1709 Statute of Anne—the first copyright law—shifted the right to copy from publishers to "authors."

This legal creation of "the author" established a tension between the cultural commons and individual acts of creativity by suggesting that creative work can be quantified and judged in terms of how it exceeds the culturally common elements and ideas from which it is composed. When can someone claim their rendition of a song they heard from someone else as their own? How do we measure the difference? Can we own a five-note sequence? One note? Is borrowing a beat "fair use"?

DIGITAL SAMPLING

As with the printing press, the development of digital samplers led to legal disputes over the use and ownership of culturally common expressions, reiterating in the musical realm the problems of recognizing sole authorship. Hip-hop has a rich history of sampling, from deft disc jockeying to mix tapes, but the confluence of affordable audio reproduction technologies and the breakout popularity of records that sampled other music, such as the Beastie Boys' 1986 *Licensed to Ill*, publicized the threat IP protection poses to artistic expression. Even now, long after the Supreme Court's 1994 ruling in favor of 2 Live Crew's fair-use claim to guitar, bass, and drum samples from Roy Orbison's "Pretty Woman," musicians are still threatened for their use of samples. Danger Mouse's *The Grey Album*—a mashup of Jay-Z's *The Black Album* and samples from the Beatles' *The White Album*—has been the target of litigation by EMI, which owns the rights to the Beatles' songs. Other music we never get a chance to hear. Public Enemy pulled the track "Psycho of Greed" from their 2002 album *Revolverlution* because of the exorbitant fee for using a sample from the Beatles' "Tomorrow Never Knows."

Our "rip, mix, and burn" culture suggests that many of us engage with these same processes of remixing and sharing cultural expressions, which blur the line between the commons and private ownership. Expanding IP protections attempt to redefine this line and to set the conditions for assessing the legality of our engagement with our own culture. Critics charge that instead of serving the interests of individuals' creative cultural expressions, such protections are designed to help the information and media industries maintain and expand markets.

THE GLOBAL EXPANSION OF IP PROTECTION

IP laws were for the most part developed by the United States and Western European nations under pressure from private industries seeking to protect current interests and create new fields for safe investment. The range of IP protections has been expanded sporadically since the eighteenth century to cover more forms of ideas and expressions for longer periods of time over a larger geographic area. But the international standardization and global implementation of national IP laws has only been achieved more recently through high-pressure trade negotiations dominated by a U.S.-led coalition of economically and politically powerful countries, who were in turn influenced by intense lobbying from multinational corporations heavily invested in knowledge-based industries such as the media.

Thus, the World Intellectual Property Organization (WIPO)—established in 1967 to "promote the protection of intellectual property throughout the world"—was bypassed by the Agreement on Trade Related Aspects of Intellectual Property (TRIPS) in 1994, and the WTO became the de facto governing body for international IP rights. All WTO member states must sign on to TRIPS, which requires that they enact IP laws modeled largely on those of the United States and European nations that were formed to protect the interests of private industries.

This has allowed multinational corporations to expand into developing nations under legal protection from the government, where they create new markets for previously acquired IPs and use their economic muscle to acquire new IPs for other markets. Not only does this give them an unfair advantage over local producers of valuable IPs, but also gives the multinationals a great deal of control over the circulation of cultural expressions in the public domain. For these reasons, many argue that the global growth of media piracy is a response to the simultaneous expansion of media markets and IP protections that greatly increase the availability of creative cultural expressions while severely delimiting how people can engage with them.

See also Branding the Globe; Communication Rights in a Global Context; Digital Divide; Google Book Search; Hypercommercialism; Innovation and Imitation in Commercial Media; Internet and Its Radical Potential; The iTunes Effect; Media Reform; Net Neutrality; Online Digital Film and Television; Online Publishing; Pirate Radio; User-Created Content and Audience Participation.

Further Reading: Bettig, Ronald V. *Copyrighting Culture: The Political Economy of Intellectual Property.* Boulder, CO: Westview Press, 1996; Cook, Curtis. *Patents, Profits, & Power: How Intellectual Property Rules the Global Economy.* London: Kogan Page, Ltd,

2002; Coombe, Rosemary J. *The Cultural Life of Intellectual Properties: Authorship, Appropriation, and the Law.* Durham, NC: Duke University Press, 1998; Halbert, Deborah J. *Intellectual Property in the Information Age: The Politics of Expanding Ownership Rights.* Westport, CT: Quorum Books, 1999; Haynes, Richard. *Media Rights and Intellectual Property.* Edinburgh: University Press Ltd, 2005; Sell, Susan K. *Private Power, Public Law: The Globalization of Intellectual Property.* Cambridge: University Press, 2003; Thierer, Adam & Wayne Crews, eds. *Copy Fights: The Future of Intellectual Property in the Information Age.* Washington, DC: Cato Institute, 2002; Vaidhyanathan, Siva. *Copyrights and Copywrongs: The Rise of Intellectual Property and How it Threatens Creativity.* New York: University Press, 2001.

Carl McKinney

PIRATE RADIO

"Radio pirates" are those who broadcast without a license. Thus it follows that the first radio pirates were actually the early inventors of the 1900s like Guglielmo Marconi and Reginold Fessindon, themselves unlicensed because, of course, there was no license to be given out at a time when the medium was only just being invented. The term "pirate broadcaster" was initially used to describe amateurs who stepped on another hobbyist's signal, and was coined at a time when there was no government regulation of the airwaves. Today, some activists prefer the term "microbroadcasters" or "free radio," arguing that they are not criminals but rather, more like revolutionary pamphleteer Thomas Paine.

Pirate radio broadcasters have emerged—and continue to emerge—all over the world, in places that lack sufficient legal means for citizens to have access to the radio waves. They operate in opposition to government-controlled airwaves as a crucial means of providing information and news during times of civil war and unrest, and for some, just for fun, or "because we can." Governments have used pirate radio as a means of broadcasting clandestine information across otherwise closed borders. Even in an era of increasingly Internet-based radio listening in the United States, FM pirate radio stations continue to emerge as forms of resistance to the corporate domination of the airwaves, and as alternative media outlets in their own right, in large part because radio is an affordable technology, easy to operate, and accessible for listening audiences.

RADIO REGULATION AND THE DEVIL?

In 1925, evangelist Aimee Semple McPherson sent a telegram to then secretary in commerce Herbert Hoover, imploring him to "Please order your minions of Satan to leave my station alone. You cannot expect the Almighty to abide by your wavelength nonsense. When I offer my prayers to Him I must fit into His wave reception. Open this station at once" (Hadden and Swann 1981, pp. 188–89).

PIRATE RADIO AROUND THE WORLD

There is a tendency to write off pirate radio stations as one-off projects of hacks and kids interfering with legitimate radio stations just for fun. Or in Britain, the common narrative around pirates is that of a haven for gang culture, drugs, and underground garage and reggae clubs. While there are certainly examples of pirate stations that fit both these stereotypes, the failure of many media scholars, policy makers, and the general public to adequately account for the impact of pirate radio is a disservice to an important site of the battle over media ownership and "citizen" access to the airwaves.

As such, pirate radio exists in many shapes and sizes. Radio Venceremos ("Radio We Will Win"), for example, broadcast as an underground guerrilla radio station in opposition to the government from the highland jungles of El Salvador during the country's civil war in the 1980s. The station was a crucial means of information for peasants and indigenous people, transmitting news, playing music, and serving as witness to war, airing live reports of air attacks, civilian massacres, and battles between guerrillas and government troops. The station broadcasts today from the capital city with a license. Pirate radio stations were also vital sources of news and information across Eastern Europe under communism, and in former Yugoslavia in opposition to Slobodan Milosevic. In Chiapas, Mexico, pirate radio continues to be an important communication tool used by the Zapatistas.

Pirate broadcasting is at times a dangerous business. Stations have been bombed or been the target of sustained government attacks and intimidation. Even in Tampa, Florida, pirate operator Doug Brewer had his station raided in 1995 by heavily armed agents from the Federal Communications Commission (FCC), FBI, and local police. During the raid, Brewer and his wife were held at gunpoint on the floor while their equipment was raided and house ransacked. "I had absolutely no political agenda—at least not until they came in here with guns," Brewer told the *Los Angeles Times*. "I just thought Tampa radio sucked and we had to do something to improve it" (Bennett 1998).

There are pirate stations like Galway Pirate Women in Ireland, broadcasting a range of programming made by and directed at women, the former KBLT in Los Angeles, a station that became an influential outpost for alternative music and hipster culture during its short life on air, or Radio Limbo in Tucson, which provided a cultural oasis in the city by playing a range of eclectic music not otherwise on air in the city. There is Reverend Rick Strawcutter of Radio Free Lenawee broadcasting in Michigan from a small room inside the Church of Our Lord Jesus Christ, battling the government over his right to broadcast, or patriot broadcaster Lonnie Kobres, who has the distinction of being the only person in the United States who actually went to jail for unlicensed broadcasting (typically the FCC confiscates equipment and may also levy fines). There are progressively radical or anarchist stations like Steal This Radio in New York, Freak Radio in Santa Cruz, and the San Francisco Liberation Radio, and radically conservative and sometimes survivalist or even white-supremacist stations. Despite deep ideological differences, these groups share a frustration with the government's system of allocating access to the airwaves. "What unites these microbroadcasters," writes Rijsmadel, "is the systematic exclusion of them and their audiences—who frequently are also participants—from their local media, be it commercial or public, radio or television."

WHY PIRATE?

Pirate radio is often the project of communities looking to fill a void on the radio and bring neighbors together. In Vermont, Radio Free Brattleboro fought their impending FCC closure with widespread support including that of the city council and Senator Patrick Leahy, himself a co-sponsor of legislation to expand low-power radio, in part because of pressure from the Brattleboro community he serves. In the United Kingdom, north London pirate Lush FM operates as a community-run station and is involved in local anti-gun and violence prevention programs. A recent survey by the British communications regulator concluded that one in six adults regularly listens to pirate radio, with the figure even higher in some of the most ethnically diverse and poorest neighborhoods in London (Ofcom 2000).

Pirate stations and their organizers have influenced policy decisions related to the allocation of radio licenses and the structure of broadcasting sectors. In the 1960s, an explosion of off-shore pirate radio stations emerged in the waters off the coast of Britain. These stations, set up on old fishing boats, served as alternatives to the monopoly the BBC had, at the time, over the airwaves. While the BBC was highly regarded for its role in providing quality news and public affairs, it offered only limited hours of pop music airplay during the height of popularity of British bands like the Beatles and the Rolling Stones. Pirate stations like Radio Caroline captured the zeitgeist of the times. As a result, many scholars credit the influence these stations had on the BBC's decision to launch less-centralized local radio services and a pop music channel (BBC Radio 1—whose first DJs included a number of former pirates like John Peel). In Hungary, the first community station in the country began as a pirate in 1991, during the early post-communist years. Tilos Rádió ("Forbidden Radio") defiantly went on air to bring attention to the fact that there were no legal means for community groups and independent broadcasters to apply for a license. Tilos was eventually licensed four years later, following the development of a media policy with strong support for community stations, and continues to be at the heart of cultural life in Budapest.

In the United States, a group of pirate broadcasters have been key actors in the movement to expand legal alternatives for community-based or amateur broadcasters. In 1986, housing rights activist Mbanna Kantako set up a radio station to serve the African American community of Springfield, Illinois. The station, WTRA, Radio of the Tenants' Rights Association, began as a community organizing tool for the housing project. The station was ignored by authorities for several years, until it broke a story about what ended up being a high-profile police brutality case. When agents came to shut down the station, Kantako went downtown to the federal building and the police station and dared officials to arrest him. When authorities realized such a course of action could backfire in the increasingly tense situation, they left him alone for years, spurring many to realize the FCC was not always ready to enforce its own regulations. WTRA is now known as Black Liberation Radio and continues to broadcast without a license, even after a raid of its equipment in 1999.

TIMELINE

1906—On Christmas Eve, Reginald Fessenden broadcasts the first-ever radio broadcast of music and voice over long distances. From an unlicensed station he built in Brant Rock, Massachusetts, his broadcast includes a reading and Christmas song, and is heard by unsuspecting wireless operators on ships as far away as off the coast of Virginia.

1937—The first experimental FM radio station, W1XOJ, is granted a construction permit by the FCC. The birth of FM—a cheaper and easier medium to build and operate than AM—eventually makes it possible for a movement of pirates to flourish.

1947—XERF, one of the most famous of the "border blaster" radio stations, begins operation from Cuidad Acuna just across the Rio Grande in Mexico. These border stations were not pirates, but represent early attempts at subverting the U.S. licensing system by broadcasting from stations licensed in Mexico near the U.S. border. Some border blasters did, however, broadcast content in violation of U.S. consumer protection law, such as a station in Kansas whose on-air healers advocated "goat gland surgery" to improve masculinity.

1958—Radio Mercur, the first known station to broadcast from a ship in international waters (the first offshore European pirate station) launches. Others, like Radio Caroline, follow in the 1960s, until passage of the Marine Broadcasting Offences Act of 1968 made such broadcasting practically illegal.

1973—The FCC refuses to renew right-wing, fundamentalist Christian radio operator Reverend Carl McIntire's radio license for station WXUR because the station did not comply with the Fairness Doctrine, which required time be given to opposing viewpoints. In response, McIntire becomes a pirate, broadcasting off the coast of New Jersey from a former WWII minesweeper, marking a new era in his long-standing fight against the FCC—a battle he eventually lost, although an important precedent is set regarding the FCC's authority to regulate offshore broadcasting.

1979—At the behest of newly created National Public Radio, the FCC eliminates class D licensing, a service used by many noncommercial, educational broadcasters. This move further fuels the explosion of pirates in the 1980s and 1990s.

1987—Mbana Kantako launches a pirate radio station in the Springfield, Illinois, housing project where he lives. The station later becomes known as Black Liberation Radio and is credited with inspiring a generation of future pirates.

1995—The FCC files a motion against California's Stephen Dunifer and Free Radio Berkeley, sparking a prolonged court battle during which time pirate radio in the

United States flourished, echoing Dunifer's call to have "a thousand transmitters bloom."

1998—West Philadelphia's Radio Mutiny and others stage the Showdown at the FCC, a protest in support of a community's right to have access to the airwaves. The highlight of the demonstration is a pirate broadcast in front of the FCC's headquarters in Washington, DC.

2000—The FCC creates the service for low-power FM radio (LPFM), allowing neighborhood-based groups the possibility to apply for low-power radio licenses. The service is curtailed soon after by Congress, which limits the areas where the service is available to the least populated parts of the country. As of spring 2007, activists like the Prometheus Radio Project are fighting to have this decision overturned.

2001—Reverend Rick Strawcutter of Radio Free Lenawee broadcasting inside the Church of Our Lord Jesus Christ is taken off air by the FCC. Strawcutter is well known among pirates for his efforts in fighting the FCC to allow low-power stations to operate.

2007—Nevada pirate operator Rod Moses obtains permission from the FCC to continue broadcasting with a special temporary authority until he can apply for an LPFM license in a yet-undetermined future application window. Permission is obtained following the intervention of U.S. Senate Majority Leader Harry Reid.

FREE RADIO BERKELEY VERSUS THE FCC

Inspired by Kantako and others, a movement of pirate radio broadcasters emerged in the 1990s that directly challenged the government's policy of ignoring community concerns. Microbroadcasters achieved some surprising victories in the courts, which threw into doubt the validity of the licensing system itself. Of significance was the case put forward by microbroadcaster Stephen Dunifer of Free Radio Berkeley, whose case compelled the court to strongly consider whether, as he claimed, under the stewardship of the FCC the public airwaves had become "a concession stand for corporate America." Though Dunifer's case was ultimately lost in the courts, a great deal of momentum was created and many otherwise law-abiding citizens were taking to the airwaves without a license as a form of protest against corporate domination of media.

Dunifer is an electrical engineer from Berkeley, California, who became frustrated with what he felt was a pro-Pentagon tenor of mainstream reporting during the first Gulf War in 1991. In response, he built a transmitter from scratch and carried it in a backpack up to the hills above Berkeley and began broadcasting. In time, the station began serving as a community station, open to programmers who contacted Dunifer and wanted to get involved. After a few years of covert broadcasting, Dunifer was caught by the FCC and fined $20,000. He vowed to continue broadcasting and publicly refused to pay the fine. The FCC then took him to court seeking an injunction against him.

His 1993 case was a turning point for the free radio movement. The National Lawyers Guild took his case, arguing the regulations were unconstitutional on the basis of the First Amendment right to free speech. They argued that the United

States's model of telecommunication regulations allows only a wealth-based broadcasting system and that the dominance of media by corporate interests is not accidental but is inherent in the design of the current regulatory framework. Dunifer made the claim that micro-radio is the "leaflet of the Nineties" and that to disallow it is tantamount to censorship. Free Radio Berkeley won an important Ninth Federal District Court decision in 1995 in which Judge Claudia Wilken refused to grant an injunction against Dunifer pending review of the constitutionality of current FCC licensing practices. It took four years for the case to make its way back through the system and in the meantime, Dunifer continued broadcasting in a quasi "not legal but not illegal" state. Dunifer eventually lost the case on technical grounds, as, since he had never actually applied for an FCC license, he was thus never officially denied one, according to the court's ultimate decision.

During the time his case was pending, however, hundreds of people across the country took advantage of the apparent lapse in the FCC's authority to regulate the airwaves and began their own unlicensed broadcasting. Accurate numbers are difficult to come by, but it seems upward of 1,000 pirate radio stations were in operation across the country in the early 1990s, echoing Dunifer's call to see "a thousand transmitters bloom." There were also conservative religious and politically right-wing stations that emerged, including some stations run by white supremacists.

Many of the politically progressive pirates responded en masse. Spearheaded by Dunifer and Free Radio Berkeley and organizer Pete Tridish (co-founder of the Prometheus Radio Project) and Radio Mutiny based in West Philadelphia, they began to mobilize. When Radio Mutiny's studio transmitter was seized by FCC agents, the group responded by demonstrating outside the Liberty Bell in downtown Philadelphia. Activists with Radio Mutiny organized a conference of microbroadcasters and the "Showdown at the FCC," in which 150 pirates gathered in Washington, DC, in October 1998. The highlight of the demonstration was a pirate radio broadcast on the steps of the national headquarters of the FCC.

LOW-POWER FM (LPFM)

By the late 1990s, the FCC had begun a serious crackdown on pirates across the country. But the sheer number of new pirate operators, and the community support many enjoyed, put the new FCC chairman William Kennard in an awkward position. Kennard admitted that the pirates had some legitimate concerns regarding the concentration of media ownership and lack of community access to the airwaves. Kennard was especially concerned about the declining number of minority-owned radio stations following passage of the 1996 Telecommunications Act. The FCC chairman announced he would prioritize creation of legitimate opportunities for new voices on the radio dial. Robert McChesney put it this way, stating: "[The pirates] showed the FCC that low-power broadcasting is here whether you like it or not. And that they're going to have to deal with it" (quoted in Markels 2000). In 2000, the FCC created a new service for noncommercial low-power radio. While issues remain regarding the expansion of the service beyond small towns and rural parts of the country, LPFM is nevertheless an important milestone toward increasing public access to the airwaves.

It is significant that this movement of pirate radio activism took hold in the period prior to and around the passage of the 1996 Telecommunications Act, a time during which the radio industry was subject to massive consolidation of ownership, reduction and, in some cases, elimination of local influence over content and programming decisions. And public radio was increasingly being criticized by some for becoming increasingly national in focus and "beige" in sound. These criticisms remain in the foreground for alternative media advocates.

CONCLUSION

In short, pirate radio is deeply woven into the cultural fabric of our media landscape, emerging in a range of contexts for a variety of agendas across all political lines. It has demonstrated the need for more media diversity and public access and less corporate and government domination of the airwaves, has galvanized a movement of media activists, and has entered the cultural lexicon as an evocative symbol of media resistance. Pirate radio is both an alternative to mainstream media and a site where important battles over communication rights are taking place.

See also Alternative Media in the United States; Conglomeration and Media Monopolies; Global Community Media; Government Censorship and Freedom of Speech; Hypercommercialism; The iTunes Effect; Media Reform; Minority Media Ownership; National Public Radio; Regulating the Airwaves.

Further Reading: Bennett, Dylan. "Rebel Radio." *Sonoma Country Independent*, May 14–20, 1998; Carpenter, Sue. *40 Watts From Nowhere: A Journey into Pirate Radio*. New York: Scribner, 2004; D'Arcy, Margaretta Mitchell. "Galway Pirate Women." In Caroline Mitchell, ed., *Women and Radio*. London: Routledge, 2000; Fowler, Gene, and Bill Crawford. *Border Radio*. Austin, TX: Texas Monthly Press, 1987; Hadden, Jeffrey and Charles Swann. *Prime-Time Preachers: The Rising Power of Televangelism*. Boston: Addison-Wesley, 1981; Hilliard, Robert L., and Michael C. Keith. *Waves of Rancor: Tuning in the Radical Right*. Armonk: M. E. Sharpe, 1998; Hind, John, and Stephen Mosco. *Rebel Radio: The Full Story of British Pirate Radio*. London: Pluto, 1985; Lewis, P. M., and Jerry Booth. *The Invisible Medium*. Hampshire: Palgrave, 1989; Markels, Alex. "Radio Active." *Wired Magazine* (2000), http://www.wired.com/wired/archive/8.06/radio.html, accessed on October 19, 2005; National Lawyers Guild. "Dunifer Brief," 2000, http://www.nlgcdc. org/briefs/dunifer.html, accessed on March 17, 2004; Ofcom. "Illegal Broadcasting: Understanding the Issues," 2000, http://www.ofcom.org.uk/research/radio/reports/illegal_broadcasting/, accessed on April 19, 2007; Riismandel, Paul. "Radio by and for the Public: the Death and Resurrection of Low-Power Radio." In Michele Hilmes and Jason Loviglio, eds., *Radio Reader: Essays in the Cultural History of Radio*. Urbana-Champaign: University of Illinois Press, 2001; Sakolsky, Ron, and Stephen Dunifer, eds. *Seizing the Airwaves: A Free Radio Handbook*. San Francisco: AK Press, 1998; Tridish, Pete, and Kate Coyer. "A Radio Station in Your Hands is Worth 500 Channels of Mush! The Role of Community Radio in the Struggle against Corporate Domination of Media." In Elliot

D. Cohen, ed., *News Incorporated: Corporate Media Ownership and Its Threat to Democracy.* Amherst, NY: Prometheus Books, 2005; Vigil, Jose Ignacio Lopez, and Mark Field, trans. *Rebel Radio: The Story of El Salvador's Radio Venceremos.* Willimantic, CT: Latin American Bureau, Curbstone Press, 1991; Yoder, Andrew. *Pirate Radio Stations: Tuning in to Underground Broadcasts in the Air and Online.* New York: McGraw Hill, 2002.

Kate Coyer

POLITICAL DOCUMENTARY: *FAHRENHEIT 9/11* AND THE 2004 ELECTION

For many, the year 2004 was a watershed moment in documentary history. Never before had so many documentaries, from Michael Moore's *Fahrenheit 9/11*, to Morgan Spurlock's *Super Size Me*, to Jehane Noujaim's *Control Room*, played to packed houses in multiplexes across the country. What seemed most compelling about this spate of documentaries was not only their popular appeal, but their *political* nature. Whether aimed specifically at the presidential election, or looking critically at the war in Iraq, documentaries in 2004 worked not only to document, but to persuade. For some critics, this was a welcome countermeasure to a media that many believed had failed in its mission to inform the public. For others, however, this was a sign that a once venerated tradition had become tainted by a new media landscape driven by strident partisanship and geared towards the production of "infotainment." But is political documentary really something new? And, more to the point, should documentary be "political" at all?

The reality is that political documentary has been around for as long as documentary itself. Indeed, documentary's earliest pioneers put the form to explicitly political uses, whether it was the agitprop of Dziga Vertov, meant to communicate the values of revolutionary Russia to its people in the 1920s, or the advocacy films of John Grierson, geared towards educating the British public about issues of social concern in the 1930s. And in the U.S. context, political documentaries have always played a central role in the development of the form. For instance, in the 1930s, progressive film collectives such as the Workers' Film and Photo League formed to champion political causes and expose the devastating effects of the Great Depression, while government-sponsored films, such as Pare Lorentz's *The Plow that Broke the Plains* (1936) and *The River* (1937), constructed powerful appeals on behalf of the Roosevelt administration. In the 1940s, Hollywood filmmakers such as Frank Capra (the *Why We Fight* series, 1943–44) and John Ford (*The Battle of Midway*, 1943) were recruited to make the case for the U.S. government's decision to enter World War II.

Later on, in the 1950s, journalist Edward R. Murrow took the government on with TV documentaries that advocated against the injustices of McCarthyism (*See It Now*, 1954) and exposed the mistreatment of migrant farm workers (*Harvest of Shame*, 1960). The 1960s and 1970s saw an eruption of political work by independent documentarians. Filmmakers like Emile de Antonio (*In the Year of the Pig*, 1969) and Peter Davis (*Hearts and Minds*, 1974) criticized both the effects of the war in Vietnam and the rationale for it, while women filmmakers tapped the powers of documentary to bolster the burgeoning feminist movement through films that were experimental in form and political in content. In recent years, political documentary has flourished in a variety of forms and venues, as institutions such as PBS and HBO have created new exhibition possibilities for nonfiction filmmaking. In 1988, PBS created *P.O.V.,* a series devoted to the development and exhibition of independently produced films. With funding from the National Endowment for the Arts and the John D. and Catherine T. MacArthur Foundation, *P.O.V.* has become a landmark showcase for nonfiction work that, in their words, "express[es] opinions and perspectives rarely featured in mainstream media." In the 1990s, HBO also established itself as a major contributor to the political documentary scene, working regularly with such filmmakers as Barbara Kopple, Spike Lee, and Rory Kennedy, among others. In 2006, HBO premiered Lee's critically acclaimed *When the Levees Broke: A Requiem in Four Acts*, his poetic treatise on the aftermath of Hurricane Katrina.

CAN DOCUMENTARY BE POLITICAL?

It can be easy to forget how prominent political documentary has been in the past, however, because the phrase itself seems to be an oxymoron. How can a film claim to be both political *and* a documentary?

Most people still consider "documentary" to be an objective style of filmmaking whose primary purpose is to record "life as it is" from a relatively neutral perspective. Film scholar Bill Nichols argues that, in popular parlance, documentary is understood to be what he calls a "discourse of sobriety." In this vein, documentary is thought to have a kind of "kinship" with other serious systems of thought, such as science or economics, because they all claim to have an objective and transparent relationship to the real world. As media scholar Brian Winston has argued, this common understanding has led to the valuation of specific kinds of documentary over others. Certain generic conventions, such as the educational tone and journalistic style of documentaries in the Griersonian tradition, or the fly-on-the-wall aesthetic of "verite" filmmakers like Albert Maysles and Frederick Wiseman, have become markers of what constitutes a "real" documentary. Genuine documentaries, it is often claimed, are those that stand apart from their subject, observe reality from a distance, and through this process produce a neutral document of the world.

This notion of documentary as neutral observation is complicated, then, when we add the term "political" to the mix. Film scholar Thomas Waugh defines political documentary as displaying a *commitment* on the part of the filmmaker. According to Waugh, committed documentaries are films that claim solidarity with a specific group or coalition, take an "activist stance" towards certain issues or goals, and work *within* and *alongside* political and social movements. In this way, political documentaries would seem to constitute the very antithesis of the documentary form as it is popularly understood. The idea that documentary should be an objective, neutral discourse stands in opposition to films that claim a commitment to particular groups and specific goals. Meanwhile, the notion that the documentarian should stand outside and apart from his or her subject, "observing" it from a distance, is clearly incommensurate with the practice of committed filmmakers speaking from within particular social movements. Seen from this perspective, political documentary starts to look a lot less like documentary proper, and a lot more like "propaganda."

POLITICAL DOCUMENTARY AS "PROPAGANDA"

Accusations of propaganda, of course, beg a similar question: what do we mean by propaganda? Film scholars James Combs and Sara Combs argue that, separated from its usually negative connotation, propaganda is any form of communication geared towards the production of messages intended to influence popular

---

A MATTER OF DISTRIBUTION

While the production of political documentaries is nothing new, the manner in which they are being seen is. One of the most compelling aspects of the *Fahrenheit 9/11* phenomenon was its spectacular success as a theatrical release, even out-grossing the other major Hollywood release that weekend, *White Chicks*, thus taking the top spot overall. However, while Moore blazed a new trail into the country's multiplexes, his was not the only unique strategy for distributing political documentary.

Filmmaker Robert Greenwald took a different tack in 2002 when he produced *Unprecedented: The 2000 Presidential Election*, a film that looked closely at the controversy surrounding the fight over presidential votes in Florida. Greenwald chose to forgo traditional routes and distribute the film himself. He set up public screenings through liberal groups, such as the Nation Institute and the People for the American Way, while at the same time making a DVD version of the film available for purchase through political Web sites such as MoveOn.org. His guerilla-distribution tactics worked: the film sold over 30,000 copies in three days.

Greenwald has replicated this strategy with subsequent films, including *Uncovered: The War on Iraq*, *Outfoxed: Rupert Murdoch's War on Journalism*, *Wal-Mart: The High Cost of Low Price* (2005), and *Iraq for Sale: The War Profiteers* (2006). The most important aspect of this strategy is timeliness—Greenwald's films are meant to be seen "in the moment." As such, they are made quickly on a low budget (often with funds from cooperating political organizations) and then distributed aggressively, utilizing incentives such as free screenings and low prices (the DVDs are often sold for $9.95). In this way, Greenwald is perhaps the quintessential "committed" documentarian of our time, working with specific political organizations to get a pointed message out in the hopes of raising consciousness and affecting change. In many ways, Greenwald is also the first political documentarian to utilize the new media landscape in an integrated fashion, combining any and all means of distribution strategies, from theaters to home video to the Internet. Indeed, Greenwald argues that his biggest contribution to the documentary field is precisely the development of what he calls an "alternative distribution model." As such, he remains an important figure in the emerging documentary landscape.

opinion in one way or another. But we might wonder, what film doesn't do this? Is any film—documentary or otherwise—devoid of messages and incapable of influence? A better question to ask might be: *what* messages are produced by any given film, and *how* are they meant to influence us? When the History Channel produces a documentary explaining how President Reagan's nuclear policy helped to end the Cold War and protect America's position in the world, we don't often think of this as a piece of "propaganda." But when a documentary challenges that perception, as Terri Nash's antinuclear film *If You Love This Planet* did in 1982, then it can be labeled propaganda, and often is—as was the case in this instance, when the Reagan administration forced exhibitors to attach a propaganda warning label to every showing of Nash's film. In fact, the real difference between these films lies in the types of messages they are producing. As Combs and Combs argue, a documentary that reproduces popular ideas and reinforces commonly held values constitutes a kind of "deep propaganda" that remains hidden precisely because the messages it puts forth are taken for granted by the culture at large. But when a film openly challenges common values and understandings, as Nash's film did, its political commitments become more obvious.

THE "TRUTH" ABOUT DOCUMENTARY

If it is agreed that all documentary is, in essence, a form of propaganda, how do we go about evaluating documentaries, in general? For many critics, the important question shifts from one about truth to one about *honesty*. As cultural anthropologist Jay Ruby has put it, every documentary is "the interpretive act of someone who has a culture, an ideology, who comes from a particular socioeconomic class, is identified with a gender, and often has a conscious point of view" (Ruby 2000, pp. 139–40). The problem is that most documentaries never own up to this fact. Indeed, as Nichols points out, the structural aspects of documentary form that we often take for granted—authoritative voice-overs and illustrative visuals or long takes, a handheld camera and the use of available light and sound—are actually stylistic *conventions* geared towards producing the *appearance* of realism. In this way, the look, sound, and feel of documentary produces a kind of "reality effect" that encourages us to accept what it says at face value.

Thus, many critics have praised documentaries that exhibit a more "reflexive" style of filmmaking. Reflexive documentaries are films that call attention to themselves *as films* by breaking with traditional documentary conventions. Reflexive documentarians often put themselves on screen, speak in the first person, and admit what they have to say is their own opinion. In this way, rather than being more "truthful," reflexive documentaries are simply more *honest* about the fact that all any documentary can do, in the end, is construct a particular interpretation of "the truth."

CASE STUDY: *FAHRENHEIT 9/11*

All of these questions about documentary suddenly became very relevant in the summer of 2004 when Michael Moore's *Fahrenheit 9/11* opened. Moore had made a name for himself with the success of *Roger & Me* (1989), his irreverent look at the disastrous effects the GM plant closings of the mid-1980s had on his home town of Flint, Michigan. His style of filmmaking incorporates a number of "reflexive" techniques. Moore, himself, appears on-screen and provides a first-person voice-over. He routinely provokes the events he films, rather than simply recording what he sees, such as when he and his cameras "ambush" corporate and public officials, producing results that are both humorous and uncomfortable. And he often employs an ironic editing scheme, in which carefully chosen music or the insertion of old film and television clips provide an extra layer of "commentary" to the visuals we see on screen. Through these and other techniques, Moore displays a style that is unquestionably political and unapologetically personal. This being the case, when it was revealed that Moore's next film would take on the president and the war in Iraq, film critics and political pundits alike took notice. *Fahrenheit 9/11* became a controversy before it even opened in the United States. The vociferous debate it spawned brings up a number of questions regarding the place of political documentary in contemporary culture.

As is often the case, the question of whether or not documentaries should be political was front and center. Critics of Moore predictably labeled the film a piece of propaganda. At best, they complained that Moore presented his information in a biased manner that ignored the "other side" and was geared more towards stoking viewers' emotions than presenting them with the facts. At worst, they called *Fahrenheit* a "pack of lies" and labeled Moore a traitor. Supporters defended Moore by citing ideas such as the freedom of speech and artistic license. Some argued that while *Fahrenheit* itself was not balanced, Moore's interpretation of events offered a much-needed counterpoint to the version usually given by the news media. Meanwhile, Moore defended himself by hiring a "war room" of lawyers to combat claims of inaccuracy, and answered accusations of bias by describing his film as a cinematic "op-ed" piece. But while *Fahrenheit 9/11* did much to provoke a widespread public discussion about political documentary, it was apparent that traditional notions of what counted as a documentary remained intact. For instance, while both supporters and detractors felt the need to bicker over Moore's committed stance on political issues, they often championed films displaying a more "neutral" aesthetic, such as the "verite"-style films *Control Room* (2004) and *Gunner Palace* (2005).

Questions over the political nature of *Fahrenheit 9/11* were not the only debates that surrounded Moore and his film. Many critics worried about the way in which Moore's narrative-driven, humorous style may have tainted a traditionally sober discourse with "show-biz" values. Should documentaries about serious issues be *entertaining*? Moore's answer to this question is an unequivocal "Yes!" He has often railed about the fact that, traditionally, documentary has hampered its own ability to provoke social change by maintaining a set of conventions that are didactic and boring—a style he refers to as the "illustrated lecture." Moore's use of dry wit and conventional storytelling are geared towards making films that are both informative *and* fun. And it's a tactic that has worked: Moore's films have continued to outsell each other at the box office, and he currently holds the top three spots for most successful documentaries of all time. But many critics worry that Moore's tilt towards entertaining means a tilt *away* from the factual. Indeed, this kind of anxiety often allows Moore's political opponents to dismiss his films out-of-hand, a tactic the Bush administration used when White House communications director Dan Bartlett told the press, "If I wanted to see a good fiction movie, I might go see *Shrek* or something, but I doubt I'll be seeing *Fahrenheit 9/11*."

Fahrenheit 9/11's popular success also raises questions about a related phenomenon. Michael Moore is not only a filmmaker—he is a celebrity, a movie star, and a political "brand name." This, of course, has its advantages. *Fahrenheit*'s boffo box-office was driven by legions of Moore fans. Indeed, many critics credited Moore's popularity alone for stoking interest in other political documentaries that year. There are, however, downsides to celebrity. Moore has become so personally connected to his films that, oftentimes, critics can't seem to separate the filmmaker from his argument. At the end of the day, Moore's personal, entertaining style might have allowed his political opponents to engage in a tactic of discrediting the filmmaker rather than the film. This issue has haunted other political documentaries with recognizable personalities, such as Morgan Spurlock's *Super Size Me* and the Al Gore film on global warming, *An Inconvenient Truth* (2006).

The most contentious debate that surrounded *Fahrenheit 9/11* and, to a lesser extent, all the political documentaries that came out in 2004, was over what political effect these films might have on the voting public. Here, of course, "political effect" was understood in the most narrow sense of the term, namely: election results. Could a film like *Fahrenheit 9/11* actually sway the election? Of course, the results of the 2004 election did not swing Moore's way, and Bush's victory led many critics to a rather damning conclusion: that the film was merely "preaching to the choir." This accusation is often directed against political documentary, and indeed, many on the right were eager to repeat it. Some gleefully argued that not only did *Fahrenheit 9/11* fail in its mission to unseat the President, but it actually *aided* in his victory. Does the election's outcome mean that we should view *Fahrenheit 9/11* as a failure? The rationale behind such declarations is specious, however, for it asks us to conclude that if Moore had not made his film, Bush would have lost, and that one documentary could wield enough power to be *the* deciding factor in a national election.

WHAT ARE WE LOOKING FOR?

Perhaps the most relevant question to ask, then, when considering the recent popularity of political films, is: "Just what do we *expect* from a documentary?" Should a documentary be a film that attempts to achieve some kind of measurable social effect? Or should it be a film that simply adds constructively to the public discourse? Should documentaries be emotionally compelling and cinematically entertaining? Or should they be "sober" affairs geared towards serious deliberation? Should a documentary strive to maintain a sense of neutrality and objectivity? Or should it admit its biases up front and present us with a compelling argument? The heated controversy over *Fahrenheit 9/11* suggests that these questions are still very much on the table. Meanwhile, political documentary as a popular form shows no signs of slowing down. As such, it is time to reconsider just what role we want documentary to play in public life.

See also Al-Jazeera; Bias and Objectivity; Government Censorship and Freedom of Speech; Media and Citizenship; Media and Electoral Campaigns; Nationalism and the Media; News Satire; Paparazzi and Photographic Ethics; Political Entertainment; Presidential Stagecraft and Militainment; Propaganda Model; Public Opinion; Public Sphere.

Further Reading: Barnouw, Erik. *Documentary: A History of the Non-fiction Film.* 2nd rev. ed. New York: Oxford University Press, 1992; Bullert, B. J. *Public Television: Politics and the Battle Over Documentary Film.* New Brunswick, NJ: Rutgers University Press, 1997; Combs, James E., and Sara T. Combs. *Film Propaganda and American Politics: An Analysis and Filmography.* New York: Garland, 1994; Ellis, Jack C., and Betsy A. McLane. *A New History of Documentary Film.* New York: Continuum, 2006; McEnteer, James. *Shooting the Truth: The Rise of American Political Documentaries.* Westport, CT: Praeger, 2006; Nichols, Bill. *Introduction to Documentary.* Bloomington: Indiana University Press, 2001; Nichols, Bill. *Representing Reality: Issues and Concepts in Documentary.* Bloomington: Indiana University Press, 1991; Rabinowitz, Paula. *They Must be Represented: The Politics of Documentary.* London: Verso, 1994; Renov, Michael, ed. *Theorizing Documentary.* New York: Routledge, 1993; Rosenthal, Alan, and John Corner, eds. *New Challenges for Documentary.* 2nd ed. Manchester: Manchester University Press, 2005; Ruby, Jay. *Picturing Culture: Explorations of Film and Ethnography.* Chicago: University of Chicago Press, 2000; Toplin, Robert Brent. *Michael Moore's Fahrenheit 9/11: How One Film Divided a Nation.* Lawrence: University of Kansas Press, 2006; Winston, Brian. *Claiming the Real: The Documentary Film Revisited/The Griersonian Documentary and Its Legitimations.* London: BFI, 1995.

J. Scott Oberacker

POLITICAL ENTERTAINMENT: FROM *THE WEST WING* TO *SOUTH PARK*

At its best, entertainment can draw us in emotionally, making us care about its subjects, and its wide appeal can attract a considerably larger audience than more sober alternatives. Both of these attributes at times make it an ideal vessel for political information and discussion. Yet some critics see entertainment as an entirely inappropriate site for politics, while yet others see entertainment as incapable of dealing with the complexities and nuances of politics. Can entertainment and politics mix?

Political entertainment is any program, song, book, film, or other cultural product whose primary purpose is to entertain and amuse, frequently (though not necessarily) for commercial purposes, yet that also offers explicit political commentary. Entertainment is laden with other responsibilities—we look to it for escape and emotional inspiration, and to cheer us up, make us laugh or cry, and stimulate our imaginations—but some media products also get political, whether through serious narrative, satiric play, critical dialogue, or imaginative fantasy. The politics in question can be governmental (critique of the president,

OUR FICTIONAL POLITICIANS

Some of history's most inspiring politicians exist in the cinema and television alone, as Hollywood has offered us many a political drama or thriller. Certainly, Jimmy Stewart's filibuster in Frank Capra's *Mr. Smith Goes to Washington* (1939) remains one of American film history's more famous scenes, and an enduring testament to the little guy fighting rampant political corruption. Or, 54 years later, Kevin Kline's depiction of the impersonator-turned-president in *Dave* offered a similar tale. Meanwhile, on the little screen, television has given the nation its first female president in *Commander in Chief* (ABC, 2005–06), its first and second African American presidents in *24* (FOX, 2001–), and its first Latino president in *The West Wing*. *The West Wing* has also offered some of the most lyrically moving presidential announcements, such as when Martin Sheen's President Jed Bartlet declares that "if fidelity to freedom of democracy is the code of our civic religion, then surely the code of our humanity is faithful service to that unwritten commandment that says we shall give our children better than we ourselves received." Screenwriters of such stories tend to oversimplify and romanticize politics, but nevertheless, often one cannot but compare screen politicians and speeches with their real life counterparts, a process that motivates discussion and debate, and that sets standards to which we are asked to hold these counterparts.

for instance), social (feminist or antiracist, for example), or even media-related (criticizing the politics behind news coverage, for instance); can range from mild and playful to deep and biting; and can include both fiction and nonfiction.

The criticisms of political entertainment tend to stem either from a belief that entertainers should stick to entertainment, and hence that the marriage of politics and entertainment is inappropriate, or, alternatively, that as entertainment, it is insufficiently dedicated to its politics, producing "politics lite" or even a mockery of politics.

POLITICS AND ENTERTAINMENT AS AN INAPPROPRIATE MARRIAGE

Many of us divide our world into work and play, seriousness and fun, and to some, entertainment is thus a zone that must remain separate from the serious world of work and politics in order to maintain its claim to entertainment. A meaningful engagement with politics requires that we come face to face with much that is ugly in the world, and hence might seem to offer little room for laughter or joy. As such, entertainment frequently, and refreshingly, offers to take us away from such uncomfortable realities. At the end of a long day's work, many people seek media entertainment as a refuge from the worries of daily existence, turning on the television, putting on a piece of music, or engrossing themselves in a film, for instance, in order to leave those worries far behind. We often welcome so warmly the imaginative universes that entertainment provides because of their difference from our lived environments; therefore, some consumers aim to protect these universes from the semblance of "invasion" by the world of politics. Particularly when entertainers espouse political beliefs, then, pundits, letters to newspaper editors, and watercooler discussion alike will often question the entertainers' right or legitimacy to interject politics into entertainment.

Proponents of political entertainment, however, point out that everything is political. Admittedly, a great deal of any film, show, song, or other product's politics will be implicit, or subtle, and thus much entertainment will neither advertise its politics, nor necessarily be aware of them. Nevertheless, family sitcoms, for instance, posit very clear notions of what a neighborhood, a family, a man, and a woman are and are not; and even a seemingly escapist program such as *The O.C.* makes numerous subtle statements about everything from racial politics to poverty to the role of capitalism. We may agree or disagree with these politics, but they are always present, regardless of the product. Indeed, if one ever finds oneself in the presence of a seemingly unpolitical text, this means only that its politics are already one's own politics, hence blinding the viewer or listener to their presence. Therefore, instead of regarding political entertainment as "pulling a fast one" on us by slipping a dose of politics into our entertainment, we might instead see it as more up front and honest. Politics is about more than just who to vote for in the next election; politics at base is about determining the ways in which all institutions and individuals should interact in society. Politics thus entails everything from what rights a parent has over their children, to what rights a community has over its public places and institutions, to millions of other decisions about what the world should look like and why. Consequently, politics inevitably fly by us in every which way in all entertainment, and so defenders of political entertainment argue that politics are always already present. We can discuss and debate *which* politics the media should embody, but we cannot wish the political out of entertainment.

POLITICS AND ENTERTAINMENT AS A DYSFUNCTIONAL MARRIAGE

Political entertainment has also been attacked, however, for being too weak. This argument is most forcefully leveled by Neil Postman in his invective against American television, *Amusing Ourselves to Death*. Postman charges American television with having become nothing but entertainment. Hence, Postman argues that entertainment has colonized politics, reducing serious issues to silly sound bites, flashy graphics, and popularity contests. To Postman, politics are a serious matter, and hence must be treated as such, and the moment that they are mixed with entertainment, the prerogatives of entertainment take over, automatically simplifying and trivializing important points in the process. Postman worries that such an approach to politics produces an apathetic and ill-informed populace, who would rather have a good laugh than ponder our future with due seriousness. A significant danger of political entertainment, then, is that in presenting itself as entertainment *and* politics, as consumers we may be engaging with entertainment alone, while only thinking that we are engaging with politics.

POLITICAL MUSIC

A great deal of popular music can be fairly trivial, calling for nothing more than one's "baby" to love one "till the end of time." In contrast, however, music has also long served as a mouthpiece of rebellion and politics. Cheaper to produce and more decentralized than film or television, music has been open to more people from more walks of life. Thus, entire genres are known for their countercultural or subcultural ethos, attitude, and lyrics, from grunge to rap, punk to rave, and often many country, blues, and/or folk songs. Moreover, music's more memorable tunes and words have frequently become rallying points for countercultural or subcultural movements, as was the case most famously with the hippie and peace movement of the 1960s and early 1970s. In such moments, the music can go far beyond being a media text, actually working as part of an active culture or subculture.

Of particular concern is entertainment media's capacity for politics. In crude terms, we could ask exactly how much politics entertainment can hold. How can a four-minute song or a half-hour sitcom treat *any* topic with due complexity? As we have discussed, many citizens are weary of overt politics in entertainment; consequently, producers of political entertainment all too often err on the side of cautiousness, adding only a light political streak. Many of the sketches on *Saturday Night Live* are illustrative here: often, they will depict political figures, and they will reference contemporary political events, but ultimately little of depth is said. For instance, a sketch lampooning President Bush will play with his malapropisms and style of speech, and will offer quick commentary on a recent presidential policy or program, but the sketch will end there. For political decisions to be meaningful, surely we as a society must make them with as much information available as possible, but sketches of the *Saturday Night Live* variety offer little if any room for background information, potentially bastardizing the issues in question as a result.

THE POLITICAL POWERS OF ENTERTAINMENT

Nevertheless, critics of political entertainment as "politics lite" run the risk of holding out for the perfect political vessel. In truth, the often abstract and highly complex world of politics is usually simplified in the telling, regardless of the setting. Ideally, each of us could and would reserve significant time to learn about, discuss, and debate key political issues. But few of us do. Thus, a pragmatic approach to political entertainment might accept that it is an imperfect vessel, even one that will at times cause more problems and misunderstandings than it will resolve, but also that in offering any politics it is performing a potentially vital service to a fragmented, sometimes uninformed society.

Moreover, political entertainment can trump its more serious counterparts by making us care. The news in particular often suffers from telling us that *everything* is worth caring about, and that everything is an important story.

But 20 seconds later, the newscaster will move on, having forgotten this supposedly most important of stories. By contrast, entertainment can harness the affective powers of fiction by introducing us to characters and stories that hit home. Fictional characters and celebrities frequently become important individuals to many citizens, and we can also invest remarkably high levels of trust and admiration in them. Certainly, they can violate this trust and admiration, but in political entertainment's better moments, they can harness such powers to attract our attention and mobilize us into action. "Free Tibet" concerts, political documentaries, and political raps, for instance, have proven powerful in mobilizing political support for otherwise hidden issues. Particularly when politicians and the realm of politics have suffered such losses in respect by many citizens, and when many citizens have turned in disgust from politics proper, entertainment at times craftily constructs a back door into politics.

Thus, for instance, in his book on *Serial Television*, Glen Creeber suggests that for all its glaring historical and cultural inaccuracies and ethnocentric outlook, the famed American miniseries, *Roots*, may have played a key role in introducing white Americans to some of the horrors of slavery and to African American culture. One could certainly imagine an educational program or documentary that would depict West African culture with more accuracy, and that would be substantially more honest and true to history. But with the powers of mass entertainment behind it, *Roots* drew huge audiences, and became one of the key popular-culture landmarks of its time.

Ironically, then, we find political entertainment in an odd position: it can trivialize politics, and as such may well be in part responsible for political apathy and misunderstanding; but it may also energize politics, make citizens care, and bring citizens to politics. Therefore, we would ultimately be wise to avoid mere generalization, and move towards evaluating specific instances of political entertainment.

CASE STUDIES

In recent years, one of the more successful instances of political entertainment has been NBC's *The West Wing* (1999–2006). Eschewing the more usual television settings of court room, police station, hospital, or family home, *The West Wing* followed the lives of the fictional President Josiah "Jed" Bartlet's White House staff in their place of work. Scripts frequently drew from ongoing political issues and discussions of the day, whether prominent (the death penalty, terrorism, or partisan politics, for instance) or backroom (such as an entire episode about the census). By giving a fictional glimpse into the lives of the world's power brokers, *The West Wing* implored its audience to care about the issues that its characters wrestled with on a daily basis, and it neatly mixed substantial and often quite sophisticated discussion of politics with an entertaining format. Moreover, in doing so, it introduced many viewers to the fineries of who does what in American politics, teaching viewers the political process. One simply could not follow *The West Wing* without necessarily engaging with the sphere of politics.

Another television show, but markedly different in tone, Trey Parker and Matt Stone's *South Park* hit Comedy Central in 1997. An animated sitcom, the show follows the lives of several young children in the small mountain town of South Park, Colorado. Infamous for its profanity, R-rated premises, and lethal sense of humor, the show quickly gained a position of notoriety as did few programs before it, but behind the swearing and the fart jokes were often some smart examinations of American life and politics. Cultural controversies from the alleged anti-Semitism of *The Passion of the Christ* to the right-to-die debate surrounding the 2005 Terri Schiavo case were dealt with satirically, adding to cultural discussion of the issues as they occurred. For instance, the Schiavo-inspired episode ended with a broadside attack on the media's ghoulish display of Terri Schiavo's dying days, and a strong moral regarding the ethics of media coverage that was largely missing from public debate at the time. Frequently using language and premises to shock, *South Park* has followed in the noble satiric footsteps of eighteenth-century satirist Jonathan Swift by using entertainment to grab its audience's attention and insert commentary into an ongoing debate. It has also managed the rare trick of mixing politics and youth appeal.

However, television by no means holds a monopoly on meaningful political entertainment. Many films, too, from *Crash* to *Brokeback Mountain*, *The Insider* to *Syriana*, *Bulworth* to *Erin Brockovich*, *Wag the Dog* to *Dr. Strangelove*, *Guess Who's Coming to Dinner?* to *All the President's Men*, and so forth, have mixed stellar performances and entertainment with political commentary. Meanwhile, music and book publishing have long been the media most known for political entertainment, with the likes of Eminem, Ani DiFranco, Rage Against the Machine, and Kanye West, and earlier favorites such as Phil Ochs, Woody Guthrie, John Lennon, and Bob Dylan in music, and a long history of uncompromising literature by writers such as Kurt Vonnegut and John Steinbeck.

LIMITATIONS

Undoubtedly, political entertainment has proven more hospitable to some ideas than others. Thus, for instance, tales of racial and gender politics are common, especially when the "bad guys" are specific, rather than a pervasive societal ill in general (though, for example, the 2004 film *Crash* serves as a notable exception). Political corruption is also most commonly dealt with when historical or fictionalized and generic. Overall, political entertainment seems most willing to take on general problems stated in the abstract, rather than engage with named policies, parties, and individuals. Multimedia corporations are still too timid in the face of potentially angry audience backlash, and too keen to protect their own interests, to open the doors of political entertainment too widely. Hence, as has been the case in all societies, we should still expect those in power to reign in and somewhat sterilize political entertainment to the best of their abilities, or simply to deflect its commentary to "safer" abstract topics with no specific incarnation.

THE ROLE OF THE AUDIENCE

Of utmost importance, though, is the audience, and thus a great deal of the potential power of political entertainment relies on how individual and communal audiences will react to and use it. If we ignore the politics, or if we use political entertainment as a substitute for a more serious engagement in politics elsewhere, then fears that "politics lite" is undernourishing us will be justified; but if we use it as a springboard to learn more and to do more, political entertainment could prove a vital component of a functioning democracy.

See also Media and Citizenship; Media and Electoral Campaigns; Narrative Power and Media Influence; News Satire; Political Documentary; Presidential Stagecraft and Militainment; Public Sphere; Shock Jocks.

Further Reading: Alberti, John, ed. *Leaving Springfield: The Simpsons and the Possibility of Oppositional Culture.* Detroit, MI: Wayne State University Press, 2003; Crawley, Melissa. *Mr. Sorkin Goes to Washington: Shaping the President on Television's The West Wing.* Jefferson, NC: McFarland and Company, 2006; Creeber, Glen. *Serial Television: Big Drama on the Small Screen,* Chapter 1. London: BFI, 2004; Fischlin, Daniel, and Ajay Heble, eds. *Rebel Musics: Human Rights, Resistant Sounds, and the Politics of Music Making.* Montreal, QC: Black Rose Books, 2003; Fiske, John. *Understanding Popular Culture.* New York: Routledge, 1989; Gabler, Neil. *Life: The Movie: How Entertainment Conquered Reality.* New York: Vintage, 2000; Hartley, John. *The Uses of Television.* New York: Routledge, 1999; Jeffords, Susan. *Hard Bodies: Hollywood Masculinity in the Reagan Era.* New Brunswick, NJ: Rutgers University Press, 1994; Jones, Jeffrey P. *Entertaining Politics: New Political Television and Civic Culture,* New York: Rowman & Littlefield, 2005; Kellner, Douglas. *Media Spectacle,* New York: Routledge, 2003; Postman, Neil. *Amusing Ourselves to Death: Public Discourse in the Age of Show Business.* New York: Penguin, 1986; Sachleben, Mark, and Kevan M. Yenerall. *Seeing the Big Picture: Understanding Politics through Film and Television.* New York: Peter Lang, 2005; Van Zoonen, Liesbet. *Entertaining the Citizen: When Politics and Popular Culture Converge.* New York: Rowman & Littlefield, 2004.

Jonathan Gray

PORNOGRAPHY

Pornography is defined in the *New Oxford American Dictionary* as "printed or visual material containing the explicit description or display of sexual organs or activity, intended to stimulate erotic rather than aesthetic or emotional feelings." While pornography involving children is widely condemned, it remains a serious international problem. Pornography involving adults, although contentious, is a massive international media industry.

Pornography—from religious, commercial, social, cultural, artistic, feminist, and gay-friendly perspectives—is variously defined, criticized, and defended. While obscenity historically has not been protected under the First Amendment, very little material has been found by the courts to meet the standard for obscenity. The pornography industry is a multi-billion-dollar one; novel technologies and media—beginning with the printing press and photography and continuing through film, home video, cable television, the Internet, and digital imaging—historically have worked to expand its reach. Researchers study the impact and effects of pornography on individuals as well as society: who uses pornography and why; how pornography influences attitudes and behaviors, including misogynist attitudes and violence against women; the history of pornography; textual analysis of stories and images; and pornography as a cinematic genre.

Feminists particularly have engaged in wide-ranging debate, with some viewing pornography as a cornerstone industry in promulgating sexist beliefs, actively oppressing women and exploiting sexuality, and others claiming pornography as a potentially liberatory genre, stressing the importance of maintaining the freedom of sexual imagination. In recent times, sexual and sexually objectifying and violent images, based in pornographic conventions, increasingly pervade mainstream culture, raising further debates as to their impact.

PORNOGRAPHY TIMELINE

1500–1800—In Europe pornography was widely used as a shock vehicle criticizing religious and political authorities.

1524—Erotic engravings by Pietro Aretino along with a series of sonnets composed in Italy.

1534—Pietro Aretino's *Ragionamenti* becomes the prototype for seventeenth-century pornographic prose.

1740s—Pornographic writings become considered a genre.

1769—The word *pornography* emerges in France.

1806—The earliest modern use of the word *pornography* found in Etienne-Gabriel Peignot's *Dictionnaire critique, littéraire et bibliographique des principaux livres condamnés au feu, supprimés ou cénures.* The pornographic tradition in France strengthens.

1857—The word *pornography* appears for the first time in the Oxford English Dictionary; Obscene Publications Act is put into practice.

Late 1800s and early 1900s—Forms of filmic pornography, stag films, begin to circulate.

December 1953—*Playboy* founded by Hugh Hefner.

1959—Obscene Publications Act removes certain restrictions from texts that had been banned as obscene/pornographic if they could be justified as art.

1965—Penthouse Media Group Inc. founded by Bob Guccione in England.

1969—Supreme Court decision, *Stanley v. Georgia*, which held that people could view whatever they wished in the privacy of their own homes.

1969—*Penthouse* comes to the United States.

Late 1960s—Full-length pornographic films begin receiving cinema distribution.

1970—Report by the Commission on Pornography and Obscenity, created by President Johnson.

1970s—Video pornography appears.

1972—First mainstream hardcore pornography film *Deep Throat* is produced and shown in both adult as well as "public" theatres.

1973—Supreme Court decision, *Miller v. California*, setting up a community-standards approach to obscenity.

1974—*Hustler* first published by Larry Flynt.

1976—Women against Violence in Pornography is formed in San Francisco.

1980s—Pornography begins to be distributed over the Internet.

1981—Andrea Dworkin's influential book *Pornography* is published.

1984—Andrea Dworkin and Catherine MacKinnon convince the Minneapolis City Council to adopt a civil rights ordinance allowing women to receive damages from the alleged harms resulting from pornography.

July 1986—Attorney General's Commission on Pornography (Meese Report) published, finding some harms from pornography.

1990s—Pornographic magazines for women (*Playgirl, Bite, For Women*) become established.

1991—With the beginning of World Wide Web/Internet, porn becomes more popular; Nancy Friday's *Women on Top* is published.

1992—Supreme Court of Canada's ruling in *R. v. Butler* incorporates some elements of Dworkin and MacKinnon's legal work on pornography into the existing Canadian obscenity law.

1994/1995—Michael Ninn produces two of the best-selling and most rented porn videos—*Sex* and *Latex*, using computer graphics and high-tech imagery.

1998—*Penthouse* reveals explicit photos of oral, vaginal, and anal penetration as well as males urinating on females.

2005—U.S. District Court drops federal case against Extreme Associates.

2005—Under new ownership, *Penthouse* returns to "softer" photos and no longer shows explicit penetration.

HISTORY

Sexually explicit and arousing stories and depictions have from earliest histories been part of human cultures—in erotic contexts as well as, often simultaneously, sacred, artistic, folkloric, and political. Modern pornography began to emerge in the sixteenth century, merging explicit sexual representation with a challenge to some, though not all, traditional moral conventions, for pornography was largely the terrain of male elites and represented their desires and points of view.

In the United States, post–World War II and spurred on by new sexological research, reproductive technologies, emerging movements for social justice, and the formation of the modern consumer economy, the state began to retreat from some of its efforts toward the regulation of sexuality. This allowed the emergence of the modern pornography industry. *Playboy* was launched in 1953, followed by a number of "men's" magazines, the large-scale production

"I ONLY READ IT FOR THE INTERVIEWS"

In the wake of hard-core pornography, many companies have been remarkably successful selling "soft-core," "artistic," or "thinking man's" pornography. Such pornography usually eschews showing the actual act of intercourse in photographic form, or close-ups in video form, and lays claim to legitimacy by surrounding itself with the nonpornographic. Leading the pack here is *Playboy* magazine, whose interviews with major intellectuals, politicians, and other cultural elites have allowed the infamous excuse for those buying the magazine that "I only read it for the interviews." By avoiding the label of hard-core pornography, moreover, producers of many such images in this vein can also declare that they are merely continuing in the age-old tradition of art's fascination with the nude. As a result, soft-core pornography fills much late night pay-cable programming, has worked its way down from the top shelf of the magazine rack, and often enjoys mainstream acceptance or at least tolerance.

and dissemination of pornographic film and video, and the burgeoning of the industry through mainstreaming as well as enhancement by new technologies. Since 1957 the Supreme Court has held that obscenity is not protected by the First Amendment. In 1973, the Court gave a three-part means of identifying obscenity, including: Whether the average person, applying contemporary community standards, would find that the work appealing to the prurient interest; whether the work is patently offensive; and whether the work, taken as a whole, lacks serious literary and/or artistic, political, or scientific value. All three conditions must be met for it to be considered obscene.

In the contemporary period, Fortune 500 corporations like AT&T and General Motors now have affiliates that produce pornography and, while it is difficult to obtain precise data, most researchers conclude that pornography in the United States annually results in profits from 5 to 10 billion dollars if not more, and globally $56 billion or more. Legal actions against pornography have virtually halted, highlighted by a 2005 obscenity case brought by the federal government against Extreme Associates, a production company featured in a 2002 PBS *Frontline* documentary, "American Porn." Extreme Associates has an Internet site for members and also makes films featuring scenes of men degrading, raping, sexually torturing, and murdering women. A U.S. District Court judge dismissed the case. There was no dispute that the materials were obscene. Rather, he found that obscenity laws interfered with the exercise of liberty, privacy, and speech and that the law could not rely upon a commonly accepted moral code or standard to prohibit obscene materials.

DEFINITION AND DEBATES

Pornography is generally associated with deliberately arousing and explicit sexual imagery, which renders it deviant for traditional patriarchal religious orientations that continue to associate sexuality with sin, while equating chastity and strictly regulated sexual behavior in heterosexual marriage with goodness.

"Family values" functions as a byword for antipornography patriarchal positions that condemn not only all sexual representations but also female sexual and reproductive autonomy, as well as any nonheterosexual and nonmonogamous sexuality. Some pornography advocates critique this heterosexist morality, identifying themselves as "pro-sex." Others defend pornography by foregrounding it as a First Amendment issue. Both groups tend to defend sexual representations, as well as diverse adult consensual sexual practices, as a form of free speech and expression, as essential to the imagination, as an element of all of the arts, and as a potentially revolutionary force for social change.

Virtually all feminists argue that sexuality must be destigmatized, reconceptualized, and defined in ways that refuse sexist moralities. The association of sexuality with sin is a feature of specifically patriarchal (male-defined and dominating) societies. Such societies control and regulate female sexuality and reproduction, for example, by designating women as the sexual other while men stand in for the generic human, by mandating heterosexuality and by basing that heterosexuality in supposedly innate gender roles of male dominance and female submission. These societies foster conditions that impose a sexual double standard, selecting some women (associated with men who have some social power) for socially acceptable if inferior status in the male-dominant family, and channel other women, girls, and boys and young men (those without social power or connections) into prostitution and pornography. Patriarchal societies give men, officially or not, far more latitude in sexual behavior, and pornography and prostitution, institutions historically geared to men's desires and needs, are the necessary "dark side" of patriarchal marriage and moralistic impositions of sexual "modesty." In this way, pornography and conventional morality, though supposedly opposites, actually work hand in glove to assure male access to women, as well as male domination and female stigmatization and subordination.

Some feminists argue that as sexuality is destigmatized, "sex work," including prostitution and pornography, can be modes whereby women can express agency and achieve sexual and fiscal autonomy. Those associated with what is defined affirmatively as queer culture, including gay, lesbian, transgendered, and heterosexual perspectives and practices that challenge conventional roles, often argue that open and free sexual representation is essential to communicate their history and culture and that social opposition to pornography is fundamentally based in opposition to sexual freedom and diversity.

Mainstream cultural critics of pornography point to the ways that contemporary pornography has become increasingly ubiquitous. They argue that pornography damages relationships between persons, producing unrealistic and often oppressive ideas of sex and beauty; that it limits, rather than expands, the sexual imagination; that it can foster addictive or obsessive responses; and that it increasingly serves as erroneous sex education for children and teenagers.

Antipornography feminists, while opposing censorship, point out that pornography is a historically misogynist institution, one whose very existence signifies that women are dominated. Pornography not only often openly humiliates and degrades women, but it brands women as sex objects in a world where sex itself is considered antithetical to mind or spirit. They contend that mainstream pornography defines sex in sexist ways, normalizing and naturalizing male dominance and female submission and, by virtue of its ocularcentric and voyeuristic base, promotes a fetishistic and objectifying view of the body and the sexual subject.

Andrea Dworkin and Catharine MacKinnon are well known for their radical feminist approach to pornography. In a model "Civil-Rights Antipornography Ordinance," they propose an ordinance that would have nothing to do with police action or censorship, but would allow complaints and civil suits brought by individual plaintiffs. The Ordinance defines pornography in a way that distinguishes it from sexually explicit materials in general. Rather, pornography consists of materials that represent "the graphic, sexually explicit subordination of women" or "men, transsexuals or children used in the place of women." Their extended discussion delineates specific elements, for example, women being put into "postures or positions of sexual submission, servility or display," "scenarios of degradation, injury, abasement, torture," individuals "shown as filthy or inferior, bleeding, bruised, or hurt in a context that makes these conditions sexual." Although several communities passed versions of this law, it was overturned in the courts as a violation of the first amendment. At the same time, courts have recognized the use of pornography as a tool of sexual harassment, one that generates a hostile climate for women workers in offices, factories, and other job sites.

Numerous feminists link the practices and underlying themes of pornography to other forms of oppression. For example, Patricia Hill Collins links the style and themes of U.S. pornography to the beliefs and practices associated with white enslavement of Africans and their descendents—including bondage, whipping, and the association of black women and men with animals and hypersexuality.

USES AND EFFECTS

Research has examined the role of mass-mediated pornography in causing harmful or unwanted social effects, including the furtherance of sexism as well as violence against women and/or willingness to tolerate such violence; profiles of those who work in pornography as well as those who enjoy it; and the potentially addictive aspects of pornography.

Research into the uses and effects of pornography has been conducted employing experimental studies, anecdotal evidence from interviews and personal stories, polling, and statistical data asserting connections between existence or use of pornography and undesirable social phenomena. Two presidential commissions studied the effects of pornography, one beginning in the 1960s and the other in the 1980s. The first concluded that there were no harmful effects; and the second concluded that sexually violent and degrading pornography normalized sexist attitudes (e.g., believing that women want to be raped by men) and therefore contributed to actual violence. These conclusions have been subjected to wide-ranging debate, for example, around the validity of information obtained from necessarily contrived laboratory experiments (usually with male students), the difficulty of defining common terms like *degradation*, the

DID YOU KNOW?

Cyberpornography and Human Intimacy

From pornography's early expression in engravings, to film and magazines, writing and research designed to understand pornography and its effects on human behavior and sexuality have occupied scholars from the social sciences to the humanities. With the rise of the Internet and the vast cyberporn industry, new questions about human sexuality have occupied researchers trying to explain the motivations and consequences of heavy use, or even what some characterize as addiction, of online pornography. Pamela Paul and other health researchers have found disturbing consequences for male intimacy in those who are habituated to cyberporn. Many men accustomed to erotic responses from online pornography reported difficulty being aroused without it, even when having sex with their wives or girlfriends. One consequence of cyberporn, then, is a loss of erotic desire during sexual intimacy. Many men reported the need to recall or imitate the acts, behaviors, attitudes, and images of cyberporn in order to achieve sexual gratification, leaving them and their female partners at a loss for creative eroticism, individual expression, and interpersonal connection. Such sensibilities in the age of the Internet need not be unique to gender or sexual preference, and more research on the effects of mediated sexual experience are necessary to understand the complex nature of the relationship between human sexuality and media.

unwillingness of people to accurately report their own behavior, the political bias of the researchers, and so on.

Internationally, feminist researchers point out links between pornography and sex trafficking and slavery as well as the use of pornography in conquest, where prostitution is imposed and pornography is made of the subjugated women as well as men. For example, during the war between Serbia and Bosnia-Herzegovina and Croatia, Serbian forces systematically raped women as a tactic of genocide and these rapes were photographed and videotaped. Sexual torture, photographed and displayed as kind of war pornography, also was practiced by U.S. troops against Iraqi prisoners in the American prison at Abu Ghraib in Iraq in 2003. Subsequently, investigators released photographs of male Iraqis sexually humiliated and tortured by U.S. soldiers. There also were pornographic videos and photographs made of female prisoners, but these have not been released. Feminist activists argue that in the case of war and forced occupation, pornography regularly is used to bolster the invading forces' morale, and to destroy the self-regard of occupied peoples who are used for pornography as well as sex tourism.

CONCLUSION

Pornography is now openly diffused throughout American culture. Not only has it grown enormously as an industry, but, in mainstream imagery, other media outlets use typical pornographic images and themes in advertisements, music videos, and video games, and to publicize celebrities or events. Pornography also has become a legitimate topic for academic study and the subject of college classes.

Research shows that more women now use pornography. As part of the feminist project of redefining sexuality, there has been a surge in erotic stories and images aimed at female audiences. Some feminists and/or those identified with queer communities have begun to produce what they consider to be subversive pornographies that challenge both traditional morality and the conventions of mainstream, sexist pornography, for example, by featuring models who are not conventionally beautiful and by valorizing nontraditional gender roles and non-heterosexist practices; by celebrating the body, sexuality, and pleasure; by acknowledging lesbian, gay, and transgender realities and desires; and by stressing female sexual desire and agency.

Some applaud this expansion of pornography as reflecting greater sexual autonomy for women as well as a liberalization of social attitudes toward sexuality. Others argue that the mainstreaming of pornography does not produce or reflect freedom, but instead represents a backlash against the women's liberation movement and furthers the commoditization of sexuality, for example, in the ways that young girls are now routinely represented, often fashionably dressed, as sexually available. The system of patriarchal domination has always, one way or another, colonized the erotic. Modern pornography furthers the interests not only of sexism, but also capitalism and other forms of domination. Sexuality, conflated with both domination and objectification, can more readily be channeled into, for example, the desire for consumer goods or the thrill of military conquest.

Visionary feminist thinkers aver that to be truly "pro-sex" we need to be critically "antipornography." Eroticism is humanity's birthright, a force of creativity, necessary to wholeness, and the energy source of art, connection, resistance, and transformation. Patricia Hill Collins urges both women and men to reject pornographic definitions of self and sexuality that are fragmenting, objectifying, or exploitative, and instead articulate a goal of "honest bodies," those based in "sexual autonomy and soul, expressiveness, spirituality, sensuality, sexuality, and an expanded notion of the erotic as a life force."

See also Advertising and Persuasion; Body Image; Gay, Lesbian, Bisexual, Transgendered, and Queer Representations on TV; Media and the Crisis of Values; Obscenity and Indecency; Presidential Stagecraft and Militainment; Representations of Masculinity; Sensationalism, Fear Mongering, and Tabloid Media; Shock Jocks; Violence and Media; Women's Magazines.

Further Reading: Brison, Susan J. "Torture, or 'Good Old American Pornography.'" *The Chronicle Review/The Chronicle of Higher Education* (June 4, 2004): B10–11; Caputi, Jane. *The Pornography of Everyday Life* (documentary film). Berkeley Media, 2006 at www.berkeleymedia.com; Collins, Patricia Hill. *Black Sexual Politics: African Americans, Gender, and the New Racism.* New York: Routledge, 2004; Cornell, Drucilla, ed. *Feminism and Pornography.* New York: Oxford University Press, 2000; Dines, Gail, Robert Jensen, and Ann Russo. *Pornography: The Production and Consumption of Inequality.* New York: Routledge, 1998; Gutfield, G. "The Sex Drive: Men Who Are Hooked on Cyberpornography." *Men's Health* (October 1999): 116–21; Hilden, Julie. "A Federal

Judge Dismisses an Obscenity Prosecution on Privacy Grounds," 2005, at http://writ.news.findlaw.com/hilden/20050131.html, accessed June 9, 2007; MacKinnon, Catharine. *Are Women Human? and Other International Dialogues.* Cambridge, MA: Harvard University Press, 2006; McNair, Brian. *Mediated Sex: Pornography and Postmodern Culture.* New York: St. Martin's Press, 1996; Paul, Pamela. *Pornified: How Pornography Is Transforming Our Lives, Our Relationships, and Our Families.* New York: Henry Holt and Company, 2005; PBS Frontline. *American Porn* (documentary), 2002; Stark, Christine, and Rebecca Whisnant, eds. *Not for Sale: Feminists Resisting Prostitution and Pornography.* North Melbourne: Spinifex Press, 2004.

Jane Caputi and Casey McCabe

PRESIDENTIAL STAGECRAFT AND MILITAINMENT

In an age of mass media, the public learns about war and understands its life and death consequences through television images and the many other sources of news narratives across the media spectrum. In addition to news, entertainment formats (frequently based on real combat) also present forceful images of war, weaponry, and the soldiers who fight and die in continuing global conflict. In recent years, a hybrid format that blurs the boundaries between fiction and nonfiction, referred to as militainment, has been employed by the media and the military to represent war in our time. In addition, defining moments in the reporting of war and conflict are increasingly stage-managed by the Pentagon and White House public relations professionals.

Militainment and stagecraft are attempts to control media imagery and the meanings of war through fictional formatting, information management, and media choreography. These sophisticated strategies raise issues about the public's ability to receive accurate information and a true picture of what war and conflict are actually like.

War is understood and interpreted, justified and judged through the media that tell the stories of war. Most civilians experience military conflict through the media, their impressions derived not from the battles in distant lands but from the manner they are rendered at home. Struggles over war's true meaning, its values and necessities, play out on movie and television screens and in the photographs of newspapers and magazines. These representations are influenced by the demands of commercial media, politics, and military pressures. By the twenty-first century, the media has become the battleground where the struggle to win the hearts and minds of the public is carried out through the increasingly persuasive media management strategies of militainment and stagecraft.

THE BATTLE OVER PUBLIC OPINION

The process of negotiating the meaning of war and its depictions has been going on for centuries, but with mass media and new digital technology, that process has come to play a profound role in global conflict. Over the last century, the American public has at times expressed both favorable and disdainful opinions about war and its necessities, and those attitudes have influenced the path of conflict. Over the years, elected officials and military planners have faced significant public opposition to war. Convincing the public that war is necessary, that all diplomatic channels have been exhausted, and that the call to military action justifies the inevitable loss of life in its wake requires persuasive and well-planned campaigns. Indeed, once war is waged, problems with battlefield logistics, military conduct, and casualty figures can be an even greater deterrent to favorable public opinion, or what has been referred to as "homefront morale." Homefront morale and the public's resolve to continue the fight depend on a complicated equation that compares the war's justification with its destructive force. Once the public perceives that the cost in human life is too high a price to pay for the stated goals, opinion quickly turns against the war effort.

By the twenty-first century, images of soldiers and civilians who inevitably die in conflict, once prevalent on television during the Vietnam War, were all but eliminated from media coverage of the war in Iraq. In the absence of pictures of death and suffering, war is more easily depicted in favorable terms, as either an exciting video game, an action-packed battle film, or a rousing victory celebration. Shaping war narratives according to these formats lessens the emotional impact that grisly images from the actual battlefield might have. In doing so, the public is removed from the killing, which in a democratic system, is being carried out in its name.

PRESIDENT BUSH AND THE THANKSGIVING TURKEY WITH TROOPS IN THE GREEN ZONE, 2003

On Thanksgiving Day 2003, Air Force One left Washington, DC, on a secret trip that would carry a small group of aides with the president to the Baghdad Airport for a two-and-a-half-hour visit and photo-op with 600 U.S. troops lucky enough to be stationed in the Green Zone. The widely published image from this trip shows a beaming president wearing an Army flight jacket, cradling a bountiful golden-brown turkey generously garnished with grapes and all the trimmings. He appears to be serving dinner to the grateful soldiers who surround him. A moment of high patriotism, the picture was ubiquitous in the days that followed, and the president's poll numbers shot up five points as criticism for his seeming indifference to the suffering of American troops was quieted.

It would take a week for the *Washington Post* to report that the president was not actually serving the soldiers, who were eating presliced turkey from canteen-style hot plates. It was six o'clock in the morning, and the turkey Bush held was inedible. White House officials rebuked those who called the turkey fake, insisting it was not a presidential prop, but a standard decoration supplied by contractors for the chow hall. In a burst of spontaneous enthusiasm, the president had raised the platter and the shutter clicked. To the company that produced a limited-edition Turkey Dinner Action Figure of the President for $34.95, it did not matter that some viewed the secret trip as a ploy, or even a cowardly act, because the president had been criticized for not attending services at U.S. military bases where the bodies of the fallen return home. It became "a piece of our nation's history."

PRESIDENT BUSH AND THE TOP GUN FLIGHT

One of the best illustrations of presidential stagecraft during the war in Iraq came after "major combat operations" were over. This dramatic visual event was staged in real time and performed by President George W. Bush. The president garnered much media attention when, dressed in a military flight suit in the cockpit of a fighter jet, he flew the plane and made a successful landing onto the aircraft carrier the *U.S.S. Lincoln*. He was welcomed by the military personnel who had just returned from Iraq. In front of a banner that hung from the ship's upper deck proclaiming "Mission Accomplished," President Bush told the country that the successful invasion of Iraq was over. The White House said the flight on the jet fighter was necessary because the carrier was too far out to sea to be reached by helicopter. In fact, a few columnists and alternative news sources reported that the ship was so close that it had to be turned around to prevent television cameras from catching the San Diego coastline in the background. More importantly, as history would show, the invasion of Iraq was just the beginning of a long, drawn-out conflict that would cost many more Iraqi and American lives. In hindsight, this incident has come to symbolically underscore a lack of military planning for a clear exit strategy from the country.

The stage-managed event was reported as news, and some television personalities, most notably Robert Novak, pointed out how well the flight suit fit the president. However, independent video editors revealed that the dramatic landing was virtually identical to visual sequences in the popular Tom Cruise film of 1986, *Top Gun* (see "Hollywood Victory," distributed by Paper Tiger Television, New York). Mainstream commercial broadcasters made few critical comments that might have exposed the flight's choreography, and question its message and purpose, most likely because such production values and fictional referencing have become standard features in commercial media's programming design.

MERGING NEWS AND ENTERTAINMENT

After the September 11, 2001, attacks on America, the Pentagon met with media industry producers and directors and requested that Hollywood join the fight against terrorism. The military and the media collaborated on such films and television programs as *Behind Enemy Lines* and ABC's *Profiles from the Front Line*. This direct request from the White House formalized what was already an ongoing relationship between the film industry and the Department of Defense. Film scripts must be given the stamp of approval from the military, and the Pentagon is quite selective in choosing which movies it officially endorses with access to bases and ultra-high-tech weaponry. The films of Jerry Bruckheimer are popular with the Pentagon, and posters of his films hang on the walls there. *Pearl Harbor* got mixed reviews from critics, but its patriotic themes passed muster with the Department of Defense, and it was well supplied by the military.

RESISTING PENTAGON INFLUENCE

The first significant film to be set in the Persian Gulf depicting Desert Storm was Edward Zwick's *Courage Under Fire* (1996). The film features Lieutenant Colonel Nathan Sterling (Denzel Washington), the leader of a tank battalion, who during the war had directed fire at a suspected enemy vehicle, only to find that he had destroyed one of his own. After the war he struggles to come to terms with this incident of friendly fire that bears an uncomfortably close resemblance to actual conduct in the war. Sterling is dispatched to investigate events surrounding the death of Captain Karen Walden (Meg Ryan), a Medivac helicopter pilot killed in action. The film's dark cast of the military goes further than friendly fire and portrays the mutiny, cowardliness, and incompetence of the soldiers Captain Walden helped save. Unable to accept orders from a woman, one soldier under her command leaves her wounded in the desert, telling the rescue pilot that she is already dead. The U.S. Army refused to supply equipment for the film unless Zwick changed the script. Refusing to depict the military and the war in a better light, Zwick made the film without assistance from the Pentagon.

When the United States began a bombing campaign over Afghanistan, press requests for access to the war were refused, but working for ABC's entertainment division, Jerry Bruckheimer shot *Profiles from the Front Line* with full cooperation from the U.S. military. The series from Afghanistan aired on ABC during the buildup to war in Iraq, and *Profiles* was the first program to present a war through the same visual and narrative style used in reality television. Television news would later take its cues from movie producer Bruckheimer when the war on Iraq began.

This first "reality show" treatment of the war on terror made no attempt to cover civilians killed in the bombing of Afghanistan, and certainly offered no pictures of that reality. Much of the media coverage of the invasion of Iraq was foreshadowed by *Profiles from the Front Line*, and Iraq became the first war to be televised in real time with embedded journalists providing videophone pictures live from the desert battlefield. These compelling images featured brave soldiers fighting, but almost no images of death or suffering. Some alternative Internet sources showed the casualties of war, some of which were shut down by the Pentagon.

THE STORY OF SAVING PRIVATE LYNCH

At one point, the initial invasion of Iraq was stalled by sandstorms and heavy resistance around the capital of Baghdad. At that point, in the early morning hours of April 2, 2003, the military announced to reporters at Central Command in Qatar that a crack commando unit had rescued a young female private named Jessica Lynch. Commandos had stormed a Nasiriyah hospital and carried her to safety in a waiting Black Hawk helicopter. The gripping story was ubiquitously described in the mainstream media as a daring raid. *Time* magazine asserted, on April 14, 2003, that Hollywood could not have dreamed up a more singular tale.

Doubts about the story's authenticity were first raised by the London *Times* on April 16, 2003. After a thorough investigation, the BBC concluded that Lynch's rescue was a staged operation. No embedded journalist accompanied the raid, and the green night footage was shot and cleverly edited by the military's own Combat Camera as proof that a battle to free Lynch had occurred when it had not. On May 18, 2003, the BBC pointed out the fictional aspects of the raid, and observed that the Pentagon had been influenced by Hollywood producers of reality television and action movies, most notably Jerry Bruckheimer.

U.S. news headlines embellished the story, saying that Jessica had fought for her life, and had sustained multiple gunshot wounds. Some added that Jessica was stabbed by Iraqi forces, and even raped. Months later, it was reported that, in fact, no fighting had occurred, but rather Lynch suffered only accident injuries when her vehicle overturned. A medical checkup by U.S. doctors confirmed that Iraqi doctors had tended her injuries, a broken arm and leg and a dislocated ankle.

The incident demonstrates the use of militainment. The rescue of Jessica was a classic rescue narrative of mythic proportions told at a difficult time in the fighting to boost American morale and public support for the war. After the Lynch story, the downed statue of Saddam Hussein in Baghdad's Firdos Square would become the icon of victory over Iraq. Only later would an internal Army study find that the statue toppling was a psychological operations maneuver—another staged event.

WAR GAMES

America's Army was the first video game created by the military and was offered free to kids to download off the Internet on July 4, 2002. It became the number-one online action game in the country with more than 3 million registered players. Players are positioned as first-person shooters, and after basic training, the advanced "marksmanship" is so realistic that the computer screen moves in time to the digital soldier's breathing under fire. The online actors are patterned after the actions of real soldiers. Though the weapons, graphics, and settings are highly realistic, the violent consequences of killing are downplayed. The enemy is faceless and masked, and when hit releases a puff of red smoke and falls to the ground. As CNN reported, "From a propaganda perspective the Army has seemingly hit the jackpot. (And the Army readily admits the games are a propaganda device)" (CNN/money.com, June 3, 2002).

When video games depict violent combat but downplay the graphic images of death or other horrific aspects of war, they offer a sanitized version of fantasy combat, even while depicting actual battles. The visual styles and compelling participation offered to gamers turn the otherwise disturbing aspects of war and killing into excitement and entertainment. The recognizable imagery of video war games has become popular as a graphic style in many feature films depicting combat. Computer-based imaging is also seen in news coverage of war, which often features digital graphics of high-tech weapons systems supplied by the Pentagon.

Video games are now used by the military for recruitment and training. The Department of Defense contracted with the company Ubisoft to help market and distribute *America's Army*. At a computer-gaming conference in early 2005, Ubisoft deployed the Frag Dolls, a group of young women gamers with names like Jinx and Eekers, to demonstrate *America's Army*. The "booth babes" posed for pictures as they played the games, inviting young men to enter and occupy the gaming space. Eekers's promotional blog about her Combat Convoy Experience can be found on the *America's Army* Web site. These and the other points of convergence between the media and the Department of Defense have led to what some critics have called the military/entertainment complex.

The ongoing merger between the entertainment and military industries, together with the use of sophisticated media managing and stagecraft by the government, have raised serious issues for those concerned with the role of the media in a democratic society, especially during times of war. The public relies on the media to report the consequences of war, but when the industry is economically and culturally invested in the technologies of war, critics question its ability to be an independent source of information. Parents and educators worry that young people, especially military recruits, will be unprepared for the actual consequences of war. The audio-visual milieu that turns war into entertainment also lessens the public's ability to feel alarm and compassion for those who die in wars carried out in its name.

See also Bias and Objectivity; Embedding Journalists; Government Censorship and Freedom of Speech; Media Watch Groups; Nationalism and the Media; Paparazzi and Photographic Ethics; Political Documentary; Political Entertainment; Propaganda Model; Public Opinion; Reality Television; Representations of Masculinity; Representations of Women; Sensationalism, Fear Mongering, and Tabloid Media; Video Games.

Further Reading: Andersen, Robin. *A Century of Media, A Century of War*. New York: Peter Lang, 2006; Hedges, Chris. *War Is a Force that Gives Us Meaning*. New York: Anchor Books, 2002; Robb, David L. *Operation Hollywood: How the Pentagon Shapes and Censors the Movies*. New York: Prometheus Books, 2004; Solomon, Norman. *War Made Easy: How Presidents and Pundits Keep Spinning Us to Death*. New York: John Wiley & Sons, 2005; Thussu, Daya Kishan, and Des Freedman, eds. *War and the Media*. Thousand Oaks, CA: Sage, 2003.

Robin Andersen

PRODUCT PLACEMENT

Product placement is the intentional and strategic positioning of brand-name products and services in various media for the purposes of advertising and brand promotion. Examples include movies, TV shows, video and computer games, comics, novels, theater productions, even news shows. Why has this practice, sometimes called "branded entertainment," grown into a $4 billion

INSERT YOUR COMPANY'S CIGARETTE HERE

"As discussed, I guarantee that I will use Brown & Williamson tobacco products in no less than five feature films. It is my understanding that Brown & Williamson will pay a fee of $500,000.00." From a letter dated April 28, 1983, signed by movie actor Sylvester Stallone and addressed to Associated Film Promotion, Los Angeles. (Legacy Tobacco Documents Library, University of California, San Francisco)

industry in just a few years? Is it merely about adding "realism" to all of these media products, as the industry routinely claims? Or is placement perhaps a stealth way of advertising to distracted or impressionable audiences? What can the phenomenal growth of product placement tell us about the state of our media and entertainment systems?

In an ever more crowded commercial media environment, advertisers and their agencies must continually search for more effective ways of reaching their target audiences. Indeed, they refer to this self-generated crowding as "ad clutter": a cacophony of advertising messages that is so busy and so overwhelming, it's increasingly difficult to reach target audiences without the distraction of other competing commercial messages. Many in the advertising industry have become disenchanted with conventional advertising methods, such as TV and radio commercials, because viewers can skip, zip, zap, or TiVo their way around these messages.

Product placement offers a way to sidestep this issue by putting the ad message *inside* the media content it would otherwise bookend. The growing use of digital video recorders (DVRs) ensures that more products and ad slogans will be incorporated into popular TV programs. Added benefits for advertisers include the enviable and often exclusive association with a celebrity, an "event" movie, or a hit TV show; and the recurrent and expanding exposure brought by syndication, repeats, reruns, cable, DVD, international distribution, and so forth.

FILMS

An increasing trend toward product placement is also found in film production. The economic benefits of using placement are substantial. One reason is that some of the massive production costs associated with filmmaking can be significantly offset by cutting deals with advertisers to feature their products: either the advertiser pays handsomely to have their product appear in the movie, or the producers save substantially by having interested advertisers provide props, uniforms, trucks, even entire sets. Product placement in films once took the form of side deals between props managers and advertisers, with the former agreeing to add a product to a scene in return for a small amount of money, but the practice is now carefully coordinated by studios, and a potentially lucrative business. Indeed, carefully negotiated deals can save movie productions millions

PRODUCT PLACEMENT TIMELINE

1982—*E.T.* features Reece's Pieces. Sales jump 65 percent.

1984—U.S. product placement (all media): $512 million.

1992—*Wayne's World:* Draped in Reebok clothes and waving Pizza Hut boxes around, Wayne declares: "Contract or no, I will not bow to any sponsor." Ironic? Sure. Fabulously targeted placement? Absolutely.

1993—*The Firm:* Gene Hackman to Tom Cruise: "Grab a Red Stripe." Sales in the U.S. go up 50 percent.

1994—U.S. product placement (all media): $1.13 billion.

1999—"BMW gave us a lot of money if we put their car in the movie. So we did." John Schwartzman, Director of Photography, *Armageddon*; "We used a TAG Heuer big clock, and I put that little TAG logo there and it saved me $75,000." Michael Bay, Director, *Armageddon* (commentary tracks, special edition DVD).

2000—*Cast Away* features 56 appearances of the FedEx logo. A FedEx spokesperson says, "We're a character in this movie."

2004—U.S. product placement (all media): $3.5 billion.

2009—U.S. product placement (all media): $6.9 billion (projected).

"A Product Placement Hall of Fame," *BusinessWeek*, http://www.businessweek.com/1998/25/b3583062.htm; "Product Placement Spending in Media 2005," (PQ Media); Gettelman, E., and David Gilson, "Ad Nauseam: Madison Avenue is Scrambling to Stick Ads Anywhere It Can, from Children's Books to Bathroom Stalls," *Mother Jones*, Jan./Feb. 2007.

of dollars. One recent deal involved the placement of one vintage Coca-Cola glass in a period scene in a movie about Bob Dylan. In return for this placement, Coca-Cola agreed to provide all the soda for the entire crew and cast for the duration of the production—a saving in the order of tens of thousands of dollars.

Such economic benefits further ensure that priority will often be given to dialogue, scenes, and entire scripts that lend themselves most readily to product placement. It also means viewers can expect to see more advertising inside movies—not just workaday "mainstream" comedies and romances (which are often positively saturated with placements—think of "star vehicles" for actors such as Tom Hanks and Adam Sandler, with Hanks's *Cast Away* providing one of the garish examples of product placement by raising FedEx to the level of virtual co-star), but also in the work of more "serious" directors.

HISTORY

The movies were recognized as a potential advertising medium very early on. In a book published in 1916 titled *Advertising by Motion Pictures*, the author Ernest A. Dench wrote: "It will probably seem rather strange to you that an invention like the cinematograph, which has achieved widespread fame as a form of entertainment, can perform the functions of advertising, but it is none the less a fact." Product placement, then, is just one advertising practice that has been long associated with film, and finds its place among other marketing strategies such as tie-ins, cross-promotions, and product merchandising. Indeed, it is a relatively new term for a practice that is almost as old as the medium of film itself. This has included payments by DeBeers to guarantee that diamonds would be mentioned in scripts, to the use of costume drama to promote the fashion industry.

Meanwhile, American television began as an advertising vehicle. The current practice of "spot advertising," in which multiple advertisers' products are shilled in commercial breaks during a program, was preceded by a system by which each program had a single sponsor. Television stars were expected to sell their program sponsor's product in a variety of venues, including the program itself. Thus, for instance, the early sitcom *I Remember Mama* would often end with the narrator glowing about the beloved Mama's insistence on making Maxwell House coffee, and even Fred Flintstone anachronistically smoked Winston cigarettes. However, with time, this practice waned somewhat, as television shows became too expensive for any one advertiser to financially support alone, and it is only in recent years that the practice is once more becoming prevalent, now often with multiple placements per program.

OUT OF THE CLOSET

The founding of the Entertainment Resources & Marketing Association (ERMA) in 1991 marked a moment of formalization of the industry, bringing product placement, as the first president of the ERMA put it, "out of the closet." No longer was placement to be understood as a sporadic, almost experimental practice. In film, particularly, the early use of Reece's Pieces in *E.T.* proved to be an enormous success, and when *Dirty Harry* used a 44 Magnum handgun, it was one of the most memorable moments in the film and became a staple of the sequels. Sales of Ray-Bans jumped when Tom Cruise wore them in *Risky Business*. These early successes established the practice, and the ERMA now represents the interests of dozens of agencies dedicated to brokering deals between advertisers and studios.

STEALTH PERSUASIONS

Product placement can be understood most simply as a form of "ad creep": a symptom of advertisers' escalating need to reach consumers in largely unfettered ways. The movies offer a wonderful environment for this: amazing sound systems, comfy seats, very few distractions, and the kind of ticket prices that would understandably make one reluctant to sully the experience with negative thoughts. The strange thing is we don't actually notice brand appearances in movies all that much, unless we're been reminded to look out for them. On the other hand, when we see an ad, it is clear to us that it has been designed to persuade us to buy a product. For this reason, when we look at ads, we do

DIGITAL PRODUCT PLACEMENT

With the development of digital editing techniques, product placement no longer even requires the actual presence of the product while filming. Rather, several companies, such as Marathon Ventures, and CanWest Mediaworks in Canada, now specialize in adding or even changing products in specific scenes after the fact. Thus, for instance, if you are watching *Will and Grace*, the various food or drinks on the characters' kitchen counter or coffee table may vary from viewing to viewing. Using this nascent approach, advertisers can capitalize on popular shows long after they've become hits, rather than taking risks on new projects. Products can also be targeted at specific foreign markets through strategic digital placement in exported shows.

---

so with a more critical eye. But because we do not expect the entertaining movie we are watching to be an advertisement, we may be skeptical about the commercial messages it contains. Indeed, placement agencies tell clients that as an advertising strategy, product placement is more persuasive because viewers do not realize that they are watching commercial messages. Viewers are more likely to assume that the characters are drinking certain sodas and wearing particular clothes because they like them, not because the director has cut a deal with those particular companies. Thus, for instance, many viewers of the teen drama *Dawson's Creek* may have been unaware that the characters' clothing was provided through placement deals with American Eagle and J. Crew, or that the characters' tastes in music were largely restricted to *Dawson's Creek* parent company Warner Bros.'s music library.

DO YOU MIND?

When placement agencies claim that most people really don't mind product placement, one wonders whether it's because we *genuinely* "don't mind" or because we remain uninformed about how hard people are working behind the scenes to get those brands before our eyes. One infamous survey done in 1993 by researchers Nebenzahl and Secunda concluded that cinemagoers don't mind placement. Their method? Asking people in movie lines whether they would prefer higher ticket prices instead. There was no third option.

Folks in the industry will claim publicly that they are simply providing realism: we live in a branded world, therefore the world on the screen would actually look "unreal" if it wasn't also saturated with brands. Critics of the proliferating commercialization of the media charge that the persistent claim of added realism is disingenuous, and point to a variety of counter arguments:

- Placement agencies work to make (or save) money through *advertising*, otherwise they'd be called "realism consultants" or some such thing.
- If we look carefully at many, many movies (often older ones) we can see multiple ways in which scenes have been crafted so as *not* to emphasize

labels, signs, and logos. Directors are highly inventive, visual people: they can choose not to focus in on the logo on the hood of the car; not to make the actors turn their soda cans to camera, and so on. Indeed, placement often renders scenes *unrealistic*, as when multiple scenes from television's *Frasier* ensure that the package of Pepperidge Farm's Milano cookies are magically pointing label-out in each of three camera angles.

- Generic, "no-name," or even invented brands have long been a part of the make-believe of the movies and television, the job of set dressers and prop masters; although the placement experts would have us believe otherwise, it seems hard to imagine moviegoers or television viewers leaving the theater or turning off the television in disgust at the lack of "real" brands. ABC's immensely successful *Lost*, for instance, offers its castaway characters only a generic, fictional brand of food, with no noticeable audience attrition as a result.
- The kinds of movies that placement agencies love—big budgets, lots of action and effects, huge opening weekends, happy endings—are rarely about "real" things. More like asteroids or giant waves hitting earth, real life dinosaurs, the White House being shot up by a spaceship, a hero who gets out of scrapes with highly unlikely gadgets, and so on.
- When, occasionally, two movies with more or less the same theme emerge from Hollywood at about the same time (e.g., *Deep Impact* and *Armageddon; A Bug's Life* and *Antz*), we would expect them both to have the same amount of product placement in them. And yet we find 18 brand appearances in *Capote* but only five in *Infamous*. (Both films are realist dramas that tell basically the same story about a specific period in the life of writer Truman Capote.)

Based on the evidence available, then, we should understand that product placement does not exist to beef up the "realism" of movies, their capacity to reflect precisely the world around us. Product placement is advertising by another name. While the negative consequences for the creative process of storytelling through the media of film or television are sometimes hard to quantify, there is no doubt that many films and television programs have been altered either before or during production—in order to accommodate products and services. Editing and pacing have been changed as the camera is held static to display a product logo. Dialogue and scripts are altered to include brands, and settings have sometimes been changed to foreground products. Manufactures pay higher sums to have the stars of the big screen mention their products, wear their clothes, and drive their cars, and increasingly, we are even seeing significant placement in trailers. For example, the trailer for *The Transporter 2* acted as an ode to Audi as much as an advertisement for the film. Film culture continues to confer artistic status to the medium, with awards given for editing, camerawork, acting, set, and costume design. Yet with product placement, the collaboration revolves around the motivation to sell, a motivation distinct from the necessities of character development, narrative, and filmic aesthetics.

PARODYING PLACEMENT

With movies such as *Wayne's World* (see "Product Placement Timeline" sidebar), Hollywood has realized the benefits of presenting its placements periodically: not only do producers still get the money, but they seemingly escape the accusation of selling out, while the advertiser receives prominent exposure and seems cool, hip, and willing to take a joke—an arrangement, therefore, calculated to bring both parties maximum benefit. In this regard, we might be more impressed by the placement parodies in, for example, the films of Kevin Smith (Nails Cigarettes; Discreeto Burritos) and Quentin Tarantino (Big Kahuna Burger; Jack Rabbit Slim's Restaurants). In *The Simpsons*, fictional brands such as Duff Beer, Lard Lad Donuts, or Laramie Cigarettes take the spotlight, thereby drawing viewers' attention to the practices of product placement, while also avoiding using this seeming lesson of media literacy as yet another platform for advertising.

THE FUTURE OF PRODUCT PLACEMENT AND THE FATE OF THE MOVIES

With the arrival of reality television, we have witnessed the summary collapse of the formal distinction between TV shows and the commercials they once sandwiched. Programs such as *The Apprentice* and *Survivor* allowed producer Mark Burnett to make vast sums in placement deals, basing entire episodes around the contestants' need to advertise a certain product in the case of *The Apprentice*, and offering the food-deprived *Survivor* cast Doritos as a way of ensuring endless paeans to the wonders of the nacho chip. Similarly, *American Idol* judges drink nothing but Coca-Cola, *The Amazing Race*'s family edition showed endless scenes of contestants gassing their cars up at BP, and *America's Next Top Model*'s reward of a Cover Girl contract ensures excited weekly mentions of the cosmetics company.

Movies, though, are not far behind, given their appeal to advertisers, and the relative lack of organized resistance to this practice. To take one example: Tom Hanks is a celebrated actor, but he's also a gift to advertisers, since he appears to have no qualms at all about cozying up to products, as demonstrated by four of the most placement-saturated movies of recent times: *Forrest Gump, You've Got Mail, Cast Away,* and *The Terminal*. Such celebrated film stars of the past were reluctant to have their names associated with the commercial necessities of advertising. but Hanks's newest film project is called *How Starbucks Saved My Life*.

Nonreality television, too, is growing more placement friendly, with numerous advertisers experimenting with "old-style" single sponsorship for one-off events, as when one season of *24* began without commercials, yet with continuous loving shots of hero Jack Bauer in his Ford SUV, and as entire episodes of the former ratings giant *Friends* revolved around the characters' love of certain products, such as Pottery Barn furniture.

Judging by industry figures (see "Product Placement Timeline") we can look forward to more and more placement, which may lead to fewer and fewer movies that do not readily lend themselves to having their scripts transformed into two-hour shills. And a new moviegoing generation that never had the pleasure of seeing placement-free movies will wonder what all the fuss was about, while the marriage of culture and consumption—of understanding ourselves chiefly through the products we choose—will be all the more entrenched.

See also Advertising and Persuasion; Branding the Globe; Conglomeration and Media Monopolies; Hypercommercialism; Independent Cinema; Media Reform; Mobile Media; Pharmaceutical Advertising; Reality Television; Runaway Productions and the Globalization of Hollywood; TiVo; Transmedia Storytelling and Media Franchises; Video News Releases.

Further Reading: Andersen, Robin, and Lance Strate, ed. *Critical Studies in Media Commercialism.* New York: Oxford University Press, 2000; *Behind the Screens: Hollywood goes Hypercommercial* (2000, 37 mins.). Media Education Foundation; *Brand Hype: A Critical Resource on Product Placement.* (www.brandhype.org). Launched 2005; Dench, Ernest A. (1916). *Advertising by Motion Pictures.* Cincinnati, OH: The Standard Publishing Company; Friend, Tad. "Copy Cats." *The New Yorker.* September 14, 1998; Jacobson, Michael F., and Laurie Ann Mazur. *Marketing Madness: A Survival Guide for a Consumer Society.* Boulder, CO: Westview Press. 1995; Galician, Mary-Lou, ed. *Handbook of Product Placement in the Mass Media.* New York: Haworth, 2004; Gettelman, E., and David Gilson. "Ad Nauseam: Madison Avenue is scrambling to stick ads anywhere it can, from children's books to bathroom stalls." *Mother Jones* (January/February 2007); Herzog, Charlotte. "'Powder Puff' Promotion: The Fashion Show-in-the-Film." *Fabrications: Costume and The Female Body,* ed. Jane Gaines, and Charlotte Herzog. New York: Routledge, 1990. 134–159; McAllister, Matthew P. *The Commercialization of American Culture: New Advertising Control and Democracy.* Thousand Oaks, CA: SAGE Publications, 1996; McChesney, Robert. *Rich Media, Poor Democracy: Communication Politics in Dubious Times.* Urbana: University of Illinois Press, 1999; Nebenzahl, Israel D., and E. Secunda. "Consumers' attitudes toward product placement in movies." *International Journal of Advertising* 12(1) (Winter 1993): 1–12; Ohmann, Richard, et al., eds. *Making and Selling Culture.* Hanover, NH: University Press of New England [for] Wesleyan University, 1996; Segrave, Kerry. *Product Placement in Hollywood Films: A History.* Jefferson, NC: McFarland, 2004; Wasko, Janet. *How Hollywood Works.* London: Sage, 2003.

Matt Soar

PROPAGANDA MODEL

In the 1980s, Edward S. Herman and Noam Chomsky formulated and applied the "propaganda model" in their groundbreaking work, *Manufacturing Consent: The Political Economy of the Mass Media.* Since that time the model has become one of the most highly contested and debated models within communication studies. Herman and Chomsky argue that elite agenda-setting media play an important role in establishing a framework for what is called "cultural hegemony." The general argument is that elite media legitimize dominant ideological principles and social institutions and defend the principal economic, social, and political agendas of powerful corporate, institutional, and state interests.

The propaganda model assumes that regularities of misrepresentation in media flow directly from the concentration of power in society. It holds that media interlock with other institutional sectors in ownership, management, and social circles, effectively circumventing their ability to remain analytically detached from the power structures of which they themselves are integral parts. The net result of this, the model concludes, is self-censorship, without any significant coercion. Media performance is understood as an outcome of market forces.

This model has been a battleground issue because it questions many of the basic assumptions of American democratic media practices, especially First Amendment guarantees of a free and open press able to provide citizens with the information they need to shape their own lives, elect their leaders, and create policies in their own interests. Yet like most critical ideas, the model challenges the media to live up to its democratic mandate and it points to the ways in which, and reasons why, the fourth estate often fails to keep the public informed. In addition, in a country that prides itself on its freedom of express and civil liberties, the model asserts that Americans are the targets of an all-encompassing propaganda environment that is almost invisible and is infrequently identified as such. Though it presents at times devastating criticisms of the media that many believe to be extreme, over the past 20 years the model has proven to be a useful tool to scholars and analysts seeking to understand the complexities of how and why the media often fail to live up to their democratic mandate.

THE FIVE FILTERS

The propaganda model presumes that a series of five interrelated filters constrain how media create news. In brief, these influences include: (1) ownership, size, and profit orientation of dominant media firms; (2) advertising as the principle source of media revenue; (3) dominance of official sources within the news; (4) flak as a control mechanism; and (5) anti-communism and/or the dominant ideology as a means of social control. Herman and Chomsky maintain that these pressures on reporting are the most dominant elements in the news production process. The filters interact, but also operate individually and one filter may have more influence at any one point in time. How particular topics, issues, events, actors, and viewpoints are represented within the news, and whether they are present at all, is bound to the structural, institutional context(s) in which news itself is created and produced. The underlying assumption is that media shape public opinion by controlling what ideas are presented and how they are treated, and also by limiting the range of credible alternatives.

According to Chomsky, social control within the capitalist democracies is so effective because ideological indoctrination is combined with a general impression that society is relatively open and free. The view of dominant social institutions as autocratic, oppressive, deterministic, and coercive can be understood as the bedrock on which the foundations of the propaganda model

FROM THE COLD WAR FILTER TO ANTI-TERRORISM

Written at the tail end of the Cold War, Herman and Chomsky's propaganda model made note of the anti-Communist filter on news at the time. Like most Americans, many journalists had been trained to vilify Communism, and thus actions of Communist or even Socialist governments were reported with suspicion and wariness, and domestic policy reporting was careful not to appear in any way sympathetic to Communism or Communist causes. The result was yet another limitation on American journalism that predetermined the frame within which much world news was set, and that restricted the sort of reporting that could take place domestically. Twenty years later, post–Cold War, remnants of a long held anti-Communism, and hence of the anti-Communist filter, have not yet passed on, but they have been replaced more prominently with an anti-terrorism filter. Rhetoric similar to the Cold War era is once again common, as journalism participates in the Bush administration's division of the world into the good guys and bad guys, lovers of freedom and forces of hate, the noble and the evil. Anti-Communism used to illicit conformity, in much the same way that anti-terrorism filter has used fear to stifle dissent and challenge long-standing civil liberties and freedoms.

As earlier, many journalists fear appearing to be "anti-American" by examining social or cultural issues behind "terrorism," or even sometimes of interrogating the complicity of Western democracies in financing and establishing "terrorists." Once more, then, much international news is framed and thereby told before a journalist even studies the facts, and much domestic policy reporting reacts to the much-hyped figure of the terrorist. As such, the anti-Communist filter has become, or, rather, has been supplemented by, the anti-terrorist filter.

---

are constructed. The propaganda model is first and foremost an institutional critique of media. It is a critical perspective, one that conceptually confronts how the interrelations of state, market and ideology constrain democracy, and it theorizes the operation of power in relation to dominant structural elements. Many scholars have embraced the model principally because it offers an attractive analytical framework, one that is oriented toward empirical research.

The propaganda model assumes that media choices pertaining to story treatment are fundamentally political choices. It predicts that the treatment accorded certain events, actors, and voices will differ in ways that serve political ends. The model has its own methodological approach to the study of news discourse.

CENTRAL METHODOLOGICAL TECHNIQUES

Some commentators have suggested that Herman and Chomsky's propaganda model does not constitute a fully fledged analysis of media discourse because no single article or book chapter has been devoted to methodology alone, and scholars have been required to consult a diverse range of books and essays

ANALYZING INTERNATIONAL COVERAGE AS "PAIRED EXAMPLES": EAST TIMOR AND KUWAIT

In the months following the August 1990 Iraq invasion of Kuwait, the Canadian News Index lists approximately 200 articles published in Canadian daily newspapers on the invasion. Most of the headlines that accompanied these articles were highly sensationalistic, purposefully designed to draw reader attention, such as "Kuwait Becomes 'Wasteland': Witnesses Recall the Horror of Iraqi Murder, Pillage and Rape" and "Atrocities Ravage Kuwait as 'Time Is Running Out.'" In stark contrast, Indonesia's 1975 invasion of East Timor was accorded an absolute low volume of news coverage within the Canadian media. The headlines reflected the overall differences in reporting. The East Timor headlines were just as the propaganda model would predict. Consider these two headlines, in comparison with the headlines noted above: "Reports Conflict on Timor" (December 9, 1975) and "Envoy Begins Timor Study in Jakarta" (January 16, 1976). The Indonesian invasion of East Timor had violated the same two basic proscriptions of the UN Charter as had Iraq's invasion of Kuwait: right to territory and self-determination. The differences in treatment accorded the two cases by the Canadian media reflected how differently the two cases were treated diplomatically. Following the Iraq invasion of Kuwait, Canada went to war for the first time in 40 years. Following Indonesia's invasion of East Timor, Canada presented Indonesia with $200 million in aid and abstained from voting on East Timor resolutions at the United Nations. Canada was the largest Western investor in Indonesia in 1975, when Indonesia invaded East Timor. Canada's strong diplomatic and material support for Indonesia continued in the years that followed, even as Indonesia imposed forced relocation, sterilization, and near-genocide in East Timor.

on this aspect of the model. Yet it is clear from their writing over the years, that using the model requires an interconnected analysis that explores the interplay among ideology, power, and social inequalities. The methodology requires that media coverage be analyzed within the political and economic context. In his political writing, Chomsky often moves easily between discussing media coverage and comparing it to the historical facts of events reporting.

The model also suggests that comparing coverage of some topics, issues, and events, as opposed to others, may enable insight into broad patterns of media practice. Finding observable disparities in media treatments of similar historical events, or *paired examples,* also provides and level of critical insight. Coverage of victims in the news offers such a comparative critique.

VICTIMS IN THE NEWS: WORTHY OR UNWORTHY?

A central methodological technique associated with the propaganda model entails analysis of how victims are represented within media texts. The model predicts that worthy victims (victims of state terror enacted by official enemy states) will be the topic of significant humanistic coverage that will evoke sympathy and mobilize public opinion and outrage. Other the other hand, unworthy victims (victims of state terror enacted by United States, Canada, allies, and client states) will be given little coverage with minimal humanization, and will be treated in ways that do not invite sympathy or indignation. Another dimension of this analysis (as well and other topics) is the inclusion or absence of photographs, since visual images have powerful influences on how news is framed and interpreted.

The methodological technique most favored by Chomsky is to explore the "boundaries of the expressible" on crucial topics according to both power and social class interests. Investigating the extent to which news coverage conforms to the boundaries of the expressible, or what can and cannot be said, entails observing what is present in the news frame and what is absent from it. Other qualitative criteria for criticism include, sources used, emphasis, placement, tone, fullness of treatment, and context.

The propaganda model assumes that public debate is set by powerful elites, and thus predicts that the primary sources of news will be "agents of power." According to this framework, boundaries of debate are effectively defined by official sources that reflect the interests of power and social class, and the model predicts that debate will conform to these interests. Concurrently, applying the model entails examining the degree to which voices challenging the range of debate are present within (or absent from) media texts, and if they are presented in favorable and/or unfavorable terms and settings. Such omissions and style of presentation are ways of understanding the extent to which news language favors an official world view that promotes existing relations of power.

The model assumes that commercial media exist within a system of power and that the media are themselves fundamentally agents of social power. This assumption emerges from the model's foundational assumptions regarding the structural organization of society.

The propaganda model suggests that media analysis should extend its qualitative criteria to include analysis of textual prominence. This involves evaluating features of media texts that reveals how they are structured or framed. Because of the top-down organization of news, headlines play a significant role in influencing readers understanding and interpretation news. The most important or newsworthy information is conveyed at the outset of media texts and are central to textual prominence. Fore-grounding and back-grounding determine what events, voices and/or facts are made explicit within media texts, and what is presented merely as trivial, or even omitted. The structure of news presentation offers another insight into the ways in which media texts are ideologically inflected.

Herman and Chomsky pay particular attention to presuppositions that undergird common sense understandings of reporting. News of a specific event may include themes from past events while simultaneously ignoring or omitting various facts and/or voices. As noted, the model suggests that analysis of historical and political-economic elements should also be firmly integrated into the media analysis.

The propaganda model and the methodological techniques associated with it allow for sophisticated analysis of media discourse that extends beyond a mere reading of media texts. Quite clearly, the model is concerned to connect text analysis with political, social and economic elements. The model originated in the United States, but recent scholarship from Canada and the United Kingdom indicate that its explanatory power is not limited by geographic borders. And while more than 20 years have passed since the model was first advanced, it is more applicable today than ever before. Similarly, many assume that the model is ideal for exploring international news coverage, but recent scholarship has demonstrated that it is well suited for analysis of domestic news events.

DEBATING THE PROPAGANDA MODEL

There have been several criticisms leveled against the propaganda model over the past two decades. Some challenge what they see as a "conspiratorial" view of media. But Herman and Chomsky have stressed that the model does not assume conspiracy or deliberate intent on the part of news gatekeepers. Because it is a structural model, it is unconcerned with the inner workings of particular newsrooms and makes no claims regarding the organizational aspects of newsroom work. It does not assume that media personnel routinely make conscious decisions to align themselves with the interests of particular elites. The model's focus is on how structural elements, including economics, impact media discourse. There exists a range of literature devoted to the social construction of news that is principally concerned with questions skewed toward newsroom practice.

THE QUESTION OF THE NEWS READERS, VIEWERS, AND MEDIA AUDIENCES

Possibly the most contentious aspect of the propaganda model for media studies scholars is the question of media effects and audience participation. The model has been challenged for seeming to present media audiences as passive and easily manipulated. Though the use of terms such *manufacturing consent* and *brainwashing* suggest a passive audience, Herman and Chomsky do not assume that viewers and readers are passively duped by the media. In fact, quite the opposite seems to be the case. Herman and Chomsky have written about instances when the media has not been effective, and Chomsky has also written at length about dissent culture and what he calls "intellectual self-defense." Although Herman has noted that they make no claims regarding the overall effectiveness of the propaganda system, Chomsky has referred to the propaganda system as inherently unstable, and he understands that audiences read texts in complex ways, an idea related to other theories about the way audiences actively participate and subvert media texts.

The propaganda model's overall program of inquiry, however, can be seen to highlight the fact that perception, awareness, and understanding are informed and constrained by the structure of news discourse. Most critical approaches to media assume that media discourses pervade subjectivity in some way, and are influential in shaping perceptions and opinions. It is uncontroversial to suggest that media *do* have various impacts, although the range of those influences, especially with regard to behavior, remains highly contested. A range of scholarship exists that provides much empirical support for the notion that media are both culturally and politically influential, having intended effects on opinion and policy.

CONCLUSION

In conclusion, the propaganda model is a critical approach, concerned with the interplay between power and ideology, and how these connect to social inequality and economic imbalances within the broader social world. It can also be seen to be a democratic approach, concerned with social injustices. Like critical discourse analysis, the propaganda model advocates an approach to the study of social forces that is accessible and can be read and understood by nonspecialist audiences. The model's foundational assumptions and program of inquiry seem today to be even more relevant than when the model was initially originated, given the globalizing economy and the ever-increasing global power and reach of large corporations, in the face of growing powerlessness among the vast majority of the world's population.

See also Audience Power to Resist; Bias and Objectivity; Children and Effects; Conglomeration and Media Monopolies; Government Censorship and Freedom of Speech; Hypercommercialism; Media and Citizenship; Media and Electoral Campaigns; Narrative Power and Media Influence; Paparazzi and Photographic Ethics; Public Opinion; Public Sphere; Sensationalism, Fear Mongering, and Tabloid Media.

Further Reading: Chen, Jean, Teresa Chen, and Jeffery Klaehn. "An Assessment of the Physical, Emotional and Economic Impact(s) of Workplace Injury in Canada and Analysis of the Ideological Formation of the Workers Compensation Board in the Canadian Media." In *Bound by Power: Intended Consequences,* ed. Jeffery Klaehn. Montreal: Black Rose Books, 2006; Chomsky, Noam. *Necessary Illusions: Thought Control in Democratic Societies.* Toronto, Ontario: CBC Enterprises, 1989; Chomsky, Noam. *Media Control: The Spectacular Achievements of Propaganda.* New York: Seven Stories Press, 1997; Chomsky, Noam, and Edward S. Herman. *The Political Economy of Human Rights, Volume One: The Washington Connection and Third World Fascism.* Montreal: Black Rose, 1979; Herman, Edward S. "The Propaganda Model: A Retrospective." *Journalism Studies* 1, no. 1 (2000): 101–102; Herman, Edward S., and Noam Chomsky. *Manufacturing Consent: The Political Economy of the Mass Media.* New York: Pantheon, 1988; Klaehn, Jeffery, ed. *Filtering the News: Essays on Herman and Chomsky's Propaganda Model.* Montreal: Black Rose Books, 2005; Klaehn, Jeffery, ed. *Bound by Power: Intended Consequences.* Montreal: Black Rose Books, 2006; Miller, David, ed. *Tell Me Lies: Propaganda and Media Distortion in the Attack on Iraq.* London: Pluto, 2003; Winter, James. *Democracy's Oxygen: How the Corporations Control the News.* Montreal: Black Rose Books, 1998; Winter, James. *MediaThink.* Montreal: Black Rose Books, 2002; Winter, James. *Lies Media Tell Us.* Montreal: Black Rose Books, 2007.

Jeffery Klaehn

PUBLIC ACCESS TELEVISION

The advent of cable television franchises across the country in the early 1980s gave rise to public access channels designed for community participation that offered alternatives to commercial television. The act of placing communications resources within the hands of community members was an attempt to empower public expression at the local level. However, public access has never become an institution within mainstream society and is continually struggling over production issues, day-to-day operations, and legislative challenges often driven by the commercial motives of mainstream media.

UN-TELEVISION: PUBLIC ACCESS AS A TV ALTERNATIVE

Regardless of the communications apparatus, public access television offers alternatives. Ideally, it is about replacing the consumer-driven imperative of commercial television with a medium directed by a community's needs. Public access is part of a decentralized public media movement that seeks to empower the community through training in production technologies without the "professional" tampering of reporters, editors, and producers. Public access conceives the video maker as organizer, activist, and catalyst. This may be a difficult concept given cultural norms that applaud individual enterprise over group processes.

COLLECTIVISM AND PROCESS

Ceding authority and debunking the individualism of auteur theory is crucial to the collective ideal of public access, whose advocates argue that community members need to be empowered through inclusion and group participation. Collectivism strives to impartially allocate power so each individual is instrumental to the group project. Successful production models that embody this more egalitarian and process-oriented approach can be found in the work of Paper Tiger Television, Deep Dish TV, and Indymedia.

PUBLIC ACCESS AS MEDIA LITERACY

When nonprofessionals begin to produce media, they often start by imitating what they have seen on mainstream TV, especially young people intent on imitating popular music videos and other commercial formats. In the effort to help those eager to move from media consumers to media producers, public access staff often incorporate media literacy into their curricula and provide instruction beyond the technical aspects of production. Workshops facilitate discussions of television's intersection with the social, political, and economic factors that influence the medium and the look of commercial programming, providing emerging media makers with the critical tools necessary to expand into creative uses of the medium and alternative constructions. Public access producers can then reapply the constructivist techniques of television in addressing personal and communal concerns.

PARTNERSHIPS AS SYNERGY OF MISSION RATHER THAN EXPLOITATION OF REVENUE STREAMS

To fulfill their mission as a community resource, public access television centers utilize partnerships with regional nonprofits. Some access centers located in cities like New York benefit from the cable operator's large subscriber base and allocate monies from the franchise to community-based organizations in the form of grants. This money is then used to purchase equipment, train members, and support production projects to increase the diversity of producers and content, while solidifying partnerships between public access centers and their community members. Notable centers like Manhattan Neighborhood Network have jump-started the communications efforts of organizations working with homeless youth, immigrants, families of incarcerated people, and other underserved populations.

At other facilities like Brooklyn Community Access Television (BCAT), educational collaborations drive many partnerships. BCAT has joined with community colleges, youth organizations, cultural institutions, and advocates for victims of substance abuse and HIV/AIDS to both create programming and learn how regional television can assist in meeting their organizational missions.

In the winter of 2007, BCAT entered into collaboration with Girls, Inc. to teach video production and media literacy skills to young women in Brooklyn. These young women, ranging in age from 15 to 16, determined that the issue of sexual harassment was most relevant to them and their community and explored the subject through research, inquiry, and the active process of video making. The young women learned all aspects of production from conceptualization and planning through production, postproduction, distribution, and exhibition. They interviewed community members, asking them why some boys and men engage in unwanted sexual advances toward women and girls. They examined mainstream media's influence on culture and how images help create the permissible environment for sexist behavior. Challenging these precepts through the construction of alternatives, these young women completed their project by screening their work to members of their community. The young women used the video to provoke discussion on a topic "normalized" by the conventions of a medium dominated by male ownership. Collaborations between organizations like BCAT and Girls Inc. return public access television to its oppositional role as agitator, reimagining television to serve our needs as citizens, residents, and people, and not just consumers.

See: http://mnn.org/; http://bcat.tv/bcat/default.asp; http://www.girlsincnyc.org/; http://girlsincnyc.blog spot.com/.

COMMUNITY AND DIVERSITY

The public access television center is conceived as a physical space that should mirror its community, reflecting the diversity of its people and issues. It is a place where isolated and fragmented publics can be brought together creating a more cohesive entity.

The center should be a space for public mediation and the cultural celebration of difference. It is the role of access centers to facilitate social engagements by organizing screenings, discussion series, panels, conferences, and parties. It should be a facility for disseminating messages but also a place to have fun.

Those who work in public access point out that the most effective centers are designed as creative environments where new thoughts are welcome, where growth and enlightenment are realized through an atmosphere of social learning. An access center can be a place where seniors with different backgrounds, including some with strong religious ties as in some Brooklyn neighborhoods in New York, can be taught editing techniques and the social construction of gender stereotypes by artists/educators from groups traditionally locked out of mainstream participation such as lesbian, gay, and transgender communities. It is a place where understanding, sharing, and community are provoked and expanded.

Diversity in programming is severely limited when cable providers make it overly arduous to produce and program a show. This opens access up only to the passionate eccentrics of the community, defining the political base of public access as fringe and not representative of the broader, more dynamic community.

COMMUNITY RESOURCE OR TELEVISION PROGRAM?

Proponents of public access explain that as one of the few alternatives functioning outside of powerful media systems, public access should continue to embrace its oppositional character. Some lament that over time it has lost its antagonistic tone by appropriating the theory and practices of commercial television. Striving for "legitimacy," some access centers are taking on the controversial role of creating content for their public access channels. However, without community involvement, programs concerning job growth or the economy, for example, are advised by local chambers of commerce rather than unions, labor groups, and other community organizations usually given little airtime on commercial and even public television.

Instituting professional programming practices at the local level would transform the nature and mission of public access. When public access programming aspires to be a regional version of CNN or NPR, it reinforces the opinion that public access television is merely a stepping-stone on the way to corporate media. Since access does not deliver lucrative markets to advertisers, it cannot be measured using a commercial broadcasting ratings system. Because of these factors, advocates argue that public access needs to be reconceptualized as a community resource rather than as a television program. They point to the history of its development and its unique vision in an age of highly centralized, corporate-dominated media institutions.

THE UNIQUE MISSION OF PUBLIC ACCESS TELEVISION

Public access has always been tied to community activism and social change, and is part of a long struggle to claim public space within emerging communications technologies. It proposes a model of television based on need rather than aroused desire and consumer satisfaction. The direct precursor to public access television in the United States was Challenge for Change, a program of the National Film Board of Canada, directed between 1968 and 1970 by George Stoney, widely considered the father of public access television. Challenge for Change held with the basic tenet that film and eventually video can be used to foster dialogue between citizens and government and thereby facilitate participatory media. The actual development of public access television in the United States is often described as an accidental boon when the diverse interests of a fledgling cable industry intersected with the progressive ideals of media educators, artists, and activists. Organizations like the Alternate Media Center at New York University, founded by Stoney, and radical video collectives like Raindance, Videofreeks, Ant Farm, Global Village, and the May Day Collective were active participants and early innovators in the young medium. Some political activists viewed new communication technologies as pathways to developing an adversary culture critical of given economic and political structures. Michael Shamberg of Raindance described how information resources are vital to social models based on human needs. Manifestos concerned with the appropriation and reimagination of communication technologies advocated for people to petition and secure public access channels.

WEAK AND DEPENDENT: THE LIMITATIONS OF PUBLIC ACCESS TELEVISION

Public access television exists through the precarious arrangement of a contractual compromise between the private, profit-seeking cable companies and local municipalities often aligned with nonprofit organizations. Since the 1980s, public access centers have been dramatically compromised as private companies, operating as commercial ventures, seek to meet the minimal obligations of their franchises. Access centers are becoming more and more the exception, while drop-off playback facilities lacking production equipment, facilities, or staff are becoming the rule. In addition, shifting political winds along with funding shortages have repositioned independent video from its use as an instrument of social change to more standardized formats. Some charge that once the emphasis on community within public access is lost, the medium will be little more than a device of artistic vanity for individuals able to take advantage of access channels.

THE CONTINUAL EROSION OF PUBLIC ACCESS

Public access television continues to be challenged from a number of quarters, particularly the cable industry, that would like to take back channels for commercial motivations. Recent legislative maneuverings have been successful at moving authority over public access from local municipalities to state capitals. These structural changes have decreased channel capacity in some states and limited operating hours in others, further contributing to the ongoing erosion of public access television. As of this writing, 23 states have either passed statewide legislation or have bills pending. Though federal bills sponsored by telecommunications companies seeking entrance to the television market failed, these continued assaults have raised alarms throughout the public access community.

PUBLIC ACCESS AND EMERGING TECHNOLOGIES

In an era of media convergence, many understand that public access centers need to stay relevant, but this does not mean that public access workers need attend the latest industry trade shows to survey new gadgets. To follow the unique mission of public access television would mean, rather, that it would take up the watchdog role of examining the convergence of media critically. Is the convergence being driven socially or commercially? Is this new development simply a better way to sell advertising and products? In terms of convergence branded as a "triple play" of services, whose interest is served, that of the communities or that of the media corporations?

The mission of public access television has not changed even as the technology has advanced. An access center's relationship to the community is still the same. Residents are trained to use technology, and centers continue to provide distribution whether the mechanism is television or the Internet. The ideals championed by George Stoney and the video collectives of the counterculture remain access's legacy into the digital age. Many access centers are introducing programs to teach community members how to produce video for the Web. Video blogging classes are increasing the community of producers and placing that community into a global environment. In these times, public access centers are becoming aggregators of media and information, collectors and distributors of digital files that are relevant and valuable to the communities they serve.

REALIZING A UTOPIAN VISION

Above all, public access television requires a utopian sensibility when looking at its prospect and processes. Paraphrasing the words of DeeDee Halleck, founder of Paper Tiger Television and consummate advocate for community media, public access is romantic, just as democracy, liberty, and the First Amendment are romantic. They are ideals valued and defended in the social consciousness of an autonomous people.

Today, public access TV is the incomplete promise of community media, and remains an unrealized ideal for direct democracy through civic engagement with media making.

See also Alternative Media in the United States; Cable Carriage Disputes; Communication Rights in a Global Context; Global Community Media; Hypercommercialism; Media Literacy; Media Reform; Media Watch Groups; Minority Media Ownership; Net Neutrality; Pirate Radio; Public Broadcasting Service; Ratings; World Cinema.

Further Reading: Boyle, Deirdre. *Subject to Change: Guerilla Television Revisited.* New York: Oxford University Press, 1985; Engelman, Ralph. *Public Radio and Television in America: A Political History;* Thousand Oaks, CA: Sage Publications, 1996; Halleck, DeeDee. *Hand-Held Vision: The Impossible Possibilities of Community Media;* New York: Fordham University, 2002; Paper Tiger Television. *Roar: The Paper Tiger Television Guide to Media Activism.* New York: The Paper Tiger Television Collective, 1991; Shamberg, Michael. *Guerilla Television.* New York: Holt Rinehart & Winston, 1971, http://saveaccess.org/.

Carlos Pareja

PUBLIC BROADCASTING SERVICE

The Right has long tried to dismantle the public broadcasting system, claiming the so-called public TV channel is too liberal and too elitist. The Left says that "creeping commercialism" and timidity are to blame for public television's undemocratic tendencies. Both camps tend to oversimplify the issue for their own purposes.

The U.S. public broadcasting system comprises hundreds of local stations and several large national bureaucracies. The most recognizable symbol of this labyrinth is PBS, the logo of the Public Broadcasting Service, which appears on all nationally distributed public television programs, designed so that the letters P-B-S vaguely resemble the human brain. Since its creation in the late 1960s,

---

A PUBLIC BROADCASTING TIMELINE

1950—Ford Foundation takes up the cause of "educational" television.

1951—Federal Communications Commission (FCC) reserves 209 noncommercial television channels for educational use.

1953—First educational TV station (KUHT-Houston) goes on the air.

1958—National Educational Television and Radio Center sets up shop in New York.

1962—National Educational Television Facilities Act is passed.

1964—Carnegie Commission on Educational Television is established; "Public Television: A Program for Action" is released in 1967.

1967—U.S. Public Broadcasting Act is passed.

1968—Children's Television Workshop begins.

1969—PBS debuts.

1972—Richard Nixon vetoes funding for public broadcasting.

1974—PBS Station Program Cooperative is launched.

1979—"A Public Trust: The Report of the Carnegie Commission on the Future of Public Broadcasting" is released.

1984—Ronald Reagan vetoes Public Broadcasting Authorization bill.

1992—Newt Gingrich seeks to abolish federal funding for public broadcasting.

1996—House of Representatives votes to slash public broadcasting's funding.

PBS has positioned itself as the "oasis" of the vast wasteland—a home for televised art, intellectual culture, education, and quality information in a sea of mass cultural mediocrity. For almost as long, PBS has also been the principal target of politically charged disputes over public broadcasting's performance in the United States.

In one of the more recent salvos, in June 2006, Republican members of the U.S. House of Representatives voted to "slash" funding for public broadcasting. Their decision reawakened a Congressional debate that spilled into newspaper articles, opinion pages, and talk shows. Because public television and public radio receive about 20 percent of their funding from annual Congressional appropriations (the rest comes from local and state governments, corporate sponsors, and private donations), these cultural institutions are particularly vulnerable to partisan political currents and must "prove" their value each time the federal purse is opened. Although Congress ultimately rejected the Republicans' plan (for now), PBS remains trapped in a cycle of controversy.

HISTORY

Public television arrived late in the United States. Whereas the United Kingdom, Canada, and many other Western democracies developed public service approaches to broadcasting that were overseen by tax-funded national broadcasting authorities, the United States took a "free-market" approach to radio and television. Not everyone supported this path: throughout the 1920s and into the 1930s, vocal educators, labor unions, and progressive reformers pressured the federal government to allocate a significant portion of the spectrum to nonprofit channels. The corporate sector's lobbying power, coupled with a distrust of "socialistic" activity in the American context, worked against this possibility, however. The 1934 Communications Act entrusted broadcasting entirely to the commercial market, presuming that private companies could turn a profit and serve the public interest as well.

In the 1950s and 1960s, fissures in the U.S. approach to broadcasting emerged. At this time, television culture was dominated by three networks (ABC, CBS, and NBC), and most programming was geared toward a huge mass audience. High-placed critics began to protest what they perceived as television's lowbrow homogeneity and worried that the nation's most popular medium did little to instruct or enlighten citizens. To correct these problems, the prestigious Ford Foundation invested considerable private resources in National Educational Television (NET), a small-scale alternative devoted to "respectable" culture (opera, live plays, British dramas) and information (documentaries, panel discussions). However, Ford's pockets were not bottomless and "educational" television remained a minor blip on the television landscape. Public investment was clearly needed to create a public alternative to market-driven commercial hegemony.

In the 1960s, the case for public television was advanced by many public figures, including former Federal Communications Commission (FCC) chair man Newton Minow and political columnist Walter Lippmann. In 1966, the philanthropic Carnegie Corporation of New York assembled a high-powered team of Ivy League intellectuals, renowned artists, university presidents, corporate executives, and other high-profile individuals to "look into" the issue; their report recommended "immediate federal action." The Public Broadcasting Act was swiftly passed by Congress and signed into law by President Lyndon Johnson in 1967, and programs carrying the PBS logo began to appear in late 1969. Defined as a "Chance for Better Television," PBS claimed a redemptive cultural identity and cultivated an aesthetic based more on pre-electronic media such as live drama and the printed word than on contemporary TV formats. Because PBS had been created to solve a range of perceived cultural problems without fundamentally altering the economic landscape of commercial television, it could not compete for the hearts and minds of TV viewers and maintain its legitimacy.

The purpose of public television was sufficiently ambiguous to allow for alternative interpretations, however. While most bureaucrats, politicians, and supporters saw the new channel as a noncompetitive and altogether nonthreatening cultural forum for quality and "enlightenment," others saw an opportunity to bring racial diversity, political debate, and countercultural values to television. In New York and other large cities in the contentious late 1960s and early 1970s, a small amount of provocative programming that challenged the social, political, and cultural status quo was produced under public television's auspices. While this alternative material comprised but a small part of the overall PBS schedule, it was offensive to conservative politicians who sought to tame PBS's nascent political bite. In 1971, President Richard Nixon vetoed public television's federal funding and set into motion the rhetorical basis of a conservative assault on PBS that continues to this day.

PBS AND CHILDREN

Children's programming is much more popular than adult PBS genres—largely because of *Sesame Street*. In 1969, Children's Television Workshop (CTW), the creators of *Sesame Street*, appropriated the look and style of popular television—including TV commercials—to "sell" cognitive and social skills to children. Contrary to prime-time PBS, which focused on small and usually upscale audiences, the goal was to reach as many kids as possible. CTW was concerned with poverty issues and *Sesame Street* received some of its funding from the Department of Health, Education, and Welfare to operate as a televised Head Start program for poor preschool children, which provided an impetus to bring "disadvantaged" child viewers, in particular, into the public television audience. Producers cleverly fused fast-paced visuals, humor, irony, storytelling, and celebrity guest stars to educational lessons, creating a brand of television "edutainment" that was spun off into *The Electric Company*, *Zoom*, and other shows. Children's programming continues to attract a cross-class, multicultural presence to PBS—but now as before, most kids tend to "drop out" of the public TV audience when they become adults.

FOR THE PEOPLE, NOT BY THE PEOPLE?
THE DEBATE OVER PBS

The disputes over PBS are predictable: while the minor details and individuals involved may change, the "positions" in the cultural battle over PBS generally do not. There are three major positions, emerging (more or less) from three sectors of society: neoconservative elites, the liberal upper middle class, and the intellectual/artistic Left. Each position claims to speak for the larger "public" being served (or not served) by the so-called public channel. Most ordinary people, however, have little voice in the ruckus over public television, or are even aware of it. PBS may be engulfed in periodic controversy, but it is off the cultural radar of most TV viewers.

The neoconservative critique of public television is based on two claims. First, it is argued that PBS programs are "slanted" in favor of people with liberal viewpoints and alternative lifestyles. This accusation is unproven and rather dubious, according to research studies of public television's content. Second, PBS is said to cater to an "elite" slice of the population, in terms of income and education—an observation that is more valid. Officially, PBS claims to reach a broad spectrum of the population, so that everyone is included in the "public" it represents. Yet, PBS also envisions "selective" people who possess college and graduate school degrees, professional and managerial occupations, and disposable income as its core audience, particularly during prime time. Paradoxically, the ability to attract such upscale viewers is part of the "distinction" that has historically defined public television's difference from commercial television in the United States. Neoconservatives point out the elitist dimensions of this mission—not to make public television more culturally democratic, but to privatize it. PBS should retain its distinction but be required to support itself commercially through the sale of advertising and merchandise, claim such critics. Or else, they argue, consumers who want "public" television should pay for it on a subscription basis.

Neoconservatives won the first battle over PBS by fusing perceptions of political bias in some programming to the larger problem of class selectivity and cultural elitism. In this way, the Right—as opposed to the Left—strategically

BUSTER

In March 2005, PBS caved in to conservative pressure by pulling an episode of *Postcards from Buster*, a children's program. In the episode, a cartoon bunny visits Vermont, where he learns to make maple sugar and is invited to dinner at the home of children with two mommies; critics objected to the inclusion of homosexual lifestyles. According to Fairness and Accuracy in Reporting (FAIR), the episode was yanked the same day that PBS received an official letter from President George W. Bush's new Republican Secretary of Education, who condemned the episode and asked PBS to "strongly consider returning the federal money that went toward its production."

FAIR Action Alert, "PBS Censors Postcards from Buster," January 31, 2005, http://www.fair.org/index.php?page=2040.

established itself as the ally of the common people. What scholars call an "authoritarian-populist tactic" has since been also used by other right-wing cultural reformers, from Pat Buchanan to Ronald Reagan to Newt Gingrich, looking to privatize PBS. Such critics do not really represent the public, which is rarely consulted and never asked what it might like to see on public television. If public television is paradoxically "for the people, not by the people," so too is the recurring conservative critique of its shortcomings.

Against the neoconservative position, liberal defenders argue that PBS brings integrity to television by providing a sophisticated alternative to market-driven infotainment. Unlike pay cable, it also "freely" disseminates enlightenment to the culturally deprived. According to this logic, PBS deserves public subsidy because it ensures the survival of "respectable" culture (as defined by educated tastemakers) while also offering the masses an opportunity to pursue informal education and cultural refinement through television viewing. The fact that most adults avoid PBS's curriculum much or all of the time is, significantly, downplayed. Instead, children's programs like *Sesame Street*, which tend to attract a much larger and more socially and economically diverse audience than does prime-time PBS, are strategically accentuated in a metaphoric battle to save "Big Bird" from budget-cutting neoconservatives. The defensive position has succeeded in preserving a token amount of Congressional funding for PBS. However, it has also reproduced the system's internal elitism and therefore constrained thinking about how PBS might serve a broader range of cultural interests and tastes.

The intellectual/artistic Left's critique of PBS emphasizes intersecting problems of political censorship and discrete commercialization. Many activist filmmakers, media reformers, and progressive scholars see in public television an unrequited opportunity for communicative democracy. Because our corporately owned media system threatens the free exchange of ideas required of democracy, noncommercial "public" media spaces are paramount to a fair and just political system. PBS's potential to provide such an electronic public sphere is said to have been undermined by its reliance on corporate underwriters who do not wish to be associated with controversial programming. Corporate funding has, over the years, led to an overabundance of "safely splendid" programming—such as imported British costume dramas and nature documentaries—that crowds out provocative material, contend critics. The watchful eyes of conservative politicians looking for liberal or unconventional "bias" is another factor in the difficulties—and sometimes outright institutional censorship—experienced by independent producers who are deemed too controversial for PBS.

The Left provides a valuable counter-explanation to the "problem" with PBS. Challenging neoconservatives in Washington, this position maintains that a stable source of noncommercial funding is what is needed to ensure PBS's journalistic freedom and protection from political bias. However, critics from this camp tend to oversimplify the role of political economics by presuming that PBS was (or would be) democratic in the absence of corporate interference. They tend to overlook the politics of cultural value by replacing "safely splendid" ideals with their own class- and education-bound view of what counts as worthwhile television. Progressive intellectuals and "censored" PBS producers often distrust

REPUBLICANS VERSUS BILL MOYERS

Conservative politicians have long monitored PBS's public affairs programs with an eye toward institutional censorship. In the early 1970s, when PBS was just getting started, Richard Nixon ordered White House staffers to scour its news and documentary programs for evidence of political and personal "bias" against the Republican president. More recently, in 2005, Kenneth Tomlinson, the Republican chairman of the Corporation for Public Broadcasting (CPB), which oversees issues of "objectivity and balance" among other tasks, secretly hired a consultant with conservative ties to "conduct an analysis of the political ideology" of guests on the PBS program *NOW* and three other public television and radio programs. According to National Public Radio, which obtained the unreleased report, the guests were graded not just on their political viewpoints, but on "whether they explicitly supported policies of the Bush White House." The CPB board is appointed by the president; Tomlinson was named chairman by George W. Bush.

Tomlinson complained that Moyers, whose journalistic commentaries have appeared on PBS since the early 1970s, was too liberal and "critical of Republicans and the Bush Administration." In addition to commissioning the study, he hired a senior White House aid to "draw up guidelines to review the content of public radio and television broadcasts."

David Folkenflik, "CBP Memos Indicate Level of Monitoring," National Public Radio, June 30, 2005, www.npr.org; Michael Sorkin, "Speech at Conference Assails Right Wing," May 16, 2005, CommonDreams.org Newsletter, www.commondreams.org.

habitual TV viewing and prefer serious information and avant-garde material over popular television formats, which they would just as soon leave to commercial channels. This failure to engage with the possibilities of popular public television has made it difficult for the intellectual Left to align itself with ordinary people in the cultural battle over PBS.

CABLE COMPETITION

As commercial cable has developed, PBS's approach to quality and informal education has become somewhat redundant to the niche-oriented goals of the Discovery Channel, the History Channel, and the Arts and Entertainment Network—as free-market conservatives and Leftist critics point out. The Right uses this redundancy as further ammunition in its quest to privatize PBS; the Left sees it as another reason to embrace provocative political programming the commercial market (no matter how many channels) is unable or unwilling to provide. There is another, perhaps more democratic possibility overlooked by this stalemate, that involves funding noncommercial versions of popular genres and formats, with no expectation of cultural or political enlightenment, along the lines of much public television in Britain. However, given the structures of U.S. broadcasting and the dominant frameworks for thinking about PBS's role, this is not likely to occur.

See also Alternative Media in the United States; Children and Effects; Global Community Media; Media and Citizenship; Media Reform; Media Watch Groups; National Public Radio; Political Documentary; Public Access Television; Public Opinion; Public Sphere; Regulating the Airwaves.

Further Reading: Consoli, John. "PBS Hones Its Pitch With New Sponsorships." *Media-Week* 16, no. 34 (September 25, 2006). http://www.mediaweek.com/mw/search/article_display.jsp?vnu_content_id=1003155605; *Current: The Newspaper about Public TV and Radio in the U.S.* http://www.current.org/; de Moraes, Lisa. "PBS's 'Buster' Gets An Education." *Washington Post,* January 27, 2005, C01; Hoynes, William. *Public Television for Sale: Media, the Market and the Public Sphere.* Boulder, CO: Westview Press, 1994; Ledbetter, James. *Made Possible By: The Death of Public Broadcasting in the United States.* London: Verso, 1998; Lewis, Justin, and Toby Miller, eds. *Critical Cultural Policy: A Reader.* London: Blackwell Publishing, 2002; McChesney, Robert. *Telecommunications, Mass Media, and Democracy: The Battle for the Control of U.S. Broadcasting, 1928–1935.* Cambridge: Oxford University Press, 1993; Ouellette, Laurie. *Viewers Like You? How Public TV Failed the People.* New York: Columbia University Press, 2002; Wildman, Sarah. "Tune In, Turn On, Fight Back." *The American Prospect Online,* July 3, 2005. http://www.prospect.org/web/page.ww?section=root&name=ViewPrint&articleId=9860.

Laurie Ouellette

PUBLIC OPINION: ARE POLLS DEMOCRATIC?

Opinion polls should, in theory, be a democratic force, closing the gap between citizens and their political representatives. However, as a form of public expression, polls are limited: citizens play little part in their subject or design, and many of the groups commissioning polls do not see them as a way of deepening democratic expression. Nevertheless, once we understand these limitations, polls can still play a role in keeping political elites in check. Further, they suggest a more progressive view of the world than the stereotypes often drawn upon to signify popular opinion.

In 1995, the democratic theorist James Bryce called for a means by which the "will of the majority of citizens" might be "ascertainable at all times." His hope was to provide a greater balance between the power of the people and of their elected officials, thereby cutting the distance between the electorate and the political elite. When George Gallup's polls made this possible in the 1920s, it seemed that we were on the dawn of a more democratic era.

But many a tale is founded on the idea that we should be careful what we wish for, and few would now regard opinion polls as the lifeblood of the democratic state. For many, polls litter rather than enhance the political landscape: they are derided as the tools of public relations consultants and spin doctors rather than lauded as the voice of the citizenry. They have contributed toward an ersatz democracy, a multiple-choice manufacturing turning active citizens into passive consumers.

So what went wrong? The answer, one might suggest, lies less with polls themselves than with the conditions in which they are produced and interpreted. Despite their limits, polls should not be dismissed as mere marketing tools or as a symbol of political superficiality. For while Bryce's vision may have been a little naive, opinion polls can have a democratic function and provide a check on political elites. Indeed, there is a case for us taking polls *more* seriously than we do now.

THE POINT OF POLLING

There has been a great deal of attention paid to the statistical shortcomings of polls. This is, in part, because they are often associated with predicting electoral outcomes: a complex matter that requires sophisticated sampling techniques (in order to predict who will actually vote, who is lying, etc.) and where the margin of victory may be less than the margin of error. In this spirit, scholars have often chided the news media for their failure to report or understand the technical aspects of polls.

If the debate about the ability of polls to forecast elections often takes center stage, we are better off seeing it as a trivial sideshow. This use of polls has very little to do with exploring or representing public opinion: their purpose is to provide a commentary on the electoral race. From a democratic point of view, this is an ultimately pointless exercise that might be done just as well by bookmakers.

Moreover, an obsession with accuracy is misplaced. Methods matter of course: there is no shortage of surveys based on ad hoc or self-selecting samples that cannot claim to be representative. But most opinion polling takes care to use sampling techniques designed to represent a broadly representative cross-section of the public. And while polls can never *predict* how people will vote with pinpoint accuracy, sampling techniques allow us to get a flavor of public attitudes using surprisingly small samples. We should not lose sight of how remarkable it is to be able to get a sense of what the population is thinking by talking to only a tiny fraction of that population.

But sampling, almost by definition, is not an exact science. Its statistical method is based on notions of probability rather than certainty. A good poll may claim to be accurate within two or three percentage points, but it does so on the basis of a level of probability (say, 95 percent). A poll that is a few percentage points out in predicting an election result is not so much "wrong" as misinterpreted.

We are, perhaps, seduced by the neat numerical precision that polls can provide. What is useful about polls, however, is their ability to suggest patterns and tendencies rather than their exactitude. Once we recognize this, we can see how the more profound limits of polls have less to do with science and more to do with the nature of the artifice. To put it another way, the issue is less *who* is asked, than *what* they are asked, in what context, and what we make of their responses.

THE PRODUCTION OF POLLS

There are three issues here. First, as many critics have pointed out, there is nothing authentic about the poll versions of public opinion (or, for that matter, many other representations of public opinion). Polls do not so much measure public attitudes as manufacture them. After all, the conversation between the pollster and the respondent bears little relation to the way people generally talk about politics and current affairs. They are based on artificial, one-sided conversations, where the pollster chooses the subjects to discuss, asks all the questions, and offers a limited range of responses. The citizen plays a part, but it is a small and tightly scripted one. For some, this makes polls less a signifier of public attitude than a poor substitute for deliberative public discussion and debate.

This does not mean that polls are necessarily bogus or manipulative: the attempt to represent public opinion can be done in a way that tries to capture people's priorities, concerns, and beliefs. But it is a form of manufacture nonetheless, and the circumstances in which polls are produced will shape the nature of the responses. Although it may be difficult to get people to profess opinions they do not hold, the poll is an unthinking apparatus that can only reveal what it has been told to look for. The beauty of polling machinery lies in its propensity for statistical sophistication, not in its understanding of the everyday.

All of which raises important questions of authorship and motive. Although polls are extremely efficient ways to gauge public responses to specific questions, they are too expensive to be viable for ordinary individuals or citizens groups. Polls are therefore bound up in a political economy that favors corporate bodies: notably business and government. While there are some institutions—notably universities or public agencies—with a genuine commitment to using polls purely as a form of democratic expression, the motives behind the commissioning opinion polls are not always so laudable. To be able to claim to speak on the public's behalf is a powerful political or marketing tool.

Some have argued that polls are democratic because they allow us to appeal to a broader citizenry than the cabal of well-heeled lobby groups who routinely try to influence the political process. This is certainly true in theory, but polls can also be used by those very same groups for their own ends. Indeed, it is the well-heeled lobbyists who are most likely to have the resources and the motive to commission them. Many polls may have thus very little to do with public consultation, and can be designed primarily as a way to highlight a consumer need, a legislative issue, or simply to grab a headline.

So, for example, Jon Kronsnik examined a poll commissioned by an insurance company, whose function was clearly to create an impression that public opinion favored legislation that insurance companies were pressing for. While the poll may have been statistically beyond reproach, he showed how it was as much an exercise in manipulation as consultation. It was designed to promote a cause, and the failure of news reports in the *New York Times* to point this out highlights the importance of understanding the political economy of polls.

Similarly, it is worth considering why news media polls tend to proliferate during election periods. This is not, in most cases, to fulfill a Brycean vision to bring political representatives closer to those who elect them. On the contrary, only rarely do we see polls that ask people which policy initiatives they really want from their politicians. Instead, we are obliged to conform to the main party agendas by simply stating who we will vote for, rather than what we want

POLLS AND THE MANUFACTURED CENTER

A common strain of journalistic thinking, in both the United States and the United Kingdom, is that the broad mass of the public occupy a space somewhere to the right of the middle of the road—a place that, in a kind of symbolic symmetry, is often referred to as "middle England" or "middle America." And while there are certainly issues where we find majority opinion in precisely that space, it is notable how often polling data cast doubt on this assumption. What we often find, instead, is that many aspects of the center/right policy leanings favored by many political and business leaders have little majority support amongst the general population.

In the United States, for example, large sections of the public are skeptical about many features of the pro-business globalization model that both main parties generally adhere to, while research suggests that if given information about the size of the military budget, most would prefer cuts of a magnitude that few political leaders would dare contemplate. In Britain, polls suggest little support for the gradual move towards the "reform" of public services through privatization and (somewhat convoluted) market mechanisms. These divergences between public and elite opinion are muffled by a conventional wisdom that assumes a population symbolized by a mythic and metonymic "middle," whose center/right leanings we could expect to be sympathetic to globalization, militarism, and a pro-business, privatization agenda.

---

them to do. During campaigns, polls are generally commissioned to inform a well-rehearsed narrative about who is winning and what the outcome might be. They are there to make news rather than to inform the democratic process, and they tell us very little about what people actually think.

POLLS AND THE NEWS MEDIA

This raises a second, more general point: in the public sphere the news media play a key role in mediating public opinion. It is not just that newspapers and broadcast news outlets regularly commission polls; polling information is much more likely to influence public policy or debate if it is in the public eye. The role polls play in the political process depends upon, to a large extent, how conspicuous they are. This means that polling information tends to become significant only when it is regarded as newsworthy.

If polls are themselves a way of mediating public opinion, then their findings are subject to another level of selection and interpretation by the news media. These two forms of mediation can often overlap: opinion polls, especially those conducted by news organizations, are often written around a news agenda. The poll thereby feeds back the narrative of news, sustaining an impression of synchronicity between the news world and public opinion.

A third issue follows from this. Our opinions about politics and public affairs are based on a series of assumptions about the world, much of which *comes* from the news media. The news media not only interpret polls for us, they provide the informational context on which our opinions are based. So, for example, if we think, on the basis of what we read, that immigration is running at unsustainably high levels and is a major burden on public services, we are more likely to support efforts to curtail it. Or if we repeatedly see experts telling us that a foreign government poses a serious and imminent threat to the security of the world, we are more likely to support military intervention against that government.

An intelligent reading of polling data will acknowledge this, and in cases where media coverage is prominent and germane to the question being asked, polls may be as much a measure of the influence of the news media as anything else. This understanding is increasingly informing opinion research, which is beginning to explore the links between knowledge and opinion. For it is here that we are most likely to see the ideological play of media influence: the media may not foist opinions upon us, but they provide an informational climate which makes some opinions more tenable than others.

Work by the Program on International Policy Attitudes (PIPA) at the University of Maryland has explored the way in which misunderstandings about foreign policy have developed, and we can see how those misunderstandings have shaped public opinion. So, for example, in 2003, their research found that a number of erroneous assumptions about Saddam Hussein were widespread among the U.S. population, and these assumptions clearly informed the case for war with Iraq. Similarly, the U.S. group Retro Poll, run by citizen activists, carries out polls exploring the relation between assumptions and attitudes, partly to demystify conventional wisdom in the mainstream news media.

In sum, the technology of polling is a useful way of finding out what people within a society think and assume about the world. But the political economy of polling and its dependence upon the news media mean that many polls are not *primarily* there to do this. The first question we should ask of polls is not to quibble about sampling, but as to who commissioned and designed them, and to what end.

TOWARD A MORE DEMOCRATIC USE OF OPINION POLLS

The media and politicians are sometimes accused of paying too much attention to polls, thereby pandering to a kind of unprincipled populism. There is, however, very little evidence for this. Politicians certainly use polls, but this generally has more to do with market research than a desire to do the people's bidding. Polls are more likely to inform matters of presentation rather than matters of policy.

The media use of polls is also very far from being a tale of slavish adherence. Research suggests that journalists tend to use polls less as a form of genuine enquiry than to bolster the prejudices of the newsroom. So, for example, King and Schudson describe how, during the Reagan era, journalists assumed their own impressions of the president—as affable and likeable—were held by a majority of the public. They thereby ignored a great deal of polling evidence to the contrary, focusing only on those snippets that supported their assumptions.

Indeed, while journalists have long been criticized for a failure to appreciate the meaning and technical limits of polls, what is more striking is their comparative absence in news reporting. It is fairly commonplace for both print and broadcast news to reference public opinion or to represent the citizenry, but most of these references are impressionistic and make no use of polling data. If the news is full of reporters making speculative assumptions about public attitudes or "vox pops" reacting to a news story, this is rarely backed up with the kind of evidence polls provide. Lewis, Inthorn, and Wahl-Jorgensen's study of how the public are represented in U.K. and U.S. television news suggests that only between 2 and 3 percent of references to public opinion in mainstream news programs involve polling data.

We can see, under these circumstances, how conventional wisdom about public opinion may have little evidentiary basis (see "Polls and the Manufactured Center" sidebar). Polls that fly in the face of journalistic assumptions, far from being newsworthy (as we might assume) tend to make little impact. So, for example, polls show far less support for cutting taxes and public spending than most journalists usually suggest. Similarly, during the BBC's coverage of the shootings at Virginia Tech in April 2007, correspondent Matt Frei suggested that most U.S. citizens did not support greater gun control—a view that fits a media stereotype but that is flatly contradicted by most polling data.

In short, there is a very real sense that paying more attention to polls would indeed, as James Bryce hoped, identify the gap between the public and their representatives. Whether they would lessen that gap is another matter, although once it becomes a conspicuous part of public debate, public opinion can be a powerful force, informing the way in which news stories are framed and played out. So, for example, media coverage of war tends to be more critical when polls show substantial public disquiet.

This is not to suggest an empty-headed embrace of opinion polling, more that we give more credence to the careful use of polling technology. There is nothing sacrosanct about the answers people give to polling questions, but if we appreciate the constraints that polls put on public expression, as well as the informational context in which people respond to them, they can be a powerful democratic force.

See also Bias and Objectivity; Media and Citizenship; Media and Electoral Campaigns; Propaganda Model; Public Sphere; Sensationalism, Fear Mongering, and Tabloid Media.

Further Reading: Herbst, Susan. *Reading Public Opinion.* Chicago: University of Chicago Press, 1998; King, E. and Schudson, Michael. "The Press and the Illusion of Public Opinion." In Charles T. Salmon and Theodore L. Glasser, eds., *Public Opinion and the Communication of Consent.* New York: Guilford Press, 1995; Krosnik, John. "Question Wording and Reports of Survey Results: The Case of Louis Harris and Associates and Aetna Life and Casualty." *Public Opinion Quarterly* 53 (Spring 1989); Lewis, Justin. *Constructing Public Opinion.* New York: Columbia University Press, 2001; Lewis, Justin, Karin Wahl-Jorgensen, and Sanna Inthorn. "Images of Citizenship on Television News: Constructing a Passive Public." *Journalism Studies* 5(2) (2004); Salmon, Charles T. and Theodore L. Glasser. "The Politics of Polling and the Limits of Consent." In Charles

T. Salmon and Theodore L. Glasser, eds., *Public Opinion and the Communication of Consent.* New York: Guilford Press, 1995.

Justin Lewis

PUBLIC SPHERE

As modern industrial life has linked the concerns and fates of millions of individuals in forms of social and political organization such as nation-states, interpersonal and mediated communication have become critical aspects of the political process. The space and mode in which such communication takes place is the "public" or the "public sphere." In the indirect, representative democracies of many Western countries as well as other forms of modern political organization, the public sphere is thus a crucial battleground and space in which citizens seek to impact on the formulation of political will.

The "public sphere"—as opposed to related yet more commonplace terms such as "the public," or "public opinion"—is primarily an academic concept that seeks to analyze forms of public and political discussion and debates in modern societies. While few dispute the immense significance of mass communication in achieving and maintaining political power in contemporary societies, the notion of the public sphere links the analysis of media industries, technologies, and content with the exploration and, crucially, evaluation of the

---

JÜRGEN HABERMAS

Jürgen Habermas (born June 18, 1929, in Düsseldorf) is a German philosopher and sociologist who has been associated with the second generation of the Frankfurt School, a group of scholars originally based at the Institute for Social Research at the University of Frankfurt, whom from broadly Marxist, yet also psychoanalytical perspectives sought to critically assess modernity and its prevalent social, cultural, and economic conditions. While Habermas's work departs substantially from many conceptual traditions of the first generation of the Frankfurt School, he shares with its most prominent exponents, such as Theodor Adorno and Max Horkheimer, an emphasis on the role of (mass) communication in the analysis of modern societies. *The Structural Transformation of the Public Sphere*, written as Habermas's habilitation—a substantial thesis that qualifies scholars in the German academic system to obtain the rank of professor—and first published in German, thus set the framework for much of Habermas's subsequent work, including his magnum opus, *Theory of Communicative Action* (1981).

Habermas himself was a professor at Frankfurt University between 1964 and 1971 and from 1982 until his retirement in 1994. In recognition of his work, he has received numerous awards and remains one of the most influential European philosophers who is still actively engaged in the public debate as in his outspoken protest against the U.S.-led invasion of Iraq in 2003.

---

depth and quality of the engagement of individual citizens in political debates and decision making, forcing us to interrogate exactly how the media speaks to, engages, and involves citizens in the political process.

THE STRUCTURAL TRANSFORMATION OF THE PUBLIC SPHERE

The concept of the public sphere attracted increasing academic attention in North America following the translation of Jürgen Habermas's critical study *The Structural Transformation of the Public Sphere* into English in 1989, nearly three decades after its original publication. In this first of his major works, Habermas undertakes a broad historical analysis into the development of public debates in modern societies. In particular, he identifies the political debates among the early modern bourgeoisie in England, France, and later Germany, as an ideal type of public debate. This early modern bourgeois public sphere preceded the arrival of media industries and their commodification of information and political debate as well as the emergence of powerful structures of government in modern nation-states interfering in a range of social, cultural, and economic processes. Thus, for a brief historical window, political communication, according to Habermas, took place in an open, unrestricted fashion, often finding its locus in publicly accessible coffee houses and salons and through the circulation of nonprofit media (such as pamphlets) written and circulated by members of the public. This emerging public sphere was inherently modern by breaking the feudal control over public communication, which had thus previously not been public at all.

Moreover, in its earliest manifestation, it embodied the qualities that Habermas identifies as the key features of the public sphere: open, unrestricted access for all citizens and a rational dialogue among all participants, which in turn is based on the separation of private and public realms, as citizens met in public places such as coffee houses where they could congregate to discuss pressing issues of the day free from coercion. Habermas's definition of the public sphere reflects these qualities: "By 'the public sphere' we mean first of all a realm of our social life in which something approaching public opinion can be formed. Access is guaranteed to all citizens. A portion of the public sphere comes into being in every conversation in which private individuals assemble to form a public body" (Habermas 1989, p. 136).

Yet, making his analysis of the structural transformation of the public sphere foremost a chronology of its historical decline, Habermas suggests that the forces of modernity also led to its demise: he identifies the increasing power and hence involvement in a range of social, cultural affairs of the modern nation and welfare state as the culprit in the downfall of the public sphere. Drawing on C. W. Mills's distinction between "public" and "mass," Habermas argues that the formation of public opinion shifted from an unrestricted communicative environment to a state of mass communication in which opinions are expressed by a small elite excluding the public from the opinion-making process: "With the interweaving of public and private realms, not only do the

A GLOBAL PUBLIC SPHERE?

Following Habermas's analysis of the emerging public sphere in England, France, and Germany, the concept of the public sphere continues to center on the modern nation-states. However, over the past half century, various transnational or even global spaces of public debate have formed: shortwave radio stations such as BBC World were aimed at a global audience during the Cold War and continue to do so today; the arrival of multichannel television in the 1980s led to an internationalization of televisual content and the rise of transnationally transmitted news networks such as CNN; and since the 1990s the Internet has provided an increasingly universally accessible forum of political information and debate alike. At the same time, pressing political concerns ranging from environmental risks such as global warming; the threats of nuclear technology and genetic engineering; questions of security and political or religious violence; and concerns over human rights, equality, and poverty all expand beyond national boundaries as well as the influence of individual nation-states and are commonly taken up in form of social movements and nongovernmental organizations (such as Greenpeace, Amnesty International, etc.). Whether, however, these spaces of transnational communication constitute a meaningful public sphere remains hotly contested: On the one hand, such transnational dialogue appears vital in the face of global challenges and risks. On the other, transnational public spheres—like other alternative public spheres—do not map onto transnational legislative and governmental structures. Conversely, supranational and region states such as the European Union have so far failed to establish a single regional public sphere to inform their democratic institutions.

political authorities assume certain functions in the sphere of commodity exchange and social labour, but, conversely, social powers now assume political functions.... Large organizations strive for political compromises with the state and with one another, excluding the public sphere whenever possible" (Habermas 1989, p. 141.) This collusion between the state and other large-scale organizations, including broadcasters and publishers, leads in Habermas's words to the "refeudalization" of the public sphere, a state in which citizens are once more marginalized or even excluded from meaningful public debate. The public debates that take place in and through mass media such as television (for example, during televised parliamentary debates, in news programs, or in talk shows) or radio (for instance, in phone-ins) are thus a "pseudo-public and sham private sphere of cultural consumption" (Habermas 1989: 160) that, by being part of a privatized nexus of mass production and mass consumption, are inherently apolitical.

CRITIQUE OF HABERMAS'S WORK

Following the belated translation of Habermas's analysis of the structural transformation of the public sphere, it quickly became one of the most widely used sources in the analysis of contemporary political communication in the

English-speaking world. Despite its popularity, however, it has attracted a substantial body of criticism. Much of the scrutiny has centered on the historical details of Habermas's account of the early public sphere. It is now widely accepted that the early bourgeois public sphere Habermas depicts is an idealization that fails to account for a number of historical realities: Habermas underplayed the significance of state institutions in the early bourgeois public sphere (see Ely 1992; Price 1995), and while he acknowledges the role of the development of capitalism and industrialism in the rise of the bourgeois public sphere, he fails to account that they also inevitably led to the formation of media industries and thus the monopolization of public debates. Most importantly, however, Habermas has come under attack for his failure to acknowledge the profound social barriers excluding vast sections of the population from participation in the early bourgeois public sphere: circles of discussion and debate in Europe's early modern coffee houses were not only limited to those who through their social status and economic capital could frequent such places—thus excluding a wide section of the population on the basis of class alone—but also discriminated on the grounds of gender, age, class, ethnicity, and/or nationality. The early bourgeois public sphere was hence far from the ideal communicative environment Habermas originally suggested.

ALTERNATIVE PUBLIC SPHERES

It is this criticism on which many media and communication scholars have focused in coming to a more optimistic assessment of the current state of the public sphere. If the early public sphere in fact excluded large sections of the population, the contemporary public sphere with different print, broadcast, and online media at their heart appears as relative progress and comparatively more democratic than its predecessor. Studies of different media, genres and texts such as television news, talk shows, or the Internet thus suggest that mass media, rather than exercising monopolistic control over public debate, offer opportunities of engagement and participation to many citizens while being widely and openly accessible. Researchers focusing on popular media content in particular have contrasted Habermas's notion of the bourgeois public sphere with a "post-modern public sphere" that expands far beyond the traditional realm of political debate, eroding boundaries between the private and the public, between politics and entertainment (see Hartley 1997; McKee 2005). As John Hartley, a leading proponent of this position, argues, "The major contemporary political issues, including environmental, ethnic, sexual and youth movements, were all generated *outside* the classic public sphere, but they were (and are) informed, shaped, developed and contested within the privatized public sphere of suburban media consumerism" (Hartley 1997, p. 182).

Habermas has in turn responded to particularly the feminist critique of his original work (see Fraser 1992) by conceding the inaccuracy of his historical analysis and acknowledging its limitations. The significance of *The Structural Transformation* thus does not lie in being a historical study: rather, it derives its value from offering a model of public debate and political communication that sets out ideals for democratic societies to aspire to, regardless of whether they have been met in the past. This normative model of the public sphere calls for the media to involve all citizens in a rational dialogue that is at the heart of all democratic decisions.

While many of these values—unrestricted access to a public realm that fosters a rational dialogue and informs political decision making—appear desirable to most of us, the ideals of Habermas's work cannot be as easily divorced from the details of his analysis. His concept of the public sphere is tied to early modern nation-states and thus to a particular social-institutional context. From this follows the possibility of multiple public spheres, in the first instance in different nation-states but secondly also within and across different nation-states following lines such as gender, sexuality, or ethnicity. Yet, the notion of multiple public spheres not only constitutes a remarkable departure from the term *Öffentlichkeit* in Habermas's original work, which literally translates as "publicness" and hence describes the state of being public rather than a given space. This opposition between public spheres and publicness highlights fundamental concerns regarding the legitimacy of contemporary political processes and the effectiveness of contemporary public discourses. Whereas publicness is inherently tied to a given political systems, public spheres (corresponding with distinct audience groups) lack a clear integration into political systems.

This disjuncture between spaces of debate and realms of political decision-making creates the democratic deficits in mediated democracies Nicholas Garnham describes: "The problem is to construct systems of democratic accountability integrated with media systems of matching scale that occupy the same social space as that over which economic or political decision will impact. If the impact is universal, then both the political and media systems must be universal" (Garnham 1992, p. 371). Alternative public spheres in the realms of popular culture, subculture, or transnational communication (see "A Global Public Sphere?") thus provide important spaces of debate, but they sever the fundamental link between citizens' participation in public debates and governance. Yet, as both the early bourgeois and the contemporary public sphere have failed to accommodate unrestricted, rational debates that translate into the formulation of laws and government actions, the concept of the public sphere continues to serve as a powerful reminder to question the working of contemporary, mediated democracies.

See also Alternative Media in the United States; Bollywood and the Indian Diaspora; Global Community Media; Government Censorship and Freedom of Speech; Independent Cinema; Media and Citizenship; Media and Electoral Campaigns; Media Watch Groups; Nationalism and the Media; Political Documentary; Political Entertainment; Public Broadcasting Service; Public Opinion.

Further Reading: Butsch, Richard, ed. *Media and Public Spheres*. Basingstoke: Palgrave, 2007; Crossley, Nick, and John Michael Roberts, eds. *After Habermas: New Perspectives on the Public Sphere*. Oxford: Blackwell, 2004; Ely, Geoff. "Nations, Publics and Political Cultures: Placing Habermas in the Nineteenth Century," in *Habermas and the Public*

Sphere, ed. Craig Calhoun. Cambridge, MA: MIT Press, 1992; Fraser, Nancy. "Rethinking the Public Sphere: A Contribution to the Critique of Actually Existing Democracy," in *Habermas and the Public Sphere,* ed. Craig Calhoun. Cambridge, MA: MIT Press, 1992; Garnham, Nicholas. "The Media and the Public Sphere," in *Habermas and the Public Sphere,* ed. Craig Calhoun. Cambridge, MA: MIT Press, 1992; Habermas, Jürgen. *The Structural Transformation of the Public Sphere.* Cambridge, MA: MIT Press, 1989 (1962); Habermas, Jürgen. "Further Reflections on the Public Sphere," in *Habermas and the Public Sphere,* ed. Craig Calhoun. Cambridge, MA: MIT Press, 1992; Hartley, John. "The Sexualization of Suburbia: The Diffusion of Knowledge in the Postmodern Public Sphere," in *Visions of Suburbia,* ed. Roger Silverstone. New York: Routledge, 1997; Holub, Robert C. *Jürgen Habermas: Critic in the Public Sphere.* New York: Routledge, 1991; McKee, Alan. *The Public Sphere: An Introduction.* Cambridge: Cambridge University Press, 2005; Price, Monroe E. *Television, The Public Sphere and National Identity.* Oxford: Oxford University Press, 1995; Thompson, John B. "The Theory of the Public Sphere." *Theory, Culture and Society* 10 (1993): 173–89.

Cornel Sandvoss

R

RATINGS

Do the ratings systems that measure the audiences for media such as television, radio, and the Web accurately reflect what the public is consuming? If not, what are the consequences? For years, scholars and industry executives alike have debated whether various audience measurements are accurate or not. Critics of such measurement systems argue that they present a distorted view of who is watching or listening, and that these distortions lead to programming that does not serve the interests of all viewers and listeners. These criticisms have become more pronounced in recent years, as the media environment grows more complex and the ratings firms introduce new—and sometimes controversial—measurement systems.

Ratings are the "currency" of the media industry. They provide information on how many people watched a particular television program or channel, listened to a particular radio program or station, or visited a particular Web site. Ratings are produced by outside (or third party) measurement firms such as Nielsen

---

TIMELINE OF AUDIENCE MEASUREMENT IN THE UNITED STATES

1929—The first radio ratings (called the "Crossleys" after lead researcher Archibald Crossley) are established by a consortium of advertisers. Telephone surveys are used to gather listening data.

1936—Two MIT professors introduce the first "audimeter" device, which automatically records radio-tuning behaviors. The rights to the device are immediately purchased by Arthur C. Nielsen.

1942—The A. C. Nielsen Company is established.

1949—ARB (later to become Arbitron) is established.

1963—Congress holds hearings investigating the integrity of ratings methodologies.

1964—The Broadcast Rating Council (later the Media Rating Council) is established by the broadcast industry to oversee and certify ratings services.

1985—Audits of Great Britain introduces the first "people meter" in the United States in an effort to compete with Nielsen.

1987—Nielsen launches its own people-meter service.

1988—Audits of Great Britain ceases operations in the United States.

1994—Congress holds hearings investigating Nielsen's effectiveness in measuring minority television audiences.

1999—Nielsen introduces the Local People Meter in Boston as a replacement to the paper diaries used to measure local TV audiences.

2004—Congress holds hearings into allegations of racial misrepresentation in the Local People Meter measurement system.

2007—After 15 years of testing and development, Arbitron officially launches its Portable People Meter in Philadelphia, with four other large markets to follow soon after.

2007—Amidst substantial controversy and industry resistance, Nielsen introduces "commercial ratings," which report audience sizes for commercial breaks rather than for individual programs.

Media Research (for television and the Web) and Arbitron (for radio). In addition to evaluating how well shows are performing, ratings also provide information on the key characteristics of media audiences—such as their average age, income, and their gender distribution, to name just a few of the demographic characteristics that ratings firms measure these days.

SETTING ADVERTISING RATES

Advertisers use ratings data to decide where to advertise and how much they are willing to spend. Media programmers use ratings data to decide how much to charge advertisers, as well as to decide which television and radio programs and Web sites to continue, and which ones to cancel. Ratings provide the ultimate measure of how programming is performing, and so survival depends upon performing well in the ratings.

Different media have their ratings calculated differently, though always by an independent third party responsible for providing independent and accurate information that both advertisers and programmers can rely on. Television ratings, for example, are provided in the United States by Nielsen Media Research. Nielsen produces its national television ratings by installing electronic "people meters" in a national sample of 10,000 television households. These households have agreed to have their viewing measured in exchange for a very small payment from Nielsen. A meter is attached to each television set in the house. Whenever a household member sits down to watch television, she or he must "log in" to the meter via an assigned button on the remote control. When that household member finishes watching television, she or he must remember to "log out." Each person in the family has a different button assigned, and demographic information about each individual is gathered by Nielsen, so that when one member of the family is watching TV—say a 13-year-old male—Nielsen knows that a 13-year-old male is watching. By gathering this information from thousands of households, Nielsen is able to produce the ratings reports that tell advertisers and television programmers not only how many people are watching each television program, but also what the composition of this audience is, in terms of characteristics such as age, gender, and income—characteristics that advertisers consider important in making decisions about where best to advertise certain products.

RADIO AND WEB RATINGS

Radio still relies primarily on a system of paper diaries that samples of radio listeners carry around with them for a week at a time. Radio ratings in the United States are produced primarily by the Arbitron Company. Participants in the Arbitron measurement system are expected to record in their diary all of their radio listening, including the station channel and call letters. At the end of the week, diaries are sent back to Arbitron via mail for tabulation and a new diary is received. Once the tabulations are complete, detailed quarterly ratings reports are produced that tell advertisers and radio stations how many (and what type of) people were listening to each station at different times of the day and different days of the week. This rather antiquated system is in the process of being replaced with an electronic system (called the Portable People Meter), in which participants carry cell phone–size devices with them that automatically pick up all radio signals the participant hears.

The World Wide Web also has a ratings system in place. The primary method of producing Web ratings involves placing monitoring software on participants' hard drives. This software keeps track of each Web site that is visited, and for how long the site is visited. This information is then automatically sent, via the Internet, back to the measurement company for tabulation. There are a few different companies involved in Web audience research in the United States, including a subsidiary of Nielsen Media Research called Nielsen/NetRatings, and a competitor called comScore. As with television and radio, participants in Web site ratings measurement provide demographic information about themselves so that the measurement company can produce ratings reports that indicate how many different people of what age, gender, and income visited a given Web site in a particular month and how long the typical visitor stayed on the site.

PROMINENT RATINGS-RELATED CONTROVERSIES IN TELEVISION PROGRAMMING

1969—NBC cancels the science fiction television series, *Star Trek*, after only three years on the air due to low ratings. The show goes on to become a surprise hit in syndication, spawning 11 feature films, five spin-off television programs (including an animated children's program), and a multitude of books and merchandising efforts.

1983—A letter-writing campaign overseen by Dorothy Swanson leads CBS to reverse its decision to cancel the series *Cagney & Lacey*. In the wake of the success of this campaign, Ms. Swanson went on to found the organization Viewers for Quality Television, which for 16 years advocated on behalf of high-quality television programs and is credited with extending the life span of a number of high-quality programs that might otherwise have been canceled.

1996—CBS first moves, and then cancels the long-running mystery series, *Murder, She Wrote*, despite the fact that the program was attracting a larger audience than competing programs on ABC and NBC in its Sunday night time slot. However, because *Murder, She Wrote* tended to attract older viewers, it was earning significantly less in advertising revenues than programs with much smaller audiences.

1996—FOX cancels *America's Most Wanted*, one of the network's highest-rated shows, reportedly because the network wanted to replace the program with a show that could be more profitable in after-markets such as syndication and DVD sales. A letter-writing campaign, which included requests from the director of the FBI, governors of 37 states, and police departments from around the country, led FOX to quickly reverse its decision.

2005—FOX revives the animated prime-time program, *Family Guy*, which it canceled in 2002 due to low ratings, due primarily to the strength of the program's DVD sales and the performance of reruns on the Comedy Central cable network.

CRITICISMS, SCIENCE, AND ACCURACY

All of these ratings systems have a number of traits in common. Perhaps the most important is that they produce ratings from a *sample* of the total audience, yet the ratings numbers are presumed to represent the total *population* of television, radio, and Web users in the United States. This may seem somewhat surprising given that these samples are in fact quite small in comparison with the total size of the audience. For instance, Nielsen/NetRatings monitors the Web usage of only 140,000 of the more than 70 million households with Internet access in the United States. Similarly, Nielsen Media Research monitors the television viewing of only 10,000 of the more than 100 million television households in the United States.

How can the television viewing habits of only 10,000 households accurately represent the tastes of over 100 million U.S. television households? The answer lies in the process of *sampling*. Ratings firms strive to develop *representative samples*. A representative sample is one that accurately reflects the characteristics of the broader population from which it was drawn. There is an entire complex science devoted to the process of sampling, and ratings firms are experts in this science, as the quality of their product depends on the extent to which it accurately reflects the media consumption habits of the population as a whole. Just as political polls project election outcomes based on surveys of representative samples of only a few thousand voters, so too do ratings firms project the media consumption habits of the population from representative samples of just a few thousand media consumers.

A key question that frequently arises in the ratings world, however, is how confident can we feel in the accuracy of these samples? We have certainly seen political polls get election outcomes wrong in recent years, so we know that sampling is an inexact science at best. Might there be reason to believe, for example, that there are too many men in the sample, or not enough African Americans? This kind of sampling error can arise for any number of reasons. Some categories of people may be less inclined to agree to participate in the measurement process. Young people, for instance, often are less willing to have their radio listening measured than older people. Similarly, Hispanic households have proven less likely to participate in the TV measurement process than white households. The more people who refuse to take part in the measurement process, the less likely that the sample that ultimately is created will accurately reflect the population as a whole.

Some segments of the viewing or listening public might be neglected for a wide range of logistical reasons. Until recently, for instance, Nielsen Media Research did not include college dormitories in its sampling. Similarly Web ratings services often have found it difficult to measure the behavior of workplace Web users since most companies have tended to forbid the placement of the necessary monitoring software on workplace computers. These shortcomings limit the extent to which the sample can accurately reflect the population as a whole. If the sample does not accurately reflect the population as a whole, then the accuracy of the ratings produced from this sample becomes questionable.

There are other potential sources of inaccuracy beyond sampling. What happens, for instance, if large percentages of the people who receive radio diaries don't bother to put them in the mail at the end of the week? Or if some people wait until the end of the week to fill their diary out but can't remember accurately what stations they listened to during the week and for how long? Or what if somebody has a friend who is a DJ at a local radio station and to help that friend out decides to write in his diary that she listened to her friend every day for three hours when in fact she didn't? These kinds of examples illustrate other very important potential sources of inaccuracy in the ratings data that the media and advertising industries rely upon every day.

What does it mean if the ratings are inaccurate? It is around this question that some of the most intense controversies surrounding audience ratings have arisen. When we consider that programmers and advertisers make their decisions based on ratings data, if the ratings are inaccurate, these organizations will make decisions that do not accurately reflect the tastes and interests of the viewing or listening public. Inaccurate ratings can, for instance, make a television show appear to be doing worse than it actually is. For instance, for years, NBC complained that the fact that Nielsen Media Research did not measure viewing in college dorms meant that the ratings for *Late Night with Conan O'Brien* (which is very popular with college students) were being undercounted, and that the show was actually much more popular than the ratings reports would suggest. Similarly, for years the system of measuring television audiences has been criticized for containing flaws that overrepresent broadcast television viewing relative to cable television viewing.

RATINGS AND PROGRAMMING FOR MINORITY AUDIENCES

The stakes get even higher when we consider the issue of programming targeting the needs and interests of minority communities. For instance, in recent years a number of industry and advocacy organizations charged that the Nielsen Local People Meter (LPM) dramatically undercounted African American viewers. The LPM is an effort to place the same technology used to calculate national TV ratings into local television markets, where, until recently, Nielsen still relied on paper diaries. As the groups opposed to the LPM argued, any undercounting of African American viewers would lead programs that target African American viewers to appear less popular. This would lead to diminished advertiser support for these programs and then to a greater likelihood that these programs would be cancelled. As a result, members of the African American community would have fewer programs targeting their tastes, preferences, and interests to choose from. In this way, what has been called "diversity of programming" would be diminished. This controversy grew so heated that in 2004 congressional hearings on the subject were held as Congress considered the possibility of directly regulating television and radio ratings firms in part to make sure that their methods sufficiently measured the viewing habits of all demographic groups. However, one key issue that arose during these proceedings involved the question of whether the new measurement system truly was inferior to the old system in terms of measuring African American viewers, or whether the issue of minority programming was being used by some broadcasters to stall the new system since the new system eliminated some of the shortcomings in the old system that artificially favored broadcast television over cable television.

The nature of this controversy helps to illustrate important truths about ratings—they are always inaccurate to some degree, and new measurement systems likely will improve upon some existing inaccuracies but also may introduce new ones. And, perhaps more important, any inaccuracies often can be helpful to some groups while being harmful to others. Some of the harshest critics of the media also point out that ratings only measure "exposure" to individual programs, and neglect to measure how audience members feel about the programs they watched (for example, how much they like or dislike individual programs). A system that measured not only audience exposure, but also audience appreciation (called Television Audience Assessment), was briefly introduced in the late 1970s, but failed to catch on with advertisers or programmers. For these reasons, the systems for providing audience ratings often become contentious battlegrounds around which media industry executives fight for measurement systems that present their programming in the most favorable light. And when new audience measurement systems are introduced that have the potential to completely reshape the media marketplace, these battles can become particularly fierce.

See also Cable Carriage Disputes; Hypercommercialism; Innovation and Imitation in Commercial Media; Media Reform; Minority Media Ownership; Net Neutrality; Online Digital Film and Television; Public Opinion; Representations of Race; Representations of Women; Sensationalism, Fear Mongering, and Tabloid Media; Shock Jocks; Transmedia Storytelling and Media Franchises.

Further Reading: Ang, Ien. *Desperately Seeking the Audience.* New York: Routledge, 1991; Bates, James, and Matthew James. "Political Opposites Costar in a TV Ratings Drama; Murdoch's News Corp. and a Minority Coalition Seek to Delay New System for Counting Viewers." *Los Angeles Times,* June 3, 2004, A1; Bermejo, Fernando. *The Internet Audience: Constitution and Measurement.* New York: Peter Lang, 2007; Bianco, Anthony, and Ronald Grover. "How Nielsen Stood up to Murdoch." *Business Week,* September 20, 2004, 88; Buzzard, Karen S. *Chains of Gold: Marketing the Ratings and Rating the Market.* Metuchen, NJ: Scarecrow, 1990; Napoli, Philip M. *Audience Economics: Media Institutions and the Audience Marketplace.* New York: Columbia University Press, 2003; Webster, James G., Patricia F. Phalen, and Lawrence W. Lichty. *Ratings Analysis: The Theory and Practice of Audience Research,* 3rd ed. Mahwah, NJ: Lawrence Erlbaum Associations, 2005.

Philip M. Napoli

REALITY TELEVISION

From the evolving *Survivor* series to *Queer Eye for the Straight Guy*, the phenomenon known as reality TV has transformed the face of television and changed the way programs are produced, distributed, and consumed. For more than a decade, reality TV has exerted considerable influence on media economics, program aesthetics, and industry practices, and raised critical issues for participants and viewers alike. Reality TV has become a battleground for media observers and critics, who charge that these popular programs expose private spaces, encourage voyeurism, and claim that entertainment is reality in competitions that often lead to ridicule and humiliation.

Reality television is simultaneously a genre, a format, a technological form, a series of experiments, a celebrity-making machine, an interactive aesthetic, and a political ideology. While its history is contested and its boundaries are fuzzy, reality TV is without doubt one of the most significant developments in twenty-first-century media.

PREDECESSORS

Many of the characteristics found in reality TV can be found in TV programs from decades ago. Bringing cameras into people's everyday lives as entertainment can be traced back to shows like *Queen for a Day* and *This Is Your Life* in the 1950s. This attention to "ordinary people" could later be found in *Real People* and *That's Incredible!*, shows that highlighted unusual abilities. Daytime talk shows continued this focus on everyday lives, as well as featuring "makeover" segments (central to later reality TV). *America's Funniest Home Videos* and

America's Funniest Pets didn't just portray everyday people—they relied on footage supplied by them.

The 1973 PBS 12-episode series *An American Family* is also a significant precursor, as it followed the lives of one family, the Louds, for seven months. *Candid Camera* was a wildly popular program that can be seen as an ancestor to recent prank-oriented programs like *Punk'd, SpyTV, Boiling Points, Girls Behaving Badly*, and *Scare Tactics*. Game shows have been a staple of television since its inception, and find new formulations in reality programs called "gamedocs" (e.g., *Big Brother, Survivor, The Bachelor/ette, The Apprentice, The Amazing Race, Treasure Hunters, Project Runway*, and *So You Think You Can Dance?*). One particular game show, *Battle of the Network Stars*, turned celebrities into the contestants (in 2005 we saw a short-lived homage called *Battle of the Network Reality Stars*). Shows like *Cops, America's Most Wanted*, and *People's Court* can also be viewed as nascent reality TV, focusing on real people from a law-and-order perspective and relying on a range of documentary, recreated, and scripted footage.

Regardless of these various influences and precursors, it is generally agreed that two programs signaled the rise of contemporary reality TV. The first is MTV's *The Real World*. Premiering in 1991, *The Real World* was an early "docusoap" following the lives of seven young house inhabitants cast by the network. *The Real World* is one of MTV's strongest franchises, and its producers, Bunim/Murray, went on to create similar shows like *Road Rules* (the cast lives in an RV and faces challenges) and the hybrid *RW/RR Challenge*.

The second major programming breakthrough was CBS's *Survivor*, premiering in 1999. Unlike *The Real World*'s cable status, *Survivor* demonstrated that reality TV could be popular and profitable on a broadcast network. Created by Mark Burnett, *Survivor* was a blockbuster gamedoc hit involving isolating contestants on an island and subjecting them to challenges. Each week, a contestant was voted off by their tribe until the finale, where the last two contestants were subjected to questioning and a vote from a jury comprised of the nine most recently exiled cast members. *Survivor*'s massive popularity not only ensured its return, but also opened the floodgates for a whole host of programming that quickly changed the face of television.

ENDEMOL

The Dutch production company Endemol is, along with Mark Burnett, the most successful reality TV producer. A hybrid of its founders' names (John de Mol and Joop ven den Ende), the company is responsible for the first international reality hit, *Big Brother*. First premiering in 1999 in the Netherlands, *Big Brother* eventually was adapted to 70 countries. *Big Brother* encapsulates two characteristics that made Endemol such a media juggernaut. First is its global outlook. Endemol recognized that it was preferable to make programming adaptable to many regions and cultures rather than sell the same show to a presumed monolithic global audience. This allowed national markets to claim they were producing local programming rather than importing foreign media products. Their second contribution is related to the first, namely the selling and promotion of *formats* rather than fully formed shows. Formats are templates (an ensemble of rules and procedures around a central idea) which can, like code, be modified depending on context. Among the Endemol empire's products are *Fear Factor, Extreme Makeover: Home Edition, Gay, Straight, or Taken?, Changing Rooms, Deal or No Deal,* and *1 vs. 100.*

FORM/GENRE

There is wide debate over the validity and accuracy of the name "reality TV." The most basic comment is that the term covers too many types of programming to be useful. What does *The Surreal Life* have in common with *Design on a Dime*, or *Punk'd* with *Queer Eye for the Straight Guy*? Some programs have a game component, others are about style makeovers; some focus on celebrities, others on ordinary people; some focus on pranking people, others on therapeutically rehabilitating them; and there is a varying degree of scriptedness in each. The wide range and sheer amount of programming make reality TV a dubious and exhaustive category.

Another more philosophical criticism leveled at the label is that these programs cannot be said to be accurately representing reality. Take the case of *The Real World:* the cast members are selectively chosen, their conditions are highly unusual (free food and booze in a lavish house), their antics are often provoked or staged, and the result is a highly edited package. Reality TV's roots in documentary styles and aesthetics (like *An American Family*) further complicates its relationship to reality.

For these reasons, a host of names have been proposed to divide reality TV into various subgenres or to clarify its representational status: gamedoc, docusoap, factual entertainment, postdocumentary television, dramality, reality sitcom, lifestyle programming, unscripted drama, actuality programs, experiment TV, virtual TV, neo-verite, and more pervasive forms of "infotainment" or "edutainment." Perhaps reality TV is not a genre at all, but an array of formats. Reality TV can be seen as a medium, a recombinant series of formats that fuses narrative, previous television genres, games, documentary styles, drama, and skills/education. Its experiments and formats have appeared on news channels (CNN's *Turnaround*) and influenced film documentaries (*Super Size Me*). More importantly, the emergence of reality TV has demonstrated that reality can be a marketing tool, and that these kinds of classifications are products of a convergence of industry, critical, and audience expectations.

CONTROVERSIAL SHOWS

Besides the ongoing debates around reality TV as a whole, a few programs generated significant controversy when they were released. A couple of months before the premiere of *Survivor* (often noted as the beginning of the second wave of reality TV), FOX broadcast *Who*

Wants to Marry a Multi-millionaire?, derided by critics as a new low in television. The program was essentially a beauty contest in which 50 women competed for a marriage proposal from a millionaire whose identity was only revealed at the end of the contest. Another FOX product that sparked outrage was *Who's Your Daddy?*, cancelled after its first episode. An adopted woman faced 25 men, each of whom claimed to be her biological father. Her objective was to discern this person via interviews. If she did so, both would win prize money, but if she picked the incorrect man, he would take the prize. The use of torture-like challenges (such as those in *Fear Factor*) has caused consternation among critics and audiences. *The Chair* and *The Chamber* premiered within a week of each other in 2002, and each depicted contestants undergoing extreme environmental disturbances testing their endurance of external stimuli for money. A few years later, a humorous version of this format found expression in *Distraction*, a quiz show that gave contestants easy questions while they underwent painful or humiliating tests (clothespins on the face, getting pummeled by food items, put in a box with insects). In the United Kingdom, however, torture took on a more serious political tone with 2005's controversial *The Guantanamo Guidebook*, which re-created interrogation scenes from Camp X-Ray. Finally, *Welcome to the Neighborhood* was a game show in which white conservative suburban residents judged which of the competing families was to win a dream house in their cul-de-sac. Among the family applicants: Hispanic, pagan, gay, African American, tattooed, and Korean. The show's trailers and promotional material were so incendiary that the series never made it to the air.

ECONOMICS

The 1980s saw a number of economic developments that set the stage for the rise of reality TV. The growth of cable and satellite technology created more video outlets for programming. At the same time, production costs were increasing (especially for directors, professional writers, and celebrity actors). To increase profits, networks and production companies cut back on labor costs. In response, a wave of strikes by numerous entertainment industry unions threw the industry into crisis. In 1988, a 22-week writers' strike delayed the opening of the fall season. Meanwhile, programming that did not rely on professional writers remained unscathed. In addition, the astronomical success of *America's Funniest Home Videos* in the early 1990s proved that nonscripted, cheap, audience-supplied content could be popular and profitable. Reality TV emerged, then, partially as a cost-cutting strategy.

Ten years later, reality TV proved that it could create blockbusters as well. *Survivor* creator Mark Burnett devised marketing and production strategies that transformed the economics of television. Television's basic pre-*Survivor* business model involved a network investing in a production company's program from the outset, taking most of the risk in hopes of big returns in future advertising. Burnett's model was this: he would pre-sell sponsorship of the program (e.g., getting Doritos to pay to place its product as one of the contestant's rewards), taking on more of the risk at the beginning. Then, because the network invested little at the beginning, he was able to keep much more of any future ad revenue.

In essence, this pre-selling puts more responsibility on shows' producers and leads to a blurring of programming and marketing (e.g., *The Apprentice*, which designs entire episode challenges around a marketing stunt for a sponsor).

AUDIENCES/INTERACTIVITY

One of the key defining features of reality TV is its integration of audiences into its programming. Audiences have been called "co-programmers" and "co-producers" by industry producers. We can think of this in terms of a broader media culture process of interactivity. First, a number of programs use audience voting to determine their outcomes (including the most popular reality TV franchise of all time, *American Idol*). Second, a number of virtual and material interactions with reality TV stars are encouraged. Viewers can chat online with contestants after an episode, and MTV hosts club events where fans can mingle with select *Real World* cast members. Finally, the fact that most of the programs are composed of "ordinary people" means that the audience (not just of any particular program, but of the genre) functions as a potential pool of contestants and participants.

Obviously this does not mean ordinary people get to design the scenarios, cast the program, edit the text, or reap the profits that producers do. But it does mean that the audience is incorporated as a variable into the design itself, and that ordinary people are transformed into players and participants whose actions can alter future arrangements.

ISSUES AND THEMES

A variety of motifs and cultural issues can be found in reality TV, and they are worth mentioning briefly. Reality TV is both symptom and cause of an intensified celebrity culture. It holds out the promise that anyone can become a star, even if briefly. Be it in music (*American Idol*), business (*The Apprentice*), modeling (*America's Next Top Model*), theater (*Grease: You're the One that I Want*), or back on reality TV (see the careers of *Survivor's* Johnny Fairplay and *The Real World's* Trishelle Connatella and Tonya Cooley), celebrities can be made in the genre. At the same time, celebrities themselves are brought closer to ordinary people. They are made into contestants (as in *Celebrity Mole, Celebrity Fit Camp, I'm a Celebrity, Get Me Out of Here!, The Surreal Life, Celebrity Boxing,* and *Celebrity Fear Factor*) or their lives are treated as ordinary people (as in *The Osbournes, Newlyweds, The Anna Nicole Show, The Simple Life, Breaking Bonaduce, Run's House, Being Bobby Brown, Hogan Knows Best, Shooting Sizemore,* and *My Fair Brady*). VH1 even calls their cluster of these shows "Celebreality."

Makeovers are another key theme in reality TV. We could even say that reality TV is a medium whose central operational imperative is *transformation*. As just mentioned, transformations occur by turning ordinary people into celebrities and celebrities into ordinary people. Home improvement and redesigning shows (such as *Extreme Makeover: Home Edition, Design on a Dime, Trading Spaces, While You Were Out, Garden Police,* and much of the lineup on the Home & Garden, Style, and Discovery Home channels) make a game out of domestic rearrangement and reorganization, as do shows in which personal transformation is fused with property improvements (as in *Pimp My Ride* and *American Chopper*).

Personal transformations occur through style overhauls (as in *Queer Eye for the Straight Guy, What Are You Wearing?, Ambush Makeover, What Not to Wear, How Do I Look?*, and *Starting Over*), seduction training (*From Wack to Mack, How to Get the Guy, Can't Get a Date*, and *Wanna Come In?*), bodily alterations (*Extreme Makeover, The Swan, Biggest Loser, I Want a Famous Face*, and *Dr. 90210*), and entire life overhauls (*Made, Camp Jim, Changing Lives, Intervention*, and *ToddTV*). Other programs' focus on transformation is more subtle, as when contestants talk about the "learning process" of encountering different types of people and living situations in MTV's *The Real World* and *Road Rules*, or CW's *Beauty and the Geek*, as well as personal growth through self-knowledge in *Big Brother, The Amazing Race*, and *Survivor*.

Youth and the nuclear family are two demographics as well as central social clusters in reality programs. Broadcast networks consistently run prime-time shows like *Trading Spouses, Wife Swap, Nanny 911, Supernanny*, and *Extreme Makeover: Home Edition*, each of which takes the nuclear family as its subject. Meanwhile, MTV targets youth around a variety of issues facing them: friendship (*Laguna Beach, Why Can't I Be You?, You've Got a Friend*), courtship (*Parental Control, Date My Mom, Next, Engaged and Underage, Room Raiders, Dismissed*), family (*Damage Control, One Bad Trip, My Super Sweet 16*), jobs (*I'm from Rolling Stone, The Assistant, 8th and Ocean, Power Girls*), and tolerance (*Boiling Points*).

REALITY ACTIVISM AND COUNTER-INTERVENTIONS

Reality TV's reliance on audience interactivity and immersion into everyday life has produced some interesting unintended consequences. The first season of *Big Brother* (U.S.) saw an ongoing series of interventions by activist fans, both online and in the material world. Tactics involved throwing tennis balls with messages into the house's yard, communicating with megaphones, and flying planes with banners (with messages like "Big Brother is worse than you think—get out now"). A group calling itself Media Jammers claimed responsibility for some of the banners and tried to influence the audience voting. Activists plotted online to convince contestants to stage a walkout and split the winnings. The houseguests came close to doing so, but after a series of producer interventions (an attempted bribe; disseminating information to one houseguest via an exiled contestant; limiting the online video feed to prevent viewers from hearing the contestants' deliberation; further controlling the communication coming in from outside) ultimately surrendered to the producers' design. Subsequent seasons eliminated the audience voting component. Culture jamming also describes the events surrounding the *Real World: Chicago* season. In a number of seasons, the *Real World* cast has encountered hostility from ordinary people, at times resulting in bar brawls and arrests (a variation of this happened when the *Project Runway* contestants left New York for

Paris, only to be pelted with eggs by a Frenchman from his apartment). This antagonism took on a humorous political tone in Chicago when 350 activists, artists, and neighbors staged a "protest" party outside of the building where the show was being taped. Chanting "Free the Real World 7," the pranksters closed down the block for hours with their exuberance, and demanded that MTV surrender its production equipment so that the people "could do something real with it."

THE POLITICS OF REALITY

Criticisms of reality TV have come from many quarters and different sides of the political spectrum. For some, reality TV is a morally bankrupt phenomenon, one that thrives on humiliation, degradation, and interpersonal conflict as spectacle. Shows like *Fear Factor, Are You Hot?*, and *Flavor of Love* highlight the basest of instincts, while programs like *The Swan* and *My Super Sweet 16* privilege superficial values of consumerism and outward attractiveness.

Other criticisms go beyond moral condemnation to address issues of representation and stereotyping. The casting of character types (often with the help of psychological consultants) designed to cause conflict on a show like *The Real World* are cited as promoting stereotypes. At times, programs take racial stereotyping as their focus (such as *Black.White.*, *The White Rapper Show*, and *College Hill*). Gender and sexual norms are reinforced in many courtship shows (as in *The Bachelor/ette, Flavor of Love, Joe Millionaire*, and *Beauty and the Geek*), while others promote typical gay characters (especially the lightning-rod program *Queer Eye for the Straight Guy*). *Survivor* and other island-setting programs (as well as the globe-trotting *The Amazing Race*) have come under scrutiny for their exploitation of exotic imagery and local cultures.

Finally, a number of cultural critics have analyzed reality TV as part of a broader shift in governing and social control strategies. Reality TV can be seen as the cultural expression of contemporary surveillance society. By playing on audience voyeurism (especially in shows like *Big Brother*), programs often seem to function to make this surveillance both natural and pleasurable. Monitoring technologies are a central component of some programs (as in *Exposed, Room Raiders, Spying on Myself*, and *One Bad Trip*). Spy techniques like disguises and deception are part of the whole prank-show subgenre (see *Punk'd, Scare Tactics, Boiling Points, Girls Behaving Badly, Spy TV, My Big Fat Obnoxious Fiance, Joe Millionaire*, and *Joe Schmo*).

Privacy is more than just a single issue in this programming: it constitutes the very material for the medium. Not surprisingly, a number of reality TV programs take place in the home, traditionally the seat of privacy. From the range of home improvement/decoration/organization programs, to the domestic displays of wealth in *Cribs*, to the experimental homes of *Big Brother* and *The Real World*, private space is increasingly becoming a spectacle. In addition to private spaces, the very relationships that comprise the private sphere (family, courtship, friendship) also find themselves the target of surveillance reality. The "confessional" (direct-to-camera interview sessions) is a staple of reality TV programming, sometimes requiring a special room for these personal revelation sessions.

Reality TV's interventions into private spaces, as critics have argued, have an educational or training component. They provide models of behavior with implications for shaping selves into citizens. Reality TV or "lifestyle" television acts as instructional programming whose effect is to encourage self-responsibility, self-entrepreneurialism, and self-improvement. According to some cultural analysts, these interventions are integral to a neoliberal form of governance, in which political solutions are outsourced to private citizens and groups, while the populace learns to become responsible by relying on various lifestyle experts. Others note that this training parallels the forms of labor required in an information society or post-Fordist economy. Programs like *The Apprentice* are obvious choices, but numerous others encourage individuals to learn the art of self-promotion, ways of being adaptable to new tasks, and working in collaborative team-based projects (e.g., *Project Runway, Top Chef, Dream Job, Kept, I Wanna Be a Hilton, The Scholar, The Contender, Who Wants to Be a Superhero?, Hell's Kitchen*). As a result, individuals learn to become flexible and to be constantly open to new experiences, but also to new program commands and external stimuli. In addition, subjects learn how to strategize and work the rules of any game so as not to get eliminated. While the programs stimulate and draw upon the powers of transformation, those desires are often organized around narrow values pertaining to competition, fame, and money.

See also Celebrity Worship and Fandom; Dating Shows; Embedding Journalists; Gay, Lesbian, Bisexual, Transgendered, and Queer Representations on TV; Hypercommercialism; Innovation and Imitation in Commercial Media; Media and the Crisis of Values; Narrative Power and Media Influence; Product Placement; Ratings; Representations of Class; Representations of Women; Surveillance and Privacy; User-Created Content and Audience Participation.

Further Reading: Andersen, Robin. *Consumer Culture and TV Programming*. Boulder, CO: Westview Press, 1995; Andrejevic, Mark. *Reality TV: The Work of Being Watched*. Lanham, MD: Roman and Littlefield, 2003; Biressi, Anita, and Heather Nunn. *Reality TV: Realism and Revelation*. New York: Wallflower, 2005; Bratich, Jack. "'Nothing Is Left Alone for too Long': Reality Programming and Making Malleable Subjects in Control Societies." *Journal of Communication Inquiry* 30 (January 2006): 65–83; Brenton, Sam, and Reuben Cohen. *Shooting People: Adventures in Reality TV*. New York: Verso, 2003; Hay, James, and Laurie Ouellette. *Guidelines for Living: Television and the Government of Everyday Life*. Malden, MA: Blackwell Press, 2007; Heller, Dana, ed. *Reading Makeover Television: Realities Remodeled*. London: I. B. Tauris, 2007; Hill, Annette. *Reality TV: Factual Entertainment and Television Audiences*. New York: Routledge, 2005; Holmes, Su, and Deborah Jermyn, eds. *Understanding Reality Television*. New York: Routledge, 2004; Huff, Richard M. *Reality Television*. Westport, CT: Praeger, 2006; Murray, Susan, and Laurie Ouellette, eds. *Reality Television: Remaking Television Culture*. New York: NYU Press, 2004; Wright, Christopher J. *Tribal Warfare: Survivor and the Political Unconscious of Reality Television*. Lanham, MD: Lexington, 2006.

Jack Z. Bratich

REGULATING THE AIRWAVES: "A TOASTER WITH PICTURES" OR A PUBLIC SERVICE?

At the heart of American broadcasting policy has been the licensing of public airwaves to private radio and television broadcasters. In exchange for their licenses, broadcasters have been required to serve the "public interest, convenience, and necessity," a phrase that continually has confused, emboldened, and troubled broadcasters, regulators, and citizens alike. What constitutes the public interest and who composes the broadcasting public have been consistent areas of contestation and conflict; at stake in these struggles have been the contours of broadcaster obligations to audiences and the parameters of acceptable governmental interventions in the workings of the broadcasting industry.

In 1961, Federal Communications Commission (FCC) Chairman Newton Minow labeled television as a "vast wasteland," and appealed to broadcasters to improve their programming and to uphold their public service obligations to audiences. Twenty years later, FCC Chairman Mark Fowler referred to television as a "toaster with pictures," which suggested that broadcasting was an industry that did not require special regulations or considerations. This comment signaled his commitment to the deregulation of broadcasting and to his vision that the public interest would be best served if broadcasters could operate in a free market unfettered by government regulations.

These two poles, the "vast wasteland" that requires active regulation of the airwaves, and the "toaster with pictures" that favors deregulation, epitomize the tension that has characterized U.S. broadcasting policy since its inception. At the core of this debate have been competing ideas about the relationship between broadcasters and the publics they serve. Some regulators have seen their interests as compatible and have insisted that the best way to serve the public is to bolster the broadcasting industry itself. Others have understood their interests to conflict and have fought to impose regulations on broadcasters to ensure that the needs of the public are met.

The history of broadcasting regulation has also been the history of public activism to influence how broadcasters and their regulators understand the meaning of the "public interest." Activists from across the political spectrum have participated in this conversation and have helped shape the direction not only of broadcasting regulation, but of the broader conversation over the role of broadcasting in American life.

A TIMELINE OF COMMUNICATIONS REGULATION

1912—Congress passes the Radio Act of 1912, which gives the Commerce Department the power to assign frequencies and to license radio operators. This act marks the first time that the federal government exerted its authority over wireless communication and crafted a policy that ranked how it was to be used.

1922–25—Commerce Secretary Herbert Hoover holds four National Radio Conferences, which bring together individuals representing the interests of the government, technicians (scientists and engineers), and representatives of the radio industry to map out a policy for broadcasting.

1927—Congress passes the Radio Act of 1927.

1934—Congress passes the Federal Communications Act and establishes the FCC.

1941—FCC issues *Report on Chain Broadcasting* that outlines restrictions and modifications on the network-affiliate relationship.

1941—FCC establishes restrictions on radio station ownership.

1943—Supreme Court rules in *National Broadcasting Co. v. United States* that the FCC has the power to regulate radio networks, and affirms that the scarcity of the spectrum legitimates the public-interest responsibilities imposed on broadcasters.

1946—FCC issues its "Blue Book," *Public Service Responsibilities of Broadcasters*, which defined for broadcasters how the FCC would ascertain whether license renewal applicants had fulfilled their public interest obligations.

1949—FCC establishes the Fairness Doctrine.

1952—FCC issues its *Sixth Order and Report*, ending the four-year freeze on licensing television stations. The FCC approves licensing stations in both the Very High Frequency (VHF) and Ultra High Frequency (UHF) bandwidths. It also reserves 242 licenses for noncommercial, educational broadcasters.

1956—FCC implements its 7–7–7 rule, which prohibits a single entity from owning more than seven AM stations, seven FM stations, and seven television stations nationally.

1960—FCC issues the *Programming Policy Statement*, which outlines 14 elements necessary for broadcasters to fulfill their public-interest obligations. It also requires broadcasters to ascertain the needs of the communities they serve.

1962—Congress passes the All-Channel Receiver Act and the Educational Television Facilities Act. The first act requires television set manufacturers to produce television sets that can receive both VHF and UHF signals. The second act allocates federal money to states to establish or enhance educational broadcasting services.

1962—FCC passes the Anti-trafficking Rule, which requires owners to wait three years before they can sell a station.

1966—U.S. District Court rules on *Office of Communication of United Church of Christ vs. Federal Communications Commission*. The case provides members of the public legal standing to participate in broadcast license renewal hearings.

1967—Congress passes the Public Broadcasting Act, which creates the Corporation for Public Broadcasting, a private nonprofit corporation to promote public broadcasting.

1969—Supreme Court rules in favor of the FCC in *Red Lion Broadcasting v. Federal Communications Commission*, thereby upholding the constitutionality of the Fairness Doctrine.

1970—FCC establishes the Prime Time Access Rule (PTAR) and the Financial Interest and Syndication Rules (Fin-Syn).

1975—FCC bans cross-ownership of broadcasting stations and newspapers.

1978—Supreme Court rules in favor of the FCC in *Federal Communications Commission v. Pacifica Foundation*.

1978—FCC establishes policies to favor minority ownership of broadcasting stations.

1981—FCC replaces the license renewal process, which had required a detailed report, with a "postcard renewal process."

1982—FCC extends terms of broadcasting licenses, which previously had been set at three years. Radio broadcasters' license terms are raised to seven years, television broadcasters' to five years.

1984—FCC eliminates the Anti-trafficking Rule.

1984—FCC raises the 7–7–7 ownership rule to a 12–12–12 rule.

1984—Supreme Court rules in *Federal Communications Commission v. League of Women Voters* that the amendment to the Public Broadcasting Act that forbids editorializing on a noncommercial station violates the First Amendment. This ruling is the first time the Court finds a broadcasting regulation to be unconstitutional.

1985—FCC eliminates the numerical cap on television station ownership and replaces it with an "audience reach" limit. The limit holds that no entity can own television stations that reach more than 25 percent of that national television audience.

1987—FCC repeals the Fairness Doctrine. Congress passes a bill to legislate the Fairness Doctrine, which is vetoed by President Reagan.

1990—Congress passes the Children's Television Act.

1995—Fin-Syn Rule and the Prime Time Access Rule are eliminated.

1996—Congress passes the Telecommunications Act.

2003—FCC proposes to relax media ownership rules. A widespread public campaign to fight further deregulation is mounted in response. The FCC receives close to 1 million e-mails and letters opposing the new rules.

2004—As part of an omnibus spending bill, Congress raises the national ownership limit of television stations from 35 percent to 39 percent.

2004—In *Prometheus Radio Project v. Federal Communications Commission*, the U.S. District Court issues a stay on the FCC's media ownership rules.

2006—FCC fines 20 CBS stations $550,000 for a 2004 Super Bowl broadcast in which musician Janet Jackson's breast was exposed on air.

BRIEF OVERVIEW OF BROADCASTING POLICY

The federal government has regulated radio since 1912, when Congress gave the Commerce Department the authority to license users of the electromagnetic spectrum. Fifteen years later, Congress passed the Radio Act of 1927, which established a temporary agency, the Federal Radio Commission (FRC), which was charged with granting broadcasting licenses to applicants who could best serve the "public interest, convenience, or necessity." The FRC initially interpreted the "public interest" as the "best possible broadcasting reception conditions throughout the United States." The FRC initially preferred stations that had the best technical equipment, a policy that favored radio networks and network affiliates, who had the capital and technology to produce quality-sounding broadcasts. The FRC also favored "general public interest stations" over "propaganda stations," for example those run by labor unions or political parties.

A concerted effort against "balkanizing the dial," the FRC privileged broadcasters with programming strategies to meet the needs of a general listenership. In its early licensing decisions, the FRC favored a broadcasting system predicated on national commercial networks and cast suspicion on other uses of radio.

During the period between 1927 and 1934, a broadcast reform movement—composed of private foundations, educators, intellectuals, churches, and others—fought for a new regulatory paradigm that would diminish the primacy of commercial, network stations within the burgeoning radio industry. The 1927 Radio Act had had dire consequences for educational broadcasters; in 1927, 94 educational institutions had broadcasting licenses, a number that dwindled to 49 by 1931. The FRC reassigned educational broadcasters to less desirable frequencies, reserving the more powerful ones for commercial broadcasters. Allies in Congress proposed legislation that would reserve a set percentage of stations for educational broadcasting. At the core of this movement was the presumption that the dominance of commercial broadcasters squandered the possibilities of radio, and consequently diminished the potential for public service that the medium offered. In response, the national networks successfully launched a public relations campaign to extol the benefits of the status quo and to publicize the educational and service capabilities of commercial broadcasters.

When Congress passed the Federal Communications Act of 1934, which reiterated almost word-for-word the Radio Act of 1927, it cemented the failure of the broadcast reform movement to realize an alternate system of broadcast regulation. The act replaced the FRC with the FCC, a permanent regulatory agency that would regulate all telecommunications—not just broadcasting, but telephony and telegraphy as well. Members of the FCC, who would be appointed by the president but would answer to Congress, would have the power to license broadcasters, allocate channels, renew broadcasting licenses, and guard the airwaves to protect the public interest. This act would remain the basis of U.S. broadcasting policy until 1996, when Congress passed the Telecommunications Act.

If initially federal regulators understood that the best way to serve the public interest was to support the growth of a stable broadcasting industry, then later the emphasis would shift to a new definition of the public interest. This new model asserted that the best way to ensure that the public's interest was met was to foster competition, diversity, and localism in the broadcasting industry. However, regulators, legislators, and the courts would disagree over the best way to accomplish these goals.

For some, the path required imposing regulations upon broadcasters. The FCC, beginning in the 1960s, required broadcasters to fill out lengthy renewal forms in which they would detail how they had fulfilled their public service obligations. In the 1970s, the FCC created the Prime Time Access Rule (PTAR) and the Financial Interest and Syndication Rule (Fin-Syn), both intended to bolster local and independent programming. The PTAR restricted stations to three hours of network programming during prime time, in the hopes that that the fourth hour would be filled by local programming. Fin-Syn forbade networks from having a financial interest in, and domestic syndication rights for, its entertainment programming. The goal of Fin-Syn was to increase the power of independent producers to gain access to airtime. The FCC also imposed ownership restrictions on how many stations a single company could own and passed rules to encourage minority ownership of broadcasting stations.

In the 1980s, the FCC implemented a new direction in broadcasting policy: deregulation of the broadcasting industry. It adopted a "marketplace approach" to broadcast regulation, one that led it to remove many of the regulations it had imposed in the past. During this decade, the FCC expanded the length of a broadcasting license to five years for television stations, seven years for radio; it also eliminated the lengthy license renewal process. The FCC also repealed the Anti-trafficking Rule, which had required station owners to wait three years before they could sell their stations. The FCC additionally reformed its broadcast ownership rules, allowing single entities to expand their holdings.

This era of deregulation was codified by Congress when, in 1996, it passed the Telecommunications Act. Among its other provisions, the act removed the national cap on how many radio stations a single company could own and raised the number of television stations a single company could own. It also diminished the ability of the FCC to revoke a broadcasting license and required the FCC to examine its media ownership rules every two years to ascertain if they still served the public interest.

REGULATING SPEECH

A persistent area of conflict in broadcasting regulation has been the tension between the First Amendment rights of broadcasters and their public service obligations. This friction is evident in the 1934 Federal Communications Act, which defined broadcast speech as speech protected by the First Amendment, but also prohibited "obscene, indecent, or profane language" and required broadcasters to allow political candidates access to the airwaves.

One of the early concerns of regulators was that broadcasters could use the airwaves as bully pulpits to promote their views. In 1941, the FCC instituted the Mayflower Doctrine, which prohibited broadcasters from editorializing on the air. By the end of the decade, however, regulators acknowledged the public-square function of broadcasting and asserted that, for citizens to participate knowledgably in democratic processes, they must have access to the arguments that affect the exigent issues of the day. In 1949, the FCC established the Fairness Doctrine. The Fairness Doctrine had two requirements: (1) broadcasters had an affirmative obligation to air issues of public concern to their communities and (2) they must provide airtime to both sides of the issue.

Broadcasters chafed at the Fairness Doctrine and argued that it violated their First Amendment rights. The Supreme Court, in its *Red Lion Broadcasting Co. v. FCC* (1969) decision, upheld the constitutionality of the Fairness Doctrine. The Court ruled that the right of the public to hear multiple viewpoints trumped broadcasters' claims to free-speech rights. In addition, the Court held that because broadcasters had access to a resource, the airwaves, denied to most people, they had different responsibilities than newspapers or other organs of the press.

Though the Fairness Doctrine typically applied to news and public affairs programming, in the 1960s the FCC expanded its reach. For example, in 1962 John Banzhaf filed a complaint under the Fairness Doctrine against CBS's New York stations; Banzhaf had requested airtime to respond to claims made in cigarette ads. The FCC decided that the Fairness Doctrine can apply to advertising and other forms of programming, a decision affirmed by the U.S. District Court.

Public interest groups in the 1960s and 1970s drew on this expanded definition of the Fairness Doctrine in their campaigns to diversify the content of broadcast programming. Specifically, one of the main activist strategies members of the public used during this period was to file with the FCC a petition to deny the license renewal of a local broadcasting station that, according to the petitioners, had violated its public interest obligations. In their petitions, activists often pointed to how stations violated the Fairness Doctrine in their news and entertainment programming, as well as in their choice of advertisements.

One of the priorities of the FCC during the deregulatory climate of the 1980s was to repeal the Fairness Doctrine. Rather than facilitate discussion over public affairs, detractors argued that the Fairness Doctrine had had a "chilling effect" on broadcasters who had shied away from controversy for fear of Fairness Doctrine–based complaints to the FCC. In 1987, the FCC rescinded the Fairness Doctrine. Congress passed a bill that made the Fairness Doctrine law, which was vetoed by President Reagan.

REGULATING DECENCY, PROTECTING CHILDREN

The impact of broadcasting on children has been a consistent concern for regulators and activists. The FCC and Congress routinely have required broadcasters to provide programming specifically for children and have worked to shield children from indecency and violence on the airwaves. Public interest groups also have targeted children as part of the broadcasting public in particular need of protection.

In the 1940s, the FCC issued its *Public Service Responsibilities of Broadcasters* (also known as the "Blue Book"). The Blue Book pointed to programming for children as a necessary component of broadcasters' public interest obligations. Indeed, when the FCC expanded the license renewal process, it required broadcasters to document the shows they had provided for children. The continued importance of children's programming has been so persistent that, in the midst of the widespread deregulation of the 1990s, Congress passed the Children's Television Act, which required broadcasters to air at least three hours each week of educational programming for children. It also limited the amount of advertising during children's programming.

Children's advocates have not always been satisfied with the efforts of broadcasters to serve and protect children. In 1968, concerned mothers formed Action for Children's Television (ACT), an organization committed to reforming network television to make it more responsible to children. In the early 1970s, ACT members successfully encouraged the FCC to examine rules regarding children's television and to develop a permanent children's unit as part of the agency's infrastructure. In addition, ACT filed a petition with the Federal Trade Commission (FTC) to ban commercials for sugar-based foods (cereals, candy) and toys on television. The ACT campaign garnered substantial public interest, drawing attention to ACT's concerns over the health hazards of manipulative television advertising and transforming cereal commercials to be more sensitive to their impact on young audiences.

The hazards of indecent programming on children also have spurred both federal regulation of the airwaves and public interest campaigns to stem its ubiquity on television. The 1934 act prohibited indecent speech from the airwaves, though what constitutes indecency has been a contested issue. In the 1970s, for example, the FCC had sanctioned a Pacifica radio station for airing a broadcast with alleged indecent language, George Carlin's "seven dirty words" routine; the station disagreed that this routine was "indecent" and questioned the FCC's authority to police its content. The Supreme Court decided in favor of the FCC in its *Federal Communications Commission v. Pacifica Foundation* (1978) decision, and ruled that the FCC has the authority to determine what constitutes indecency and to prohibit indecent broadcasts when children were likely to be part of the broadcasting audience.

Congress, in the 1996 Telecommunications Act, also acted to protect children from indecent programming. It required television manufacturers to install a V-chip in television sets that would allow parents to block programming unsuitable for children. The act also required the television industry to develop a ratings system, similar to that of the motion picture industry, which would alert viewers to programming inappropriate for children. Both the V-chip and the television ratings system would come under attack, the former for being difficult to use, the latter for being difficult to understand.

The brief exposure of Janet Jackson's breast during the halftime show of the 2004 Super Bowl catapulted the issue of broadcasting decency into the national headlines and onto the FCC's agenda. The Parents Television Council (PTC), a watchdog group founded in 1995, solicited hundreds of thousands of people to complain to the FCC that the airing of the breast constituted an indecent broadcast. The FCC in 2006 fined 20 CBS stations for this broadcast. Since the 2004 Super Bowl incident, the FCC has increased the number and amount of fines for indecency it has imposed on broadcasters.

REGULATING OWNERSHIP

The FCC and Congress continually have considered the impact of who owns the media on service to the public interest. Broadcasting policy has addressed concerns over horizontal integration (how many broadcasting stations a single company could own) and vertical integration (whether a single company could have holdings in multiple media markets). People who favor restrictions on media ownership have claimed that the consolidation of media threatens diversity, competition, and localism—the core values of the public interest. Those who oppose restrictions counter that concentration can help promote these values; they currently also argue that the rise of new technologies like DVD players and the Internet have diversified the media landscape, eliminating the need for ownership restrictions.

In 1941, the FCC imposed its first restriction on media ownership: it prohibited a single company from owning more than one same-service (AM or FM) station in the same market. Five years later, it stated that a company could not own more than one national radio network. In 1964, the FCC put restrictions on TV station ownership, ruling that an entity under specific circumstances could own at most two stations in the same market. In the 1970s, the FCC also prohibited cross-ownership of a newspaper and a broadcasting station in the same market and cross-ownership of a radio and television station in the same market. The FCC also placed caps on how many broadcasting stations a company could own nationwide.

The turn to deregulation loosened many of these ownership restrictions. The 1996 Telecommunications Act raised the national limit on how many television stations a company could own and erased a national limit on radio station ownership. In 2003, the FCC voted to further relax media ownership restrictions and was met by heavy public and congressional opposition.

At stake in these battles over media ownership has been a fundamental disagreement over the relationship between media ownership and media content. On the one side, people argue that diversity in ownership promotes diversity in viewpoints expressed over the air. On the other, detractors posit that what promotes diversity of views is the diversity of media outlets available to consumers, regardless of who owns them. It is a battle that may persist as a mainstay on the FCC's agenda, as media concentration and the development of new technologies continue to change the media landscape.

See also À La Carte Cable Pricing; Cable Carriage Disputes; Children and Effects; Communication Rights in a Global Context; Conglomeration and Media Monopolies; Government Censorship and Freedom of Speech; Media and the Crisis of Values; Media Reform; Minority Media Ownership; National Public Radio; Net Neutrality; Obscenity and Indecency; Pirate Radio; Pornography; Public Access Television; Public Broadcasting Service.

Further Reading: Brainard, Lori A. *Television: The Limits of Deregulation*. Boulder, CO: Lynne Rienner, 2004; Creech, Kenneth. *Electronic Media Law and Regulation*. Boston: Focal, 2000; Douglas, Susan J. *Inventing American Broadcasting, 1899–1912*. Baltimore: Johns Hopkins University Press, 1987; Hendershot, Heather. *Saturday Morning Censors: Television Regulation Before the V-Chip*. Durham, NC: Duke University Press, 1998; Horowirz, Robert Britt. *The Irony of Regulatory Reform: The Deregulation of American Telecommunications*. New York: Oxford University Press, 1989; Krattenmaker, Thomas G., and Lucas A. Powe, Jr. *Regulating Broadcast Programming*. Cambridge, MA: MIT Press, 1994; McChesney, Robert. *Rich Media, Poor Democracy: Communication Politics in Dubious Times*. Urbana: University of Illinois Press, 1998; McChesney, Robert. *Telecommunications, Mass Media and Democracy: The Battle for the Control of U.S. Broadcasting, 1928–1934*. New York: Oxford University Press, 1993; Ray, William B. *FCC: The Ups and Downs of Radio-TV Regulation*. Ames: Iowa State University Press, 1990; Smulyan, Susan. *Selling Radio: The Commercialization of American Broadcasting, 1920–1934*. Washington, DC: Smithsonian Institution Press, 1994; Streeter,

Thomas. *Selling the Air: A Critique of the Policy of Commercial Broadcasting in the United States.* Chicago: University of Chicago Press, 1996.

Allison Perlman

REPRESENTATIONS OF CLASS

U.S. media simultaneously ignore class-based inequalities and convey the mythical idea that anyone can rise above their socioeconomic origins if they just work hard enough. While representations of class are not as controversial as the media's treatment of gender and race, they are no less important as cultural indicators of unequal power relations.

Did you ever notice how many doctors, lawyers, and business executives populate the fictional and nonfictional worlds of U.S. television? Like other forms of commercial media, TV dramatically overrepresents the lives—and lifestyles—of well-educated, upper-income professionals. As social critic Barbara Ehrenreich points out, about 70 percent of people in the United States can be considered "working class," in that they perform monotonous (and often low-paid) forms of manual and service work, labor for wages instead of salaries, and often do not have college degrees (Ehrenreich 1998). Yet, we rarely see their experiences on the job, in the community, or at home reflected on the screen. As numerous media scholars have shown, when working-class people do appear in the media, they are often shown to be pursuing the American dream of upward mobility— or else they are often blamed for failing to "pull themselves up by the bootstraps." Given the stigma ascribed to working-class people by mediated images and discourses, it is not surprising that most Americans reject that label. According to

---

TITANIC

The 1997 blockbuster *Titanic* reworked the cross-class romance narrative—a staple of Hollywood film—at a moment of growing class polarization. In the midst of corporate downsizing, cuts to social welfare programs, and looming economic recession, the film offered a feel-good story about a poor artist who is traveling in steerage and a pampered socialite who is traveling first-class. Defying the steep social hierarchy inherent to the two-tier spatial organization of the ship, Jack and Rose fall in love and eventually come to reject the European-coded class hierarchies of the "bygone" era depicted by the film. Celebrating Rose's voluntary downward mobility and situating vivid social and economic inequalities squarely in the past, *Titanic* reaffirmed the American dream of classlessness at a moment of impending doubt about the future of the middle class. Filmed in Mexico to exploit the cheap labor of "runaway" movie production, the film offered a quintessentially American fantasy in which the structural inequalities of the global capitalist order can be overcome by the choices of plucky individuals.

See Laurie Ouellette, "Ship of Dreams: Cross Class Romance and the Cultural Fantasy of Titanic," in *Titanic: Anatomy of a Blockbuster*, eds. Gaylyn Studlar and Kevin Sandler (New Brunswick, NJ: Rutgers University Press, 2002).

cultural analyst Benjamin DeMott, the media perpetuate a political paradox, in that the majority of people in the United States prefer to identify as middle class, despite their unequal access to society's material and educational resources.

SELLING THE DREAM: COMMERCIALISM AND CLASS REPRESENTATION

Commercialism is a powerful filter when it comes to class representation. Take the case of television. In the late 1940s and early 1950s, when TV was getting its start, the major networks broadcast "urban, ethnic, working class family sitcoms" as well as live anthology dramas that dealt with the everyday realities of working-class life (Boddy 1992). By mid-decade, however, all of these programs had been cancelled or drastically modified to meet the promotional demands of the consumer economy of which television was an integral part. Sponsors preferred stories about well-to-do suburban families; social realism, they claimed, didn't foster the "right" mood for selling products. By accommodating the advertising system from which it profited, TV also constructed white, heterosexual, upper-middle-class family life as an idealized cultural "norm." Although we now have many more broadcast and cable channels available to us, television's class bias hasn't changed much. Indeed, many critics argue that the fragmentation of the television landscape can never foster class diversity because the emphasis is still on selling products to the "right" customers.

CHEATS, REDNECKS, AND BUFFOONS: PATHOLOGIZING CLASS INEQUALITY

What sociologists call "class" stems from a combination of education, income, and culture in capitalist societies: a person's job, schooling, and family origins are indicators of class position, and these factors in turn shape a person's lifestyle and "taste" in everything from beer to television programs (Bourdieu 1984). Class differences are not inborn but are socially produced within unequal power relations. The upper classes are not inherently more intelligent, ambitious, or sophisticated than the majority of the population: they simply control more financial, educational, and cultural resources and are able to pass these resources from one generation to the next. Why then do people appear to accept relatively stable class hierarchies? One reason is that the U.S. media soften the harsh injustices of the capitalist class system by perpetuating intersecting fantasies of individual class mobility and "classlessness."

Media representations of class promote the notion that anyone can transcend the circumstances of their birth if they work hard enough. This logic is democratic in that it subverts efforts to regulate and maintain "fixed" class positions common to aristocratic societies. However, it also has a troubling flipside in that it assumes that wealth is something to be gained individually (rather than shared socially) and that the identities, tastes, habits, and lifestyles of the upper-middle class are inherently superior and thus universally desired. Moreover, most individuals are not able to "overcome" class disadvantages and inequalities on their own, particularly at a time when social programs (such as federal student aid) designed to level the playing field have been cut and the gap between haves and have-nots has grown wider. Because the media ignore the structural circumstances that work against class fluidity, class differences are all too readily ascribed to individual pathologies and lifestyle choices.

The news media's construction of the "welfare mother" exemplifies this pattern. Since welfare reform gained political currency in the 1980s, news stories have coded the typical recipient as young, female, irresponsible, lazy, immoral, and often black—even through white people have historically benefited most from need-based government programs. Blending ideologies of race, gender, and class, news discourse has attributed systemic poverty not to the persistence of social inequalities or the uneven distribution of resources, but rather to the pathological ethics, work habits, and character flaws of poor people and poor women of color in particular. In so doing, say media scholars, the news has supported a policy trend based on the argument that social welfare programs designed to soften the harshest blows of the capitalist economy are no longer necessary (Gilens 2000).

Fictional media also tend to represent working-class life as a "deviation" or pathology. Poor and working-class characters are underrepresented in entertainment genres; when they do appear, they are often slotted into one-dimensional roles such as criminal or servant/helper. When working-class people take the lead, they often play for laughs. In a study of TV sitcoms, media scholar Richard Butsch found that working-class men are almost always depicted as stupid, lazy, and narrow-minded buffoons who deserve their low-paying, low-status jobs. Indeed, characters from Ralph Kramden (*The Honeymooners*) to Archie Bunker (*All in the Family*) to Al Bundy (*Married with Children*) and Homer Simpson (*The Simpsons*) are little more than caricatures of bad taste, vulgar habits, muddy thinking, and undeveloped morals. These representations situate working-class men as hapless "others," says Butsch—fodder for voyeuristic amusement, but not positive identification or political action (Butsch 1992).

JUST DO IT: CLASS MOBILITY AND SELF-TRANSFORMATION

The patterns of representation discussed so far coexist with the discourse of class mobility in U.S. media. The inflation and normalization of class privilege is tolerated in part because the media also circulate rags-to-riches mythologies and how-to advice for achieving the good life. Hollywood is a major source of these inspirational stories. From *Good Will Hunting* (about a janitor who is discovered to be a math genius) to the *Rocky* series (about a working-class boxer who becomes world champion), Hollywood films have often taken dramatic class mobility as a central theme. While male characters often rise on the basis of their hard work and individual talent/merit, women's mobility on screen has traditionally been linked to beauty capital and romantic trickery. In the gendered class fantasies played out in classic Hollywood films like *Sabrina*, *Pretty Woman*, and *Born Yesterday*, for example, a woman's good looks are her ticket out of the dingy world of class oppression.

ROSEANNE

When it comes to working-class representation on TV, *Roseanne* (ABC Television, 1988–97) is the exception to the rule. Based on the comedy of Roseanne Barr, this family sitcom explored the trials and tribulations of a white, blue-collar family of five from the vantage point of its feisty matriarch. *Roseanne* brought a distinctly feminine—and often explicitly feminist—face to the working-class hero, who has been historically coded by labor organizers as male. The program dealt regularly with "downbeat" issues such as workplace discrimination, low wages, lack of job security, unemployment, and social discrimination, which are routinely ignored by other sitcoms and by TV news, even though they impact many people. While *Roseanne* didn't delve too deeply into the politics of capitalism, it did express the everyday injustices and resentments it breeds. For many critics, *Roseanne* remains the most dignified portrait of working-class life to ever appear on television in the United States.

See Julie Bettie, "Class Dismissed? Roseanne and the Changing Face of Working Class Iconography," *Social Text* 14, no. 4 (Winter 1995).

Popular journalism complements these Hollywood mythologies by focusing on their real-life equivalents. As DeMott points out, "humble" socioeconomic origins claimed by pop stars like Britney Spears, sports figures like Michael Jordon, and CEOs like Donald Trump are accentuated as can-do parables by our celebrity-oriented media culture. This affirmative discourse tempers the stigmatized view of the working class by affirming that anyone, regardless of birthright, can aspire to follow in the footsteps of these successful and admired individuals. While most people recognize this as an unlikely fantasy, the growth of the self-help industry, combined with cultural trends like reality TV, promises ordinary people the chance to "make over" themselves in more believable ways and offer instructions for doing so. Programs from *Dr. Phil* to *I Want to Be a Hilton* to *What Not to Wear* promise to help facilitate individual class mobility by teaching people how to develop a "winning attitude," dress for success, or perfect their manners and personality. These programs acknowledge that class is partly a matter of access to "approved" cultural resources, and in so doing they may demystify the way that class inequality is perpetuated. However, the programs inevitably downplay the shared politics of class oppression and help to perpetuate the same class-based cultural hierarchies they claim to alleviate at the individual level.

DON'T ENVY THE RICH

While media promote self-transformation techniques and fantasies of class mobility, they also characterize the super rich as dysfunctional, greedy, and out of control. From Hollywood films like *Wall Street* to television programs like *The Simple Life* and *My Super Sweet Sixteen*, these cautionary tales present privileged elites as objects of moral scorn rather than envy or emulation. Yet, whether it is corporate raiders or leisure-class prima donnas who we love to hate, these mediated personifications of excess ambition and/or inherited privilege do little to challenge the class bias perpetuated by U.S. media. The structural inequalities that produce extreme wealth are deflected onto individual character flaws in these cautionary tales of wanting too much or wandering too far from our place in what DeMott calls the myth of the "imperial middle." Ultimately, unflattering representations of the rich encourage us to accept profound class inequalities, not challenge them.

Representations of the "noble" poor complement this particular strand of media discourse. Every so often, poor people are not stigmatized but are instead validated for possessing better ethics, morals, and character than the rich. For example, the poor hero of the film *Charlie and the Chocolate Factory* is far more likeable than the spoiled rich children he encounters. Sometimes, as in Hollywood's version of the Charles Dickens novel *Great Expectations*, lower-income characters achieve spectacular upward mobility, only to denounce the superficial riches—and people—they find populating the land of plenty. Other times, they hold on to their "poor" values symbolically. In *Charlie and the Chocolate Factory*, for example, young Charlie ends up owning the factory, but prefers to live in the same run-down house where he was born, and thus the dilapidated house is moved into the gleaming factory. Either way, these stories deflect structural inequalities, discourage class envy, and confirm the idea that fixed class positions are irrelevant in the "classless" society.

CLASS AND IDENTITY POLITICS

Media representations of class (particularly in the United States) have not provoked as much criticism as representations of gender and race, for several reasons. The myth of classlessness makes it difficult to think critically about class inequality, despite its presence in our lives. Working-class people are encouraged to aspire to mobility dreams and transform themselves on an individual basis instead of embracing their shared class status as a rallying point for broader socioeconomic changes. There is no positive "identity politics" associated or emerging from the working classes, partly because working-class life is deeply stigmatized, and partly because the myth of the American dream encourages us all to chase materialism and pursue self-betterment.

See also Communication and Knowledge Labor; Digital Divide; Global Community Media; Minority Media Ownership; National Public Radio; Public Access Television; Public Broadcasting Service; Reality Television; Representations of Masculinity; Representations of Race; Representations of Women Sensationalism, Fear Mongering, and Tabloid Media.

Further Reading: Boddy, William. *Fifties Television.* Urbana: University of Illinois Press, 1992; Bourdieu, Pierre. *Distinction: A Social Critique of the Judgment of Taste.* Cambridge, MA: Harvard University Press, 1984; Butsch, Richard. "Class and Gender in Four Decades of Television Situation Comedies." *Critical Studies in Mass Communication* (December 1992); DeMott, Benjamin. *The Imperial Middle: Why Americans Can't Think Straight About Class.* New Haven, CT: Yale University Press, 1990; Ehrenreich,

Barbara. "The Silenced Majority," in *Race, Class and Gender: An Anthology*, 3rd ed., ed. Margaret L. Andersen and Patricia Hill Collins. Belmont, CA: Wadsworth Pub. Co., 1998; Gilens, Martin. *Why Americans Hate Welfare*. Chicago: University of Chicago Press, 2000; Grindstaff, Laura. *The Money Shot: Trash, Class and the Making of TV Talk Shows*. Chicago: University of Chicago Press, 2002; Jhally, Sut, and Justin Lewis. *Enlightened Racism: The Cosby Show, Audiences, and the Myth of the American Dream*. Boulder, CO: Westview Press, 2001; Kendall, Diana. *Framing Class: Media Representations of Wealth and Poverty in America*. New York: Rowman and Littlefield, 2005; Kumar, Deepa. *Outside the Box: Corporate Media, Globalization and the UPS Strike*. Urbana: University of Illinois Press, 2007; Lipsitz, George. "The Meaning of Memory: Family, Class, and Ethnicity in Early Network Television Programs," *Cultural Anthropology*, 1, no. 4 (November 1986): 355–87; Media Education Foundation. *Class Dismissed: How TV Frames the Working Class*. VHS (2005; 62 min.). Northampton, MA; Wray, Matt. *Not Quite White: White Trash and the Boundaries of Whiteness*. Durham, NC: Duke University Press, 2006.

Laurie Ouellette

REPRESENTATIONS OF MASCULINITY

What does it mean to "be a man," and how do the media answer this question for us? Masculinity is probably most often assumed to be a natural phenomenon that is coextensive with the biological condition of maleness. In the latter part of the twentieth century, however, social scientists began to make a distinction between sex (male and female; both biological conditions) and gender (masculinity and femininity), and to view the latter as a socially constructed phenomenon, something that is created and maintained by the operation of a complex set of social institutions and structures. The media in particular have been seen as having a key role in shaping our ideas about what masculinity is, and in producing ideals and norms of masculinity through the images of and narratives about masculinity that they circulate. These images of masculinity often conflict with each other, making masculinity itself a highly contested category and raising questions about what masculinity is and what it means.

HISTORY

The impetus to create representations of masculinity is not a particularly recent development. Some of the earliest examples of representations of masculinity date back to ancient Greek statuary such as the much-copied Discobolus of Myron (460–450 B.C.). These statues, and their Roman successors, provided idealized images of the male body, muscular and virile. Often these images represent men engaged in sporting activities that serve to magnify the impression of physical power associated with our ideas about what masculinity is. Although there have been numerous changes in what is considered to be the masculine norm since the time of the ancient Greeks, the ideal of masculinity captured in Greek statuary has proven to be an enduring one. Its influence can be detected in the way that the male body is portrayed in some of the art of Renaissance

Italy and is particularly pronounced in statuary created by the Nazi regime in Germany in the 1930s and 1940s. It is an ideal of masculinity that still persists to some extent today, sometimes in a greatly exaggerated form found within the relatively marginal subculture of body builders, but also in more main-stream representations of masculinity (see the discussion of Stallone, Willis, and Schwarzenegger below).

The longevity of these idealized images of masculinity and the widespread adoption of these ideals within an array of different cultural contexts can have the effect of endowing this ideal of masculinity with an aura of naturalness; in effect, repeated exposure to these images conditions our everyday understand-ing of what a man should be like, so much so that we assume that it is men's nature to be muscular, athletic, and competitive. However, more recent thinking on the subject suggests that it is more accurate to think of gender not as natural condition but as a set of practices that are performed by the individual, a "script" that is acted out. Understood in this way, it is possible to see that the singular term, masculinity, is not really adequate to describe the variability and com-plexity of every way of performing manhood, and for this reason it has recently become more usual to talk about masculinities in the plural and to recognize that there may be significant variations between different types of masculinity. Most particularly, ideas about masculinity have been subject to historical and geographical variation: what it means to be masculine may be very different at different historical times and in other parts of the world. Even in a particular historical moment and geographical location, there will be considerable varia-tions in masculine types, particularly when gender intersects with other major components of social identity such as race and ethnicity to produce specific masculine identities.

FEMALE MASCULINITY

If masculinity is nothing more than an elaborate masquerade, if the relationship between masculinity and the male body is merely an arbitrary convention rather than an essential one, then is it possible to have masculinity without the male body? Yes, according to certain thinkers working within "queer theory," most notably Judith Halberstam. Halberstam argues that the most complicated and interesting manifestations of masculinity are to be found not in the normative straight white male but in the more transgressive forms of gender iden-tity encountered in women who perform masculine identities: the "stone butch," the "drag king." These gender performances are not perverse or deviant appendages to normative gender configurations, but illustrate the constructedness of all gender identities and reveal the role played by power in elevating certain normative identities to privileged positions of widespread acceptance.

This detachment of masculinity from the male body may be most striking when witnessed in overtly gay and lesbian contexts, but these are not the only manifestations of the phe-nomenon. Several well-known, mainstream Hollywood movies have utilized images of pow-erful, muscular women: Linda Hamilton in *Terminator 2: Judgment Day* (1991), Demi Moore in *G.I. Jane* (1997), and Sigourney Weaver in *Aliens* (1986) and *Alien 3* (1992). Additionally, actress Hilary Swank won the Oscar for Best Actress in a Leading Role for her performance as the cross-dressing Brandon Teena in *Boys Don't Cry* (1999).

PERFORMING MASCULINITY

The idea that gender (masculinity and femininity) amounts to a performance of a particular kind of identity can be traced back to the late 1920s, when psychoanalyst Joan Riviere published a now famous article, "Womanliness as Masquerade," in which she suggested that women who operated in a male-dominated field adopted a façade of femininity as a defense against any feeling that they may be challenging the men they worked with. The idea that elements of our identities may be something that we perform, rather than inherent qualities that we possess, gained further ground in the 1950s when sociologist Erving Goffman suggested in *The Presentation of Self in Everyday Life* that our everyday social interactions amount to an act of self-presentation or identity performance. The idea that our identities are performative rather than inherent has been very influential on recent critical thinkers such as Judith Butler who, in *Gender Trouble*, argues that masculinity and femininity are nothing more substantial than pure performances of gender: scripts that are learned and internalized by individuals and, as such, are unstable and open to variation and challenge.

FILM AND MASCULINITY

In modern times, writers on gender and culture have come to regard the media as a key institution for shaping our conceptions of masculinity. Not only are many media representations literally performances, but the media are seen as a key source of the images of masculinity that shape contemporary ideas about what it means to be a man. Representations of masculinity abound in all media, of course, but our focus here is on film. As the preeminent medium of entertainment for the first half of the twentieth century, and with many blockbusters of the latter part of the twentieth century centering action on lone male hero figures, film has been a key source of debate about how masculinity is represented in the media. We could also argue that many of television's key scripts for men were learned from film, such as the hard-nosed detectives of the *CSI* and *Law & Order* franchises that reference heroes of film noir.

Much of the debate over representations of masculinity in film has focused on what representations are acceptable, particularly so far as the depiction of male sexuality is concerned. For much of what is known as Hollywood's classical period (from around 1915 to the early 1960s), Hollywood operated a system of self-regulation known as the Production Code, which provided rules governing what sorts of representations were morally acceptable in Hollywood films. In 1934, Joseph Breen became head of the Production Code Administration. Breen, a staunch Catholic, held deeply conservative views about the depiction of sexuality, particularly homosexuality, and this limited the extent to which what Breen frequently referred to as "pansies" or "sissy types" could be explicitly depicted onscreen.

Notwithstanding this strict regulation of the screen, filmmakers found ways around the code, incorporating into their films subtle (and sometimes not so subtle) hints at homosexuality. Notable examples include *Bringing up Baby* (1938), which contains a memorable scene in which Cary Grant, wearing women's clothing, exclaims, "I just went gay all of a sudden!" and *Rope* (1948), in which the relationship between the two central characters, Brandon Shaw (John Dall) and Phillip Morgan (Farley Granger), two young men who share an apartment and who together murder a third man for thrills, has been understood by critics to be a thinly veiled depiction of homosexuality. Further well-known examples of filmmakers' efforts to evade the constraints of the Production Code include *Some Like It Hot* (1959), in which Tony Curtis and Jack Lemmon spend most of the movie passing as women, and *Spartacus* (1960), in which Tony Curtis's character, Antoninus, becomes the "body servant" of Laurence Olivier's character, Marcus Licinius Crassus.

Since the demise of the Production Code in the 1960s, filmmakers have had greater scope for exploring the complexity of masculine identities. In *Midnight Cowboy* (1969), for example, the traditional rugged western tough-guy figure, familiar from countless earlier movies featuring unambiguously heterosexual actors such as Gary Cooper and John Wayne, receives a rather different treatment when Joe Buck (Jon Voight) comes to New York and is drawn into the world of male prostitution. In one exchange that tells us much about changing attitudes toward masculinity in America between the western movie's heyday in the 1950s, and the time of *Midnight Cowboy*'s release, Joe's friend, Ratzo Rizzo (Dustin Hoffman), tells Joe that his western clothing is "strictly for fags," to which Joe responds, "John Wayne! Are you tryin' to tell me he's a fag?"

CASE STUDY: THE 1950s "CRISIS OF MASCULINITY"

It is common now to read about masculinity "in crisis," or, alternatively, of the "crisis of masculinity." However, what this "crisis" amounts to, what caused it, and where it came from are difficult to pin down. Indeed, it is probably more accurate to talk about periodic crises that surface from time to time in response to particular social circumstances rather than a singular crisis afflicting a monolithic and transhistorical masculinity. The suggestion that masculinity is in crisis belongs to the post–World War II period and predominantly to Anglophone Western cultures. The origins of this idea can perhaps be attributed to the shifts in gender roles that were brought about by World War II and the decades that followed. In the 1950s, social changes brought about a perceived "crisis" concerning masculine identity and the role of men in society.

During the 1950s, anxieties about masculinity arose from conflicts between different conceptions of what a man should be. The tough, invulnerable masculine type that had dominated representations of masculinity during the war was less appropriate for a postwar world in which commerce and consumerism replaced combat and fear as the defining features of society. While more traditional representations of men as rugged, tough individualists did not disappear—see the films *High Noon* (1951), *Shane* (1953), or *The Searchers* (1956), for example—

new stereotypes of masculinity that reflected these new priorities also began to appear in movies.

One of the key stereotypes of masculinity during the 1950s revolved around the twinned concepts of the "breadwinner" and the "domesticated male." This figure reflected both traditional assumptions about men's economic position in the family as well as a more progressive belief in the need for a more equal distribution of responsibility in the home between men and women. This latter aspect provoked concern that traditional qualities of manhood were being eroded. Consequently, this stereotype of 1950s masculinity quickly became a figure of ridicule. In January 1954, *Life* magazine published a humorous article titled *The New American Domesticated Male*, which poked fun at these men who struggled to conform to the demands of work and home life. The following year, moviegoers were presented with one of the most memorable portrayals of this new type of man in Nicholas Ray's *Rebel Without a Cause*. While James Dean's portrayal of one of the era's other key ways of representing men—the rebel—is probably the best-remembered feature of the movie, the film's depiction of masculinity in crisis is enacted through Jim Stark's (Dean's character) relationship with his father, Frank (Jim Backus), an almost cartoonish vision of the domesticated male. Jim longs for a father he can look up to as a role model, someone who can show him how to be a man, but Frank is a timid man who is afraid of his domineering wife and possesses no authority in the home. In a key scene, Jim catches his father

MASCULINITY AND RACE

Within much of the debate about masculinity, it is possible to overlook one of the fundamental assumptions that often underlies both representations of masculinity themselves and discussion about those representations: that the presumed normative masculine identity is white. In the past, representations of nonwhite masculinities have either been sidelined or have only taken center stage when they are presented as a problem. Despite the existence of distinctive and assertive nonwhite masculinities—the Black Panthers and the Nation of Islam, for example, or the identities assumed by young men influenced by gangsta rap, which may be less formally constituted but are no less distinctive, and signal clear affinity with an identifiable community—and despite the undoubtedly increased visibility of race in recent years, white male characters generally remain the central figures, even in apparently liberal-minded cultural productions. In *The Shield* (FX, 2002–), for example, while numerous African American and Latino characters occupy positions of authority, their actions are repeatedly undermined by the actions of a white male detective, Vic Mackey (Michael Chiklis). Similarly, while *24* (Fox, 2001–) may provide the first representation of an African American U.S. president, his attainment and continuing possession of power relies almost entirely on the actions of the maverick agent Jack Bauer (Kiefer Sutherland), a white man. The construction of Bauer's character most closely resembles that of the western heroes of numerous films from the 1950s: the maverick, the outsider, the man who does "whatever a man has to do," and his role in underpinning a representation of a nonwhite president illustrates the extent to which conservative values and assumptions continue to inform representations of racially marked masculinities.

tip-toeing around the house to avoid waking his sleeping wife, while attending to domestic chores and wearing a frilly apron. The scene captures perfectly the fears that are compressed into the term "crisis of masculinity": fear that men were yielding power and authority to women; that they were, in the process, thereby becoming feminized; and that these powerless, feminized men were unable to provide adequate male role models for the next generation of young men.

These fears remained central to 1950s anxieties about masculinity for the remainder of the decade. In 1958, *Look* magazine published a series of articles under the rubric "The Decline of the American Male," and later that year collected these articles together in a book of the same title. These articles state clearly the nature of the 1950s crisis of masculinity: the fear that the man of the time was "no longer the masculine, strong-minded man who pioneered the continent and built America's greatness" because "from the moment he is born, the American boy, is ruled by women." And, thus dominated by women, the domesticated male of the 1950s would be "demasculinized" and incapable of acting as a role model for his sons, whom he "either deserts...because he is too busy making a living, or confuses...because he does the same household chores as the boy's mother."

The "breadwinner" and "domesticated male" stereotypes were by no means the only visions of masculinity in 1950s America. As indicated earlier, the more traditional "tough guy" survived through the decade in certain films and the "rebel" became an important motif in the representation of younger men. The introduction of *Playboy* magazine in 1953 also revitalized the "bachelor" as a masculine type (single men above a certain age had previously been regarded as sexually suspect). Perhaps, after all, it is this fragmentation and proliferation of possibilities for masculine identity that was at the heart of the "crisis" in the 1950s, since it spelled the end to any clear, unequivocal understanding of what it means to be a man.

CONTEMPORARY REPRESENTATIONS OF MASCULINITY

In the same way that representations of masculinity in the 1950s reflected the concerns of the time about the position of men in society, it is possible to detect in more recent representations of men some of the anxieties that dominate discussion about men and the relationship between the sexes. In the 1980s, much attention was given to a new masculine type, the "New Man." The New Man represented a more sensitive type of masculinity, a man who embraced women's equality and undertook his fair share of domestic chores, who was in touch with his "feminine side" and unafraid to show emotion. However, just as the figure of the domesticated male of the 1950s had produced anxiety and concomitant efforts to restore more conventional visions of masculinity, the "New Man" was also rapidly counterpointed by a resurgence of more traditional masculine figures that emphasized the familiar "manly" characteristics of muscular physicality and rugged individualism, for example the characters developed by actors such as Sylvester Stallone in the *Rambo* series of films (1982, 1985, 1988), Bruce Willis in the *Die Hard* series (1988, 1990, and 1995), and Arnold Schwarzenegger in the *Terminator* series (1984, 1991, 2003).

Toward the end of the millennium, these continuing anxieties about the character of masculinity were evident in an expanding array of "pop-psychology" paperbacks concerned with masculinity, by authors such as Anthony Clare and Guy Corneau. As in the 1950s, fragmentation and the loss of a coherent sense of what it means to be a man again became key themes. Nowhere are these themes more evident than in the film *Fight Club* (1999). Here the key narrative device involves the revelation that the two central male characters—Tyler Durden (Brad Pitt) and the narrator (Edward Norton) are in fact one person; that Durden is a projection of the narrator's ideal of masculinity. *Fight Club* presents a powerful metaphor for the loss of a sense of masculine identity that characterizes contemporary debates about masculinity "in crisis." The name of Norton's character is never revealed; he is known only by a number of pseudonyms and through a series of depersonalized emotions that he uses to refer to himself—"I am Jack's smirking revenge," and so on—creating a strong impression of the loss of any sense of self. Although *Fight Club* ultimately restores the narrator to a more normative masculinity by positioning him within a romantic couple—with its implications of family, stability, settling down, and so on—most of the film provides a remarkable vision of the ambiguities that beset contemporary masculinities and of the conflicts that follow from the loss of clearly demarcated gender roles.

See also Body Image; Dating Shows; Gay, Lesbian, Bisexual, Transgendered, and Queer Representations on TV; Narrative Power and Media Influence; Presidential Stagecraft and Militainment; Reality Television; Representations of Class; Representations of Race; Representations of Women; Shock Jocks; Violence and Media.

Further Reading: Butler, Judith. *Gender Trouble: Feminism and the Subversion of Identity.* New York: Routledge, 1990; Clare, Anthony. *On Men: Masculinity in Crisis.* London: Arrow Books, 2001; Cohan, Steven. *Masked Men: Masculinity and the Movies in the Fifties.* Bloomington: Indiana University Press, 1997; Cohan, Steven, and Ina Rae Hark. *Screening the Male: Exploring Masculinities in Hollywood Cinema.* New York: Routledge, 1993; Corneau, Guy. *Absent Fathers, Lost Sons.* Boston: Shambhala Publications, 1993; Ehrenreich, Barbara. *The Hearts of Men: American Dreams and the Flight from Commitment.* London: Pluto, 1983; Halberstam, Judith. *Female Masculinity.* Durham, NC: Duke University Press, 1999; McCann, Graham. *Rebel Males: Clift, Brando and Dean.* London: Hamish Hamilton, 1991; Osgerby, Bill. *Playboys in Paradise: Masculinity, Youth and Leisure-Style in Modern America.* Oxford: Berg, 1991; Penley, Constance, and Sharon Willis, eds. *Male Trouble.* Minneapolis: University of Minnesota Press, 1993; Perchuk, Andrew, and Helaine Posner, eds. *The Masculine Masquerade: Masculinity and Representation.* Cambridge, MA: MIT Press, 1995.

Mike Chopra-Gant

REPRESENTATIONS OF RACE

In the new millennium, in a country where discrimination based on race is now illegal and visual culture is becoming more diverse, are racial depictions getting better? What constitutes or creates "better" representations, and is improvement only relative?

The representation of race has been a topic of discussion since the beginning of film exhibition at the turn of the twentieth century and even more since the start of television broadcasting in the late 1940s. In fact, the questions, public debates, and private reactions connected to the representation of race in culture precede film and television, having a history in theater, literature, and journalism. What makes race such a powerful cultural, intellectual, and political issue is that it is also deeply personal. Race is something that is not only represented, it is something that is perceived; hence, race is about how an individual is understood (or misunderstood), and how a person is ultimately treated (or mistreated) in society. Film and television play an important role in communicating—sometimes dictating—social roles and social hierarchies according to racial, class, gender, sexual, national, and religious identities.

TIMELINE

1950s—*Amos 'n' Andy* airs and is canceled after two seasons as a result of strong NAACP protests.

The Nat King Cole Show is canceled due to lack of sponsorship and poor ratings.

Television westerns replicate the film genre's tendency to depict Native Americans in homogeneous ways as either threatening enemies to Western expansion, or as a peace-loving people in need of modern assistance.

1950s–60s—Civil rights movement is broadcast on national television news.

1960s—Asian servant characters such as Hop Sing in *Bonanza*, Kato in *The Green Hornet*, and Mrs. Livingston in *The Courtship of Eddie's Father* appear.

Julia premieres, starring Diahann Carroll and produced by Hal Kanter specifically as an apology for earlier depictions of African Americans; the program becomes controversial, liked and disliked by African American as well as white American viewers for its "unrealistic" portrayal of a beautiful African American nurse.

1960s–70s—Vietnam War receives increasing, and increasingly negative, coverage, along with antiwar protests.

1970s—Norman Lear produces a number of social commentary series such as *All in the Family* and several spin-offs, *Maude*, *Good Times*, *The Jeffersons*, and *Sanford and Son*.

Chico and the Man, starring Freddie Prinze, was similar in format to *Sanford and Son* in its portrayal of a father/son–like relationship between an auto garage owner and a mechanic, Chico. It broke ground as a successful series with an ethnic lead character. The series included the same producers as *Julia* (Hal Kanter) and *The Courtship of Eddie's Father* (James Komack).

Several popular television programs emerge that represent whiteness in nostalgic ways, for example, *The Waltons*, *Little House on the Prairie*, and *Happy Days*.

1980s—*The Cosby Show* rises to the top of the ratings and remains the number-one program for most of the decade. (The working-class, feminist series *Roseanne* eventually rivals *The Cosby Show* in the late 1980s.)

An era of affluence and excess is ushered in during the Reagan years, reflected in television programs such as *Dynasty* and *Dallas*, which were about extremely wealthy white businessmen and their families who had made their fortunes in the oil industry.

1990s—The Rodney King beating is caught on home videotape.

The LA uprisings are seen across the country, even internationally, as representing "race riots" and civil unrest in the United States.

O. J. Simpson is seen driving a white Bronco in a slow-speed police car chase; the O. J. Simpson trial becomes one of the most watched media events in television history. Reactions to the O. J. Simpson trial and its verdict are clearly divided along racial lines, demonstrating, on one hand, a distrust in the criminal justice system that many have had for deeply historical reasons, as well as, on the other hand, a return to tropes of black masculinity (as threatening) and white femininity (as idealized and innocent) that informed people's judgments.

2000s—The attack on the World Trade Center on September 11, 2001, marks a new era in the representation of American patriotism and national identity, often positioned in opposition to "undemocratic" or "extremist" Others.

The Oprah Winfrey Show celebrates its 20th year. The program has become the most popular daytime talk show on television, and Oprah Winfrey is not only one of the most powerful people in the business of media, but she is an undeniably influential figure in the culture and politics of American life today.

WHAT IS A STEREOTYPE? WHAT IS THE FUNCTION OF A STEREOTYPE?

While there are specificities to different racial and ethnic groups, there are also commonalities in the general pattern of maintaining a status quo social hierarchy (social order) through the use of images and stories in American media culture. These images have taken the form of visual tropes or deep-seeded stereotypes such as: black men as threatening, black women as "sassy," Asian and Asian American women as exotic yet passive, Asian and Asian American men as lacking "masculinity," Latinos assumed as being noncitizens, Native Americans as so-called "noble savages," and more recently, those who look to be Middle Eastern as "suspected terrorists"; the suspicion of those who are Islamic as so-called enemies to democracy has become particularly intense since the start of the second war in Iraq in 2003, with news images being perceived by some with a sense of threat. This list names just a few of the associations linked to images of racialized figures that we see on television. All, however, contribute to a larger discourse of ideal whiteness—and Americanness—by representing nonwhite races in a lesser or undesirable position.

A stereotype is a kind of iconic shorthand; it is a "controlling image" that involves a process of objectification, subordination, and justification (Hamamoto 1992, p. 4). The function of a stereotype is to display and express power. Using stereotypes is not only a way to disempower, debase, or humiliate the target of a stereotype, it is also a means to benefit the comparative figure, that is, the lead character in relation to, literally, the supporting character. Often, the "racial sidekick" serves to enhance white (and often male) superiority in the text; examples include Tonto to the Lone Ranger, Kato to the Green Hornet, the buddy genre, as well as a long history in film and television of the racialized servant. Racial stereotypes have been part of our visual and cultural lexicon since the first interactions between people of different races. How can we move beyond stereotypes in representational culture, on the part of both creators of television as well as consumers of it?

ON SCREEN

The place to start when thinking about race and representation is to consider what we see (or do not see) on television and in film. Background characters or supporting roles played by actors of color are far more common than lead roles. Stereotyped images are more common than rich, complex characters of color. While the quantity of characters of color is a concern, it is the quality of the roles that must be assessed. There has been, no doubt, an increase in the number of actors of color working and appearing in the media overall; African American faces are seen frequently, Latinos have become more noticeable, there are a handful of Asian Americans when there used to be one or none, though there are virtually no identifiable Native Americans populating the television and film landscapes except as requisite props in a Western setting. While one could argue that progress is being made inasmuch as there is steadily an increase in the number of faces and actors of color appearing on the small and big screens since previous decades, the questions to ask about these appearances include:

- Are these characters important to the main plotline, and are the performers equally promoted as cast members if the series is popular or the film is a hit?
- Do these characters of color challenge and perhaps even disrupt traditional expectations of certain racial groups, or are they attached to stereotypical notions in updated costume?
- Can such roles potentially widen the imagination of viewers, not only in terms of representing race, but also in terms of representing race relations in a multicultural country such as the United States? Ideally, new roles for performers of color would be integrated into a popular vision that does not reproduce racial hierarchy and is not solely about white subjectivity—in other words, we need more film and television roles that share the perspectives of racial characters in substantive ways.

BEHIND THE SCREEN/BEHIND THE SCENES

How do these kinds of roles get created? Before an actor gets on television or is seen in a film, before she or he is even able to audition for a part, the role has to be written. Writers who have unique and lesser-known stories to tell can widen and deepen the range of characters represented in the media, and conscientious nonminority writers can expand their work to be more inclusive or less super-ficial in writing characters of color. Casting directors have the powerful ability to cast in creative and diverse ways; for example, even if a part does not specifically call for a "minority" actor to play it, the casting director could intervene in the process by suggesting or hiring an actor of color. *Grey's Anatomy's* Sandra Oh, for instance, is an actor who has been cast in parts not originally intended as "an Asian role." In a visit to the University of California, Santa Cruz in May 2004, she informed my students that one of the biggest challenges she faced as a performer was to be allowed to audition for roles that writers, producers, and casting di-rectors didn't expect or see an Asian face in. Oh has taken charge of such roles with talent and charisma, and has helped expand peoples' expectations of who a person of Asian descent is, what she can be like, and how she acts.

Producers and show runners also have the power to include or exclude sub-stantive rather than stereotypical characters of color in their films and television programs, and to lobby for a media piece that is innovative in the way that it represents race and race relations. Ultimately, executives are the ones whose de-cisions affect which films and programs are greenlit, which will be championed and promoted, and which will be placed in the advantageous slots on the movie release or television schedule.

IN FRONT OF THE SCREEN

Where does the viewer fit in this discussion of race and representation? Is there anything that audiences can do to affect change? Network executives, ad-vertising sponsors, studios and their investors depend on audiences to watch their programs and to pay to see their films. Viewing practices can be gauged through such mechanisms as the Nielsen ratings (which measure how many people watched a certain television broadcast) to determine what programs to develop and place on the schedule, or through focus-group surveys of soon-to-be-released films to determine, for example, what kind of ending viewers prefer.

Executives and producers create films and programs based on what they *anticipate* audiences will like, based on what they assess has *already* been popu-lar. The primary goal in making most of mainstream film and television is not to produce beautiful art or to stimulate critical thinking, but rather, to create audiences (through the creation of "entertainment"). This usually maintains the status quo, that is, idealized stories of white (upper-)middle-class families, heroes, and heterosexual (monoracial) romances have worked in the past and therefore, executives bank on similar fare to work in the future. When the tele-vision programs *Lost* (2004–) and *Grey's Anatomy* (2005–) became unexpected hits, an industry term emerged: "multicultural casting." Moreover, because mul-tiracial casts were deemed popular, other networks offered new programs with that similar concept, for example, *Heroes* (2006–). A somewhat racially diverse cast existed in programs like *ER* (1994–), but a deliberate "rainbow coalition" cast became a major trend only because one network tried it in two programs. It is important to realize that these two programs had people of color employed as writers, producers, and executives who, together, created this new television format; but equally if not more important, it took audiences' acceptance and rallying around such representations of race and race relations to establish multicultural casting as a legitimate and significant new form.

Changes and improvements can happen because the system allows for (or more precisely, cannot prevent) social input—the media industry can be pushed because it relies on individual viewers, and more specifically, categories of viewers. The most coveted and valuable set of viewers for executives, marketers, and advertisers is the 18-to-34 demographic, and therefore, the viewers in this group have the most power to influence what stays on the air and what innovative, unusual, untraditional programs might get canceled. The choice of programs and films that one watches and supports makes a difference in the kinds of representations—of society, family, friendships, lifestyles, values—that continue to be seen and circulated in popular culture. The media industry is neither inherently conservative nor progressive. Film, and television in particular, are formations that can sustain the status quo, contain counter-hegemonic stories and images, and yet also facilitate advancements and absorb changes in the representations of race and race relations.

THROUGH ACADEMIA, AND THROUGH SOCIAL ACTIVISM

It seems a tautology to believe that viewers aren't interested in seeing African Americans in serious dramas or Asian American men as romantic lead characters, and therefore, that is why television programs and films with such stories aren't made. Researchers and students in fields such as sociology, psychology, communications, and film and television studies theorize, analyze, and collect data about diversity in the media. Ideally, the work of academics will reach and interface with those working in the media industry. Activist organizations also work to affect changes in the way that Hollywood represents race, race relations, and American culture.

The National Association for the Advancement of Colored People (NAACP) has been vigilant about film and television representations since the birth of cinema marked by protests against D. W. Griffith's *Birth of a Nation* in 1915. Founded in 1909, the NAACP is one of the oldest and most influential civil rights organizations, concerned with many realms including the media. In the fall of 1999, the NAACP protested just before the new television season was to begin. The concern was that in the line-up of 26 new shows, none had any major characters of color. How, at the turn of the new millennium, in the United States, could not a single show be offered with a lead who was not white? From whence did this come—from unimaginative and racist writers, producers, and networks, or from dull and complacent audiences? It took the tenacity and organization of the coalition of ethnic media watch groups who joined the NAACP, American Indians in Film and Television, the National Asian Pacific American Legal Consortium, and the National Latino Media Council, to threaten boycotting television networks in order to bring about some changes. In some cases, the changes were last minute; in others they were seemingly superficial (an industry term, "coloring up," emerged)—but there have been changes nonetheless.

While protesting in front of a station or studio does not affect ratings in a direct sense, it can serve to embarrass executives (or viewers), forcing them to at least consider the grievances at hand. The NAACP has succeeded in serving as a materialized voice shouting into the halls of executive and production offices. Consciousness-raising can help to increase audiences' awareness about, and hopefully their desire for, more complex characters of color in film and television. Media culture is contradictory: on one hand it is hegemonic; on the other hand, because hegemony is a social existence that people are not coerced into but consent to, it is contestable. Media culture needs to be contested.

HOW IS DIVERSITY DEFINED? WHY IS DIVERSITY IN THE MEDIA VALUABLE?

Professor George Gerbner, who conducted research on television representations of gender roles, racial characters, class, and occupational categories for over three decades, states in the Media Education Foundation's video *The Electronic Storyteller* that "To be invisible in visual culture is to not have power in society."

In studying the topic of race and representation in the media, there is production and business on one hand, and reception and culture on the other, although the two realms are clearly connected. Diversity is housed in many fields: diversity is a cultural issue, an issue of politics; it is an issue in the marketplace (in systems of business); diversity is also a moral issue, a moral imperative for some. What makes approaching the goal or notion of "achieving diversity" challenging is the that people working on it are coming from different worlds, or different worldviews.

The question of how to define diversity in terms of representation remains open; for example, it has yet to be determined what the standard is that marks an adequate number or fair representation of racial characters. Must it be proportionate to the percentage of African Americans, or Latinos, or Asian Americans, and so on, in U.S. society? This leads us back to the quantity-versus-quality question, and perhaps there ought to be goals other than sheer/mere numbers. In terms of employment, the question remains: at what point will we know we have arrived at an equitable distribution of opportunity in the industry? Moreover, it is not easy to tangibly or materially monitor and secure that a process of production is diverse (Robinson 1996).

Beyond the numbers, ensuring a diversity of ideas—on screen, behind the screen, and ultimately, in front of the screen out there in "the real world"—is the goal of increasing diversity and improving the representation of race in Hollywood. Working towards diversity is part of a process of social change through media culture and media consumption. Viewers make up a consumer group as well as a social body and a *political* and ideological constituency—we are all viewer-citizens who are actively (though sometimes unconsciously) engaged in cultural production and in the generating of social values. Diversity in the representation of race and race relations on television and in film is important because such images and stories can limit or expand our expectations, about others as well as about ourselves.

Are racial depictions in American television and film getting better? In general, yes, though there are still moments of egregious and racist representations of people of color to be aware of, and to contest. We can be cautiously optimistic, and yet acknowledge that many of the improvements are relative to shifts in society about race in general. Therefore, the question to focus on should be: are the media industry and its consumers active in improving racial depictions? The answer to this question remains open, as the goal of racial equality has yet to be fulfilled. Progress is being made, certainly, but we still have work to do.

See also Audience Power to Resist; Bollywood and the Indian Diaspora; Dating Shows; Islam and the Media; Media and Citizenship; Media Literacy; Minority Media Ownership; Nationalism and the Media; Parachute Journalism; Reality Television; Representations of Class; Representations of Masculinity; Representations of Women; Sensationalism, Fear Mongering, and Tabloid Media; Shock Jocks; Tourism and the Selling of Cultures; World Cinema.

Further Reading: Bodrogkhozy, Aniko. "'Is This What You Mean by Color TV?' Race, Gender, and Contested Meanings in NBC's *Julia*." In *Private Screenings: Television and the Female Consumer,* ed. Lynn Spigel and Denise Mann. Minneapolis: University of Minnesota Press, 1992; Children Now Publications. "Fall Colors: Prime Time Diversity Report," available for 1999, 2000, 2001, 2002, 2003 at http://publications.childrennow. org/; Coleman, Lionel (dir.). *I'm the One That I Want.* New York: Winstar TV and Video, Cho Taussig Productions, 2000; Davis, Angela, and Neferti X. M. Tadiar, eds. *Beyond the Frame: Women of Color and Visual Representation.* New York: Palgrave MacMillan, 2005; Downing, John D. H., and Charles Husband. *Representing Race: Racisms, Ethnicity and the Media.* Thousand Oaks, CA: Sage, 2005; Ferguson, Robert. *Representing Race: Ideology, Identity and the Media.* London: Arnold, 1998; Fiske, John. *Media Matters: Race and Gender in U.S. Politics.* Minneapolis: University of Minnesota Press, 1996; Gray, Herman. *Watching Race: Television and the Struggle for "Blackness."* Minneapolis: University of Minnesota Press, 1997, 2002; Hamamoto, Darrell. *Monitored Peril: Asian Americans and the Politics of TV Representation.* Minneapolis: University of Minnesota Press, 1994; Hunt, Darnell, ed. *Channeling Blackness: Studies on Television and Race in America.* New York: Oxford University Press, 2005; Hunt, Darnell. *Screening the Los Angeles 'Riots': Race, Seeing, and Resistance.* Cambridge, MA: Cambridge University Press, 1997; Kim, L. S. "Be The One That You Want: Asian Americans in Television Culture, Onscreen and Beyond." *Amerasia Journal* 30, no. 1 (Winter 2004): 125–46; Leung, Linda. *Virtual Ethnicity: Race, Resistance and the World Wide Web.* Burlington, VT: Ashgate, 2005; Media Education Foundation. *Reel Bad Arabs* (film), 2006; Noreiga, Chon. *Shot in America: Television, the State, and the Rise of Chicano Cinema.* Minneapolis: University of Minnesota Press, 2000; Riggs, Marlon (dir.). *Color Adjustment.* San Francisco: California News Reel, 1992; Robinson, Russell. "Hollywood's Race/Ethnicity and Gender-Based Casting: Prospects for a Title VII Lawsuit." *Latino Policy and Issues Brief* no. 14 (December 2006). http://www.chicano.ucla.edu/press/briefs/documents/LPIB_14December2006_001.pdf; Torres, Sasha. *Living Color: Race and Television in the United States.* Durham, NC: Duke University Press, 1998.

L. S. Kim

REPRESENTATIONS OF WOMEN

Media representations of women have been the focus of feminist critique for decades. Critics charge that media images represent exceedingly narrow forms of femininity that function to perpetuate and uphold the status quo in a patriarchal society. Women are most often portrayed as victims, especially of sexual violence. In addition, media representations send mixed messages to women, calling on them to be virginal and innocent yet sexually alluring and adventurous, independent in their thinking yet committed to pleasing men. These contradictions cause many women to experience a conflicted relationship with mass media.

Women were being represented visually long before the advent of modern media, and analyses of centuries-old painting and sculpture demonstrate gendered conventions in the visual construction of women. But the proliferation of media in our lives today has upped the ante in the debates over media representations. This is especially the case since scholars began to recognize that the media perform a key ideological function in helping to define the ways a society understands the world, and therefore have a significant political impact. This works in large part through the development of stereotypes, which simplify complex situations into routine ways of thinking that come to seem natural or common sense. These stereotypes are most effective when they are plausible and when they are not transparent about the value system that guides them.

To understand how gender stereotyping works, it is important to know that scholars distinguish the biological differences represented by the terms "male" and "female," and the social, historical, and cultural meanings of "feminine" and "masculine" that have come to be associated with these biological differences. Notions of femininity and masculinity, in other words, are socially constructed and create a commonly understood form of gender difference. This then functions to create a gender hierarchy and the power structure that such a hierarchy justifies and maintains. In sports for example, this hierarchy promotes the idea, represented in media, that male athletes are important for their athletic abilities, while female athletes are primarily interesting in terms of their femininity and sexuality. This reinforces the notion that female athleticism is less important or less interesting than male athleticism, a notion that research has shown to be widespread among sports fans of both sexes. This gender hierarchy in turn supports *patriarchy*, a system in which men dominate decision making and have authority over women and children.

Stereotypes of women create images and expectations about what women "are really like," in addition to policing those images culturally by presenting them as a means of comparison against those who do not fit them. Critics of media representations of women argue that the world's actual diversity of women is challenging to male authority, so that the media's transformation of this reality into manageable images of what femininity should look like comforts men, especially those who actually do wield power.

Yet critics also point out that there is a diversity of women and women's experiences, so that we must not *essentialize* them, thereby assuming that all women share the same experiences. Any individual's experiences and perspectives depend on a multiplicity of factors, including her race, age, sexual orientation, and class experiences. While it is important not to essentialize women by assuming a common experience shared by all women, it is also important to recognize the similarity of the constraints placed upon all women by virtue of their being female in a patriarchal world.

In order to understanding the power of stereotypical media images, it is also important to be aware of the concept of *intertextuality*, which recognizes that an individual text never stands alone but that the multitude of images that pass by our eyes every day constantly refer to and build upon each other. This is increasingly the case in the contemporary age of technological convergence, where media are converging in digital platforms. This means that when we think about media representations, we must recognize that they have an impact beyond the intentions of individual authors and media makers. Their intentions form only a component of how texts are understood by audience members, each with their own experiences and social positions that shape how they read and understand media texts. Nevertheless, feminist critics have been quick to point out that while audience members read a text differently based on their individual experiences, the utopian vision of some scholars who celebrate the audience's control over the construction of meaning from media texts is unrealistic. While the audience may be active in interpreting media texts, the media do play a key ideological function in developing ritualized ways of presenting images of the world that exclude as much as they include, and that emphasize certain aspects of reality while downplaying others.

LAURA MULVEY AND THE MALE GAZE

Laura Mulvey's 1975 article, "Visual Pleasure and Narrative Cinema," provided a groundbreaking conception of the viewing audience that changed the way media spectatorship would thereafter be understood, researched, and theorized. At a time when most scholars were analyzing stereotypes in the media, Mulvey took the pleasure viewers feel in the experience of watching movies as her starting point. She argues that classical Hollywood films prioritize the perspective of the masculine subject both visually and through narrative by forcing the audience to regard the text through the perspective of the (heterosexual) male. The female body thus becomes an object of the camera and of male desire, and women characters' experiences onscreen are presented with an eye to how men would react to these events. Mulvey coined the term "male gaze" to describe how men are the subjects doing the looking while women are objects to be looked at. This also means that women viewers must experience the narrative secondarily, through identification with the male subject. They must learn to perceive themselves as objects to be scrutinized, and thus to watch themselves being watched by others. In this way, Mulvey argues, films make voyeurs of both male and female members of the audience so that the act of objectification becomes a source of pleasure in the viewing experience.

Mulvey's essay helped establish feminist film theory as a legitimate field of study. It was groundbreaking in its recognition that sexism can occur not only through media images, but also in the ways that a text is presented, whose perspective is privileged in that presentation, and what that says about the intended audience. The essay provoked heated debate and critique, which Mulvey answered in a follow-up article entitled "Afterthoughts on 'Visual Pleasure and Narrative Cinema.'"

STEREOTYPICAL IMAGES OF WOMEN

In the twentieth century, images of women in the media have largely been linked with a consumerist lifestyle and a rather domesticated version of femininity, and these stereotypical ways of representing women are consistent and enduring over time and across media forms. A large body of research has shown that sex stereotypes such as women's "compassion" and men's "aggressiveness," for example, lead people to expect men and women to have different personal characteristics that relate in turn to their integrity and their different areas of competence.

In addition, feminist researchers have for decades pointed out the artificial yet stereotypical divide between the public sphere, largely assumed to be the domain of men, and the private sphere of the home, stereotypically the domain of women. This public/private divide has reinforced notions of women as incompetent in the public sphere, and even when successful professional women are the focus of media attention, they are often represented in ways that emphasize their competence in the private sphere, rather than their professional abilities. Early studies of media images, for example, demonstrate that in the Victorian era, lifestyle magazines modeled, through their editorial and content, a specific class-based, "proper" lifestyle that placed women firmly in the private sphere of the home. Women's first inroads as media makers, such as in children's programming, the writing of women's magazines, or by focusing on issues such as health, education, and welfare, functioned to reinforce rather than challenge the public/private divide. Also, women's comparatively late start as media producers meant that once they did enter the media field, they had to enter on male terms and emulate the actions and voices of men. While women have made increasing inroads both as media makers and in media images, the public/private dichotomy remains persistent in the popular media.

The most common representation of women in the media is as victims, most commonly of sexual violence. Other consistent media images include women as hypersexualized or as whores; women as nurturing and caring, based on their role as mothers; and women as inscrutable and dangerous. Women are often represented as monstrous creatures, including as vampires, witches, and beings possessed by otherworldly life forms. While men appear in some of these roles as well, what differs in these representations is that women appear monstrous and dangerous specifically *because of* their sexuality, or their identity as *female*. This is mirrored in the common practice of representing women as body parts to be fetishized, rather than complete human beings. Another growing concern is the increasing eroticization of very young girls, and the linking of childlike innocence and vulnerability with the potential for becoming a victim of violence. This is especially alarming when combined with representations that suggest that women are only teasing when they reject men's advances, and that when they say "no," they really mean "yes."

An issue of special concern in relation to representations of women involves the media's narrowly conceived image of female beauty, in particular the overwhelming emphasis on thinness. The standard of female beauty stereotypically portrayed in the media is unrealistic for the vast majority of women, yet all women must deal with the personal and social consequences of such a narrowly defined sense of what makes a woman beautiful. As a result, most girls and women report feeling alienated from and dissatisfied with their bodies, and many develop problematic relationships with food and dieting. (For more information, see "Body Image.")

Many of the commonplace media representations of women (and the expectations they engender) involve contradictory messages about how women should behave. On the one hand, women are expected to be chaste and pure, but on the other, they are also encouraged to be sexually adventurous. Women are told to be tolerant of those who are different, while at the same time they are fed image after unending image representing an especially narrow version of feminine beauty. Women are told they should be independent and free-thinking, while at the same time they are consistently coached to please the men in their lives. As Susan Douglas points out in *Where the Girls Are*, these contradictory messages "make us the schizophrenics we are today, women who rebel against yet submit to prevailing images about what a desirable, worthwhile woman should be." This causes women to develop a conflicted relationship with mass media, and makes the transition to adulthood especially difficult for girls.

In addition to the often contradictory messages and stereotypical representations that do exist, it is important to recognize the significant absences in media representations of women: women of color, lesbians, disabled women, and older women make few appearances in the media. When representations of lesbians do appear, for example, they paint these women as unusual by focusing on their "deviant" sexuality, rather than representing them as leading normal lives. In addition, the vast majority of studies in English on women in the media focus on Western cultures and almost always on white women, although this has been changing in recent years.

Yet it is not images alone that define representations of women in media; this also occurs through mediated voices. Whereas men are often presented in media

---

SUSAN FALUDI AND *BACKLASH*

Susan Faludi is a Pulitzer Prize–winning journalist and author whose book *Backlash: The Undeclared War against American Women* (1992) argues that the 1980s ushered in a backlash against feminism characterized by a slew of negative stereotypes against working women. These included the claims that large numbers of working women were suffering burnout and other consequences of stress, childless women were depressed and confused and found themselves facing a crisis of infertility, and single women were facing a shortage of eligible men. News reports also maintained that single working women were more depressed than other women, that large numbers of professional women had decided to forgo their jobs in order to stay at home with their children, and that single women over 30 had a very small chance of getting married. In essence, Faludi argues, the popular media was promoting the idea that the women's movement was women's worst enemy.

Using data from a wide variety of government and university studies, the popular press, and personal interviews, Faludi interrogated and debunked these myths about the status of women that were current at the time she was writing. She critiqued the press for not challenging these myths and for reinforcing the idea that feminism is to blame for the (supposed) unhappiness of women. She argued that if women are indeed unhappy, this stems from the fact that the struggle for equality remains unrealized. She also pointed out that the backlash is a historical trend that tends to appear when women have made substantial gains in their struggle for equal rights.

---

as the voices of experts and authority, women's voices are often featured in "soft" areas, such as advertisements for baby products, cleaning goods, pet foods, or luxury items, particularly those aimed at male purchasers (such as chocolates and perfume). In addition, stereotypes about "feminine discourse" include social (rather than linguistic) concepts such as gossip, bitching, and nagging, for which there are no masculine equivalents. This concept of a "feminine discourse" in contrast to more masculine forms of communication is especially prominent in debates about gendered representations in the stereotypically "feminine" genre of soap operas.

WOMEN AND/IN SOAP OPERAS

Soap operas have been widely studied, perhaps because they are hugely popular in both Western and non-Western countries. One significant debate that has arisen from these studies is whether or not soap operas represent a form of "feminine discourse" that is cause for celebration, or whether this conception reaffirms gender essentialism and the image of women as more concerned with relationships and talk, rather than action. The conventional view is that soap operas are a women's genre, and therefore do reproduce "feminine discourse." Critics argue, however, that the gap between the male and female audience for soaps is not as large as most people suppose, and that if soaps are deemed "feminine" *because* they deal with everyday problems and are set primarily in the private sphere, then this further perpetuates, rather than proving, a gender essentialism.

While some scholars have argued that soap operas provide a positive image of gossip and that female soap opera fans gain pleasure from the texts in ways that undermine patriarchy, others find little evidence that this playful use of soaps subverts dominant discourses. While soap operas do provide a wider variety of images of women than other media, research on the contents of soap operas indicates that soap characters are represented as flawed individuals, living complicated lives that nevertheless remain within the expectations of patriarchy. Structural answers to complex problems are not addressed in these programs, so that violence against women, racism, teenage pregnancy, drug abuse, and other issues are always represented as problems facing individuals rather than society as a whole. These representations in turn suggest that the solutions to these problems are also individual rather than social concerns, thereby ignoring the structural constraints facing women in a patriarchal society.

WOMEN AND/IN SPORT

Sport is recognized as an expression of the sociocultural system and as mirroring the values of the society in which it takes place. It provides a society with ideas about honor and heroism, and its games are often seen as symbols of personal or larger social struggles. For this reason, critics of the gendering of sport and sports media argue that the playing field itself can be seen as a metaphor for gender values in the United States, and that by limiting women primarily to stereotypical support roles such as cheerleader and spectator, the media function to maintain the status quo assumption that women should be subservient to men. In addition, the emphasis on violence in sports is also a concern for critics who argue that this practice socially sanctions violence and, combined with sexually charged media representations, antagonism towards women.

Perhaps most telling about the media and their impact on sport, however, are the findings of research examining the media treatment of female athletes. Since the passage of Title IX federal legislation in the early 1970s that prohibited discrimination on the basis of sex for federally funded education programs, the number of females involved in sport has risen significantly. Yet the portrayals of female athletes have reinforced the gender hierarchy in sport, paradoxically functioning to resist fundamental social change while simultaneously representing such change as an indication of progress in gender equity.

While media representations in sport feature a growing number of women, there is nevertheless a consistent underreporting and underrepresentation of female athletes in sporting events. When women are represented, they are depicted as participating primarily in individual and aesthetic sports (such as figure skating and gymnastics) rather than team sports. Female athletes are consistently marginalized or trivialized through photographs depicting them in passive roles, coverage that focuses on their physical appearance rather than their athletic abilities, their representation as having character flaws and emotional instability, or images of female athletes on screen while the accompanying commentary focuses on male athletic performance. In sport as in other media genres, women are represented with a focus on their sexuality rather than their abilities, as exemplified in media coverage of tennis player Anna Kournikova. This also implies that only the most glamorous female athletes are worthy of media coverage, and the general absence of minority, lesbian, and disabled women athletes in media coverage sends the message that sport should be limited to white, heterosexual, nondisabled women. Thus, in maintaining stereotypical images of femininity and masculinity, the media have functioned in sport as they have in other genres to maintain the status quo and the superiority of men, even while paying lip service to progress.

THE MOMMY WARS

Physically placed on opposite sides of the aisle on the set of the Dr. Phil show, female participants in the episode "Mom vs. Mom" found themselves pitted against each other in a showdown between stay-at-home moms and working mothers. Shortly after its opening segments, the show got nasty, with participants insulting each other and audience members "meowing" the mothers onstage. This event was an extreme example of how entrenched ideals of the "perfect" mother combine with the demands of a consumer society to place mothers in a no-win situation.

Feminist critics note that the "Mommy Wars" as constructed in mainstream newspapers and magazines and on the daytime talk shows are simplistic, a diversion that redirects public attention from the real problem: the lack of support and respect for caregiving in the United States. Media representations of the Mommy Wars make the assumption, for example, that stay-at-home moms never return to the workplace, and working women never leave it. This does not reflect the reality that women move in and out of the workforce, that one-third of U.S. women work part-time, that there are an increasing number of stay-at-home dads, and that both women and men are finding new and creative ways of handling the balance of work and home life. It also ignores those women who do not have children.

Ultimately, critics argue, by pitting mothers against each other, the media-constructed Mommy Wars let politicians off the hook. Dividing women destroys their ability to act as a unified interest group to push for change. As critics point out, the Mommy Wars do not lead to questions about the workplace itself; rather they prompt women to judge and undermine other women. They also divert attention from the role of men, who increasingly wish to play a bigger role in family life, and negate the issues facing the growing number of single mothers who do not have the option of staying at home to raise their children. And lest we forget, critics point out that the sensationalism and controversy surrounding the Mommy Wars helps to sell newspapers, magazines, TV shows, and radio broadcasts.

A positive development has been the growing number of mothers working to change the degree of support for all families. These women have called for a halt to the Mommy Wars. Shortly after the Dr. Phil show "Mom vs. Mom" aired, two of its guests considered to be on opposing sides of the Mommy Wars publicly called on mothers to stop the hostilities and work together to improve the status of families and the lives of children. Their statement redirected the argument from one about women to one about families and children, and urged mothers to "set aside any negative reactions you have to 'mommy war' comments and join us in moving beyond this media-exaggerated conflict." They called for increased flexibility in the workplace for parents, including the kind of paid parental leave enjoyed in almost all countries outside the United States, a lower tax burden on families, and health insurance for children. Organizations involved in the effort agree they are facing an uphill battle, since they are calling for a cultural shift from a focus on conflict and consumerism to a commitment to compassion. These groups nevertheless remain committed to pushing for change, not least for what that will mean for our children.

WOMEN AND/IN THE NEWS AND POLITICS

Women remain underrepresented in most areas of the news, including in their work as politicians (and therefore news makers). They are featured much less often than men in the programming itself, and as anchors, reporters, commentators, and experts. They are also underrepresented in technical areas and in decision-making positions in the media; women still only represent a small percentage of media executives, with white middle-class men occupying the vast majority of positions at all levels. In addition, decades of research have shown that the five journalistic norms—objectivity, news values, the use of official or institutional sources or "experts," work routines that privilege certain types of news, and structural constraints—all privilege a patriarchal worldview. This results in media coverage dominated by images of male professionals, while professional women remain largely absent, further reinforcing the idea of the public sphere as masculine.

These trends harm the interests and performance of women media workers and politicians, since (male and female) journalists seek out few women as sources, not in outright dismissal of their talents, but because of unconscious tendencies to see women as less qualified. Scholars have found that U.S. journalists tend to rely on symbiotic relationships with a limited range of "official," almost exclusively male sources, primarily political and military figures, and then to report directly what they say, at times even glorifying them. As a result, the culture of most newspaper and broadcast organizations as well as the political arena is still being defined in predominantly male terms.

News and politics, therefore, as with most media content, overwhelmingly reflect male perspectives on the world. Yet feminist critics of this situation do not assume that an increase in women in these areas will necessarily improve the situation. Some argue, in fact, that women often actively choose not to go into the news or politics rather than deal with the need to survive in these male-dominated fields. But more importantly, for a woman to be successful, she has to be willing to play with the boys on their own terms, or at least to put up with a masculinized environment in which she is not as valued or as well paid as her male colleagues. This is arguably apparent in the recent increase in attractive young women news anchors, very often partnered with older, more serious male counterparts. In these instances, the male anchor generally introduces the more serious, leading stories of the newscast, while the younger woman introduces the human interest or other "soft" stories aired later in the program.

Research has also shown that inadequate coverage of women is a worldwide phenomenon. Rarely do media quote women, let alone focus on their concerns, and when women are featured on screen, men overwhelmingly dominate the discussion. The "public" as represented in the news is also male-dominated, in that more men than women are asked to provide "man-on-the-street" interviews. Women also tend to be featured in stories about accidents, disasters, and domestic violence rather than in stories that feature their abilities or expertise, and stories about political or economic success are almost always about men.

Researchers have demonstrated that the sex of a woman is always the media's focus when she is producing or making the news. This is in large part because the economics of the media industries rely on the commodification of women as cheap labor (still consistently cheaper than their male counterparts) and their sexualization as employees and in media images as ways of using sex to increase the bottom line. Female politicians are far more often referred to by age than their male counterparts, and comments on their clothing, hairstyle, and other stylistic concerns are often included in coverage of their activities; this is not the case when male politicians are covered in the news. Women in the news industry have described the same phenomenon, whereby their physical appearance is far more a focus than their professional abilities. In addition, comparison of news coverage of male and female politicians has shown that female politicians are often referred to in comparatively unflattering and highly personal terms, and that while male politicians are usually referred to by their surnames, the media often use female politicians' first names. Even the few positive portrayals of female politicians and news workers, however, often gloss over the difficulties these women have faced in balancing their professional and personal lives, thereby reproducing gender inequities by implying that women who cannot balance these aspects of their lives have somehow failed.

In addition, scholars have critiqued the concept of "objectivity" as journalism's primary claim to legitimacy in U.S. news, arguing that the concept is highly problematic and reflects a male view of the world. The concept assumes that reporters can get at the "truth" of any situation by adhering to certain procedures, regardless of their gender, race, and class experiences. A belief in the possibility of "objectivity" assumes that a journalist has the needed insight to ask government officials and corporate representatives tough questions, and that such experts do not have agendas of their own. Some female journalists argue, therefore, that true "objectivity" requires that male values be balanced by female ones in a given news account or range of accounts, and that this must be accomplished by hiring equal numbers of male and female journalists as well as by using equal numbers of male and female sources. Others argue that the concept of "objectivity" must be jettisoned altogether, and that the news should be working instead to present a multiplicity of viewpoints on a given issue.

MOVING FORWARD

One concern of feminist scholars is that despite the decades of challenge to media representations of women, the balance of power remains largely unchanged. They point out that contradictory or challenging images of women do not necessarily lead to social change. For example, while there has been an increase in lead female roles in crime shows and action movies that functions to challenge normative assumptions about the role of women in society, these representations still largely conform to stereotypes of normative femininity in that the characters are most often white, slender, and conventionally attractive, are presented as less capable than their male counterparts, and are frequently relegated to the role of sidekick. In addition, strong female role models are often represented as exceptions, and their presence has been used as an excuse to criticize and deny the need for feminism. Strong women are often represented as deviant and dangerous, and tend to get their just deserts in the end; take *Thelma and Louise*, for example, in which the two drive themselves off a cliff at the end of the movie. Sigourney Weaver in *Alien*, while widely recognized as the first significant female action hero in the science fiction genre, is still commodified as a sex object and made available for the *male gaze* (see "Laura Mulvey and the Male Gaze"). The popular heroine Lara Croft of the virtual game *Tomb Raider* is another example of a recent crop of tough but highly eroticized heroines in media texts that provide paradoxical readings. *Buffy the Vampire Slayer*, for example, can be read as empowering for women, but also as a male Lolita fantasy. Nevertheless, the increase in female role models in the media does provide women and girls with more strong female role models than ever before.

Feminist critics have increasingly called attention to the ways in which ownership issues affect content. They argue that representations of women in the media will not change substantially until there is significant change in the gender makeup of those who construct and produce media images, as well as those who make content and hiring decisions. It is hoped that such changes will transform the masculinized culture of contemporary media and the images they produce, and offer women a diversity of media images that more accurately reflects them and their experiences.

See also Advertising and Persuasion; Body Image; Dating Shows; Gay, Lesbian, Bisexual, Transgendered, and Queer Representations on TV; Pornography; Reality Television; Representations of Masculinity; Representations of Race; Shock Jocks; Women's Magazines.

Further Reading: Byerly, Carolyn M., and Karen Ross. *Women and Media: A Critical Introduction*. Malden, MA: Blackwell Publishing, 2006; Carter, Cynthia, G. Branston, and S. Allan, eds. *News, Gender and Power*. London: Routledge, 1998; Creedon, Pamela J., ed. *Women, Media and Sport*. Thousand Oaks, CA: Sage, 1994; Douglas, Susan. *Where the Girls Are: Growing up Female with the Mass Media*. New York: Random House, 1994; Faludi, Susan. *Backlash: The Undeclared War against American Women*. New York: Doubleday, 1991; Inness, Sherrie A., ed. *Action Chicks: New Images of Tough Women in Popular Culture*. New York: Palgrave Macmillan, 2004; Macdonald, Myra. *Representing Women: Myths of Femininity in the Popular Media*. New York: Edward Arnold, 1995; Mulvey, Laura. *Visual and Other Pleasures*. Basingstoke: Macmillan Press, 1989; Norris, Pippa, ed. *Women, Media and Politics*. New York: Oxford University Press, 1997; Steiner, Leslie Morgan, ed. *Mommy Wars: Stay-at-Home and Career Moms Face Off on Their Choices, Their Lives, Their Families*. New York: Random House, 2006; Tuchman, Gaye. *Making News: A Study in the Construction of Reality*. New York: The Free Press, 1978; Tuchman, Gaye, Arlene Kaplan Daniels, and James Benet, eds. *Hearth and Home: Images of Women in Mass Media*. New York: Oxford University Press, 1978; Wolf, Naomi. *The Beauty Myth: How Images of Women Are Used against Women*. New York: William Morrow, 1991.

Lisa Brooten

RUNAWAY PRODUCTIONS AND THE GLOBALIZATION OF HOLLYWOOD

The United States has a long history of dominance in the global export and circulation of movies and television programming. However, in our current era of rapid media globalization, American film and television producers have begun to actually take their projects outside of the United States in search of less expensive production conditions in other countries. These enterprises, which are referred to as "runaway productions," have increased at such a dramatic rate that American media industry critics have lobbied for legislation to encourage producers to bring their projects—and the jobs they provide—back home. Runaway productions are also not without detractors in their host countries, where concerns have been raised about a new form of American media imperialism in which domestic labor and financial resources are seen to fuel the Hollywood machine at the expense of local media production.

The Director's Guild of America (DGA) defines runaway productions as any American movie or television program that is developed specifically with the intent of being broadcast or screened in the United States but is filmed entirely in another country. These projects fall into two categories: (1) creative runaways and (2) economic runaways. Creative runaway productions are those that are shot on location outside of the United States for aesthetic reasons such as unique physical landscapes or exotic locales that are integral to the plot or "look" of a movie or television project. Economic runaways, on the other hand, are developed outside of the United States for the primary purpose of saving money on production and labor costs and thereby increasing the profit potential of the final product.

Creative runaways are not a new phenomenon. Since the early days of the Hollywood studio system, some movie directors have chosen to film their projects outside of Los Angeles—and the United States—to add artistic value to the story. This form of "locations shooting" reached a high point in the 1970s when a new generation of American movie directors sought a higher degree of realism and authenticity in their films than could be achieved in the more artificial environment of the studio backlot or soundstage. These individuals unintentionally blazed the trail for future economic runaways by establishing strong working relationships with policy makers, producers, and other creative media personnel in countries such as Canada and the United Kingdom, as well as other countries throughout Europe. Those working within the Hollywood industry were not overly concerned about creative runaways as such productions tended to be intermittent, few in number, and often of the lower-budget, artistic variety. However, the economic runaways that followed in their path a decade later would become a major source of alarm for the Los Angeles production community. These subsequent runaway productions not only tended to be big-budget feature films but also television movies and, even more disturbing to those in Los Angeles, ongoing television series and serials.

"HOLLYWOOD NORTH"

Countries that facilitate American runaway productions are always concerned about the vulnerability of their locations industries. For instance, when the lead actors of *The X-Files* demanded that the series relocate to Los Angeles so that the cast could be closer to their families, media insiders forecasted the start of a trend where other shows would follow suit and "run back home." These fears were exacerbated when the Canadian dollar began to rise in value in 2005—almost reaching parity with the U.S. dollar—and it was assumed that the Vancouver production service sector would collapse in the face of reduced economic incentives. These dire predictions have, thus far, not been realized. New American television series such as *Men in Trees* (ABC), *Smallville* (WB), and *Supernatural* (WB) have located in Vancouver to fill *The X-Files* vacuum, despite the less-than-favorable currency exchange rate. So, while a permanent relationship between "Hollywood North" and Los Angeles can never be guaranteed, there are signs that a combination of economic and more intangible creative factors have somewhat solidified the relationship between the two cities.

ECONOMIC RUNAWAY PRODUCTIONS

Television and movie productions "run away" from the United States to countries that offer particular cultural and economic advantages such as favorable currency exchange rates, linguistic and cultural similarity to the United States, and the presence of a relatively developed domestic audiovisual industry that can be incorporated into the American production. For these reasons Canada, Australia, and Britain have become the most important service locations for American runaways. Canada, in particular, successfully exploited several competitive advantages to attract American productions and thus over 80 percent of runaways are located there.

For the past two decades, the strength of the U.S. dollar in comparison with the Canadian dollar meant that American producers could gain more value for every production dollar spent if they filmed their project in a Canadian city. This resulted in significant savings for higher production values considering that at one point in the 1990s the U.S. dollar was worth more than $1.40 Canadian. However, currency exchange rates were not all that Canada had to offer. Because Canadian urban and rural areas look similar to their American counterparts, it was easy for producers to make it appear that their movie or television series was set in the United States. The fact that Canadians look and sound very similar to Americans also allowed U.S. producers to cast local actors in secondary roles and thus save the expense of bringing an entire troupe of actors with them from Los Angeles or New York. Moreover, Canada offered a critical mass of production crews who had received quality training within the well-established domestic public broadcasting system.

The Canadian federal and provincial governments were quick to realize the economic potential of establishing the country as the premier site for American runaway productions and developed a range of financial and infrastructure incentives to ensure the longevity of the country's new "locations industry." These included the provision of tax rebates and credits for every American production facilitated in the country as well as the construction of studios and soundstages that could accommodate U.S. blockbuster films. Investments were also made in postproduction facilities that would enable the Americans to complete all facets of their projects within Canada. The success of these efforts is witnessed not only in the hundreds of American movies and television series now filmed in Canada but also in the number of jobs and ancillary profits that have been generated by economic runaway productions. Servicing U.S. productions has become a multibillion-dollar industry in Canada.

CASE STUDY—"HOLLYWOOD NORTH": VANCOUVER, BRITISH COLUMBIA, CANADA

Audiences in the United States probably do not realize that Vancouver is the third-largest production site for American movies and television series after Los Angeles and New York. And for those who have heard of Vancouver's success in establishing itself as the major locations service industry in North America, it was probably the television series *The X-Files* that brought the city to their attention. The series' creator, Chris Carter, needed a forest for a UFO landing scene in the show's first episode and, as forests are scarce in Los Angeles, he headed north to Vancouver to find the backdrop he needed. What began as a creative runaway, or single location shot, became the most famous economic runaway in the television industry. Carter found that Vancouver not only offered him the requisite scenery and atmosphere he wanted for *The X-Files* but also a solid production infrastructure that included state-of-the-art studio facilities and crews that had garnered years of experience working on other American runaway productions. As a result he made the city the permanent production home for *The X-Files* and his two later series *Millennium* and *The Lone Gunmen*.

The X-Files was the apex of a larger 20-year economic strategic plan for British Columbia. In 1978, the provincial government created the B.C. Film Commission with the mandate to attract and facilitate international film and television production as a means to diversify a resource-based economy that was vulnerable to the boom–bust patterns of global commodities markets. While the B.C. Film Commission set about promoting the city of Vancouver to Los Angeles–based producers, the province invested millions of dollars in building studio space to secure potential runaway productions. Today, Vancouver is home to the largest special-effects stage in North America and, consequently, has been able to attract high-budget feature films such as *Jumanji*, *Blade*, and the *X-Men* franchise. This investment in infrastructure gave American producers the confidence to completely relocate their projects to Vancouver. The first, and most influential, was Stephen J. Cannell, who went further than most producers and built North Shore Studios in the 1980s for his series *21 Jump Street*, *Booker*, and *Wiseguy*. Cannell's positive experiences laid the groundwork for other American producers to "run away" to British Columbia.

CHRIS HADDOCK

Canadian writer and director Chris Haddock is an example of the new cross-border cultural producer that has emerged from the globalization of the Hollywood industry. Haddock gained experience writing for the American runaway action-adventure series *MacGyver*, which filmed in Vancouver in the 1980s. The professional network and experience he developed in the locations industry enabled him to establish his own production company, and he now develops crime and suspense dramas for both American and Canadian television networks. He was the first producer to sell a Canadian television series to a major U.S. broadcast network: CBS. This series, *Da Vinci's Inquest*, was already a prime-time hit for the Canadian Broadcasting Company (CBC) and became a critical and audience success in the United States, where it was acclaimed for its edgy feel and unique storytelling (and it did not even hide the fact that it was set in Canada). The series has been sold in 85 countries and Haddock continues to develop new television and film projects for both Canadian and American distribution.

Vancouver was able to edge out other Canadian cities, such as Toronto and Montreal, in the competition for American runaways because of the province's unique physical landscape. The diversity of locations available in a coastal province that also includes a glacier mountain range and a dry, rugged interior region means that producers can find almost any type of natural setting to suit their stories. Vancouver can be, and has been, the stand-in for Tibet, Montana, California, and numerous other places. The added bonus for American producers is that they can oversee their productions in Vancouver and—within the span of a two-hour flight—be back in Los Angeles for office meetings or family time. This confluence of factors earned the city the moniker "Hollywood North" and made it the global model for other aspiring runaway locations cities.

RUNAWAYS AS OUTSOURCING

Canada's success in attracting and keeping American runaways generated a heated response from members of the Los Angeles production community. They argued that every job offered to a Canadian actor or crew member was one that was lost to an American and, at the same time, every dollar spent on production in Canada was one not invested in the United States. They saw runaway productions as similar to other forms of labor outsourcing, such as that found in the automobile and information technology industries, in an age of economic globalization. Consequently, the major audiovisual labor unions—including the Directors Guild, Producers Guild, Screen Actors Guild, and Writers Guild, among dozens of others—came together to form the Runaway Production Alliance, an association that lobbied the American government to introduce legislation that would stem the tide of economic runaways from Hollywood. In 1999, the Directors Guild and the Screen Actors Guild commissioned a study that found that the number of runaway productions between 1990 and 1998 had increased by 185 percent, with an economic loss of over $10 billion to local production spending, merchants and hotels, and lost tax revenues. They estimated that more than 23,000 jobs in the entertainment industry had been lost to runaways, particularly in the more technical sectors of production: costuming, lighting, transportation, catering, and the like.

The Runaway Production Alliance's lobbying efforts were rewarded when the American government legislated the American Jobs Creation Act in 2004 and included provisions that offered production incentives for film and television projects that stayed in the United States. It is too soon to tell whether these incentives will prove sufficient to reverse the trend in economic runaways. The runaway productions industry has matured to the extent that major Hollywood studios have invested directly in infrastructure development in other countries. As the Directors Guild/Screen Actors Guild study reported, in the year 1998 alone Fox built a multimillion-dollar studio facility in Australia while Paramount and Disney both built studios, soundstages, and production offices in Vancouver. These companies are now so firmly entrenched in other countries that the new American production incentives may prove too little, too late.

In this respect, runaway productions must be seen as a component of larger processes of economic globalization. Media companies, just like any other type of corporation, have taken advantage of trends toward the deregulation of domestic monopolies as well as foreign investment legislation in order to consolidate their operations. Today, the majority of American media organizations are part of larger global conglomerates that no longer view national borders as an obstacle to their goals.

RUNAWAYS AS PRODUCTION IMPERIALISM

Given the economic gains the country has made from U.S. runaway productions, it might be surprising to note that there are Canadian critics of the domestic locations industry. In Canada, the structure of media policies and the national public broadcasting network itself was developed in relation to concerns about cultural imperialism from the United States. This fear is based on the presumption that the cultural identities of smaller nations are threatened when the media products of a larger nation come to dominate the viewing habits and leisure time of their citizens. As most major Canadian cities are within a few hundred miles of the U.S. border, Canadian audiences have freely watched American programming since the inception of television. And American movies dominate Canadian theater screens as most of these venues are owned by U.S. companies. Some of the criticisms of Canada's evolution into "Hollywood North" extend this argument to imply a possible new form of production imperialism. Here, Canadians are not only audiences for American movies and television programs but now they are helping to produce them as well. Consequently, Canada becomes a branch plant for the Hollywood industry and the domestic resources that are invested in economic runaways create profit for those headquartered in Los Angeles, where control over decision-making remains. In turn, Canada becomes merely a backlot where anything that can identify the country is erased and transformed to look like someplace in the United States—the ultimate form of cultural imperialism, you might say.

This form of production imperialism is also seen to negatively impact those with the least decision-making power in both the Canadian and American industries: the production crews and other "noncreative" personnel. Cross-border labor cooperation becomes impossible as members of Canadian and American audio-visual trade unions are forced to compete with one another to attract and maintain productions in their respective communities. The potential here is what some media researchers have called "the race to the bottom"—characteristic of economic globalization in general—wherein laborers may agree to cuts in wages, benefits, and working standards in order ensure that jobs remain within their community.

BLIND SPOTS

Debates that focus on the economic dimensions of runaway productions tend to neglect the dynamic changes occurring from the creative elements of transnational production relationships. In this respect, processes of economic globalization are also intricately tied to cultural globalization. As these industries become increasingly mobile, we now find cultural producers working across borders and contributing to the emergence of new creative networks and partnerships. These have led to new types of television programs and movies produced through international co-ventures—where producers from two or more countries work together to develop a story—which may offer not only a greater quantity of programming, globally, but also greater diversity in the forms (or genres) or topics that we see broadcast or exhibited on our screens. These new global productions also help feed the increased demand for media content as television channel capacity grows exponentially. And even the DGA study noted that television and film production in Los Angeles has increased annually despite the corresponding increase in runaway productions. Servicing runaways can also provide creative opportunities for workers in the locations city as they can garner greater skills and financial resources to invest in projects for development in their domestic television and film sectors. Therefore, the creative and economic aspects of runaway productions must never be seen as mutually exclusive of one another.

See also Bollywood and the Indian Diaspora; Branding the Globe; Communication and Knowledge Labor; Communication Rights in a Global Context; Conglomeration and Media Monopolies; Cultural Imperialism and Hybridity; Hypercommercialism; Independent Cinema; Nationalism and the Media; World Cinema.

Further Reading: Allen, Scott. *On Hollywood: The Place, the Industry.* Princeton, NJ: Princeton University Press, 2005; Elmer, Greg, and Mike Gasher, eds. *Contracting Out Hollywood: Runaway Productions and Foreign Location Shooting.* Oxford: Rowman and Littlefield, 2005; Florida, Richard L. *The Flight of the Creative Class: The New Global Competition for Talent.* New York: Harper Collins, 2005; Gasher, Mike. *Hollywood North:*

The Feature Film Industry in British Columbia. Vancouver: UBC Press, 2002; Hartley, John, ed. *Creative Industries.* London: Blackwell, 2005; Hozic, Aida. *Hollyworld: Space, Power and Fantasy in the American Economy.* Ithaca, NY: Cornell University Press, 2002; Miller, Toby, Nitin Govil, John McMurria, and Rick Maxwell. *Global Hollywood 2.* London: BFI Publishing, 2005; O'Regan, Tom, and Ben Goldsmith. *Cinema Cities, Media Cities: The Contemporary International Studio Complex.* Brisbane: Australian Key Centre for Cultural and Media Policy, 2003; Spaner, David. *Dreaming in the Rain: How Vancouver Became Hollywood North by Northwest.* Vancouver: Arsenal Pulp Press, 2003; Tinic, Serra. *On Location: Canada's Television Industry in a Global Market.* Toronto: University of Toronto Press, 2005.

Serra Tinic

SENSATIONALISM, FEAR MONGERING, AND TABLOID MEDIA

Telling a friend that he or she looks sensational may be an effective way to give a compliment, but describing a newspaper as full of sensationalism is considered a disparaging remark, and is usually reserved for what has been coined the tabloid media. Tabloid TV and newspapers may be popular, but they constitute a major battleground issue with critics who charge them with doing a disservice to democratic society. Others say they measure the limits of our constitutional right to freedom of expression. Sensationalism in the news has a long history with very negative connotations, yet despite these condemnations it still attracts attention and faithful audiences. In spite of accusations that sensational stories appeal to base instincts, defenders point out that news without an audience is not useful. Critics counter that news produced only to titillate an audience can also be dangerous.

Recognizable sensationalism in the media is found most frequently in stories about crime, celebrity, sex, disasters, and violence, which are often presented with lurid details that shock the sensibilities and arouse emotional reactions. Sensationalism refers not only to the content, but also the style of presentation. Such stories focus on attention-grabbing devices that hail viewers and readers to stay tuned or buy the newspaper because of a jaw-dropping cover. Sensational news is not necessarily false, but it is often times misleading. Researchers have also found that sensationalism, especially with regard to crime and violence, can have serious social consequences (see "Did You Know? CBS and Fox: From Wrestling to News to "Reality/Comedy Hybrid").

DID YOU KNOW?

CBS and Fox: From Wrestling to News to "Reality/Comedy Hybrid"

With no journalistic expertise, former beauty queen Lauren Jones made the transition from being a WWE wrestler to becoming a news anchor for CBS affiliate KYTX in Tyler, Texas, in June 2007. Female journalists have been systematically marginalized throughout the news business, but Jones was retained in an attempt to boost the ratings of the self-described "Eye of East Texas." KYTX had been mired in a ratings slump, so station owner Phil Hurley recruited Jones, who also had previous experience as one of "Barker's Beauties" on the game show *The Price is Right.* Publicity photos announcing the new position pictured Jones in an alluring pose wearing a leopard-print V-neck top and a red miniskirt on the set. Zap2IT. com reported that she also had on-camera skills from a former stint as the "Hobo Bikini Model" on *Wonder Showzen.*

When Hurley hired Jones, the CBS affiliate also provided the premise for *Anchorwoman,* a new FOX reality TV show billed as a "comedy/reality hybrid" that premiered in August 2007. The FOX press release promoting the series promised that Jones would have ample opportunities for conflict with other station celebrities including reporter Michelle Reese and anchor Annalisa Petraglia. KYTX is also the home of the beloved mascot, Stormy the Weather Dog, and industry reports wondered if Jones would get along with Stormy. With the hire of Jones, the collaboration between CBS and FOX represents a qualitative leap in sensational megacorporate media practices and a stunning merger of news with the reality-show production values of shock, voyeurism, and revealing titillation. It also represents a step backward for women with aspirations to serious journalism who continue to be evaluated on their ability to allure instead of by their professional skills and dedication to keeping the public informed.

Critics hold that media sensationalism stems from increased bottom-line management and that media have been on a downward spiral, increasingly looking for stories that boost ratings and sell papers instead of reporting that informs the citizenry about important issues of the day. The axiom for some of the worst local television news has been historically, "if it bleeds, it leads," a phrase that indicates the preference for graphic television footage. While the visual nature of television lends itself to sensational news coverage, and dramatic footage can often drive the news agenda, the pioneers of sensationalism forged a path long before the video camera was invented.

THE AGE OF YELLOW JOURNALISM

Attention-grabbing news is not unique to the present media landscape. The print media employed the strategies and styles of the tabloid press in earlier times during the era of "yellow journalism." At the end of the nineteenth century, the penny press had been flourishing for 50 years and editors were proud of producing newspapers everyone could read, presenting news from the rest of the world and from their own reporters. Then two publishers, William Randolph Hearst and Joseph Pulitzer, bought newspapers and began a competition that led to the newspaper wars of the New York City press barons. Hearst, who owned the *New York Journal*, and Pulitzer, who published the *World*, tried to outstrip each other in circulation, and in doing so began the long historical run of media sensationalism in the American press. This era of newspaper competition was coined "yellow journalism" due to the two publishers' fight over which paper would gain more readers by carrying a popular cartoon strip that featured the Yellow Kid as its main character. The publishers also competed for readers and sales in other ways. They tried to beat each other out in getting the latest news, but they went far beyond scooping the competition. They turned to different types of stories, from crime and violence to exposés about the sex lives of the wealthy, to boost circulation. They encouraged their reporters to try various gimmicks to attract attention. One of the most expensive stunts was a trip around the world mimicking Phineas Fogg's 80-day whirl written by Jules Verne. Pulitzer had reporter Nellie Bly (aka Elizabeth Cochrane) travel the global sending dispatches back for publication in the *World*. Hearst hired another reporter to follow Bly who wrote articles for his *Journal*.

SENSATIONAL REPORTING AND THE SPANISH AMERICAN WAR

One of the most notorious cases of sensational reporting was coverage leading up to the Spanish American War of 1898. On the island of Cuba, insurgents had rebelled against oppressive Spanish rule as early as 1868, but in 1895 revolution was rekindled when the United States imposed tariffs on Cuban exports, an action that led to massive unemployment and economic hardships. After coverage of the French and Indian War increased circulation for the *New York Journal*, William Randolph Hearst understood that war coverage was good for business. So when Cubans tried to free themselves of Spanish rule, Hearst sent reporter Richard Harding Davis and artist Frederick Remington to cover the situation. After a few months in Cuba, Remington cabled his editor and complained that there was no war and therefore, nothing to draw. Since he could not actually see the fighting, he was bored and wanted to return to the United States. Reportedly, Hearst sent a return telegraph to Remington that read: "Please remain. You furnish the pictures, I'll furnish the war." A century later, with complete access to all Hearst historical documents, biographer David Nasaw confirms that no such cable from Hearst can be verified. (As Nasaw documents, reference to the message first appeared in the 1901 autobiography of *Journal* reporter James Creelman.) Nevertheless, these words are memorialized as a way to remember this period. The stories in Hearst's *Journal* were embellished with simplified and exaggerated narratives of damsels in distress and patriotic fervor against Spanish colonialism in North America. Sensational swash-buckling coverage in the *Journal* caused circulation to soar. The Spanish American War of 1898 may not have been started by the press, but its eager support by the American public is understood to be a result of sensationalistic reporting.

Media interest in stories that attract attention but fail to adequately explain world events and their causes has not abated. The proliferation of plays, movies, books, and essays pondering the rise of media sensationalism and the dangers it

---

THE O.J. SIMPSON CASE: OR, WHY IS EVERYONE WATCHING A SLOW CAR CHASE ON A FREEWAY?

On a June evening in 1994, television stations across the country interrupted their programming to show footage from a Los Angeles television station. Viewers watched as police cars chased a white Ford Bronco on the L.A. freeway. Why became clear as the chase continued: a football hero-turned-celebrity pitchman, O.J. Simpson had been charged with murdering his ex-wife, Nicole Simpson, and her friend, Ron Goldman. Simpson was running away from arrest. The public was captured, and the sheer quantity of media reporting made history. The three broadcast networks aired 874 stories about the Simpson case in 1995; CNN had broadcast 388 hours of O.J. Simpson by the time the jury began deliberating in 1995; Court TV aired footage from "pool" reporters and made it available to all other television outlets; book deals were made for millions of dollars.

It had all the necessary elements for a sensational news serial; crime, drama, and hot pursuit of a fallen football hero. Simpson had won the Heisman Trophy, became a sports commentator, and went on to appear in commercials for a car rental company. The entire country came to recognize the familiar footage of the athlete hurtling over luggage in the TV advertisement. The story themed one of the most iconic white racial fears; a black man was charged with killed a white woman. Simpson's legal defense team became known as the "dream team," with well-known lawyer F. Lee Bailey. In front of a predominately black jury, compelling evidence was presented of racial prejudice on the part of the arresting police officers. As the trial progressed other social issues emerged, including domestic violence and orphaned children. And the unbelievable drama was set against the backdrop of America's storied land of Hollywood. Although O.J. Simpson was found not guilty by the court in 1995, most of the public did not agree, but opinion was divided along racial lines. African Americans were more likely to believe Simpson was innocent and treated badly at the hands of law enforcement and the court system, a belief underscored by unequal treatment of people of color in the criminal justice system.

The fallout from the O.J. Simpson episode led to many social realizations. Racism remained an enduring feature of American society. The inordinate coverage brought attention to many social issues. Viewers were informed about the U.S. justice system. They learned how a judge can control a courtroom, or lose control of it; what evidence is admissible and how it can be presented; and that a jury can be sequestered to allow for media coverage. Spousal abuse and violence against women, topics often hidden from public view, were brought into the open, and the media augmented coverage with reports on what victims can do to protect and defend themselves. In an unusual rejection of shocking, sensational media fare, in 2006 public outrage prevented Rupert Murdoch's media empire from publishing Simpson's book, *If I Did It*.

---

poses for professional journalism all attest to the social problem, yet it continues. Some scholars argue that it comes about as a result of economic forces; others suggest that technology has fostered more sensational reporting; and others still find positive content in some sensational news, arguing that it attracts attention to issues that would otherwise be ignored in public discourse.

CONSTRAINTS FACED BY JOURNALISTS

Studies find that most journalists understand their role and responsibilities in a democratic society. They see themselves as members of the fourth estate who serve a public service function, keeping those in power accountable to an informed citizenry. This position tasks the media to be a watchdog over government. Herbert Gans and others find that professional journalists value their role in helping the public remain free by participating in self-governance. But good reporting takes resources, time, and legwork. Many media managers and owners run their companies as businesses rather than journalistic enterprises. With the increasing corporatization of the media, returning profits to stockholders often takes resources out of the newsroom. Under such economic constraints, reporting has shifted toward sensational stories that are easier to get and report quickly. Research and investigation into stories about health care, education, transportation, and housing take time, skill, and staff support. Such reporting must be carefully prepared, studied, and presented in some detail. Experts must be consulted and legal actions sometimes taken to uncover information guarded by those in positions of wealth and power. With existing commercial demands on media, many journalists and editors admit that this type of support is increasingly scarce in the newsroom.

CONGLOMERATION AND THE NEWS

During the era of yellow journalism, individual publishers owned their own papers. Beginning in the 1980s, business-friendly deregulation allowed single corporations to buy numerous media outlets including cable companies, production companies, publishing houses, and broadcast stations. Today such centralization of ownership has changed the landscape of American media. Most newspapers and television networks, including local radio and TV stations, now belong to large conglomerates that are publicly owned and nationally based. The resulting ownership structure has left most media outlets far removed from the communities they are mandated to serve.

GENERIC NEWS

Media corporatization and centralized ownership have resulted in the convergence of programming on different media owned by any single company. News that is produced for a number of stations, cable services, and publication simultaneously is referred to as generic news. Because generic news is centrally produced for distribution across the county, stories often focus on topics of national interest instead of reporting on regional or community concerns.

Changing corporate ownership has affected local news reporting in other ways as well. When stations in the same region belong to one corporation, owners will often pool newsroom production, uniting the news staff who must then share the same news library and resources. The same editors and reporters will produce the news for the various outlets, and also write the news for the converged Web site. Though communities may have the same number of stations, fewer reporters will be producing the news. In this way, corporations return profits to their stockholders by making news cheaper to produce, but with reduced news budgets and staff, reporters are racing to get stories out. Corporate profits also demand increased circulation and ratings and these combined economic requirements have ratcheted up the need for quick, attention-grabbing content. Today reporters often fill the news hole with the easiest reporting on crime, celebrity, scandals, sports, and entertainment. Newsrooms send staff reporters out to cover the ever-present accidents, fires, and burglaries, and treat each as if they were the worst in history. Covering the weather has become a prominent feature of much local news reporting, and it is easily hyped with dire predictions about "your morning commute" as the unwitting journalist reports "live" in the street, drenched from rain or snow, in what has become the excessively dramatized daily weather report. Such exaggerated treatment of often trivial topics has become a favorite target for political satirists such as Jon Stewart on *The Daily Show*.

TIMELINESS AND THE SERIALIZED SCANDAL

Sensational news is often the latest installment of the hottest scandal. In these cases, the speed of news-gathering and reporting allows for little reflection and requires rapid response and repackaging of stories already in circulation. A shocking story that captures national headlines can become highly cost-effective as it is serialized into a continuous stream of reporting that fills up the news cycle and offers the latest details to a public eager for the hottest revelation. This type of coverage has resulted in the excessive treatment of stories such as the O. J. Simpson murder trial, the Monica Lewinsky scandal, and the fall of celebrity socialite Paris Hilton, just to name a few. As journalists chase the same story lest they be left out, they become desperate to find another detail, angle, or personal intrigue, and reporters and news anchors often fill in the blanks with endless speculation, dubious assertions, or groundless rumors and gossip, much of which simply does not classify as serious journalism. Media critics and analysts argue that in many of these cases, news is hard to distinguish from popular fictional genres such as soap operas and crime dramas. As news merges with the formats and genres of fictional programs and narratives, it serves to reinforce fundamental cultural and social beliefs instead of offering unvarnished accounts of events of the day.

SYNERGY AND INFOTAINMENT

With fewer and fewer resources available to gather and produce meaningful news, and with increasing expectations for ratings-producing content, newsrooms come to rely on the entertainment divisions of the parent company for news content. The latest contestant expelled from this week's network reality show will be featured as a newsmaker. Tie-in stories from network programs feature the characters and real-life dramas of those who act in and are portrayed on fictional TV, and news agendas feature topics driven by entertainment programs. This strategy also serves to promote the network and its programming in a marketing compliment known as synergy. Such convergent content transforms much of non-fiction programming, especially local news, into little more than infotainment.

THE NEWSMAGAZINES

Newsmagazines are another focus of criticism, with much of the condemnation coming from former news figures such as Walter Cronkite and established journalists such as long-time CBS producer Don Hewitt. These professional insiders view the current state of journalism through a highly negative lens. They point out that newsmagazines are produced by network entertainment divisions and must compete with other fictional fare aired during prime time on other channels. Viewers come to expect entertaining plots and emotional sagas punctuated with shocking revelations in programming fare better suited to deliver audiences to advertisers than informed citizens to the voting booth.

GEORGE GERBNER AND THE IDENTIFICATION OF "MEAN WORLD SYNDROME"

George Gerbner held one of the most prestigious positions in the field of communication in the American academy. For 25 years, from 1964 through 1989, he served as dean of the Annenberg School for Communication at the University of Pennsylvania. There he helped shape one of the most significant and influential projects to be undertaken in media research. It is often claimed that there are so many other influences on behavior and perceptions that it is impossible to measure the effects of television, yet Gerbner did just that. In 1968 he founded the Cultural Indicators Research Project, which tracked and catalogued the content of television programs. The project designed a complicated methodology, one that sought to find a cognitive media influence, not a simple behavioral effect between viewing and engaging in violent behavior. Surveys were designed that recorded the impact that programming had on viewers' perceptions and attitudes. The findings exposed disturbing truths about the influence of television on the public. The research identified a "mean world syndrome," finding that heavy doses of crime and violence on TV reinforced the worst fears in the minds of viewers. Heavy viewers perceived the world as a scary place and experienced a heightened sense of danger. Gerbner took the findings out of the groves of academe and into the halls of Congress, where he hoped to have some effect. His testimony before a subcommittee on communications in 1981 is as relevant today as it was then. Gerbner said the deeper problem with violence-laden television is that "fearful people are more dependent, more easily manipulated and controlled, more susceptible to deceptively simple, strong, tough measures and hard-line postures.... They may accept and even welcome repression if it promises to relieve their insecurities."

CRIME AND FEAR-MONGERING

Even a casual news consumer will not have missed the flood of stories about scary criminals, unsafe streets, and what some media watch groups term simply "mayhem." Local news usually garners the worst of these criticisms, but the stunning increase in such visceral fare on the flagship network news programs is a measure of the transformations of news in the corporate age. Long-time journalism educator W. Lance Bennett notes that during the 1990s there was a precipitous rise in the number of crime stories that aired annually on the three network evening news programs on NBC, CBS, and ABC. From 1990 to 1998, the number of crime stories rose from 542 to 1392. The increased popularity of news about violent crime occurred at a time when the actual levels of most violent crimes in American society had dropped significantly. This disjuncture between the news reality and the social reality of crime is also reflected in the reporting of homicides. Writing in the *Washington Post*, Richard Morin noted that between 1993 and 1996, the number of murder stories increased by 700 percent. During this same period, the actual murder rate dropped 20 percent. Robert Entman and others have also demonstrated the disproportionate number of African American criminal perpetrators featured in scary mug shots on late-night local news.

TECHNOLOGY, NEW MEDIA, AND SENSATIONALISM

The greater speeds with which audiences can be measured have increased the tendencies for news outlets in all formats to play to fear, outrage, and the vicarious story. Now that reporters are also racing to get their stories on the Internet, they are seeking as many "hits" as possible, and computer technology allows those hits to be counted and reported instantaneously. Reporters and their owners are finding out immediately which stories, and which aspects of those stories, are getting attention. As much as the professional ethics codes hold that journalists should not pander to lurid curiosity, as the media converge and move toward the Web, such tendencies continue. As visual images augment online content, they also attract browsers with stories that satisfy the curious and expose the private.

IMAGERY AND SOUND

Many critics find a connection between the visual aspects of news reporting and the tendency toward sensationalism. Here too, visual imagery has long been employed as an attention-grabbing device. There has always been an interest in using type and woodprints to highlight print and newspaper stories. When the half-tone process was invented in 1880, photographs were easily inserted into newspapers and it became much easier to arouse the reader's emotions and curiosity. Lurid photos of condemned criminals being executed made the front page.

With the advent of radio broadcasting, announcers read newspaper copy over the air and learned to use their voices with the microphone to enhance the delivery of the news. Reporting during World War II, legendary CBS broadcast journalist Edward R. Murrow pioneered verbal pacing to enhance immediacy. With "This…is London," a phrase he used to open his stories of the bombing of Britain, Murrow was bringing the war home to listeners in the United States; but it was also the beginning of using the technology to elicit emotional responses from the audience, a major aspect of sensationalism.

When television was added to the media mix, the camera would be driven to find ever more evocative images. Because television has the ability not only to tell the news but to show it as well, there was increased pressure for visuals. Talking heads in front of the camera did not take full advantage of the medium, and news producers began to understand that dramatic action kept audiences "glued" to the screen. To get onto the evening news, reporters would have to supply images to help tell the story. The technical progression from television camera to portable camcorders to microwave relays and satellites all encouraged live coverage of news. With the start of CNN news on cable television, the need for colorful graphics and dramatic imagery only increased. As more 24/7 news channels delivered over cable and satellite competed for audiences, visual and audio techniques pioneered unprecedented dramatic packaging.

Nowhere were these audiovisual techniques employed to produce greater drama than with the 2003 invasion of Iraq. Cable and network shows added music, sound techniques, and pulsing special effects awash in red, white, and blue to introduce war coverage of Iraq. After the rush to war and its promotion on mainstream media, the papers of record (the *New York Times* and the *Washington Post*, most proximately) were compelled to apologize for their failure to verify the war's justifications. Many media scholars charged that, steeped in sensationalism, the mainstream media failed to prepare the country for the real consequences of war, such as the chaos and death that followed a conflict little understood, and without significant public commitment. Without engaging in serious debate from numerous sources, including the voices of dissent, and in the absence of information able to provide adequate understanding of war's costs, the public was deprived of its right to participate from an informed perspective on the significant national security decisions made in the aftermath of the 9/11 attacks.

INTERNATIONAL NEWS

Well before the invasion of Iraq, international news coverage on American media had been the topic of criticism, tending in equal parts toward the sensational, or forgotten amidst the proliferating consumer and lifestyle fare. Although the world is more globally connected than ever, most American media companies steadily reduced their coverage of foreign news and closed international news bureaus during the last two decades of the twentieth century. Television networks cut their reporting staff under pressure from corporate owners to reduce operating costs and increase profits, measures that deprived Americans of the ability to follow developments in countries across the globe. The lack of breadth and depth of foreign news has long engendered harsh evaluations, with critics charging that coverage of the world is not sufficiently complex across

WOMAN FALLS THROUGH A GRATE

Consider the stories and headlines that appeared in different newspapers on the same day. The *New York Daily News* (May 18, 2007) headline read "HER GRATE ESCAPE." On the same day another tabloid, the *New York Post*, led with "GRATE! ANOTHER CON ED PLUNGE." But the *New York Times* ran the story, "Senators in Bipartisan Deal on Broad Immigration Bill." The story about the woman's mishap was featured in the Metro section on page 6 in the *Times* with the headline, "Manhattan: Woman Falls Through Sidewalk Grate." What is important to note is that the next day the papers reported that Con Edison was going to check all of their grates. The coverage brought action.

the news spectrum. These critiques are encapsulated in the phrase "coups and earthquakes," which is also the title of one book about international news reporting, and conveys the idea that foreign countries are brought to the attention of the American public only when they experience a disaster or government overthrow. Even then, the coverage is only justified by the drama and sensational images that attract viewers. Such infrequent and sensational reporting fails to allow readers and viewers to understand the economic and political causes of such events, or to be able to evaluate the long-term solutions to those and other global problems. Under these conditions, increasingly complex global issues remain underreported, with news managers often asserting that the public is uninterested in international news. Critics and other news professionals counter that it is up to journalists and editors to make the world comprehensible in a way that interests the public.

BENEFITS OF SENSATIONALISM

The harmful and beneficial aspects of sensationalism continue to be debated. There are different perspectives that point to the positive effects of sensationalism and its ability to attract attention to social problems and its role in shaping values. Some argue that sensationalism encourages the public to engage in the political life of the country. Though scandal coverage can be titillating, it is nevertheless important news when a local politician is caught taking bribes. Indeed, when houses catch fire and cars are involved in traffic accidents on crowded highways, reporting these stories brings people important information.

Some critics also note that "real" or "hard" news is often elite news, catered more to an upper-middle-class audience than to the broad spectrum of the American public as a whole, and that it is also often inordinately concerned with masculine interests. As such, some either defend sensationalism as reflective of a democratization of the media, or at least see it as an outgrowth of the tendency of "hard" news to alienate many viewers.

Some analysts also make the case that sensationalism serves society by codifying social beliefs and values. When we see the sinner get caught, the underdog triumph, and the hero fall, we are clarifying our notions of good and evil, right and wrong, justice and injustice. The President Clinton/Monica Lewinsky story

(1998) of a young intern becoming involved sexually with the U.S. president was one such story. As James Carey argued in *Communication and Culture*, the stories in the media demonstrate the forces at work in our world and serve to help us shape our value system.

CONCLUSION

The tilt toward sensationalism can be very slippery. News that misleads the public prevents it from accurately determining which course of action to take, which bill to support, and which politician deserves to lead. Important news can be trivialized and trivial matters given undue attention. Infotainment can lead to a cynical public, one that no longer trusts the accuracy and intentions of the press. Many argue that the public-interest function of journalism must be remembered and reasserted in the age of increasing sensationalism. As stated in a code of ethics written in 1923, "The right of a newspaper to attract and hold readers is restricted by nothing but considerations of public welfare" (Wright 1996). A more recent code rearticulates the need for journalists to be honest and fair. They are enjoined not to oversimplify or to report facts and information out of context. The media and the public struggle to find a shared set of values and practices able to fulfill the information needs of a democratic, self-governing society. The media are to attract us and inform us; give us what we want and what we need.

See also Anonymous Sources, Leaks, and National Security; Bias and Objectivity; Conglomeration and Media Monopolies; Government Censorship and Freedom of Speech; Hypercommercialism; Media and Citizenship; Media and the Crisis of Values; Media Watch Groups; News Satire; Obscenity and Indecency; Paparazzi and Photographic Ethics; Parachute Journalism; Presidential Stagecraft and Militainment; Public Opinion; Ratings; Representations of Race; Representations of Women; Shock Jocks; Video News Releases; Violence and Media.

Further Reading: Allen, Craig M. *News Is People: The Rise of Local TV News and the Fall of News from New York.* Ames: Iowa State University Press, 2001; Bennett, W. Lance. *News: The Politics of Illusion*, 6th ed. New York: Pearson, 2005; Carey, James. *Communication as Culture: Essays on Media and Society.* New York: Routledge, 1988; Cunningham, Brent. "We Went Berserk." *Columbia Journalism Review* 40, no. 4 (November/December 2001): 118–99; Downie, Leonard, and Robert Kaiser. *The News About the News: American Journalism in Peril.* New York: Alfred A. Knopf, 2002; Emery, Michael, Edwin Emery, and Nancy Roberts. *The Press and America: An Interpretive History of the Mass Media.* Boston: Allyn and Bacon, 1999; Ettema, James S., and Theodore Lewis Glasser. *Custodians of Conscience.* New York: Columbia University Press, 1998; Gans, Herbert J. *Democracy and the News.* New York: Oxford University Press, 2003; Hartley, John. *Popular Reality: Journalism, Modernity, Popular Culture.* London: Arnold, 1996; Iyengard, Shanto, and Jennifer A. McGrady. *Media Politics: A Citizen's Guide.* New York: W. W. Norton, 2006; Krajicek, David J. *Scooped! Media Miss Real Story on Crime while Chasing Sex, Sleaze, and Celebrities.* New York: Columbia University Press, 1998; Kroeger, Brooke. *Nellie Bly: Daredevil, Reporter, Feminist.* New York: Times Books, 1994; Langer, John.

Tabloid Television: Popular Television and the "Other News." New York: Routledge, 1998; McChesney, Robert W. *The Problem of the Media: U.S. Communication Politics in the Twenty-First Century.* New York: Monthly Review Press, 2004; McManus, John H. *Market Driven Journalism: Let the Citizen Beware?* Thousand Oaks, CA: Sage Publications, 2005; Nasaw, David. *The Chief: The Life of William Randolph Hearst.* New York: Houghton Mifflin Company, 2000; Postman, Neil, and Steve Powers. *How to Watch TV News.* New York: Penguin, 1992; Project for Excellence in Journalism. "Understanding News in the Information Age." http://www.journalism.org; Rapping, Elayne. *The Looking Glass World of Nonfiction Television.* Boston: South End Press, 1987; Richard Morin, "An Airwave of Crime: While TV News Coverage of Murder Has Soared—Feeding Public Fears—Crime is Actually Down." *The Washington Post National Weekly Edition,* August 18, 1997, 34; Sloan, Bill. *"I Watched a Wild Hog Eat My Baby!" A Colorful History of Tabloids and Their Cultural Impact.* Amherst, NY: Prometheus Books, 2001; Society of Professional Journalists. "Code of Ethics." http://www.spj.org/ethicscode.asp; Sparks, Colin, ed. *Tabloid Tales: Global Debates over Media Standards.* Lanham, MD: Rowman and Littlefield, 2000; Spence, David R. *The Yellow Journalism: The Press and America's Emergence as a World Power.* Evanston, IL: Northwestern University Press, 2007.

Margot Hardenbergh

SHOCK JOCKS: MAKING MAYHEM OVER THE AIRWAVES

The emotional persuasiveness of person-to-person communication over the radio has been evident since the birth of the medium. Something about a voice emanating out of the very air commands an audience's attention. Many radio personalities have employed that power without any thought to pushing the envelope of acceptable speech, while others have engaged in questioning their limits almost without license. When does public speech possibly pollute the airwaves and has the very medium itself been shocking audiences, in one way or another, throughout its history?

The term "shock jock" has come into vogue as a shorthand designation for a radio personality who uses the power of his or her microphone in order to either rile up or titillate the audience. One can distinguish between two types of shock jocks. First are those with an ideological axe to grind who ridicule if not ravage the views of their opponents. The currently most popular of those figures (Rush Limbaugh, Michael Savage) tend to be conservative in their politics, although those in opposition to their positions have established a beachhead, the Air America network, to counter their preeminence on the dial. The second type of shock jock appeals to listeners through either disregarding or intentionally deflating the rules of publicly permissible speech as propounded by the Federal Communications Commission (FCC). The currently most popular of those figures (Howard Stern; Opie and Anthony) litter their broadcasts with sexual innuendo if not on occasion outright obscenity. The ultimate aim of both camps, admittedly, comes down to ratings and the maximization of their share of the audience, yet in some cases, shock jocks act in a deliberate manner in order to convince the public to adopt their positions and act upon them in such a way as to influence public life.

RADIO AS A SHOCKING MEDIUM

While contemporary shock jocks engage in a form of extreme public speech not heard by past generations over the airwaves, the very medium of radio has possessed a capacity to shock since its very beginning. Admittedly, audiences accepted and accommodated radio as a form of public communication in relatively short order after the first national broadcast by the RCA network in 1921. However, we should recall that each consumer invites the participation of others into their lives by choice. In its essence, radio can be thought of as a kind of desired or designated intrusion, a fact that was authoritatively demonstrated in recent times by the excessive amplification of boom boxes. Once radios became reasonably affordable, around 1927, the technology came to be thought of as a kind of acoustic hearth, though audiences expected those who entertained them to wipe their shoes, so to speak, before they crossed the threshold of their homes.

This desire not to be disturbed or dismayed by what was broadcast over the air particularly applied to announcers and later disc jockeys, the predecessors to and, in some cases, influences upon present-day shock jocks. On-air personalities received considerable leeway to display the full range of their idiosyncrasies, but announcers were expected to be virtually invisible and extinguish any quirks from their personalities. Some compared the phenomenon of their voices to God, as they came invisibly out of the very air, and they were expected, like the deity, to promote and not abuse community standards.

ROCKIN' IS OUR BUSINESS

This trend began to change with the emergence of the disc jockey, a position that while not inaugurated by Martin Block and his show *Make Believe Ballroom* in 1934 is by many associated with him as its originator. He gave a name and defined personality to a figure that heretofore remained anonymous, even if the music he played was the audience-friendly pop tunes of the day. Disc jockeys adopted an even more colorful role with the emergence of rhythm and blues and subsequently rock 'n' roll in the 1940s and 1950s. They broke the moderate mold not only by the type of music they played but also and more importantly through the manner with which they presented it. Individuals like Hunter Hancock of Los Angeles, the black announcers on Memphis's WDIA (Nat Williams and Rufus Thomas), and most famously Alan Freed of Cleveland and later New York injected a more raucous tone to their position. They concocted idiosyncratic vocabularies, solicited the opinions of their teenage listeners, and enthusiastically advocated the music they played. Even now, tapes of their broadcasts retain a vibrancy and audacity that time has not erased.

Many parents and some politicians feared the power these men held over their children and worried that the repertoire they featured threatened the very fabric of society. Some less open-minded citizens even called attention to and chastised the disc jockeys for playing music that they felt encouraged racial integration. When government investigations called attention to the fact that many of these men accepted payments for records they played, known at the time as "payola," hearings were held in Washington and some careers ended, Freed's most notably. The furor that followed toned down the audacity of the disc jockeys, as less threatening figures, like *American Bandstand*'s Dick Clark, adopted a posture that parents found acceptable. Nonetheless, the transformation of the on-air announcer from a virtual nonentity to an audacious individual with a definite personality was complete.

VOICES IN THE NIGHT

Some individuals saw in radio the opportunity to speak, person to person, through a microphone and conceived of their broadcasts as a sphere of self-expression. None, perhaps, succeeded more in shocking portions of the public with his adoption of the airwaves as a kind of personal podium than Jean Shepherd. It was not that he had a polemical axe to grind, but, instead, Shepherd thought of the medium as a means for transforming the minds of his listeners toward a more imaginative, even anarchic way of thinking. Some think that Shepherd single-handedly invented talk radio, even though his antics had their predecessors, like Los Angeles's Jim Hawthorne, who from the 1940s to the 1960s played records backwards and invited listeners to call in, only to hold his receiver up to the microphone and allow them to address the audience at large. Shepherd started his pioneering broadcasts on New York's WOR in 1955. Much of the time, he engaged in a kind of storytelling about his youth that one hears today in the monologues of Garrison Keillor about Lake Wobegon. (The popular film *A Christmas Story* [1983] adapts Shepherd's work and employs him as its narrator.) He also would sometimes solicit his listeners to engage in group actions that bear a surprising resemblance to the contemporary phenomenon of flash mobs; he would announce a time and place for them to meet and engage in some spirited action, a practice he called "the Milling." Other times, he urged them to throw open their windows and shout slogans to the open air, something like the broadcaster Howard Beale in the film *Network* (1976). Station owners and some listeners found Shepherd disturbing as he not only broke conventions but also refused to bend to preconceived formats. His ultimate aim, he stated, was to combat "creeping meatballism," a poetic phrase for objectionable forms of conformity.

EXPLODING THE PLAYLIST

If Shepherd shocked some by treating his broadcasts as a kind of public conversation, then the advocates of free-form radio in the 1960s triggered equally aggressive responses by expanding, if not exploding, the barriers that existed as to what kind of material, either music or speech, might be broadcast. Most disc jockeys were cobbled by playlists dictated by management and exercised little to no influence over their choices. Even if they did, their shows were routinely defined by particular genres of expression. It was considered unfashionable to mix together disparate styles; rock was kept apart from country, or rhythm and blues from concert music. The airwaves were, in effect, ghettoized, with little intermingling of material. Correspondingly, audiences tended to associate themselves with distinct bodies of sound and self-censored what they did not want to hear.

This straightjacket upon the repertoire presented on radio was removed in large part by the practices advocated by the San Francisco–based disc jockey Tom Donahue. A veteran of a number of markets, Donahue quit KYA in 1965 when controls over his material reached the breaking point. He turned instead to the newly emerging technology of FM and the opportunity presented by the troubled station KMPX to initiate a new approach. Starting in 1967, Donahue exhorted his fellow disc jockeys to play the kind of music they would for their friends and disregard any form of niche thinking. The result was a kind of sonic smorgasbord that paralleled the mashing together of forms of expression that could be heard in the city's premier music venues at the time: the Fillmore West and the Avalon Ballroom. Donahue encouraged his news staff to adopt a similarly unorthodox stance, and it resulted in what the news director, Scoop Nisker, characterized as "the only news you can dance to." Other stations, particularly on the FM bandwidth, followed Donahue's lead. Much as audiences appreciated the transformation, the radicalization of radio staff dismayed the owners of KMPX. They objected to the spillover of anarchy from the airwaves to the office spaces. This led to a strike, and, eventually, Donahue's migration to KSAN. Freeform radio itself eventually fell prey to the segmentation that affected American society as a whole, when the antiwar movement and the counterculture of the 1960s collided with the self-involvement of the following decade. Many if not most radio stations returned to a predetermined and circumscribed playlist, yet for many the shock of hearing such a wide array of sounds remains one of the high points of the radio medium.

SEVEN DIRTY WORDS

Donahue's expansion of the forms of expression included on radio itself drew upon certain programming practices of the noncommercial network known as the Pacifica Foundation. A group of stations in New York, Los Angeles, Washington, DC, Berkeley, and Houston, the foundation was founded by Lewis Hill in 1949. The inaugural signal, KPFA in Berkeley, initiated the organization's commitment to spurning advertising as well as government or corporate support, and to permitting free speech over its airwaves. Over the years, the organization has assimilated any number of points of view and styles of presentation, some of which resemble the first-person mode of Jean Shepherd (Bob Fass's "Radio Unnameable," heard on New York's WBAI) while others promote specific segments of the political or social spectrum, though customarily from a left-of-center perspective. Many listeners, should they chance upon a Pacifica station by accident, would be shocked and find the range of voices a virtual cacophony, the adoption of off-center ideologies strident in the extreme. Faithful consumers, however, regard Pacifica as the lone exception to the medium's virtual expulsion of radical perspectives and acceptance if not promotion of the almighty dollar.

The most shocking element of Pacifica's history and a groundbreaking influence upon what kind of speech could be aired occurred when WBAI broadcast an infamous track, "Seven Words You Can Never Say on Television," from comedian George Carlin's 1972 *Class Clown*. (A routine featured on Carlin's subsequent album, *Occupation: Foole* [1973], covered much of the same material.) This list of commonly used expletives was perhaps not officially prohibited from radio, yet a complaint to the FCC was made by a father who heard the track with his son. The FCC did not reprimand WBAI but put the station on notice that "in the event subsequent complaints were received, the Commission will then decide whether it should utilize any of the available sanctions it has been granted by Congress." Pacifica appealed the notice, which was overturned by the Court of Appeals. The FCC brought the matter to the Supreme Court, which came down in favor of the FCC in 1978. This decision codified indecency regulation in American broadcasting. Even though subsequent rulings amended its dictates, such as the provision that some questionable speech is permissible

SHOCK-JOCK POLITICS

Depending upon one's perspective, whether or not any individual amounts to a shock jock depends upon where one stands in the political spectrum. For those on the right, Rush Limbaugh speaks truth to power; for those on the left, Al Franken holds those who wield power inappropriately to the fire of necessary criticism. Nonetheless, sometimes individuals are hired and promoted to the public as fair and polite when even a cursory investigation of their public activities reveals that they are partisan in the extreme.

Take the hiring by CNN Headline News in January 2006 of Glenn Beck to host a one-hour prime-time talk show. The president of the network, Ken Jautz, describes Beck as follows: "Glenn's style is self-deprecating, cordial; he says he'd like to be able to disagree with guests and part as friends. It's conversational, not confrontational."

However, when one consults Beck's comments on the air prior to his hiring, they do not come across as either civil or conversational. They seem little more than one-sided invective. For example, he apparently so loathes the antiwar politician Dennis Kucinich that he stated in 2003, "Every night I get down on my knees and pray that Dennis Kucinich will burst into flames." The next year, he crossed the line even more emphatically when he characterized Michael Berg, the father whose son was beheaded in Iraq, as "despicable" and a "scumbag" because he deigned to criticize President George W. Bush.

Perhaps the most indefensible, if not alarmingly over-the-top, comment from Beck came in his attack on the filmmaker Michael Moore. In 2005, he mused on the air about killing him: "I'm thinking about killing Michael Moore, and I'm wondering if I could kill him myself, or if I would need to hire someone to do it. No, I think I could. I think he could be looking me in the eye, you know, and I could just be choking the life out—is this wrong?"

It remains a quandary what is more disturbing: that CNN would hire and defend a man who makes these kinds of statements or whether he was being anything other than disingenuous when he inquired of his audience if his sentiments were over the top?

if children are not part of the audience, the decision holds to this day. There remains a window of opportunity for shocking language between the hours of 10 P.M. and 6 A.M., but, otherwise, none of the seven dirty words should pass the lips of anyone heard over the air during the course of the rest of the day.

CAN THEY SAY THAT?

The jumping-off point for the present-day profusion of shock jocks is hard to isolate. Nonetheless, it remains clear that while the announcer on WBAI took the words out of George Carlin's mouth, these current performers do not achieve any of their audacity secondhand. It is also important to stress how virtually all of them emerged from more mainstream broadcasting as disc jockeys as well as how much they acknowledge their debt to and the influence of on-air personalities from the past, like Jean Shepherd. Some may as well have watched, or even been fans of, two short-lived television figures who virtually broke through the third wall of the screen, so vehement were their opinions: Joe Pyne and Alan Burke. Pyne broadcast a syndicated show from Los Angeles from 1965 until his untimely death from cancer in 1970; Burke appeared in New York City from 1966 to 1968 and turned to Miami-based radio during the 1970s and 1980s. It may seem more than a bit of a leap from the "Shut up, creep!" of Pyne and Burke to the outright obscenity of the current shock jocks, but a lineage between the two certifiably exists.

Other legal and institutional factors contributed to the emergence of the shock jocks. During the course of the Reagan administration, the FCC began to lean less heavily on the regulatory throttle, in particular so far as station ownership was concerned. More and more entities were brought up by broadcasting conglomerates, such as Clear Channel, and owners sought formats that could appeal across broad geographical and ideological segments of the population. Sexual innuendo, frat-boy shenanigans, and spirited diatribes against one's opponents fit the bill. Also, the regulations regarding the need for all sides of an issue to be publicly aired became trimmed, so that the aggressive defense of polemical positions did not require any counterpointed alternative. The adoption of the airwaves as a personal soapbox therefore acquired the sanction both of the law and the corporate bottom line.

Don Imus unleashed his loose cannon on WNBC in New York City in 1971; Howard Stern joined him there in 1982; Rush Limbaugh began his career in 1984 in Sacramento, California; Michael Savage unleashed his vitriol fist over San Francisco's KGO in 1994. While all four of them commonly stretch the boundaries of taste and legally protected speech, each operates under his own agenda. Stern, the "King of All Media," aims to goose the adolescent mentality of listeners any way he can; Imus oscillates between the outrageous and the ideological, maintaining a need both to crack a crude joke and tweak the sensibilities of those he considers unwise or effete; Limbaugh engages his loyal listeners as a virtual cheerleader for their common conservative social and political philosophy; and Savage savages that which he dislikes with an acid tongue and the utter conviction of a true believer. All four men have also successfully engaged in media other than radio, publishing books and appearing in films or on recordings. Each maintains a loyal and considerable following as well as receives some of the highest salaries in broadcasting.

None of them continue, however, without opposition or outcry. The phenomenon of the shock jock certainly has been a mainstay of columnists and op-ed writers for some time, and many individuals need only the slightest provocation to bang the drum about these men's latest foolhardiness or faux pas. Most notably, the comedian Al Franklin published a best seller, *Rush Limbaugh Is a Big Fat Idiot*, in 1996 and subsequently achieved his own on-air slot with Air America as a proponent of the liberal opposition. At the same time, sanctions of a more serious nature have been threatened against shock jocks. Stern in particular tussled repeatedly with the FCC, and some feel that part of the reason he signed up with the satellite system Sirius radio in 2006 was in order to circumvent the restrictions applied to terrestrial broadcasting. For the most part, these broadcasters continue in their established modes of calculated offense, engaging their fans as broadcasting's bad boys and shocking their detractors as near-criminal abusers of the public airwaves.

CRASH AND BURN

The phenomenon of shock jocks in general and Don Imus in particular occupied a brief but heated news cycle in April 2007. For years, Imus committed and subsequently apologized for a number of definitely offensive and debatably funny comments that amounted to little more than sophomoric exercises in sexism and racism. From referring to the African American journalist Gwen Ifill as a "cleaning lady" to characterizing Arabs as "ragheads" to denigrating the African American sports columnist Bill Rhoden as a "*New York Times* quota hire," Imus has engaged for years in a free-for-all of invective. While one might argue that these comments amount to protected speech in the service of comedy, albeit a fairly sophomoric category of comedy, they nonetheless come across as hurtful, possibly hateful, and certainly mean-spirited.

One of the paradoxes of Imus as a personality, however, remains that this schoolyard potty mouth coexists in a kind of Jekyll-Hyde or symbiotic relationship, depending upon one's perspective, with a thoughtful, well-prepared, and consistently intelligent interviewer. Many individuals who frequent Imus's microphones praise him as one of the most astute and committed commentators on the public airwaves; *New York Times* columnist Frank Rich repeated these remarks at the climax of Imus's latest, and most incendiary, collision with the limits of free speech. For years, the program oscillated back and forth between the cerebral and the coarse, and many listeners, and some participants, chose to ignore the elements of that dialogue that offended or bored them.

This process came to a head on April 4, 2007, when Imus, and his cohort, Bernard McGuirk, dismissed the Rutgers University women's basketball team as "nappy-headed hos." This was Imus's retort to McGuirk's characterization of the predominantly African American squad as "some hard-core hos." Almost immediately, a torrent of anger ensued, and two days later Imus apologized for the dialogue: "It was completely inappropriate and we can understand why people were offended. Our characterization was thoughtless and stupid, and we are sorry." Imus, however, ratcheted up the anger when he appeared on the Reverend Al Sharpton's radio program on April 9 and referred in passing to some of his critics as "you people." Plans were set in place for him to meet with the team and its coach. However, due to the public anger, loss of sponsors, and complaints from other African American employees at NBC, the network fired Imus and ended *Imus in the Morning* immediately. The meeting with the Rutgers squad proceeded, and their coach reported that the team members did not themselves call for Imus's firing.

Aside from the heat and fury of the moment, the question remains whether Imus's firing will trigger more focused attention upon shock jocks, but even more if the possibility of censorship will extend to those of a more right-wing persuasion who engage in invective and rancor on as regular a basis as did Imus.

See also Government Censorship and Freedom of Speech; Hypercommercialism; Media and the Crisis of Values; Media Watch Groups; Obscenity and Indecency; Public Sphere; Ratings; Representations of Race; Representations of Women; Sensationalism, Fear Mongering, and Tabloid Media.

Further Reading: Colford, Paul. *Howard Stern: King of All Media.* New York: St. Martin's Press, 1996; Douglas, Susan. *Listening In: Radio and the American Imagination.* New York: Times Books, 2000; Fisher, Marc. *Something In the Air: Radio, Rock, and the Revolution that Shaped a Generation.* New York: Random House, 2007; Franken, Al. *Rush Limbaugh Is a Big Fat Idiot.* New York: Random House, 1996; Imus, Don. *God's Other Son.* New York: Simon and Schuster, 1999 [1981]; Laser, Matthew. *Uneasy Listening: Pacifica Radio's Civil War.* London: Germinal Productions, Ltd., and Black Apollo Books, 2006; Laser, Matthew. *Pacifica Radio: The Rise of an Alternative Network,* rev. ed. Philadelphia: Temple University Press, 2000; Limbaugh, Rush. *The Way Things Ought to Be.* New York: Pocket Books, 1992; Post, Steve. *Playing in the FM Band.* New York: Viking Press, 1974; Savage, Michael. *The Political Zoo.* Nashville: Nelson Current, 2006; Shepard, Jean. *In God We Trust: All Others Pay Cash.* New York: Doubleday, 1966; Shepard, Jean. *Wanda Hickey's Night of Golden Memories and Other Disasters.* New York: Doubleday, 1976; Stern, Howard. *Private Parts.* New York: Simon and Schuster, 1993; Walker, Jesse. *Rebels on the Air: An Alternative History of Radio in America.* New York: New York University Press, 2001.

David Sanjek

SURVEILLANCE AND PRIVACY

The rise of an information-based economy and the threat of terrorism in the post–Cold War era have created a climate in which individuals find themselves subjected to increasingly comprehensive forms of commercial and state surveillance. Debates over the consequences of an emerging surveillance society have focused on the tradeoff between the perceived benefits of surveillance, including security and convenience, and the potential threat to privacy and individual autonomy. These debates take place amid shifting cultural expectations and norms about privacy reflected in a media culture that increasingly portrays surveillance as a form of entertainment and equates willing submission to monitoring with both celebrity and security.

BACKGROUND

Thanks in part to the capabilities of new information and communication technologies and in part to the development of strategies for political and economic control in an information-dependent world, we are living in an increasingly monitored world. Surveillance has become a uniting theme not just in the worlds of marketing and policing, but also in popular culture and even in interpersonal and family relationships as individuals adopt monitoring practices modeled by authorities. Parents, for example, can install monitoring devices in their children's cars and children can load keystroke-monitoring software on their parents' computers. The forms of anonymity and privacy associated with modernity are likely to continue to erode as we find our financial transactions, our personal information, and even our movements throughout the course of the day subject to increasingly pervasive forms of commercial, state, and peer surveillance. The future envisioned in Steven Spielberg's thriller *Minority Report*, in which retailers customize advertising based on biometric monitoring and the government uses location-tracking devices to police traffic, is neither as far off nor as improbable as it might seem.

In part, the move toward increased surveillance is driven by its supposed benefits, including increased security and convenience. We routinely accept forms of state or police monitoring—airport security checks, closed-circuit video cameras,

---

SEARCH ENGINES AND YOUR PERSONAL INFORMATION

In August of 2006, the Internet service provider AOL publicly released a database of Internet search terms entered by 658,000 AOL subscribers over a period of three months. The company replaced the names of subscribers with numbers in order to protect their anonymity, but in some cases the search terms themselves provided ample data for identification purposes, as demonstrated by the *New York Times*, which tracked down one user based on a series of keywords that provided clues about her location and last name. The release of the search data, which the company later described as a mistake, was originally intended as a form of outreach to the research community designed to foster the development of data-sorting techniques. Although AOL removed the data from its research Web site shortly after its release, the data had already been downloaded several hundred times. The release demonstrated how much information Internet users routinely disclose about themselves, very likely without considering the potential consequences. Earlier in the year, it was revealed that the government had sought search-term records from some of the nation's most popular search engines as part of its attempt to control access to online pornography. The owners of three major search engines including AOL reportedly complied, demonstrating that search engines don't just provide users with information, they gather information about them that can be used by both commercial entities and the state.

---

and so on—in the hopes that these technologies will reduce the threat of crime and help to keep us safe. We are also coming to accept more comprehensive forms of commercial monitoring as we surrender detailed information about our shopping habits and preferences by using loyalty cards, credit cards, or shopping online. Often, but not always, we are provided with the offer of compensation, convenience, or customization in return for providing personal information to marketers.

However, as monitoring practices become more sophisticated, powerful, and pervasive, critics worry that the potential for abuse increases and that the emerging surveillance society threatens to erode forms of personal autonomy and privacy that we have come to associate with democratic freedom. Given the rapid development and decreasing cost of technologies that gather, store, and sort personal information, combined with the increasing demand for such information, it is likely that concerns over the threat to privacy will only increase in the foreseeable future. As a society we will be forced to decide what legal limits we want to impose on the development and deployment of surveillance technologies, since neither state agencies nor commercial entities seem likely to do so on their own.

SURVEILLANCE

Any discussion of the apparent conflict between surveillance and privacy should start with the disclaimer that the concept of privacy is a culturally and historically variable one, and that of surveillance an ambivalent one. Typically the conflict is framed as one in which surveillance plays the role of villain and privacy that of victim. But surveillance has numerous beneficial uses in contemporary society, and we depend upon forms of state and commercial monitoring for security as well as efficiency and convenience (Lyon 2001). The government's collection of census data, for example, helps shape the allocation of political representatives in the United States as well as the distribution of government benefits. The operation of a democratic society is predicated on the ability of elected representatives to monitor the wants and needs of their constituents, and the complex financial systems upon which we depend rely on strategies for identification and verification to prevent fraud and facilitate commerce. Finally, we depend on government oversight to ensure that both individuals and private corporations follow the law.

STATE SURVEILLANCE

Its practical uses notwithstanding, the notion of surveillance tends to retain sinister overtones, not least because it implies unequal relations of power. Engaging in the practice of surveillance means more than just gathering information; it means exerting some form of control over those who are subjected to it. This fact is most obvious in the case of surveillance by the state, which can bring its policing and military power to bear on those whom it monitors. When state surveillance power is not held publicly accountable, it can be abused by those who exercise it, as, for example, in the case of attempts by the FBI to use information about the private lives of Martin Luther King, Jr. and John Lennon for political manipulation and blackmail. But even when surveillance power is not deliberately abused, as long as it is backed up by the threat of force, it serves as a form of social control, fostering conformity with the rules set by those who exercise it (Foucault 1977).

COMMERCIAL SURVEILLANCE

Although private companies do not have armies to impose their will on the populace, their ability to use information about consumers to make decisions about whether to provide them with access to goods and services might still be considered a form of power. Marketers gather information about consumers to determine ways to target them more effectively, and in so doing may help reinforce economic and informational barriers experienced by underprivileged or minority populations (Gandy 2001). In the future, as data gathering becomes more invasive and marketing more sophisticated, we may have to worry about advertisers finding ways to target us at moments when we are most vulnerable, impressionable, or insecure. The ability, for example, to determine when consumers are most likely to make an impulse purchase based on data about their past behavior or even their vital signs might be considered a form of surveillance-based power.

At the same time, surveillance-based entertainment has proven to be an effective way for media outlets to produce inexpensive content. The reality TV genre not only markets voyeurism as a form of entertainment, it puts a game-show face on the post–Cold War specter of Big Brother, portraying willing submission to monitoring as a form of self-expression, therapy, and democratization of celebrity culture. Surveillance, such shows imply, can be good fun and good for us.

PRIVACY

Many of the concerns over the use and abuse of surveillance center upon the threat it may pose to privacy, the right to which, although not written into the U.S. Constitution, is generally considered to be a core attribute of a liberal democratic society. Privacy scholar Jeffrey Rosen, among others, has argued that privacy plays a crucial rule, paradoxically, in providing the distance necessary to maintain personal, political, and professional relationships. Not only are there spheres of our private lives over which we wish to maintain control, but our acceptance of the social roles of others relies on particular aspects of their lives remaining private. Our ability to interact with some individuals as employers, others as family members, and still others as teachers or students depends on the ability of all concerned to selectively disclose information about ourselves— to retain some sense of control over which aspects of our lives are available to whom. Consequently, the threat posed by surveillance is not simply the prospect of abuse—that state or commercial agencies might use information gathered about individuals for illegitimate purposes—but of a loss of autonomy.

The privileging of the private realm as a locus of freedom and autonomy is a historically distinct development that corresponds to the rise of the middle class in modernity. Hannah Arendt points out that in the Athenian polis, the realm of privacy was equated with unfreedom—a realm relegated to the satisfaction of the most basic of human needs and functions (food, shelter, reproduction). In the modern era, it becomes—at least for bourgeois men—a site of refuge from the demands of public and professional life. For women, however, the private realm tended to remain a site of domestic labor and dependence. The feminist rallying cry that the "private is political" highlighted the way in which the construction of the private sphere served as cover for the exploitation and disempowerment of women.

PRIVACY PROTECTION

In part as a response to past abuses of state surveillance power, and in part as an expansion of constitutionally guaranteed protections against illegal searches and seizures of citizens' property, the legislature has placed limits on the ability of intelligence agencies to monitor the populace. However, these limits have been challenged by government agencies in their pursuit of national security during the post-9/11 era.

Shortly after the attacks on the World Trade Center and the Pentagon, the U.S. Department of Defense created the short-lived "Information Awareness Office" to coordinate intelligence efforts in fighting terrorism. One of the goals of the office was to create a "database of databases" that would aggregate information about citizens contained in both public and private databases as a means of identifying suspicious behavior. Because of concerns over such programs, the office was shut down in 2003. However, the government continues to enlist the aid of private companies to assemble and scour electronic databases of information about U.S. citizens and residents in the name of national security (O'Harrow, Jr. 2005). Critics of such efforts point to the lack of government accountability associated with covert surveillance. Supporters invoke the notion of a trade-off between privacy and security and argue that in the post-9/11 era citizens need to surrender their expectations of privacy in the name of safety. But the history of government agencies using surveillance against law-abiding citizens was repeated in the post-9/11 era, when police and law enforcement officers infiltrated peace groups and others opposed to government policy and the Iraq war.

SURVEILLANCE TECHNOLOGIES

The advent of digital technologies and of networked, interactive communication devices is helping to make surveillance cheaper, easier to conduct, and more powerful. Recent developments on the cutting edge of surveillance strategies include biometric detection and identification technologies, including "smart" cameras designed to "recognize" individuals based on traits including their facial features, retinas, and even the way they walk.

The rapid development of digital information-gathering and storage devices has facilitated the creation of searchable electronic databases. Digitization is making it easier to transfer, copy, compare, and combine personal information stored in both public and private databases. State and commercial entities can use search algorithms to sort through such data and identify both potential consumers and potential suspects—a process commonly referred to as data mining. When millions of records can be stored on portable hard drives, it also becomes easier to steal, copy, or circulate this information.

As we go online to shop, to stay in touch, and to work, we generate an ever more comprehensive portrait of searchable electronic data about ourselves. Search engines collect information about the keywords we use to surf the internet, browsers gather data about the sites we visit online, ATM machines keep track of where we withdraw money, and cell phone companies can monitor our movements throughout the course of the day. We are rapidly moving toward what Bill Gates has described as a "fully documented life"—one in which all of our movements and transactions are redoubled by information about them that can be digitally stored and searched.

BLURRING THE BOUNDARIES

In the United States, there has been a tendency on the part of the populace to distinguish between state and commercial surveillance and to be more concerned about the former. In the post-9/11 era, however, the distinction between these two forms of surveillance is becoming increasingly blurred, as government officials seek access to commercial databases to identify potential security threats. Database companies are building lucrative new markets in government security contracts, many of which are classified—sometimes, ironically, in the name of privacy protection (O'Harrow, Jr. 2005).

GOVERNMENT SURVEILLANCE AND NATIONAL SECURITY

One of the ongoing debates in the government's declared war on terrorism is likely to be just how much surveillance power it should be granted in the name of national security. In December 2005, the *New York Times* revealed that President George W. Bush had authorized a covert National Security Agency program to monitor international telephone conversations of U.S. residents suspected of links to potential terrorist threats. The program was controversial because it sidestepped laws requiring the government to obtain search warrants through a special court designated for this purpose by the Foreign Intelligence Surveillance Act. The program was deemed illegal by a U.S. district judge in 2006, but the decision was appealed by the government. Republican legislators responded to the controversy by seeking to pass legislation that would officially sanction the wiretapping program. The legal back-and-forth is part of an ongoing struggle between a government seeking surveillance power in the name of national security and a populace wary of unaccountable state monitoring.

PRIVACY PROTECTION

Although there is no right to privacy as such in the U.S. Constitution, a patchwork of privacy protection has been pieced together, largely in response to perceived threats as they emerged. The Constitution protects citizens against "unreasonable search and seizure" and requires state authorities to demonstrate probable cause for such searches. However, it has little to say about the threat of commercial surveillance or invasive news coverage—something that was addressed by the attempt to formulate a common-law right to privacy by Samuel Warren and Louis Brandeis in 1890. The Privacy Act of 1974, passed in response to revelations about abuses of government surveillance activity, placed restrictions on the ability of the government to gather information about private citizens and required a measure of government accountability, as did the subsequent Foreign Intelligence Surveillance Act of 1978.

With respect to commercial surveillance, there have been occasional proposals for an e-commerce privacy act that would regulate the use of information gathered online. Objections regarding the cost of such regulations have sidelined these proposals, with the result that, with the exception of certain information, including financial and medical records, online privacy policies are largely the result of industry self-regulation. As such, they remain subject to change and only minimally enforced (Solove 2004). At the same time, private companies have demonstrated that their financial interests may well trump privacy concerns, as demonstrated by the admission by Internet giant Yahoo! Inc. that it had turned over data to the Chinese government that was used to convict a Chinese journalist of leaking state secrets.

FUTURE PROSPECTS

There is little doubt that both state and commercial imperatives will continue to encroach on personal privacy, and it seems likely that a time will come when legislators will be forced to further clarify the limits of both types of surveillance. Until then, some people are relying on technological solutions such as Internet browsers that anonymize personal information and encryption technology that protects e-mail and telephone communication. Public-interest groups such as the Center for Digital Democracy and the Electronic Privacy Information Center attempt to counter public habituation to the prospect of an increasingly monitored society by providing the resources and rationale for policies that preserve citizens' control over their personal information. At stake is the preservation of a core value of democratic society—one whose protection may well have to be bolstered by a multifaceted critique of surveillance not just as an unwanted intrusion but as a form of coercive control that can be used for purposes of social sorting and economic exploitation (Gandy 2001).

See also Advertising and Persuasion; Anonymous Sources, Leaks, and National Security; Blogosphere; Communication Rights in a Global Context; Google Book Search; Government Censorship and Freedom of Speech; Media Reform;

Net Neutrality; Piracy and Intellectual Property; Public Opinion; Ratings; Reality Television.

Further Reading: Arendt, Hannah. *The Human Condition*. Chicago: University of Chicago Press, 1958; Calvert, Clay. *Voyeur Nation: Media, Privacy, and Peering in Modern Culture*. Boulder, CO: Westview Press, 2000; Foucault, Michel. *Discipline and Punish: The Birth of the Prison*, trans. Alan Sheridan. New York: Vintage, 1977; Gandy, Oscar. "Dividing Practices: Segmentation and Targeting in the Emerging Public Sphere." In *Mediated Politics: Communication in the Future of Democracy*, ed. W. Lance Bennett and Robert M. Entman, 141–59. New York: Cambridge University Press, 2001; Gandy, Oscar. *The Panoptic Sort: A Political Economy of Personal Information*. Boulder, CO: Westview Press, 1993; Gates, Bill. *The Road Ahead*. New York: Penguin, 1995; Kant, Immanuel. "An Answer to the Question: 'What Is Enlightenment?'" In *Political Writings*, ed. Hans Reiss, 54–60. New York: Cambridge University Press, 1991; Lyon, David. *The Electronic Eye: The Rise of Surveillance Society*. Minneapolis: University of Minnesota Press, 1994; Lyon, David. *Surveillance Society*. Milton Keynes: Open University Press, 2001; O'Harrow, Robert, Jr. *No Place to Hide*. New York: Free Press, 2005; Parenti, Christian. *The Soft Cage: Surveillance in America from Slavery to the War on Terror*. New York: Basic Books, 2004; Risen, James, and Eric Lichtblau. "Bush Let U.S. Spy on Callers without Courts." *The New York Times*, December 16, 2005, 1; Rosen, Jeffrey. *The Unwanted Gaze: The Destruction of Privacy in America*. New York: Vintage, 2000; Solove, Daniel. *The Digital Person: Technology and Privacy in the Information Age*. New York: New York University Press, 2004; Warren, Samuel, and Louis Brandeis. "The Right to Privacy." *Harvard Law Review* 4, no. 1 (1890): 193–220; Whittaker, Reg. *The End of Privacy*. New York: The New Press, 1999.

Mark Andrejevic

TELEVISION IN SCHOOLS

Using television for classroom teaching has been embraced and challenged in many forums that have been linked to the regulation of networks and initiatives to address teacher shortages. It has generated controversial pedagogical programs and business propositions dating back to the initial introduction of the medium. While the medium introduced significant potential for bringing expanded and up-to-date content to students, at issue are the place and value of mass or popular culture in education; the influence of commercial entities on school curricula; the incursion of advertising into the school day; and more broadly, the enveloping of young people's lives in consumer culture.

The educational potential of television has inspired much discussion and debate from the earliest introduction of the medium. Like many innovations in communication technology, television presented new ways of conceiving education and curriculum. Schools have historically been seen as in need of reform, and the widespread availability of television coincided with particular stresses in the United States in relation to classroom overcrowding, teacher shortages, and the need for educational materials that address current or timely content. In light of these "crises," television provided certain advantages over earlier media such as books. It was argued that television technology could allow a small cadre of expert teachers in various subjects to reach a multitude of students in classrooms with teachers who wouldn't need to be trained in as many subject areas. Unlike textbooks, content could be broadcast live or recorded shortly before each lesson. This would allow material to be updated and revised on a continual basis. Television was also seen as a way of allowing students access to distant places that were becoming more and more relevant to their lives in an era of rapid globalization and U.S. involvement in regions throughout the world.

The discussion of these educational potentials has always been met with strong reactions and concerns. It is important to note that there are distinct controversies surrounding the use of television technology per se and commercially produced television. There are those who have challenged the use of television out of a concern for the loss of live interaction between students and teachers. They point out the one-way nature of the viewing/listening experience shaped by the technology. From a more traditionalist perspective, many educators, parents, and advocacy organizations have opposed TV in schools, arguing that it potentially displaces teaching of core skills (reading, writing, arithmetic) and the canon of classic literature. In this regard, the overall negative influence of film and television inside and outside of school has often been construed as contributing to a decline in literacy and high culture. Some progressive educators and organizations see the importance of addressing television content in school curriculum as part of developing media literacy, some arguing for the need to provide children tools to critically analyze media, but also suggesting the benefits of tapping students' interests and expertise in mass culture as a means of fostering higher levels of engagement. From both ends of the political spectrum there has been significant opposition to commercial television or advertising to captive student audiences.

HISTORICAL OVERVIEW

School-based use of television can be understood as part of a series of audiovisual technologies that were introduced to the educational system since the later half of the nineteenth century. The founding of major U.S. museums in this period was closely linked to belief in visual experience as a means of education that was particularly powerful and accessible. This was particularly significant in this period of increasing linguistic and cultural diversity due to waves of European and Asian immigration. We can speak of a visual, and later, audiovisual education movement that spawned the adoption of heavily illustrated dictionaries and textbooks by schools. U.S. schools in the first few decades of the twentieth century purchased stereoscopic viewers and millions of stereographic image sets. This was followed by a broad embrace of 35-mm slide sets, and later film strips accompanied by audio cassettes. Film was used in schools beginning in the 1910s, but due to expense was limited to larger and wealthier schools. Smaller-format 16-mm film, which was introduced in 1924 for home or amateur filmmaking, began to be used for newsreels, and allowed for affordable, greatly expanded production and projection of educational films beginning in the 1930s. Shortly after its introduction, radio began to be used for education in the late 1910s, and gained extensive use in schools by the 1930s. When television became widely available in the late 1940s, it was practically predetermined that its educational potential would be exploited, despite significant continued opposition to audiovisual media in schools. Following this continuum, since the mid-1990s computers and networked communication have become embraced by schools, displacing some of the focus on and debate around classroom uses of television, but not all.

The 1950s saw the first major wave of implementation of television usage in schools, paralleled by the licensing of the first educational channels at the beginning of the decade. Some of these channels were directed at in-school audiences and others were meant to provide alternatives to the mainly entertainment-related commercial stations. In 1952, against the opposition of commercial broadcasters, the Federal Communications Commission (FCC) set aside a portion of the airwave bandwidth for educational use. A major force that underwrote lobbying for this move was the Ford Foundation, which had emerged as the leading proponent of educational television (ETV) in the United States. The foundation promoted ETV through two of its largest programs: the Fund for Adult Education (FAE), which was directed at public education outside of schools, and the Fund for the Advancement of Education (TFAE), which was focused on school and college education. While the FAE became the leading force behind educational education, the TFAE funded an array of influential experimental programs designed to be models for demonstrating the efficacy of teaching by television. These programs encompassed large schools and some entire districts and continued into the mid-1960s.

Notable examples were carried out in New York City's Chelsea school district, and Hagerstown, a suburb of Washington, DC. In 1957, the fund published a report by Alexander Stoddard titled *Schools for Tomorrow*, which stressed the teaching of very large classes to alleviate classroom crowding and limit numbers of teaching positions needed. He also argued that broadcast lessons would bring a wider range of subject matter and a higher caliber of teaching to remote and rural schools. The report was presented to superintendents of districts throughout the country in order to solicit their cooperation in pilot teaching projects as part of the Ford Foundation's National Program. Based on this effort, the foundation funded modestly sized experiments with the introduction of ETV in over 800 hundred primary and secondary schools in municipalities throughout the United States, along with several more comprehensive studies. Approximately 200,000 students were involved in these projects. Along the lines suggested in *Schools for Tomorrow*, almost all of these projects employed television to reach exceptionally large classes: up to 175 in elementary classes, and from 200–500 in junior and senior high schools. And the foundation also supported a much-publicized large-scale ETV experiment in American Samoa, an island under American control in the South Pacific that was carried out by its affiliate, the National Association of Educational Broadcasters, using closed circuit television (see "Early Experiments in ETV" sidebar).

It is worth noting that the promotion of television in schools was linked to an important shift that was taking place with regard to the role of the federal government in U.S. educational policy. From the nation's founding until the 1950s, educational policy had been the largely unchallenged domain of state governments. Attempts to shift some control over education to the federal government were framed by what was perceived as a crisis in education that began in the years immediately following the Second World War. The goal of remaining

EARLY EXPERIMENTS IN ETV

ETV was one of numerous responses to the highly publicized crisis in U.S. public schools during the 1950s and 1960s—a crisis that included a shortage of qualified teachers, overcrowding of schools, concerns about the quality of education (specifically as means of supplying the nation's scientific brainpower), and debates about busing in response to the ruling in *Brown v. Board of Education* in 1954. One of the largest initiatives was the Samoan Educational Television Project, which aimed to replace all traditional education in American Samoa with televised broadcast lessons. Although there were a number of large test projects in U.S. cities, control of education policy is in the hands of individual states, so the federal government created this program in a U.S. protectorate (much like a colony), where it could fully control a system-wide experiment.

competitive, if not dominant, in an increasingly global culture was put forth in arguments for shifting power over education from the local and state governments to the federal level. With the rapid development of communications technologies, the struggle for a technological edge in the Cold War became a strong justification for centralization of education and at the same time an argument for employing these very technologies in teaching.

CRITICAL VIEWING AND PRODUCTION-ORIENTED CURRICULA

Much of the initial push to use television in schools involved implementation of programs with specifically educational content designed to replicate, supplement, or supplant school curricula, and was often motivated by a vision of automation, centralization, and efficiency. By the beginning of the 1960s, educational uses of audiovisual media came to be framed against what Newton Minow, then chairman of the FCC, described as "a vast wasteland." He was speaking to what educators and advocates of learning and much of the public had come to see as television's threat to literacy.

Perhaps ironically, in the decades that followed, many educators responded by bringing television, even commercial television, into the classroom. The response most openly embraced within official curricula during the years leading up to the early 1970s was the so-called inoculation or moral approach, described by James Halloron and Marsha Jones as an attempt to address the harmful or dangerous qualities of mass media. This approach advocated teaching students about television so that they could resist its negative influence. By the mid-1970s, a growing number of educators began to argue for the need for curricula that helped to promote critical viewing practices, a tendency that had strong proponents in England and Australia. The key difference being that by this point there was a broader understanding that, for better or worse, mass media serves an important role, and that rather than trying to protect youth from it, educators would do better to develop skills for analyzing and interpreting what they view. This embrace of promoting media literacy has spawned a variety of approaches

EDISON PREDICTS THE FUTURE OF EDUCATION

"Books will soon be obsolete in the schools. Scholars will soon be instructed through the eye. It is possible to teach every branch of human knowledge with the motion picture. Our school system will be completely changed in ten years."

Thomas Edison in the *New York Dramatic Mirror*, July 9, 1913 (Saettler 1990)

with differently inflected goals and justifications. Advocates of critical pedagogy including Henry Giroux, Peter L. Mclaren, and others have suggested the importance of valuing and respecting students' knowledge and expertise in the realm of mass media culture in order for education to be authentically engaging with their lived experience. Steven Goodman, founding director of the Educational Video Center in New York City, is one of a number of pioneers of approaches that aim to facilitate critical viewing practices while engaging students in video or television production. The work of these in-school and after-school programs is rooted in the belief that students can learn a great deal about the biases and gaps in mass media representations by engaging with representational practices within their own local communities.

CHANNEL ONE: COMMERCIAL EDUCATIONAL TELEVISION AND THE PRIVATIZATION OF SCHOOLS

By far, the largest incursion of television into U.S. schools has taken place under the auspices of the business initiative Channel One, which provides schools with loans of television, video, and satellite technology in return for a commitment to have their students watch its daily 12-minute news program replete with product placement and two minutes of advertising. Founded in 1989 by Whittle Communications, and currently owned by Primedia, Channel One is watched by 7 million middle school and high school students throughout the country. This amounts to nearly 30 percent of U.S. teenagers. Participating schools agree to have 80 percent of their students watch 90 percent of daily programs.

It is not surprising that any single entity with such influence on education would draw a great deal of concern and scrutiny from parents, educators, government officials, and anyone concerned with teens and young adults. And indeed Channel One has. Critics across the political spectrum have challenged the ethics of requiring students to watch commercial advertising, essentially questioning the right to sell students' time and attention to advertisers within a compulsory education system. This has aligned conservative groups and leaders (including the Family Research Council; Focus on the Family; American Family Association and Phyllis Schlafly; and the Southern Baptist Convention) with consumer advocates (such as Ralph Nader) and liberal and progressive groups (including the National Education Association, the American Federation of

Teachers, the Media Education Foundation, and the American Academy of Pediatrics). Resistance has also been expressed at the level of school governance: both New York and California school systems banned Channel One from their public schools, though California later lifted its ban.

The criticisms of Channel One extend beyond the advertising embedded in their programs. Many have argued that the programs do not represent serious educational content and that less than half of the material is actually news-related. And some feel strongly that Channel One represents a model of education that is authoritarian, taking from educators the responsibility for making decisions about how and what to teach their students. Medical and parent groups have objected to the lifestyle and dietary models promoted by the program.

In light of this criticism and organized opposition, it is striking that Channel One has been able to gain such broad penetration within U.S. schools. It is worth noting that the rise of Channel One was coincident with several other tendencies that have placed pressure on schools, perhaps influencing them to negotiate agreements with private businesses that would have seemed unlikely in the past. These include the advocacy of school choice and voucher systems that allow families to opt out of the public system and shift tax dollars to private schools; the increasing popularity of home schooling; and the proliferation of commercially run for-profit charter schools.

CONCLUSION

Debates over television's place in classrooms and schools continues, in large part because television represents so many different things to different people: to some, it offers solutions to educational dilemmas; to others it promises to offer the very future of education; while to others its mode of delivery and its preferred images represent an apotheosis of education. Debates over television in schools are, therefore, effectively debates over what both education and television are, and, importantly, what they should or could be.

See also Advertising and Persuasion; Children and Effects; Digital Divide; Hypercommercialism; Media Literacy; Product Placement; Public Access Television; Public Broadcasting Service; Youth and Media Use.

Further Reading: Aronowitz, Stanley, and Henry Giroux. *Postmodern Education: Politics, Culture, and Social Criticism.* Minneapolis: University of Minnesota Press, 1991; Boddy, William. "The Beginnings of American Television." In *Television: An International History,* ed. Anthony Smith. New York: Oxford University Press, 1995; Buckingham, David. *After the Death of Childhood: Growing Up in the Age of Electronic Media.* Cambridge, MA: Polity, 2000; Buckingham, David, and Julian Sefton-Green. *Cultural Studies Goes to School: Reading and Teaching Popular Media.* London: Taylor and Francis, 1994; Clark, Richard. *Learning From Media: Arguments, Analysis and Evidence.* Charlotte, NC: Information Age Publishing, 2003; Cuban, Larry. *Teachers and Machines: The Classroom Use of Technology Since 1920.* New York: Teachers College Press, 1986; De Vaney, Ann, ed. *Watching Channel One: The Convergence of Students, Technology and Private Business.* Albany: State University of New York Press, 1994; Goldfarb, Brian. *Visual Pedagogy: Media Cultures in and beyond the Classroom.* Durham, NC: Duke University Press, 2001; Goodman,

Steven. *Teaching Youth Media: A Critical Guide to Literacy Video Production and Social Change.* New York: Teachers College Press, 2003; Halloran, James D., and Marsha Jones. "The Inoculation Approach." In *Media Education: An Introduction,* ed. Manuel Alvarado and Oliver Boyd-Barrett. London: British Film Institute, 1992; Lankshear, Colin, and Peter L. Mclaren, eds. *Critical Literacy: Politics, Praxis, and the Postmodern.* Albany: State University of New York Press, 1993; Molnar, Alex. *Giving Kids the Business: The Commercialization of America's Schools.* Boulder, CO: Westview Press, 1996; Saettler, Paul. *The Evolution of American Educational Technology.* Westport, CT: Libraries Unlimited, 1990; Seiter, Ellen. *Sold Separately: Children and Parents in Consumer Culture.* New Brunswick, NJ: Rutgers University Press, 1993.

Brian Goldfarb

TIVO: TIMESHIFTING AMERICA

At the turn of the twenty-first century, television transformed from a self-contained medium controlled by broadcasters into a key part of broader digital technology systems. One major innovation that helped lead this change was the digital video recorder (DVR), best known by the brand name TiVo. How did TiVo transform television, and who ended up better or worse in its wake?

In 1999, two rival companies introduced similar products that would eventually change the way that Americans watch and think about television. Both ReplayTV and TiVo marketed DVRs, devices that shifted control of the television schedule away from networks and into the hands of viewers. At first glance, a DVR seems to be little more than a high-tech videocassette recorder (VCR), allowing viewers to easily record programs onto a compact hard drive instead of bulky tapes. But the functions and possibilities of DVRs proved to be much more of a radical break from conventional television viewing than even the devices' inventors had probably anticipated, challenging long-established norms of television production and reception.

THE BROADCAST TELEVISION MODEL

Throughout the last half of the twentieth century, television was the dominant mass medium in the United States, offering the most popular leisure time activity for most Americans, and trailing only sleeping and working as a dedicated portion of everyday life. Viewers took the basic system of watching television for granted—channels were received over the air or later through cable or satellites, and the programming on each channel was scheduled and controlled by the broadcaster. If you wanted to watch television, you had to watch whatever was airing at that moment on whichever channels you received. Viewers learned when their favorite show was on, and *TV Guide* became the magazine with the highest circulation by helping viewers navigate the television schedule.

The television industry took advantage of their ability to schedule programs by developing clever techniques to attract viewers—running similar shows together in *line-ups*, placing new shows after an established *lead-in*, placing

TIVO FOR KIDS

One of the most interesting facets of a new technology's adoption is how it redefines how a generation engages with a medium. For children growing up in DVR households, television is a very different experience than it was for previous generations. When such children ask, "What shows are on?" they are not referring to the TV schedule—rather they mean, "What is on the TiVo's menu?" The transmission of television via a predetermined schedule is a foreign concept to a DVR child, even though this has always been one of the defining elements of television as a medium. For such children, all television is part of an ever-changing menu of programming to be accessed at their convenience, not a steady stream of broadcasting to be tapped into at someone else's convenience. Scheduling practices that can often define a generation's media memories, like Saturday morning cartoons, are irrelevant to TiVo children, who always have their favorite shows waiting on demand. When DVRs become commonplace, how will the TiVo generation view the media?

a weaker show in a *hammock* between two hits, and *counterprogramming* against another network's hit to appeal to a different audience. Specific time slots were developed to appeal to particular audiences, such as daytime soap operas for stay-at-home women, Saturday morning cartoons for kids, and prime time for the largest mass audience. The most important scheduling technique for networks was the placement of advertisements within a single program, paying for the network's operation by charging sponsors to access the attention of a show's viewers. The entire commercial broadcasting system depended on the ability to attract viewers via a consistent schedule of programming with embedded advertising slots that could be sold to the highest bidder.

PLAYBACK CULTURE

DVRs were not the first technology to threaten this model of broadcasting. The VCR emerged as a popular device for consumers in the late 1970s and early 1980s, offering viewers the ability to both record television broadcasts and play back prerecorded videotapes. While the ability to record broadcasts was a major feature of the VCR, the device's popularity was driven by the video rental market, as consumers used their televisions to watch films on demand. The practice of *timeshifting* television programming using the recording function of VCRs was far less common, popular only with a minority of technologically savvy viewers, dedicated fans, and video collectors. In part, this was due to the notoriously complicated procedures needed to program a VCR to record, leading to widespread jokes about unprogrammed VCR clocks flashing 12:00 due to confused users. With a VCR, timeshifting was a practice that required extra effort, planning, and technological savvy.

While DVRs enable a similar possibility of timeshifting, they offer more than just a sophisticated VCR. DVRs take the signal from cable, satellite, or an antenna and digitally record the content to a hard drive. A TiVo is always recording the signal it receives, buffering 30 minutes of programming to allow viewers to pause live television, rewind live material, or record an entire program even while partway through. With a VCR, you must actively choose to timeshift, going through the often fraught process of programming your machine to record a program, and then later using the VCR to play it back. With a DVR, you are always in the timeshifting mode, as it is actively standing by, ready to timeshift. If timeshifting is an exceptional practice for a VCR, it is the norm with TiVo—our default mode of using a DVR is to reject the schedule-driven framework that traditionally structures the experience of watching television, replacing it with an on-demand viewer-controlled mode of viewing.

Once most DVR users get the hang of its fairly simple user interface, which mimics a standard computer menu system, watching live TV becomes a last resort. While the typical television viewer of the twentieth century used the schedule to shape and determine what and how to watch, TiVo takes the schedule offline, enabling viewers to turn the various options within the television schedule into a menu of potential files to be downloaded into one's own personal collection of programming. This menu-driven mode of viewing is heightened by a DVR's electronic program guide (EPG), an interactive grid of the television schedule providing future television programs, episode titles, and descriptions, all to be recorded at the push of a button, a development that has also helped lead to the declining relevance of *TV Guide*.

LEARNING TO WATCH TV AGAIN

DVRs discourage modes of viewing more typical of conventional television—channel surfing is rare, as the EPG provides a quick assortment of identifiable options if the menu of recorded programs doesn't hold any appealing options. TiVo users need not arrange their own schedules to view a program, as it reschedules any "appointment television" and overrides scheduling strategies like hammocks and lead-ins. With a DVR, television rarely is "just on," as anything deemed worth recording deserves more attention than background viewing. And the feeling that "nothing is on" becomes nearly extinct—a well-maintained DVR always has worthwhile options on tap customized for the viewer's tastes. These ways in which we have traditionally watched television, both technologically and culturally, disappear as the DVR interface becomes the default mode of engaging with television. This becomes particularly significant as many aspects discouraged by TiVo, like indiscriminate audiences, aimless surfing, and background viewing when nothing's on, are facets of television that have been negatively linked to condemn the medium. Critics often characterize watching media like television as an inherently passive "lean-back" practice when compared with more interactive and engaging "lean-forward" media like computers—DVRs make television viewing more like using computers, getting presumably passive viewers to lean forward and engage actively in their own viewing practices.

The rise of the DVR has transformed the ways that the industry operates—even though DVRs are by no means as widespread as other technologies like

VCRs and DVD players, the industry has tried to adapt to how DVRs change the underlying practices of commercial television before the devices are commonplace in most homes. For the industry, the most significant shift in television viewing is that DVR users are much less likely to watch advertisements, using the technology to fast-forward through commercial breaks. Sponsors recognize this threat, and thus are less willing to pay for ad spots that will be actively avoided by technologically savvy viewers. The threat of DVRs has helped lead to a dramatic rise in product placement in programming in the 2000s, making sponsored promotions a key component of the program itself. Additionally, the industry recognizes that without scheduling techniques to guide viewers to their programs, they need to develop strategies to attract audiences to individual programs more than established line-ups.

One of the most significant aspects of DVRs is how they fit in with a broader logic of *technological convergence*. In the digital age, media that have traditionally been distinct are coming together via computers and other digital technology—users can browse, store, and consume their photographs, music collection, and video files on personal computers and portable devices like iPods. Television has had a bumpy role as part of convergence strategies, as early devices like WebTV failed to catch hold with consumers and the bandwidth demands made online video a rarity for years. But through devices like TiVo, video game consoles like Xbox and PlayStation, the rise of digital HDTV sets, and innovative broadband video distribution, televisions are becoming part of a home network of digital devices, rather than stand-alone boxes that only receive broadcast signals. DVRs offer features like TiVoToGo™ that allow users to transfer television programs across home networks to personal computers and mobile devices. This technology has emerged alongside the television industry offering its shows via online distribution through iTunes or the networks' own Web sites. Such developments suggest that not only will the television schedule cease to be the defining structure for accessing programming, but that the television screen itself will serve as only one option for viewing the content we traditionally think of as "television."

It is hard to predict what the future of DVRs will bring. Viewers who have adopted the technology are passionate about the opportunities and control that it offers, with many TiVo owners becoming active promoters of DVRs as the only way they would ever watch television. Certainly, for such TiVo devotees, the ability to control what and when they watch seems central to their new understanding of how television can be experienced and enjoyed. The industry views the rise of DVRs as inevitable, and thus is preparing new strategies to make programming profitable even when viewers control the schedule and can fast-forward through ads. While most insiders predict that DVRs will eventually become as commonplace as the VCR, there will be a transitional stage of a DVR divide where significant numbers of television households will be DVR users while a large number watch via traditional means. How the industry addresses these two different constituencies will vary, probably guided by which group is viewed as the most lucrative audience to sell to by advertisers. However, such technological shifts are difficult to anticipate—certainly few would have predicted in 1999 that an unknown technology firm would create a device that would trigger such a profound transformation of how television had been watched and aired for more than half a century.

See also The DVD; Internet and Its Radical Potential; The iTunes Effect; Net Neutrality; Online Digital Film and Television; Product Placement; Ratings.

Further Reading: Boddy, William. *New Media and Popular Imagination: Launching Radio, Television, and Digital Media in the United States*. New York: Oxford University Press, 2004; Cubitt, Sean. *Timeshift: On Video Culture*. New York: Routledge, 1991; Jenkins, Henry. *Convergence Culture: Where Old and New Media Collide*. New York: New York University Press, 2006; Lotz, Amanda. *The Television Will Be Revolutionized*. New York: New York University Press, 2007; Marshall, P. David. *New Media Cultures*. New York: Arnold, 2004; Mittell, Jason. "TiVoing Childhood." *Flow* 3, no. 12 (2006): http://idg.communication.utexas.edu/flow/?jot=view&id=1472; Spigel, Lynn, and Jan Olsson. *Television after TV: Essays on a Medium in Transition*. Durham, NC: Duke University Press, 2004.

Jason Mittell

TOURISM AND THE SELLING OF CULTURES

As a huge global industry, tourism spans the world, and makes objects of people, places, meanings, and experience. A vast publishing and media apparatus promotes this: visitor's guides, travel literature and programs, holiday brochures, route maps, and itineraries. As pleasure- and treasure-hunt, tourism commodifies culture and turns local lives into service support in several ways. It is true that tourism can be presented as an educational boon, and we have to take seriously the ideology that travel broadens the mind, though surely this has its privileges. As market for the strange, the curio, the souvenir, and the remote, tourism brings all "Chinese Walls" battered and bruised into the guidebooks and snapshot albums of the bargain-hunting hordes, for good and ill. The reduction and destruction of everyday lives that tourism visits on the peoples and places of the "underdeveloped" world are inevitable consequences of global inequality: the wealthy travel for relaxation or self-interest, the rest of the world smoothes the way. This divide at the heart of tourism prevails even as some may make the case for travel as a force for cultural preservation; as an opportunity for exchange; or to see tourism as solidarity and as a kind of charitable aid. On the whole, tourism suffers from a bad press on this what we sometimes call our lonely planet.

Tourist sites and experiences are glossed in promotional literature with a well-known and now instantly recognizable code: sunsets over palm fringed beaches; temples and monuments in jungles or deserts; curious modes of transport—the camel, the elephant, the auto-rickshaw or canoe; smiling cherubic youth; feathered warriors; or remote Masai women in costumed undulating dance. The adventure of tourism in the so-called third world mixes these exotics with pleasure getaways—luxury resorts (swimming pools just meters away from pristine beaches seem clearly excessive), home comforts, and promises of safety, running water or fully-catered adventure treks (with Nepalese Sherpas perhaps to carry any real weight, and political concerns safely tucked away in the nontourist peripheries, beyond the register of mainstream journalism or guided itinerary).

Ever-increasing numbers of people in the developed world seem motivated by a need to escape the routines of salaried employment so as to enjoy sunscreen-smothered leisure time on a remote beach, quaffing tropical drinks with mini-umbrellas, all served by pretty much anonymous Others called Enrico, Joy, or Tran. But it must also be considered redeeming to some degree that tourists might be genuinely and ethically motivated by an interest in the experience of other cultures and in meeting people different from those they usually find in the comfort of their familiar surrounds. Certainly, with global conflict and paranoia at a premium, the importance of intercultural exchange cannot be understated. A growing market exists for "ecotourism" in particular, where travelers (strictly differentiating themselves from the masses of "tourists") follow trails and "off the beaten track" pathways that cater to those who wish to "tread lightly" on apparently fragile foreign soil. There is certainly merit in avoiding those forms of tourist infrastructure that have required wholesale rezoning of residential land into golf courses and the like. If an alternative tourism can thereby skirt the repurposing of all aspects of a given local economy into a touristic service sector, souvenir shopping, and adventure playground (read here the transformation of seafront areas into hotel strips, the lowering of water tables via demand for swimming pools and fantasy garden-scapes) then this must be credited as an advance on mass tourism. But we must also ask if those who wish to tiptoe through remote and pristine lands do not also inevitably bring the tourist hordes in their wake—opening up new curiosities for the expansive hunger of development.

The trouble with much tourism literature has been that it must ignore the politics of commodification, inequality, and exploitation at the exact moment that these matters are the very basis of the possibility of "third-world" tourism. If there were no wealthy tourist elite (or relative elite) looking for leisured rest and/or exotic experience outside of their everyday world; equipped with incomparably larger wallets, travelers cheques, and credit cards beyond the grasp of locals; and supported with a massive infrastructure and the paraphernalia (from deck chairs and ocean liners, climbing equipment and jet skis, even the accoutrements of adventure tourism, etc.) there would be no tourist economy. As a consequence, in a competitive market, the travel magazine version of the world of tourism must present the beach, the pina colada, the "interesting" cultural life of others, as packaged and ready for sale. The educational dimension of culture then becomes a secondary consideration. Inequality is reduced to cultural difference, and may sometimes be presented as something the tourist economy can even alleviate. Some tourists, moreover, see their travels as a form of charity, grandiosely imagining their contribution as consumers to entail a global redistribution of the wealth that allows them to travel in the first place. In Denis O'Rourke's film *The Good Woman of Bangkok*, you can hear sex tourists brag that their custom keeps Thai women from a life of poverty. In the Americas, spring-break festivities in the Caribbean or in South America occlude a more urgent educational agenda. In South East Asian hotels, the arts of Wayang Kulit

THE BANANA PANCAKE TRAIL

From Cape Tribulation in Australia to Marrakech in Morocco, there is the budget-traveler phenomenon of the cozy guest house or traveler hostel in which trusted comforts from home are served up to weary travelers. This can be glossed as the "banana-pancake trail," which serves as a shorthand—an obviously gratuitous reference to the ubiquitous back-packer snack—for the contradictory adventure of experience of "otherness" that third-world travel can be. In search of otherness but in need of the comfortable trappings of home, backpacker discussion in the guest houses and lodges is so often about where travelers are from, what they would like to eat when they get back, how the food gives them "Delhi-belly" or similar, the mosquitoes, the toilets, the rip-off taxis. Quite often, such discussions go on while the traveler is served cola or chai or French fries by a 12-year-old who has worked since dawn, seven days a week, sending money home to the rural periphery that the traveler will rarely see.

---

and Gamelan, not to mention less salubrious traditions, are maintained through nightly performances for businessmen who pay top dollar for entertainments they need not fully understand. Or rather, they pay for the experience of difference, of not understanding otherness. The exotic is its own reward—does it matter that these traditions are reduced in cultural importance on the way? Some would argue against such traditionalism.

THE BENEVOLENCE OF TOURISM AND CHARITY WORK

A guilty secret resides at the heart of third-world tourism. Holidays in other people's misery seem inappropriate and though the beaches are beautiful, the tsunami was a tragedy. The equation can be resolved by charitable donation or by the presence of the tourists themselves. After the Asian tsunami of 2004, re-building of destroyed tourist resorts in India, Thailand, Sri Lanka, and Indonesia was soon followed by calls for the tourists to return, as part of the reconstruction. There is a cultural maintenance aspect here that deserves attention: In circumstances of dire wealth disparity and limited economic means, the tourist economy provides cultural workers with an expressive outlet. Ritual forms morph into entertainments, but are nevertheless preserved—albeit in museumized forms. This is a difficult evaluation to make—as many of the needed tourist dollars are not actually spent in the affected countries when one takes into account the destinations of profits from tourism after airline ticketing, charter and package tour bookings, hotel and food chains (McDonald's and Coca-Cola all over Thailand, for example) and even sale of travel guides and the market in television travel shows. Ultimately, only a very small percentage of the economic return from global tourism reaches local entrepreneurs in each case: the structure of colonialism prevails where the brochures are printed in the United States; the airlines are based in Paris, Denver, or Frankfurt; the booking agencies in London or Tokyo.

In recognition of this, a subcategory of traveler (also known as backpackers, ecotravelers, or development workers) seeks out charitable works; a few days at a Mother Teresa clinic, or volunteer washing of elephants at a nature reserve or similar. This kind of benevolence is authorized and approved in many travel guides, and in newspaper advertisements and documentary programs, through the mechanism of a heart-tugging image of an always-smiling child that would be the necessary motivator for even a gesture ("send just a few coins") of care or concern for dispossessed human beings. Clearly charitable activities, even where they "help" a bit, are also part of the benevolent self-deception of the tourist gaze serving to deflect meaningful recognition of gross economic privilege, and, along the way, turning guilt itself into a commodity form. The consuming "gaze" is self-deceiving if the traveler really believes that a few days of volunteer work in Calcutta (see Hutnyk 1996) can excuse a month of hedonism on the beach in Goa. Similar logics justify the carbon-footprint calculations of even the most well-meaning environmental traveler—to walk in the pristine rain forest and leave a "soft footprint" is still to treat the planet as an object for rapacious use, locals be damned.

SOUVENIRS

Tourists collect experience, but we have to have mementos to remind ourselves that the fantasy was real—the same photographs of the smiling kids, various knickknacks and trash purchased from the local flea market, from the beach trader, from the state emporium, or from the airport departure lounge. Thus, trinkets are then displayed on shelves at home, gathering dust, or gifted to relatives and friends not lucky enough to have been there. Postcards similarly gloat and preen. The overarching theme here is that the world experience is reduced to mere bric-a-brac. The complex global forces of capital, of work and leisure, of the division of labor and the vast networks of information and infrastructure—planes, hotels, servants, right through to Kodak processing labs and Internet travel blogging—is miniaturized in handy squares or convenient packets that can fit neatly onto the luggage rack. The idea of the souvenir is reduction itself—the veneer of the trinket, the face, ironically, of exploitation writ large. That we have learned not to read these signs in any wider register is also part of the sanctioned ignorance that tourism authenticates.

POST-TOURISM

As tourists and travelers will be the first to proclaim of course, we are, many of us, fully aware of this hypocrisy, so much so that the inauthentic has become a part of the quest—and may be called "post-tourism" in one of those not-quite-ironic neologisms (Urry 1990) that allow the nominated suffix to continue beyond its justified shelf life. Searching out the most gaudy, plastic, outrageous object allegedly proves one has not been duped by the exotica-merchants. To be in pursuit of the authentic is an essentialist trap, but to have continued past this to accept inauthenticity as part and parcel of the contemporary mixed-up

ON POSTWAR TOURISM

I am assured by the Swedish anthropologist Victor Alneng, who knows these things, that Lonely Planet impresario Tony Wheeler had his eyes set on Afghanistan for some time. As evidence, Victor translated from a Swedish newspaper interview in September 2002 the following insights into the wheeler-dealer's thinking: Wheeler: "When a place has been closed there is always a group of people that want to come there first. After them come the large hordes of travelers." Reporter: "So what destinations will be the next big thing, after East Timor?" Wheeler: "Angola and Afghanistan will come eventually. Maybe also Iraq. We were on the verge of sending one of our writers to Afghanistan as early as last summer, but it proved to still be very difficult to travel outside Kabul. Information ages quickly, so we chose to wait a little" (Translation by Victor Alneng, Swedish text available at http://www.dn.se/DNet/road/Classic/article/0/jsp/print.jsp?&a=56544).

and "complex" world still leaves commodification intact. A grinning fascination with the curio and knowing awareness of the predicaments of exoticization does not in actuality undo any of the structures of inequality that such "post-tourists" would wish to avoid. What kind of self-deception is this that extends tourist purchase to the most esoteric of objects at the same time as it can buy up the mundane? I have seen tourists purchase gaudy plastic tap handles for their metropolitan bathroom fittings, or plastic models of the Taj Mahal, with flashing lights, as a tongue-in-cheek, high-kitsch souvenir. Arguably, post-tourist irony here does not break with trinketization at all, but rather confirms the process, and extends it exponentially.

TRINKETIZATION

The word trinketization will stand for the process of downgrading the material cultures of the world into a grand compendium of trash. The anthropologist Claude Lévi-Strauss famously lamented this when he saw the detritus of the West thrown back into the face of humanity; this trash culture has now become the detritus of all our lives, and we revel in it. Does this not suggest the need for a political diagnosis of tourism as rampant exploitation? The argument here is not for an end to tourism; it is thoroughly unlikely that could even be considered and the planetary consequences are obscure; but might we look towards the remote possibility of a still better tourism, an ethical and even revolutionary tourism? What of those travelers who expressly seek out meetings with the Maoists in Nepal, who march in hope of a meeting with the reds of the Himalaya, or those who travel to learn from the Ogoni in Nigeria of their struggle against the multinationals? There are travelers who go to seek sun and friendship, and this seems worthy, but others go further and seek out local authors, artists, performers: a cultural exchange program is not a forlorn idea. I have seen a travel group barter performances with street musicians in a way that was only possible on the basis of the same commercial exchange that the critic of tourism in me deplores. Mass tourism is destructive, but there are those who take seriously the possibility of alternatives that do more than just talk the talk—*for* a new tourism perhaps?

WHAT THEN OF TOURISM CONCERN, AND SO FORTH?

Isn't the solution to relax, to stop moralizing against tourism and against those who claim tourism could be better (soft-footprinters)? For tourist resorts and pleasure peripheries to circumvent the attacks of critics, there needs to be problem-solving of issues like employment security, wage reform (in many cases, actual wages would be a start), workplace regulation, civic responsibility, impact on water table (the beach hotels in Goa are particularly irresponsible, as in many other coastal areas), cultural uplift, political support, promotional drive, sustainable movement. Organizations such as Tourism Concern (http://www.tourismconcern.org.uk/) aim to merge a critique of the destructive aspects of mass tourism with maintenance of the adventure of travel; Tourism Concern claims to "fight exploitation" and seems to do so with a positive and progressive compromise that would mitigate destruction. In case after case, I find this overly optimistic, but the orientation of the critique is perhaps the best we have. Coupled with consumer advocacy and environmental concern (vapor trails and aircraft pollution lead to global warming—"Is that journey necessary?") there seems just the glimmer of hope that the exponential rise in travel may not destroy us all—but current forecasts seem bleak. Second only to the war economy as a site of expansion and investment, the global-mediated market of tourism strips all demand. The tourist hordes resemble an all-consuming plague and the planet is ravaged as if by locusts, thereby chewed into bits.

LIMITATIONS

The trouble with making the case that tourism turns everything into trinkets is that a theoretical approach that pursues this line is in danger of becoming a part of the problem as well. The world becomes a kaleidoscope of fascinating sites in the same way that theoretical analysis all too easily can latch on to any example and use it for its argument—just like I used the example of meeting "the reds" as a case for better tourism. What would not be subject to postironic touristic exoticization? The *Guardian* newspaper today, as I write (December 20, 2006), reports the mayor of war-torn Grozny planning tourist visits and mocking the idea with the question, "But will bullet proof vests be supplied?" Yes, we can imagine how the war-devastated landscape of the Chechnyan city might become a stop on some adventure tour, which might also then take in other "dark tourism" sites, not all of them inappropriate as places to visit—holocaust memorials, Iwo Jima, former prisons, and locations of famous battles (Gallipoli) might also be on the itinerary. To call this trinketization would miss the emotional purchase of such investments, despite the raw fact that investment is also behind the touristification of war. The problem with trinketization here is that analytical purchase is also often reduced to a facade in much of what passes for the study of tourism, as if replicating the exotic gloss of the brochures also amounts to an adequate examination of the global predicament (for several examples of this, see Clifford 1997). What chance is there that travel really broadens the mind of the analyst also?

See also Cultural Imperialism and Hybridity; Global Community Media; Nationalism and the Media; Paparazzi and Photographic Ethics; Parachute Journalism; Representations of Race; World Cinema.

Further Reading: Alneng, Victor. "'What the Fuck Is a Vietnam?': Touristic Phantasms and the Popcolonization of (the) Vietnam (War)." *Critique of Anthropology* 22, no. 4 (2002): 461–89; Clifford, James. *Routes: Travel and Translation in the Late Twentieth Century.* Cambridge, MA: Harvard University Press, 1997; Crick, Malcolm. *Resplendent Sites, Discordant Voices: Sri Lankans in International Tourism.* Chur: Harwood Academic, 1994; Frommers. *Guide To India.* London: Frommers Guides, 1984; Hitchcock, Michael, and Ken Teague, eds. *Souvenirs: The Material Culture of Tourism.* Aldershot: Ashgate, 2000; Hutnyk, John. *The Rumour of Calcutta: Tourism, Charity and the Poverty of Representation.* London: Zed, 1996; Jules-Rosette, Benetta. *The Message of Tourist Art: An African Semiotic System in Comparative Perspective.* New York: Plenum, 1984; Lennon, J. John, and Malcolm Foley. *Dark Tourism: The Attraction of Death and Disaster.* London: Cassell, 1999; MacCannell, Dean. *The Tourist,* reprint of 1976 version with a new introduction. New York: Random House, 1989; MacCannell, Dean. *Empty Meeting Grounds: The Tourist Papers.* New York: Routledge, 1992; Olalquiaga, Celeste. *The Artificial Kingdom: A Treasury of the Kitsch Experience.* London: Bloomsbury, 1999; Phipps, Peter. "Tourists, Terrorists, Death and Value." In *Travel Worlds: Journeys in Contemporary Cultural Politics,* ed. Raminder Kaur and John Hutnyk, 74–93. London: Zed, 1999; Spivak, Gayatri Chakravorty. *Critique of Postcolonial Reason.* Cambridge, MA: Harvard University Press, 1999; Urry, John. *The Tourist Gaze: Leisure and Travel in Contemporary Societies.* Newbury Park, CA: Sage, 1990.

John Hutnyk

TRANSMEDIA STORYTELLING AND MEDIA FRANCHISES

While media franchises have long offered official toys, bed linens, trading cards, and the like, in recent years, several media franchises have begun to use multiple media platforms to tell stories. The narrative of *The Matrix,* for instance, unfolded across three films, a video game, comics, and a series of anime short films. Such initiatives can be criticized for being yet more instances of corporate synergy, whereby media producers squeeze more money from their consumers, sometimes carrying them in the process from advertising venue to advertising venue. However, they also potentially expand the story world and the prospects for viewers' creative means of engaging with stories, thus contributing to the development of a new form of multimedia storytelling.

Taken by itself, the term "transmedia" simply describes the process of content moving or expanding from one medium into another. As such, transmediation can describe practices ranging from *adaptation* (e.g., turning a novel into a film) to *merchandising* (e.g., creating action figures in the likeness of film characters). However, the notion of *transmedia storytelling* is more specific, and is used to describe the process of further developing a coherent narrative (or elaborating a narrative universe) by distributing related story components across multiple media platforms.

One compelling example of transmedia storytelling came in 1998, when producers of the teen drama *Dawson's Creek* launched a promotional Web site called Dawson's Desktop. At the time, most Web sites developed for television shows worked as "virtual press kits," letting visitors read short character and actor biographies, browse plot summaries, and download production photos or short video clips. Dawson's Desktop took a different approach: rather than providing information *about* the show, it offered new content that *extended* the show's narrative in between episodes and let visitors feel as if they were entering the world of the show itself. Visitors to the site were able to explore what appeared to be the title character's personal computer, reading his e-mails and logs of

1980s MEDIA FRANCHISES

While most major media franchises of the 1980s expanded to include both licensed merchandise (toys, clothing, breakfast cereal) and transmedia components (films, television series, video games, comic books), many of the most popular franchises were actually financed and launched *by* merchandisers to help sell their products.

Disney	*The Wuzzles* (1985)
	DuckTales (1987)
	Chip 'n Dale Rescue Rangers (1989)
Hallmark	*Shirt Tales* (1982)
	Rainbow Brite (1984)
American Greetings	*The Care Bears* (1985)
Tonka Toys	*Pound Puppies* (1985)
Tyco Toys	*Dino-Riders* (1988)
Mattel Toys	*He-Man & the Masters of the Universe* (1983)
	She-Ra (1985)
Hasbro Toys	*Transformers* (1984)
	G. I. Joe (1985)
	Jem & the Holograms (1985)
	Inhumanoids (1986)
	My Little Pony (1986)

Ironically, one of the catchphrases introduced in *Jem & the Holograms* might as well have been a catchphrase for the entire decade: "Showtime, synergy!"

However, as some short-lived examples demonstrated, not *all* toys and entertainment characters were capable of supporting transmedia franchises: one animated series, *Rubik, The Amazing Cube*, revolved around the Rodriguez siblings, a group of three children who learned that their Rubik's Cube would come to life and lead them on magical adventures when all of his colored squares were lined up correctly.

his online conversations with other characters, seeing the Web sites he visited, and so on. Dawson's Desktop was updated before and after each episode, and at random intervals during the week, to include new e-mails in which Dawson or other characters discussed events of the most recent episode. From this main site, fans could also follow links to other fictional sites, including a Web site for Dawson's high school newspaper and a site for the show's bed and breakfast, complete with a guestbook and 360-degree virtual tour.

However, while Dawson's Desktop had a commercial aspect, allowing fans to purchase *Dawson's Creek*–branded merchandise, it also allowed for a new type of interaction between television viewers and television content. Dawson's Desktop contributed to the story world, providing viewers the opportunity to read characters' reflections on events, as well as reactions to events not discussed on the television show. It is also important to note that Dawson's Desktop was free; while the site generated a limited amount of revenue through the sale of merchandise, and helped to promote the show, it offered little or no direct remuneration. This raises a series of interesting questions. In particular, we might ask: how are we to make sense of such a Web site and such an investment? What function(s) do sites like Dawson's Desktop provide for their accompanying programs? And, most importantly, are these transmedia extensions being developed primarily to tell better stories, or to generate higher profits?

MAKING MONEY FROM SYNERGY

A key principle of *corporate synergy* is to make as much money out of a media product as possible. Recently, media corporations have moved to establishing significant networks of *horizontal integration*, wherein a conglomeration will work with or purchase companies whose businesses work alongside one another (as when News Corp owns both a movie and a television studio), and *vertical integration*, wherein a conglomeration will work with or purchase companies up or down stream from one another (as when News Corp owns the Fox Network and multiple Fox broadcast stations). As these forms of integration become more common, corporations increasingly move to repurpose material across their various companies. Rather than perpetually developing new stories and characters, synergy draws upon existing entertainment properties, with preestablished audiences, and attempts to generate as much revenue as possible. As a result, if a movie is successful, not only will it likely receive a sequel, but the company owning it may authorize a spin-off television show, a comic book, a line of toys, a musical, cross-promotional deals with fast-food companies, an amusement park ride, and so on. Meanwhile, each "platform" serves as an advertisement for the others, and hence for the whole, thereby allowing media corporations to make money from their advertisements.

The most significant shift toward horizontal integration and media franchising came in the 1930s, when Walt Disney introduced a new business model that he described as *total merchandising*. Under this model, all Disney products served dual purposes: branded merchandise, television shows, animated movies, and amusement park rides all simultaneously functioned as entertainment *and* as advertisements for every other Disney product. Disney's characters were not the first to be featured on merchandise or appear in multiple media, but they were almost certainly the first characters designed to serve as entertainment "brands." Today, Disney continues to expand its total merchandising model, using almost every film and television series it releases as the basis for a franchise, complete with toys, amusement park rides, merchandise, comic books, and fast-food tie-ins, not to mention resale on DVD and VHS.

Star Wars, too, proved a watershed moment in the evolution of both blockbuster films and blockbuster synergy: *Star Wars* toys sold like few other consumer items in history, producing over $100 million in profits for toy company Kenner and selling over 42 million units in their first year alone, and the franchise later expanded to include several spin-off television shows, multiple video

THE *LOST* EXPERIENCE: TRANSMEDIA NARRATIVE AS INTERACTIVE TELEVISION

Lost's most ambitious transmedia experiment to date was, without question, a summer-long interactive narrative campaign (or "alternate reality game") called "The *Lost* Experience." Developed as a collaborative venture between the show's producers and broadcasting affiliates on several continents, the *Lost* Experience required players to work together and seek out clues both on and offline that would advance an original narrative developed for the game, which provided a wealth of insights and clues into the core mysteries depicted on the television series. In order to fully immerse players in *Lost*'s narrative world, the *Lost* Experience unfolded across a wide range of media platforms and sites, including the following:

- *Lost*'s fictional Hanso Foundation ran fake advertisements on television and in national newspapers, providing URLs and other clues for players.
- Players could "hack" into voice-mail systems and e-mail accounts to access private messages and hidden content, and could exchange instant messages with several of the game's characters.
- Content was distributed on a range of preexisting commercial Web sites, including Amazon, Blogger, MySpace, and YouTube, to make the game seem more real.
- More than a dozen fictional Web sites were launched, including sites for the Hanso Foundation, a blog for one of the main characters, and several message boards for players to share "conspiracy theories."
- A series of podcasts was released, culminating in a live event where players could call in, share their theories, and interact with one of the characters.
- Several of the game's characters appeared in public: one character was interviewed on *The Jimmy Kimmel Show*, while another interrupted a *Lost* panel at the San Diego ComicCon 2006 to accuse *Lost*'s producers of participating in a conspiracy.
- Fake "Apollo Candy Bars," which had appeared on *Lost*, were distributed in public locations around the world, with over a thousand containing codes that needed to be entered online to complete the story.

games, and a second trilogy of films among its rapidly growing army of products and platforms.

Examples of synergy and transmedia franchising are particularly prominent in children's media, since children represent a vast, ongoing market for entertainment products. The 1980s, in particular, brought an explosion of youth-focused media franchises. Countless film, television, and comic book characters were introduced (or reintroduced) as transmedia franchises, complete with comic books, multiple cinematic releases, animated television series, and a wide range of toys and branded merchandise. In fact, during the 1980s, many of the most popular entertainment franchises were launched not by media companies, but by merchandisers and toy manufacturers looking to build audiences (and markets) for their properties (see "1980s Media Franchises" sidebar).

PLAYING WITH SYNERGY

Criticism of media synergy is rampant, especially that directed toward children, as corporations are seen as taking advantage of children's desires to fit in with peers, and charged with persuading them to believe, for example, that their favorite TV characters chose their own clothes, when often what they are watching is the outcome of a merchandising contract. In this way, they are accused of promoting conformity and creating legions of consumer zombies who will follow wherever the Mighty Morphin Power Rangers, Pokemon, or He-Man may lead.

However, while adults may see such franchises as exploitative, to see children's involvement with such media franchises as nothing more than mindless consumerism overlooks the appeal that such franchises hold for children. *Star Wars,* Care Bears, or G. I. Joe toys empower children to "participate" in their fictional worlds by giving them control of the characters and allowing them to construct their own narratives. While much of the resulting play may simply mimic the narratives depicted on television or film, it can also provide a space for creativity and imagination, allowing children to repurpose characters or re-write scenarios to reflect their own interests, desires, and needs. This does not mean that all media franchising offers such benefits: in many cases, the products of media synergy are still developed primarily to generate revenue. But while branded bed linens, breakfast cereals, and soft drinks encourage children to consume *products*, it is important to recognize that toys, games, and many other franchise products can enable children to interact with, and take control of, a franchise's stories, themes, and characters.

Arguably one of the greatest experiences of watching a good film or television show is the experience of entering its world for just a moment. Such play with synergy may therefore promise yet more involvement. Such was the case, for instance, with Daniel Myrick and Eduardo Sanchez's *The Blair Witch Project* (1999), which positioned all of its promotional materials as "real," as with the film itself, which purported to show the last days of three missing teenagers who went into the woods near Burkittsville, Maryland, never to return. *The Blair Witch Project*'s clever pretense of reality helped lend the film added authenticity and scare factor, hence increasing the viewing experience for many viewers. Yet it was the film's promotional materials arguably more than the film itself that lay claim to depicting a "real event," thus showing how promotional materials can become part and parcel of the story, and of an audience's enjoyment of that story.

THE YEAR OF *THE MATRIX*

Following the success of *The Matrix* in 1999, creators Larry and Andy Wachowski released two sequels, *The Matrix Reloaded* and *The Matrix Revolutions*, in 2003. Rather than positioning the films as mere sequels, however, the Wachowski brothers insisted on using the films as components in a larger, more elaborate, and more interactive transmedia narrative. Rather than simply reproducing key moments from the *Matrix* films, the Wachowskis developed the *Matrix* "spin-offs" to expand their narrative canvas, using an array of media forms—including comics, video games, animated short films, and more—to provide new original content that enhanced and extended the events of the films. This year-long rollout of *Matrix*-related content led many journalists to refer to 2003 as "the Year of the Matrix."

The videogame, *Enter the Matrix*, allowed players to guide two supporting characters from the films through the events that occurred in between their on-screen appearances, and in doing so, to discover additional details and plot points that were referenced in the films. *Enter the Matrix* also incorporated almost two hours of exclusive narrative-expanding scenes written by the Wachowskis, and featuring the film actors, which were later added into a "director's cut" of the film as part of a 10-disc DVD collector's set.

The Wachowskis also oversaw the development of a series of nine short anime films, collectively called *The Animatrix*. Four of these films, written by the Wachowskis themselves, were particularly important to the larger *Matrix* narrative, including *The Second Renaissance, Parts 1 & 2*, which depicted the historical events that led to the franchise's central conflict between humans and machines, and *Final Flight of the Osiris* (often described as *The Matrix 1.5*), which depicted the events between the first and second films of the trilogy. While all nine films of *The Animatrix* were released on DVD, however, four of the films were made available for free on the Matrix Web site in the months leading up to the release of the second film, and *Final Flight of the Osiris* was shown in theaters before screenings of Stephen King's *Dreamcatcher*.

But if "the Year of the Matrix" worked to demonstrate the possibilities for transmedia storytelling, it also illustrated the inherent challenges of these possibilities: many reviewers and viewers accused the film of exploiting the success of the first film, and perceived projects like *The Animatrix* and *Enter the Matrix* as crass attempts to cash in on fan enthusiasm. Others, lacking the desire to piece together the narrative from so many different components, simply felt that the Matrix had become too complicated and demanding, and found the films difficult to understand. These problems indicate the degree to which transmedia stories must now carefully balance some viewer's desires to dig deeper into the story world with other viewers' desire not to feel left out.

THE NEW ERA OF TRANSMEDIA STORYTELLING

From this framework, we might then understand today's expansion of storytelling across media as providing greater opportunities for involvement, and as representing development in narrative form and technique, not just an explosion in cross-media promotion. The Web site for season 1 of Fox's hit television show, *24*, for instance, included links to the fictional White House and access to the main characters' Counter Terrorism Unit personnel files, both of which provided information not in the television show, and yet that also allowed audience members to better understand the characters and the world they lived in. The first season of *24* was also followed by the publication of a book, *24: The House Special Subcommittee's Findings at CTU*, which let viewers review transcripts, diagrams, and other important documents used during meetings of a fictional congressional committee that convened to discuss the events shown during the season.

More recently, elaborate transmedia campaigns have been developed around elaborate television programs such as *Lost* (ABC) and *Heroes* (NBC) to serve a range of creative, promotional, and financial purposes. For example, *Lost* has all of the standard trappings that make up modern media franchises: visitors to the show's official Web site can purchase clothing, action figures, collectible trading cards, key chains, posters, soundtrack albums, a board game, and so on. However, the show's producers have also experimented with several more innovative and compelling transmedia extensions. These experiments include:

- Launching a Web site for the fictional Oceanic Airlines (www.oceanic-airlines.com), whose Flight 815 crashed during the pilot episode, thereby establishing the show's narrative premise. The Web site contained clues and possible leads for solving mysteries within the show.
- Publishing *Bad Twin*, a detective novel "written" by one of the show's minor characters, which appeared on-screen during the second season and tantalized fans by providing additional material that could be scavenged for narrative clues.
- Producing *The Lost Diaries*, a series of short videos slated for distribution as exclusive cellular phone content, and written as "home videos" shot by one of the show's main characters.
- Writing and running "The *Lost* Experience," an elaborate alternate reality game (ARG) that unfolded across several media platforms, and provided viewers with additional narrative details as reward for solving a series of challenges (see "The *Lost* Experience: Transmedia Narrative as Interactive Television").

Yet, while *Lost*'s producers have been able to pursue these types of synergistic storytelling innovations, corporate synergy also continues to manifest itself in more crass and exploitative forms. One excellent example is the set of "Official *Lost* Jigsaw Puzzles," which promise fans exclusive access to "secret" information about the show's mysteries: viewers who purchase and complete all four puzzles, place them together, turn them over, and shine an ultraviolet light on them will be able to view an important map that appeared as a fleeting (and incomplete) on-screen image during the show. Unlike the examples above, these puzzles have no place in *Lost*'s larger narrative; instead, they take advantage of the show's mysteries, and sell otherwise unremarkable merchandise by "bundling" it with exclusive "insights."

CONCLUSION

One of the clear signs that transmedia storytelling might be developing new ways to tell stories, and not just new platforms from which to reap profits, is that many writers and directors are becoming intimately involved in the transmedia proliferation of their products. *The Simpsons*' creator Matt Groening plays a key role in developing *Simpsons* products; *Lost* executive producers Carlton Cuse and Damon Lindelof were outspoken critics of *Lost*'s early "novelizations" and are now more closely involved in sculpting the show's transmedia existence; the Wachowski brothers were active in writing *The Matrix* into and across various media (see "The Year of *The Matrix*"), and so forth. Indeed, some transmedia platforms are now experiencing legal challenges and slowdowns as writers and cast members are demanding to be paid separately, arguing that their contractual obligation to take part in promotional activities does not cover all such platforms. And, as many transmedia tales have also been synergistic goldmines for their corporate parents, often the economics of the media industries have encouraged media corporations to vigorously pursue and solicit projects that can cross various media. Concerns regarding the hidden persuasions of product placement and the monopolistic tendencies of synergy continue to exist, but they are now being accompanied by some writers' and consumers' excitement at the prospect of yet more developed story worlds.

See also Advertising and Persuasion; Children and Effects; Conglomeration and Media Monopolies; Hypercommercialism; Innovation and Imitation in Commercial Media; Product Placement; User-Created Content and Audience Participation.

Further Reading: Allen, Robert C. "Home Alone Together: Hollywood and the 'Family Film.'" In *Identifying Hollywood's Audiences: Cultural Identity and the Movies,* ed. Melvyn Stokes and Richard Maltby, 109–31. London: BFI, 1999; Bennett, Tony, and Janet Woollacott. *Bond and Beyond: The Political Career of Popular Hero.* London: MacMillan, 1987; Brooker, Will. "Living on *Dawson's Creek*: Teen Viewers, Cultural Convergence and Television Overflow." *International Journal of Cultural Studies* 4, no. 4 (2001): 456–72; Engelhardt, Tom. "The Shortcake Strategy." In *Watching Television,* ed. Todd Gitlin, 68–110. New York: Pantheon, 1986; Fleming, Dan. *Powerplay: Toys as Popular Culture.* Manchester: Manchester University Press, 1996; Gwenllian-Jones, Sara, and Roberta E. Pearson, eds. *Cult Television.* Minneapolis: University of Minnesota Press, 2004; Jenkins, Henry. *Convergence Culture: When Old and New Media Collide.* New York: NYU Press, 2006; Lancaster, Kurt. *Interacting with Babylon 5: Fan Performances in a Media Universe.* Austin: University of Texas Press, 2001; Lavery, David. "Introduction: The Semiotics of Cobbler: *Twin Peaks*' Interpretive Community." In *Full of Secrets: Critical Approaches to Twin Peaks,* ed. David Lavery, 1–22. Detroit, MI: Wayne

State University Press, 1995; Meehan, Eileen. "Holy Commodity Fetish, Batman!" In *The Many Lives of Batman: Critical Approaches to a Super Hero and His Media,* ed. Roberta E. Pearson and William Uricchio. London: BFI, 1991.Sansweet, Stephen J. *Star Wars: From Concept to Screen to Collectible.* San Francisco: Chronicle Books, 1992; Telotte, J. P. *Disney TV.* Detroit, MI: Wayne State University Press, 2004.

Ivan Askwith and Jonathan Gray

U

USER-CREATED CONTENT AND AUDIENCE PARTICIPATION

The rise of user-created content has altered the relationship between media producers and consumers. The volume and quality of material produced by audiences is seen as evidence by some of the democratization of the media space. At the same time that spaces dedicated to user-created content blossom, large media companies are incorporating audience-produced content into their products and inviting audiences to participate. This trend has raised questions, however, about content ownership, the value of cultural labor, and the right to use commercial media content and make meaning.

The rise and high visibility of user-created content is associated with both the development of consumer-level digital production and editing tools, and the maturation of the Internet as a platform enabling "push-button" publishing of text, images, video, and audio. Though tied to more recent technological and cultural developments, particularly the convergence of media devices and platforms, and the emergence of Web 2.0, user creativity, and its incorporation by professional media agencies has a longer history. The "letter to the editor" in the newspaper is a good example of early modes of audience participation in mainstream media. Magazines too have long invited audiences to submit content such as articles, personal stories, and recipes. Radio has made extensive use of the audience in the form of talk-back and call-ins. Similarly, television programs such as *America's Funniest Home Videos* relied heavily, if not wholly, on user-created content. Outside of these narrow, sanctioned media spaces, community and activist media sectors, as well as fan productions, have long demonstrated the creative capacity of nonprofessional media producers.

The development of digital camera technologies and domestic-level editing software equipped media consumers with tools previously locked in the domain of media professionals. Throughout the 1990s, multimedia applications became an important part of the home computing and electronics market, sometimes becoming central to product differentiation. Apple's 2001 campaign for iTunes, for instance, touted the software's ease for managing music and compiling mix albums, encouraging users to "rip, mix, burn." The development of the Internet as an open platform offered publishing and distribution options outside of publicly regulated spectrum and free of the necessity to invest in complex expensive machinery (such as large printing presses). Equipped with technology and skills, more and more audience members have become media producers, creating and distributing their own content.

Describing activities ranging from writing fan fiction, categorizing content, and editing photographs, to lip-synching to pop songs, reassembling video materials, and creating bedroom confessionals, user-created content exists at the friction point between a skilled and technologically enabled audience and a media industry looking to regain market share. Media markets have been continuously fragmenting since the 1970s as new services (cable, satellite) and new devices (VCR, DVD, video game consoles) competed for audiences' time. No longer enjoying a monopoly over either the production or distribution of media content, large media producers see user-created content as both a competitor and a new strategy to engage their audience.

CURRENT TV

Run by a company lead by former U.S. Vice President Al Gore, Current TV combines user-created content and professionally produced material. The station is presented as an attempt to democratize television production. Available via cable and satellite since 2005 (with a second network in the United Kingdom and Ireland launched in 2007), 30 percent of the content on Current TV is user-created. Users create 3- to 7-minute "pods" that are submitted to a voting process that registered members of the Current TV Web site participate in. Videos "greenlit" through this process are placed on the schedule amongst other short-form programming, which is a mix of documentary; news and current affairs; informational; and entertainment content, including a number of programs produced by Internet search company Google. The station encourages advertisers to engage its viewers to produce advertising, compensating users for advertising screened on Current TV and requiring advertisers to purchase the content should they wish to use it on other platforms.

While in many ways providing a space for "everyday" young people, Current TV's emphasis on high visual quality means it is far from an open system and it has been criticized for favoring content that too closely resembles traditional television fare. Though it supports user-created content, the network has to compete in a system still ruled by the logics of subscription television, meaning it must produce content watchable on a television in a lounge room. Furthermore, the sequencing of content on television requires consistency in quality, a situation not readily experienced, nor it seems required, online.

COMPETITION

Grassroots or citizen reporting and Internet journalism are a good example of the rise of user-created content as a competitor to established media. Whether frustrated by a lack of local coverage, interested in niche topics not more widely reported, close to the action at a crucial moment (see Owen 2005), or disenfranchised with corporate media, citizen journalists, bloggers, and social news sites have emerged as significant alternatives to the mainstream press. It has been heavily debated (and at times litigated) whether blogging and citizen reporting constitutes journalism and should be afforded the same legal protections as "professional" newsgathering, so that, for instance, in December 2004, Apple filed suit against numerous blogs that were reporting rumors about Apple products, while in 2005, blogger Josh Wolfe was detained over his refusal to hand over to police footage shot at a political protest. At the same time, though, user-created news activities have prompted a renegotiation of the relationship between established news services and their audiences. In part as a response to citizen news, most mainstream news services have introduced opportunities for users to participate, submit pictures, comment on stories published online, or participate in officially run news blogs. Citizen journalism has both prompted discussion about the distinctions between professionals and amateurs as well as forcibly transformed news reporting from a one-way lecture into a conversation.

Similar questions about the blurring of lines between professionals and amateurs are raised by sophisticated user-created projects such as Wikipedia. An online encyclopedia project, Wikipedia operates on a belief that over time accurate entries will be produced by informed, well-meaning participants. Maintaining an open editing policy, Wikipedia challenges the expert paradigm, recognizing knowledge can come from nonformal sources of expertise, such as the detailed knowledge produced by fans and enthusiasts. The project is often criticized for valuing the consensus of the crowd over the credentials of individual authors writing entries. This criticism is frequently rebutted by pointing out that on the whole, Wikipedia has been found to be no less reliable than professionally reviewed sources such as the *Encyclopedia Britannica* (Terdiman 2005). While this may be true, Wikipedia often strains under its own policy of openness as users with vested interests wrestle to have their perspectives on a topic included and vandals deface entries under the cover of anonymity.

CO-OPTION

While Wikipedia is a nonprofit organization, mobilizing user creativity is a strategy increasingly adopted in businesses, leading to the rise of what are referred to as prosumers (Toffler 1980) or produsers (Bruns 2005)—"productive" consumers or users. By providing spaces for users to participate, some media corporations are attempting to incorporate user creativity within the established value chain of media production. This value chain places the professional media producer on one end, the media consumer on the other, and the transfer of content for profit from producer to consumer in between.

User creativity, however, recasts the audience as a media producer, somewhat disrupting this model. Typically, media corporations have claimed ownership and exclusive rights over content submitted to them, while policing the permitted uses of content they produce. As such, news services, for instance, claim the right to use (usually for free) and re-license (usually for profit) user-submitted photos. This model has become more problematic with the rise of services where users are the predominant content producer. For instance, virtual world Second Life provides an open play space where users can build objects and create artifacts their avatars can interact with and move amongst. Early into its existence, Second Life's creators Linden Lab changed the rules of participation, assigning the intellectual property rights to objects to the users who created them. This has led to a flourishing "virtual economy" within Second Life where users on-sell virtual goods. This is a virtual economy not everyone can participate in, however. As much as digital publishing tools enable "everyday" people to participate in the media space, this participation requires access to technology and an Internet connection, as well as a certain degree of technological and creative skill. As such, while user-created content is enabled by the rise in consumer-level digital tools, the continued existence of a digital divide means some people face technological, social, economic, and cultural barriers to participation.

RECENT DEVELOPMENTS IN USER-CREATED CONTENT

1989—*America's Funniest Home Videos* premieres on the ABC Network. At the time of publication, the program, based on Tokyo Broadcasting System program *Fun TV with Kato-chan and Ken-chan*, is still on the air.

July 1995—*MTV News: Unfiltered* premieres. Viewers called MTV and pitched stories about their life. The network headed out to shoot short (no longer than 4 minutes) stories on Hi-8 video, which were then edited together into a hosted program. The program is cited as a key inspiration for Current TV (see below).

December 1995—Web-hosting service GeoCities launched (after a brief period as "Beverly Hills Internet"). While a paid premium service was later added, GeoCities continued as a free service even after its acquisition by Yahoo! in 1998.

September 1997—User-submitted "nerd" news site *Slashdot* is launched (http://www.slashdot.org). *Slashdot* is one of the longest established user-submitted news sites on the Web.

August 1999—Pyra Labs launches *Blogger*, a free Weblog publishing tool. Google acquired the service in February 2003. The simple interface and free site-hosting helped to popularize the format.

October 1999—iMovie, a consumer video editing program based on the code used for professional digital editing software, is bundled as a standard offering from Apple Computer Inc. iMovie was later joined by iTunes, iPhoto, iDVD, GarageBand, and iWeb, the last four of which are digital editing programs.

July 2003—Social networking site MySpace launches. Allowing users to create Web page profiles customized as they like, and connected to their friends' profiles, the service quickly becomes a key site for both identity expression and marketing. News Corporation acquired the service as part of a US$580 million deal in July 2005.

April 2003—The public beta of Second Life opened, opening the virtual world (version 1.0 officially launched in June 2003). Later in 2003, Second Life allowed users to retain intellectual property rights over the content they create. Teen Second Life, a separate "grid" of the virtual world restricted to users aged 13 through 17, opened on January 1, 2006.

October 2004—New York rap outfit Beastie Boys gives camcorders to audience members attending their Madison Square Garden concert with the instructions to film the concert. The footage was edited together into the film *Awesome; I Fuckin' Shot That!* and premiered at the 2006 Sundance Film Festival.

November 2004—"User driven social content" Web site *Digg* launches. *Digg* is one of the most successful user-created news sites, with a feature set often copied.

February 2005—YouTube launches. The site enables users to post short video clips that can be viewed and voted upon by other users. YouTube allows people to embed the content on their blogs and Web sites.

July 2005—Photographs from cell phones make their way into the mass-media coverage of the bombings in the London underground. These photos are some of the most compelling images of the event.

August 2005—Al Gore's Current TV commenced broadcasting in the United States in August 2005, featuring 30 percent user-created content. Current TV launched a second cable service in the United Kingdom and Ireland in March 2007.

June 2006—Lonelygirl15 first appears on YouTube. Mimicking the confessional style of teen video blogs, the series sparks speculation over whether the video diaries hosted by "Bree" are genuine or not. In September 2006, it was revealed to be a narrative experiment by fledgling filmmakers Mesh Flinders and Miles Beckett.

October 2006—Google buys YouTube for US$1.65 million.

December 2006—*Time* magazine announces "You" as the "Person of the Year."

February 2007—User-generated commercials for Doritos premiere at Super Bowl XLI.

RE-USE

User creativity raises further questions of ownership as productive audiences adapt, interact with, and build upon commercially produced popular culture. Though the confessional video journal might be seen as the public face of video-sharing sites, creative reworkings of popular culture such as mashups, fan tribute videos, and re-edits of movie trailers are also predominant. Similarly, many fan Web sites trade fan fiction—original stories featuring characters from their favorite texts. These forms of collage, manipulation, and creation are not intrinsically new, but the distribution options provided by the Internet have raised the profile and exposure of this sort of activity.

Some copyright owners have responded by using legal tools such as those provided by the Digital Millennium Copyright Act to have these works taken down. They see these uses as unauthorized, violating copyright laws that bestow the right to profit from creative endeavors on the original creator. Where the title of a property may be registered as a trademark, copyright owners have also used trademark law to have works removed. These actions are seen as necessary to protect both the commercial investment in the creative property, which in many cases is substantial, and to reduce potential confusion over what is, and what is not, an official product. This latter concern has been heightened by the increasing quality of amateur productions. Fan film *Star Wars: Revelations* (available at http://panicstruckpro.com/revelations), for instance, sports CGI effects almost as impressive as the official *Star Wars* films, despite being produced on a fraction of the budget.

An alternative perspective sees this re-use of commercially produced media as noninfringing and legitimate in an age of digital content and productive audiences. Lawrence Lessig argues that people have long remixed their culture through activities such as quoting favorite lines or using television episodes as the basis for jokes. Technology has finally caught up with this practice to enable this remixing to make use of the content itself. Similarly, Henry Jenkins suggests that user creativity represents a similar range of behaviors traditionally understood as folk culture—culture produced outside of the commercial realm.

Seeking to capitalize on creative audiences, some media producers have invited audiences to remix their content. A number of musicians have released tracks expressly inviting audiences to remix them. In a promotion for director Richard Linklater's 2006 film *A Scanner Darkly*, permission was given for the trailer to be re-edited using online video site JumpCut. Similarly, in early 2007 the SciFi Network made audio and video clips of *Battlestar Galactica* available for download, encouraging users to mashup the clips with their own content and send the clips back to the network where a prize will be awarded for the best video.

MEANING

In addition to questions about the right to use content, user creativity has raised questions about the meanings cultural goods have. Policing unauthorized uses of commercial content is a process that aims to ensure copyright owners are in charge of how these goods are represented. Permitting productive audiences to use copyright material exposes copyright owners to risks that their content will be used for purposes they may not have anticipated and may not agree with. While some have no qualms about this—indeed the Creative Commons licensing system was developed with permitting re-use in mind—others are particularly wary.

A similar competition, conducted by General Motors for their Chevy Tahoe SUV in March 2006, provided users with music and video of the Tahoe and invited them to make an ad for the brand. Some of the entries Chevy received back were highly critical of the car, poking fun at Chevy drivers and criticizing the motoring industry. In a somewhat surprising decision, Chevy decided to allow these entries to remain on the competition site, along with the more glowing endorsements. Chevy's response was that they had always anticipated some negative responses, that the brand could weather it, and that it would be disingenuous to remove critical videos. While this opinion may not be held by all who propose such campaigns, this perspective is indicative of the way user creativity is changing the relationship between media producers and media consumers.

See also Audience Power to Resist; Blogosphere; Cultural Appropriation; Digital Divide; Global Community Media; Media Literacy; Mobile Media; Net Neutrality; Online Digital Film and Television; Online Publishing; Pirate Radio; Public Access Television; Transmedia Storytelling and Media Franchises; Youth and Media Use.

Further Reading: Benkler, Yochai. *The Wealth of Networks: How Social Production Transforms Markets and Freedom.* New Haven, CT: Yale University Press, 2006; Bruns, Axel. *Gatewatching: Collaborative Online News Production.* New York: Peter Lang, 2005; Davis, Joshua. "The Secret World of Lonelygirl15." *Wired* 14, no. 12 (December 2006): 232–39; Garfield, Bob. "The Youtube Effect." *Wired,* 14, no. 12 (December 2006): 222–27; Gillmor, Dan. *We the Media: Grassroots Journalism by the People, for the People.* Sebastopol, CA: O'Reilly, 2004; Grossman, Lev. "Person of the Year: You." *Time,* 168, no. 26 (December 2006/January 2007): 38–41; Grossman, Lev. "Power to the People." *Time,* 168, no. 26 (December 2006/January 2007): 42–58; Jenkins, Henry. *Convergence Culture: Where Old and New Media Collide.* New York: NYU Press, 2006; Jenkins, Henry. "Interactive Audiences? The 'Collective Intelligence' of Media Fans," In *Fans, Bloggers, and Gamers,* 134–52. New York: NYU Press, 2006; Lasica, J. D. *Darknet: Hollywood's War against the Digital Generation.* Hoboken, NJ: John Wiley and Sons, 2005; Lessig, L. *Free Culture.* New York: Penguin, 2004; Owen, James. "London Bombing Pictures Mark New Role for Camera Phones." *National Geographic News,* July 11, 2005, http://news.nationalgeographic.com/news/2005/07/0711_050711_londoncell.html; Rose, Frank. "And Now, a Word from Our Customers." *Wired* 14, no. 12 (December 2006): 227–31; Tapscott, Don, and Anthony D. Williams. *Wikinomics: How Mass Collaboration Changes Everything.* New York: Portfolio, 2006. Terdiman, Daniel. "Study: Wikipedia as Accurate as Britannica." *CNet News.com,* December 15, 2005, http://news.com.com/2100-1038_3-5997332.html; Toffler, Alvin. *The Third Wave.* New York: Bantam Books, 1980.

Joshua Green

VIDEO GAMES

Video games are an important entertainment industry and common leisure pursuit, played by people the world over. However, video games continue to be deeply controversial. Playing video games is often viewed as mainly the activity of adolescent boys, and games are seen as isolating and antisocial, creating a generation of socially dysfunctional and unfit children. Worse still, it is alleged that the often high levels of violence in many video games encourage heightened aggression in the vulnerable young minds of those who play them.

Though the origins of digital gaming can be traced back to the 1950s, it was not until the late 1970s and 1980s that digital gaming began to develop as a common leisure activity. Today, video games are a major global industry. Global game sales exceed U.S. $21 billion, with the largest game market still undoubtedly in the United States, where game sales in 2005 were in excess of $7 billion. A recent poll by the Entertainment Software Association (ESA) suggested that 42 percent

---

GAME TERMINOLOGY

The term "video games" is sometimes used to refer to all forms of electronic/digital games played on games consoles, computers, arcade machines, cell phones, and other gaming hardware, while others use it specifically to refer only to console games. To avoid confusion, some authors and organizations have adopted other terms such as "digital games" or "entertainment software" to refer to all forms of electronic gaming.

---

of all Americans planned on purchasing at least one game in the following year. Games sales are now comparable to cinema box office takings and today more video games are sold in the United States and United Kingdom than books.

GENDER

Contrary to popular belief, video game playing is not restricted solely to male adolescents. The ESA suggests that 69 percent of video game players are over the age of 18. Though digital gaming is by no means a level playing field when it comes to gender, the ESA suggests that 38 percent of gamers are female, and in Johannes Fromme's study of over a thousand German schoolchildren, almost a third of girls (and 55.7 percent of boys) claimed to "regularly" play digital games, while it has been suggested that in Korea women make up to close to 70 percent of gamers (Krotoski 2004).

However, statistics on game-playing patterns, particularly in relation to gender, can hide continuing discrepancies and imbalances between the gaming patterns of men and women. Studies suggest that on average women continue to be less likely to play video games than men, and those who do play tend to play a lot less frequently than their male counterparts. In particular, these discrepancies are much greater for adult men and women. This is most likely because women's leisure time continues to be more restricted and fractured than men's; and because video games continue to be created and marketed primarily towards men and feature "masculine" themes, such as violence and male participation sports, with female characters often absent or sexualized within games (Crawford and Gosling 2005). Technology also continues to be primarily "controlled" by men (such as the placing of game machines in "male" spaces, such as the bedrooms of male siblings), which means that game machines and gaming are infrequently seen as belonging to women within households.

VIDEO GAME TIMELINE

1952—Cambridge University doctoral student Alexander "Sandy" Douglas produces a computer version of "noughts and crosses" (tic-tack-toe).

1958—Physicist William Higinbotham at Brookhaven National Laboratory produces a basic tennis simulation.

1962—A team of researchers at Massachusetts Institute of Technology produces a game called *Spacewar*, which becomes the first distributed game, circulated between computer labs.

1972—The first commercial home video-game console, *The Magnavox Odyssey*, launches.

1973—Atari launches the arcade version of *Pong*.

1975—Atari demonstrates *Home-Pong* at toy industry exhibition.

1977—Atari launches the Video Computer System (VCS).

1980—Release of *Space Invaders, Pac Man,* and *Battlezone*.

1981—IBM releases the 8088 processor, leading to the first IBM PCs.

1983—Nintendo produces the Famicom and Mario makes his first appearance in *Donkey Kong.*

1986—Sega releases the *Master System.*

1988—Nintendo launches the Gameboy.

1994—Sony launches the Playstation.

1996—Lara Croft makes her appearance in the first of many *Tomb Raider* games.

1998—Rockstar launches the first *Grand Theft Auto* game in the series. *Lineage* released by NCSoft.

1999—Sony Online releases the first version of *EverQuest.*

2000—The arrival of the Playstation 2.

2001—Microsoft joins the console market with the Xbox.

2003—Nokia releases the NGage, a gaming device with mobile telephone capabilities.

2004—Arrival of *World of Warcraft* from Blizzard Entertainment.

2005—Release of Xbox 360, the Playstation Portable (PSP), and Nintendo DS.

GAMING AS VIOLENT

It is evident that violence or violent themes and/or action are present in a large proportion of video games, with some of the most successful and popular games such as the *Grand Theft Auto* series or *God of War* involving high levels of violent content. Games are now being used for military training and recruitment, such as *America's Army.* Because of this, some express concern that violence in video games could/can lead to heightened aggression. In particular, due to the "interactive" nature of gaming, some authors suggest that violence in video games could potentially be more damaging than that seen in television and film. While television viewers are (largely) passive, video games often require players to actively direct the (in-game) aggression, and hence the aggression/violence is more "participatory" (Emes 1997).

However, the relationship between violent games and gamers (as with violence on television and viewers) is far from conclusive. In particular, such research has been heavily criticized for its often inconsistent methodologies and small and unrepresentative sample groups. It has also been criticized for overestimating the ability of games to influence the specific attitudes and behavior of individuals and/or groups, and for seeing gamers as passive and vulnerable to representations of violence within games (Bryce and Rutter 2003).

GAMERS AS "MOUSE POTATOES"

A further criticism often leveled at video gaming is that it is an antisocial and isolating activity, producing a generation of passive "mouse potatoes." However, this wholly negative attitude towards video gaming continues to be questioned in ongoing research. One study of over 200 London schoolchildren found no evidence to suggest that those who regularly played video games had fewer friends (Colwell and Payne 2000). Gamers are not "absent," but rather constitute active participants within the games they play. Digital gaming is an expression of human

MASSIVELY MULTIPLAYER ONLINE ROLE PLAYING GAMES (MMORPGS)

One of the biggest gaming phenomena of recent years has been the rapid growth of MMORPGs, such as *World of Warcraft, EverQuest,* and *Lineage.* These games allow the player to create characters ("avatars") that they control, and to play out adventures in an online world inhabited by other players from all over the (real) world. Games often allow characters to develop careers, not just as warriors or wizards but also professions such as dancers, miners, or doctors; some games also allow players to own vehicles, pets, and property (such as houses and shops) and even get married. These games have proved hugely popular with many players, with *EverQuest* frequently referred to by gamers as "EverCrack," due to its "addictive" qualities. Nick Yee, who runs a research Web site (the Daedalus Project) on MMORPGs, suggests that nearly 19 percent of over 2,900 gamers who completed his online survey stated that they play MMORPGs over 30 hours per week and over 40 percent in excess of 20 hours per week, and the current (in March 2006) number of players of *World of Warcraft* now exceeds 6 million—greater than the population of Libya.

---

performance and can be a very sociable activity—with gamers playing each other online, meeting up at conventions, and more commonly, playing with friends or family members. In particular, research undertaken for the Interactive Software Federation of Europe suggests that 55 percent of gamers play with others.

Likewise, the argument that playing video games can negatively affect levels of sport participation has been challenged by several authors. For instance, Fromme's study of German schoolchildren found no evidence to support the assertion that playing video games reduces a child's participation in sport. On the contrary, he suggested that his survey had produced some evidence to suggest that "daily use" of digital games was positively associated with increased levels of sport participation. Similarly, a study of U.K. undergraduate students found no evidence to suggest that playing video games could have a negative affect on patterns of sport participation, but rather that sport-related video games could actually inform and increase both the interest and knowledge of sport of some game players (Crawford 2005).

GAMING THEORY

Video games have also grabbed the attention of researchers eager to understand the interaction between gamers and the games they play. However, different researchers and authors have adopted different approaches to studying video games. In particular, it is possible to identify a divide between theorists (such as Murray) who have sought to understand video games by drawing on and developing a film and media studies approach, and those (such as Frasca) who adopt a more psychologically influenced focus upon patterns of play (a perspective called "ludology").

Adopting a media/film studies approach to video games does not simply mean that video games are viewed as "interactive" films, but it provides certain "tools" to help gain a more in-depth understanding of video games. For instance, some argue that games can be understood as a "text," just as any other media form, such as a book, television show, or film. This text can then be studied to look for meanings, both obvious and hidden, within these. From this perspective, it is also possible to study the narratives (stories and themes) within games in the same way we can with film, or study the rules and conventions of gaming using similar tools to those employed in understanding poetry.

However, there are those who question whether video games can be understood as a "text" in the same way as "older" media forms (such as television, radio, and cinema), as, unlike these, video games are not set and rigid, but can vary depending on how the player interacts with them (Kerr et al. 2005). This is a similar argument offered by a "ludology" approach, which suggests that while traditional media (such as films) are "representational" (i.e., they offer a simple representation of reality), video games are based around "simulation," creating a world that gamers can manipulate and interact with.

Nevertheless, the degree of flexibility within a game should not be overemphasized. In particular, the degree of "interactivity" a gamer has with, or over, video games has been questioned by numerous authors. For instance, new technologies (such as DVDs) are frequently introduced and sold to the market using the selling point of their increased "interactive" qualities. The user's level of control or interaction with the medium, though, is still restricted by not only the limitations of technology but also the aims of the designers and manufacturers.

A limitation with early studies that draw on both film/media or ludology approaches is that in many cases gamers were frequently seen as isolated individuals, rather than understood within a wider social setting. However, there is an increasing awareness of the need to include an understanding of the role and importance of gaming within its social setting, such as how people talk about games with friends and family, how they fit into our leisure patterns and everyday lives, and how they can inform some people's identity and sense of who they are (Crawford and Rutter 2007).

Video gaming today is a major leisure and cultural activity, engaged in by many people all around the world, often taking up a sizable proportion of their leisure time. As with any cultural activity, it is impossible to categorize this as either wholly "good" or "bad." Video games are often violent and can be sexist, homophobic, and racist—as can any media form, such as film, music, and literature. However, video games are also an important industry; they allow people to relax, and can be a source of conversation and identity for many. It is therefore important that we understand gaming within a wider social and cultural setting, sometimes as shocking, sometimes awe-inspiring, but more often a relatively normal and mundane pastime engaged in, and discussed, by many.

See also Children and Effects; Digital Divide; The DVD; Online Digital Film and Television; Presidential Stagecraft and Militainment; Transmedia Storytelling and Media Franchises; Violence and Media; Youth and Media Use.

Further Reading: Bryce, Jo, and Jason Rutter. "Gender Dynamics and the Social and Spatial Organization of Computer Gaming." *Leisure Studies* 22 (2003): 1–15; Colwell, John, and J. Payne. "Negative Correlates of Computer Game Play in Adolescents." *British Journal of Psychology* 91 (2000): 295–310. Crawford, Garry. "Digital Gaming, Sport and Gender." *Leisure Studies* 24, no. 3 (2005): 259–70; Crawford, Garry, and Victoria K. Gosling. "Toys of Boy? The Continued Marginalization and Participation of Women as Digital Gamers." *Sociological Research Online* 10, no. 1 (2005): http://www.socres online.org.uk/10/1/crawford.html; Crawford, Garry, and Jason Rutter. "Playing the Game: Performance in Digital Game Audiences." In *Fandom: Identities and Communities in a Mediated World*, ed. Jonathan Gray, Cornel Sandvoss, and C. Lee Harrington. New York: New York University Press, 2007; Emes, Craig E. "Is Pac Man Eating Our Children? A Review of the Effects of Video Games on Children." *The Canadian Journal of Psychiatry* 42 (1997): 409–14; Entertainment Software Association. *Essential Facts about the Computer and Video Game Industry*. 2006. http://www.theesa.com/archives/files/Essential%20Facts%202006.pdf; Frasca, Gonzalo. "Simulation versus Narrative: Introduction to Ludology." In *The Video Game Theory Reader*, ed. Mark J. P Wolf and Bernard Perron, 221–36. New York: Routledge, 2003; Fromme, Johannes. "Computer Games as a Part of Children's Culture." *Game Studies* 3, no. 1 (2003), http://www.gamestudies.org/0301/fromme/; Gee, James Paul. *What Video Games Have to Tell Us About Learning and Literacy*. New York: Palgrave, 2004; Kelly, R. V. *Massively Multiplayer Online Role-Playing Games*. Jefferson, NC: McFarland, 2004; Kerr, Aphra, Pat Brereton, and Julian Kücklich. "New Media—New Pleasures?" *International Journal of Cultural Studies* 8, no. 3 (2005): 375–94; Krotoski, Aleks. *Chicks and Joysticks: An Exploration of Women and Gaming*. London: Entertainment and Leisure Software Publisher's Association, 2004; Murray, Janet H. *Hamlet on the Holodeck: The Future of Narrative in Cyberspace*. Cambridge, MA: MIT Press, 2001; Newman, James. *Videogames*. New York: Routledge, 2004; Rutter, Jason, and Jo Bryce, eds. *Understanding Digital Games*. Thousand Oaks, CA: Sage, 2006; Vorderer, Peter, and Jennings Bryant, eds. *Playing Video Games: Motives, Responses, and Consequences*, Mahwah, NJ: LEA, 2006; Wolf, Mark J. P., and Bernard Perron, eds. *The Video Game Theory Reader*. New York: Routledge, 2003; Yee, Nick. *The Daedalus Project*. 2006. http://www.nickyee.com/daedalus.

Garry Crawford

VIDEO NEWS RELEASES: A HIDDEN EPIDEMIC OF FAKE TV NEWS

Of all the public relations tactics to shape news content, video news releases (VNRs) are the most intrusive and widespread. VNRs are sponsored video segments that mimic independent news reports, but promote the sponsor's products, company, or preferred policies. Television stations routinely air VNRs during news programming, but almost never disclose them to viewers. Since the sponsors that fund VNRs, the public relations (PR) firms that produce them, and the TV stations that air them all benefit from nondisclosure, how can viewers' "right to know" where their news comes from be protected?

The public expects that "news" is information that has been gathered and verified by a journalist acting as a fair observer. A fair observer may have a point of view, but should avoid—or at least fully disclose—any potential, perceived, or real conflict of interest.

"Fake news" occurs when PR practitioners adopt the practices and/or appearance of journalists, to insert persuasive messages into news media. While fake news is obviously bad news, it's very good for PR. For example, praise for Brand X has much more credibility when it is relayed by a seemingly independent reporter or commentator, rather than an actor in a commercial or a Brand X spokesperson in any setting.

The dominant form of fake news is the VNR. VNRs are sponsored, prepackaged video segments and additional footage created by PR firms, or by publicists within corporations, government agencies, or nonprofit organizations. A VNR presents its sponsor's message using a format and tone that mimic independent television news reports. Nothing in the material for broadcast identifies the

THE LIFE CYCLE OF A VNR

VNRs are usually part of larger PR campaigns, launched to burnish a client's image, improve product sales, respond to negative developments, or support policies favorable to the client. Broadcast PR firms often work as subcontractors to the firm leading the overall PR campaign. In addition to producing VNRs, broadcast PR firms may arrange satellite media tours—a series of TV interviews conducted remotely, which often follow a script similar to the VNR—or produce the radio equivalent of a VNR, called an audio news release (ANR).

Once a PR firm scripts, films, and edits a VNR, it distributes and promotes the segment to TV newsrooms. Common VNR delivery methods include satellite and online video channels, as well as the video feeds of such major news companies as CBS, FOX, CNN, and the Associated Press. In its 2003 annual report, the firm Medialink Worldwide boasted that its VNRs, ANRs, and print materials "reach more than 11,000 newsrooms" and "more than 11,000 online multimedia newsrooms." The firm D S Simon Productions promises, on its Web site, to maximize TV broadcasts of its VNRs, with "300 targeted pitch calls to broadcast networks, network affiliate news feeds, national cable outlets, regional cable networks, and syndicated shows, as well as local network affiliates and independent TV stations."

After receiving a VNR, TV newsroom staff can incorporate the footage into newscasts in various ways: by airing the entire, prepackaged and narrated segment; by airing an edited version of the prepackaged segment; by mixing and matching footage from the prepackaged segment with additional unnarrated video footage provided by the PR firm, called B-roll; or by mixing any of the VNR video with other video footage. A study by the Center for Media and Democracy found that the vast majority of VNR-derived news segments did not contain *any* independently generated video. In nearly 85 percent of the VNR broadcasts documented, all of the video and information presented in the aired news segment came directly from the VNR package.

Using electronic tracking systems, broadcast PR firms determine how widely a VNR is aired. The firms share this information with the client that sponsored the VNR. Firms may also boast about high VNR placement rates to prospective clients, as a way to prove—as one D S Simon Productions advertisement asserts—that "we get you on television."

segment as a VNR or discloses its sponsor. VNRs are just one of many deceptive PR techniques. Yet, they represent a substantial degradation of the modern information environment, for two reasons. One is that television is the most popular news source in the United States. The other is that inserting VNRs into TV newscasts is a widespread and undisclosed practice.

WHO'S BEHIND YOUR NEWS?

Indeed, VNR use appears to be near universal. Nielsen studies in 1992, 1996, and 2001 found that 100 percent of TV stations surveyed aired VNRs. In 2003, the chair of the major broadcast PR firm Medialink Worldwide told a radio reporter, "Every television station in America with a newscast has used and probably uses regularly this material from corporations and organizations that we provide as VNRs." In the 1990s and early 2000s, many TV stations increased the amount of time allotted to news programming while either decreasing newsroom budgets or simply maintaining them at previous levels. This trend made VNRs increasingly popular among newsroom staff. "Local broadcasters are being asked to do more with less, and they have been forced to rely more on prepackaged news to take up the slack," explained Project for Excellence in Journalism director Tom Rosenstiel and political science professor Marion Just in a March 2005 *New York Times* op-ed piece.

The number of VNRs produced and delivered to TV newsrooms is significant. An academic study from December 2000 credited Medialink Worldwide with producing 1,000 VNRs annually, "roughly double the number of its nearest competitor." That study, by Mark Harmon and Candace White at the University of Tennessee, also stated that "a typical newsroom may have ten to fifteen VNRs available per day." In 1990, the magazine of the Society of Professional Journalists estimated that 5,000 to 15,000 VNRs are distributed each year.

VNRs usually arrive in TV newsrooms as part of the station's satellite or online video feeds (see "The Life Cycle of a VNR" sidebar). Such feeds offer a wide range of video, from independently produced news segments to VNRs to advertisements. Some TV newsroom personnel have claimed that they have mistaken VNRs for "real" news, since both can be downloaded from the same source. However, video providers claim to have clearly segregated VNRs from real news in their feeds, following the controversy over Bush administration VNRs (see below). In addition, as they enter newsrooms, nearly all VNRs list their sponsors in the opening frames. These frames are used to inform newsroom personnel only; they are neither intended for nor formatted for broadcast. Nonetheless, PR executives often point to them as evidence that they have done their ethical duty.

Despite these measures and despite journalistic codes and TV station policies that call for clear identification of all VNR footage, disclosure to news audiences is exceedingly rare. In a two-part study that tracked nearly 70 VNRs released in 2005 and 2006, the Center for Media and Democracy documented 140 VNR broadcasts during TV news programming. In only two of those broadcasts did the TV station provide clear disclosure of the source of the VNR footage to news viewers.

Peter Simmons, an Australian academic with Charles Sturt University's School of Communications, has written that "individual journalists and public relations practitioners perceive their work to be enhanced when news release material is used without disclosure." Another finding of the Center for Media and Democracy's study supports his assertion. When one PR firm started mentioning the sponsors at the end of its prepackaged VNRs, using on-screen labels and verbal statements, TV stations removed these notifications and *still* failed to provide disclosure to viewers in 12 out of the 15 instances documented.

CASE STUDY: "OIL LOBBYIST'S 'NEWS' DENIES INCONVENIENT TRUTHS"

In June 2006, the broadcast PR firm Medialink Worldwide put out a VNR titled, "Global Warming and Hurricanes: All Hot Air?" The firm identified "TCS Daily Science Roundtable" as the client behind the segment. But Medialink didn't disclose that TCS Daily is a Web site published by Tech Central Station and was, at the time, a project of the Republican lobbying and PR firm DCI Group. Or that DCI Group counts among its clients ExxonMobil. Or that ExxonMobil gave the Tech Central Science Foundation $95,000 in 2003, for "climate change support."

The VNR features Dr. William Gray and Dr. James J. O'Brien, who are identified as "two of the nation's top weather and ocean scientists." Gray denies that there's any link between global warming and the severity of recent hurricane seasons. "We don't think that's the case," he says. "This is the way nature sometimes works."

In reality, the link between climate change and hurricane severity has not been disproved. Peer-reviewed scientific studies on the issue have reached conflicting conclusions, though an in-depth analysis reported in September 2006 found "a large human influence" on rising sea-surface temperatures, which lead to stronger hurricanes. The same month, *Nature* magazine reported on a position paper from federal scientists that linked intensified hurricanes to global warming; the document was reportedly quashed by the Bush administration.

Drs. Gray and O'Brien are meteorologists with extensive experience predicting hurricanes. However, neither of them are impartial. In June 2006, Gray told the *Denver Post* that global warming is a "hoax," something that "they've been brainwashing us [with] for 20 years." O'Brien is associated with corporate-funded organizations that question climate change, as a member of Tech Central Station's "Science Roundtable" and as an expert at the George C. Marshall Institute.

Sadly, none of these affiliations, caveats, or complexities were communicated when WTOK-11 (Meridian, Mississippi) aired as "news" an edited and revoiced version of the TCS Daily VNR on May 31, 2006. Viewers were also not told that the segment was paid for and scripted by oil company lobbyists.

WHAT'S THE LAW?

Much of the debate over disclosure has focused on VNRs from the U.S. federal government. In 2004, the Bush administration was revealed to have funded VNRs on such controversial topics as the No Child Left Behind education policy and the Medicare prescription drug plan. A March 2005 *New York Times* exposé detailed the undisclosed broadcast of Bush administration VNRs on Iraq, Afghanistan, and airport security, among other issues, while noting that VNR use also occurred in the Clinton administration.

The nonpartisan investigative arm of Congress, the Government Accountability Office, ruled in 2005 that any government VNR that does not make its source clear to news audiences constitutes illegal covert propaganda. However, the Bush administration's Justice Department and Office of Management and Budget dismissed that ruling, claiming that government VNRs are permissible, as long as they are "informational." Temporary measures passed by the U.S. Congress required "a clear notification" for government VNRs, without defining what that means. These measures have since expired, leaving how and whether to disclose government VNRs to the discretion of the federal agency and the television stations involved.

Commenting on the debate over government VNRs, Federal Communications Commission (FCC) Commissioner Jonathan Adelstein wrote, "The surprising thing, though, is nobody bothered to mention that there are separate disclosure requirements enforced by the FCC under the Communications Act." As summarized in an April 2005 public notice from the FCC, the Act's sponsorship identification rules require that "whenever broadcast stations and cable operators air VNRs, licensees and operators generally must clearly disclose to members of their audiences the nature, source and sponsorship of the material." The FCC also asserts in the notice, "Listeners and viewers are entitled to know who seeks to persuade them."

However, as of early 2007, whether and how the Communications Act (which was written in 1934) and its sponsorship identification rules (which reflect the radio payola controversies of the 1950s) apply to VNRs remained controversial questions. The FCC has not penalized any TV stations for airing VNRs without disclosure. The agency did open a VNR investigation in August 2006, sending letters of inquiry to the owners of the 77 TV stations named in the first part of the Center for Media and Democracy study.

Lawyers representing the public relations industry and broadcasters have challenged applying the Communications Act to most VNRs. They maintain that the Act only requires VNRs to be disclosed if the segments deal with controversial or political issues, or if TV stations are paid to air them.

Advocates of VNR disclosure have made three basic arguments, with regard to current laws and regulations. One is that the Communications Act's sponsorship identification rules apply when payment is made anywhere up or down the chain of production of broadcast material. Since sponsors pay PR firms to produce VNRs, the sponsor must be revealed to news audiences when a VNR is aired. The second argument is that VNRs save TV stations

HOW CAN I TELL WHAT'S A VNR?

Unfortunately, it's difficult even for savvy viewers to identify undisclosed VNR footage that has been inserted into television newscasts. PR firms are adroit at wrapping their clients' messages in a TV news–like tone, and some TV news is bad or even promotional without being sponsored by undisclosed clients. Still, there are characteristics common to VNRs, which viewers can consider VNR "red flags." These include the following:

- There is no local footage for local TV newscasts
- No local people are interviewed, again for local TV newscasts
- There are positive mentions of particular products, companies, or policies
- No reporter is shown on location, or the reporter shown does not usually appear on the station

---

thousands of dollars in production, filming, and editing costs for each minute that VNR footage substitutes for the station's own reporting. Therefore, a VNR represents a substantial in-kind contribution or "consideration" paid to TV stations, which also triggers the Act's sponsorship identification requirements. The last pro-disclosure argument points to TV stations' obligation to serve the "public interest, convenience and necessity," as described in the Communications Act. In exchange for their free use of the public airwaves—a limited and valuable resource—stations agree to act as public trustees. Broadcasting promotional segments while denying viewers the information needed to evaluate what's being presented as "news" is clearly not in the public interest. Therefore, airing undisclosed VNRs violates the terms of stations' licenses, as well as the Act.

Whether current laws and regulations mandate VNR disclosure is not an academic question. If the FCC were to begin actively requiring VNR disclosure, all TV stations—broadcast and cable—would feel the effects. Moreover, all VNRs—whether sponsored by public or private entities—would likely be covered. This is an important point; as of early 2007, all of the disclosure measures debated and passed by Congress applied to government VNRs only. Yet, companies fund the vast majority of VNRs. In 2004, the chair of the Medialink Worldwide firm told a trade magazine that government agencies account for only 5 percent of his business.

It is possible that new rules, legislation, and/or court decisions may be deemed necessary to clarify TV stations' obligations with regard to VNR disclosure. This is not surprising, and may well be the best way for Congress and the FCC to catch up to what has been a common media practice for decades.

DEFENDERS OF THE STATUS QUO

As might be expected, the broadcast PR firms that produce VNRs don't want independent oversight of their industry. Broadcasters' groups have taken a similar stance. As controversies about undisclosed VNRs have surfaced repeatedly over the years, these groups have steadfastly promoted industry self-regulation and opposed any government action.

In 1991, the nonprofit organization Consumers Union released a report called, "Are Video News Releases Blurring the Line between News and Advertising?" In 1992, *TV Guide* ran a cover story on VNRs titled "Fake News." In an accompanying editorial, *TV Guide* suggested that "when a TV news organization includes film or tape prepared by an outside source in a broadcast, the label 'VIDEO SUPPLIED BY [COMPANY OR GROUP NAME]' should be visible for as long as the material is on screen." In response, the Public Relations Society of America (PRSA) promoted a voluntary "Code of Good Practice for Video News Releases." The chair of the firm Medialink Worldwide explained at the time, "When you see a potential problem, whether real or imagined, you respond. We're taking a page right out of the crisis management textbooks."

In 2004, after the Government Accountability Office found some government VNRs to be covert propaganda, PRSA suggested that publicists not use the word "reporting" when narrating VNRs. In June 2005, PRSA called for "vigorous self-regulation by all those involved at every level in the production and dissemination of prepackaged broadcast materials."

On behalf of broadcasters, the Radio-Television News Directors Association (RTNDA) issued new ethical guidelines for VNR use, following the March 2005 *New York Times* exposé on Bush administration VNRs. In June 2005, RTNDA told the FCC that an "informal survey" of its members had confirmed their adherence to voluntary disclosure standards. Shortly afterward, RTNDA's president compared VNRs to the Loch Ness monster, telling the *Washington Times*, "Everyone talks about it, but not many people have actually seen it."

In 2006, following the first part of the Center for Media and Democracy's study and the FCC's subsequent launch of its VNR investigation, 15 broadcast PR firms announced the formation of a new lobbying group, the "National Association of Broadcast Communicators." This group subsequently issued joint statements with PRSA, objecting to the FCC investigation. RTNDA went further, asking the FCC to halt its investigation and casting aspersions on the Center for Media and Democracy and its research. The PR industry and broadcasters' groups additionally claimed that any VNR disclosure requirements would abridge broadcasters' First Amendment rights and impede the "free flow of information."

In response, Peter Simmons asked about "the quality of the information flowing freely to the public." He added, "When information flows as news, the public's interest is best served when it can make decisions about the credibility of the information based on clear identification of the source and balanced discussion of motives." Such sentiments echo the FCC's stated principle, that "listeners and viewers are entitled to know who seeks to persuade them."

While the debate over TV stations' VNR disclosure responsibilities continues, broadcast PR firms are increasingly exploring online venues for VNRs, including news Web sites, video blogs, video search engines, video podcasts, and cell phones. "Hurt by public criticism of VNRs, possible Federal Communications Commission oversight, and a shrunken news hole, these companies are looking for ways to survive," the trade publication *PR Week* reported in December 2006. "Making the Internet a bigger part of their offerings could be the answer." Many PR professionals believe that focusing on online communications will allow them to better target audiences, while limiting potential oversight. From a public-interest perspective, this is a troubling proliferation of fake news. Unlike the VNRs streaming into TV newsrooms, those posted online often don't make clear what they are or who paid for them. And, unlike television, Internet news providers are not licensed and cannot be held accountable for nondisclosure of sponsored material.

The fake news problem has become so large that it requires a multipronged approach to address it. Multiple scholars and public-interest advocates argue that "old media" disclosure requirements must be clarified and strengthened, so that television broadcasts of VNRs (along with radio broadcasts of audio news releases; see "The Life Cycle of a VNR" side bar) are clearly disclosed to news audiences. They also advocate for collecting more information on the intrusion of fake news into "new media," so that effective online disclosure standards can be developed. Lastly, they call for a serious public discussion of what is news, what are news providers' responsibilities, and what it means in the digital age to have the right to know "who seeks to persuade" you.

See also Advertising and Persuasion; Hypercommercialism; Media and the Crisis of Values; Media Reform; Product Placement; Propaganda Model; Regulating the Airwaves.

Further Reading: Andersen, Robin. *Consumer Culture and TV Programming.* Boulder, CO: Westview, 1995; Farsetta, Diane, and Daniel Price. "Fake TV News: Widespread and Undisclosed." Center for Media and Democracy, April 6, 2006, http://www.prwatch. org/fakenews/execsummary; Farsetta, Diane, and Daniel Price. "Still Not the News: Stations Overwhelmingly Fail to Disclose VNRs." Center for Media and Democracy, November 14, 2006, http://www.prwatch.org/fakenews2/execsummary; Goodman, Amy, and David Goodman. *Static: Government Liars, Media Cheerleaders, and the People Who Fight Back.* New York: Hyperion, 2006; Hazen, Don, and Julie Winokur. *We the Media.* New York: The New Press, 1997; McAllister, Matthew P. *The Commercialization of American Culture: New Advertising, Control and Democracy.* Thousand Oaks, CA: Sage, 1996; Stauber, John, and Sheldon Rampton. *Toxic Sludge Is Good for You! Lies, Damn Lies and the Public Relations Industry.* Monroe, ME: Common Courage Press, 1995.

Diane Farsetta

VIOLENCE AND MEDIA: FROM MEDIA EFFECTS TO MORAL PANICS

Concerns about media and violence have historical roots going back to the Victorian era when the newly emerging middle classes expressed anxiety over the working class reading "penny dreadfuls" instead of more wholesome fare such as "morally uplifting" literature. The modern era, on the other hand, led to numerous studies that have become known as the "media effects" literature, which has sought to demonstrate a causal connection between media representations and acts of real violence. While some claim to have demonstrated behavioral effects of media violence, critics charge that the research is flawed in various ways. Many also claim that debates over media and violence are often a cover for other anxieties that remain too threatening for many people to talk about. What are the real issues being concealed by the debates over media and violence?

For the past 40 years, researchers have been investigating what effects exposure to violent images have on children and adults, especially with regard to stimulating aggression or aggressive thoughts. The results of this mountain of studies remain inconclusive with causal links between images of violence and actual violent or aggressive behavior hard to track with any degree of accuracy. Early studies attempted to document the impact that violent movie images had on children, followed by television images and now video game interactions. Critics say these research models are flawed, and suffer in differing degrees from inadequately defined objects of study, inconsistent definitions, misapplied research methodologies, experimental limitations, and grossly simplified models of human behavior. Nevertheless, these studies have shaped public debate on the relationship of media technology, play, and child development. A brief word is in order about what concepts these studies have been based upon and the definitions of violence and aggression that underlie them.

The obvious question to ask is what is meant by "violence" and "aggression" with regard to media and its effect on people. The problem resides in both the conflation of real violence with its representation in TV, film, or video games and in what activity is presumed to be violent or aggressive. In some studies, the Three Stooges, Roadrunner, and Bugs Bunny are placed in the same category as horror slasher films and real news violence, simply based on the actions of the characters involved—who hit whom, how often, and so on. There is no meaningful distinction drawn between real and fictional violent representations, or between types of fictional violent representations and their contexts. The second point is the meaning of "effects." It is presumed that media have effects on people, but what those effects are is presumed to revolve around aggressive or passive activity, as if these are the only ways to understand how media influences individual behavior. For example, we rarely ask what kind of effect book reading, bicycling, or playing football have on subjects unless we have a predetermined answer in mind. Thus, some people would object to others reading certain kinds of books because of the violent or sexual imagery conveyed through words. However, this speaks less to the position of the reader and more to the concerns of the one objecting to the material. In other words, what is measured, if anything, is more the subjective concern of the researcher or the offense to those who would act as moral arbiter, and less the actual effect on the subject in question. Those skeptical of media effects studies charge that researchers consistently draw spurious causal connections between data that remain mere correlations, and point to the following conceptual confusion and logical flaws: (1) the simplistic theories of self used by some psychologists and child development specialists; (2) the moral agendas of political figures and those with a religious or cultural objection to media representations; and (3) legitimate concerns by parents who perceive their children as "out of control."

MODELS AND TRADITIONS OF RESEARCH

Social learning theory, developed by psychologist Alberto Bandura in the 1970s, is a modification of B. F. Skinner's behaviorist theories applied to adolescents and aggression. His research attempted to understand the interactions between the self and environment (reciprocal determinism) and set the initial standard for conducting studies of media and violence. Based on principles of observational learning or modeling therapy and self-regulation, Bandura illustrated his points with the famous Bobo doll studies. In these experiments he had a fellow experimenter strike a Bobo doll, designed for that very purpose, while children observed on a TV monitor. When given the Bobo doll the same children proceeded to strike the doll as they had witnessed. This was considered evidence that children "model" the behavior of others. What was not considered was the "meaning" the Bobo doll had for the children. The doll was designed to be struck, so this tells us little about aggression connected to modeling behavior, other than the children figured out this is what you are supposed to do with this type of toy. What was demonstrated was more the authority of the experimenter than any inherent aggression as a by-product of modeling behavior.

Bandura claimed that effective modeling depended on various degrees of attention, retention, motor reproduction, and motivation. He argued that children model the behavior of adults and other children, including media representations, hence, the concern over the consumption of violent media images. While this can explain the fact that people do model the behavior of others, even virtual others, it cannot explain what that modeling means to the individual. The issue of motivation is central, but cannot be answered by this type of behaviorist framework, because it does not offer an explanation for how interpretation can modify behavior. How do children, in fact, understand violent media representations, and do they make distinctions between real and fictional violence?

Anderson and Bushman's General Aggression Model (GAM), based on the earlier work of Bandura and others, attempted to go beyond the limitations of social learning theory, assigning priority to feelings, thoughts, and physical responses to violent media in specific situations leading to a presumed interpretation on the part of the subject. The problem, however, resides in how the GAM understands violence and aggression. The GAM perspective is often guilty of conflating the violence of horror films and "shooter" video games with the supposed earlier violence of Pac-Man, argued as desensitizing the public to real life violence. Again, the issue is one of understanding the differences between real-life aggression and violence and fantasy aggression or violence. This conflation is made consistently by critics of violent media representations.

The catharsis model, meanwhile, assumed that consuming violent media works to *lower* aggression, to "let off steam." A favorite position of defenders of violent films, TV shows, and video games, the catharsis model was based on the work of Seymour Feshbach and Robert D. Sanger, in *Television and Aggression: An Experimental Field Study*, conducted in 1971. This model attempted to offer evidence that people can benefit from consuming violent fantasies since they can give us a safe way of coping with our anxieties and general fears. Unfortunately, their studies have not been adequately replicated and remain more of a hypothesis than a testable reality.

The cultivation theory of George Gerber, former dean of the Annenberg School for Communication at the University of Pennsylvania, proposed a broader cultural or ideological critique of violent media. Often referred to as the "mean world syndrome," cultivation theory used content analysis and surveys, avoiding the problems of the experimental laboratory setup. Cultivation theory argued that heavy consumption of media led to the cultural effects of political passivity and a greater tolerance for real-world violence. The problem here is that fearful people may be drawn to watching more television for a variety of reasons, which points out the additional problem of not addressing individual variations in how people consume and understand media.

CRITICS OF EFFECTS RESEARCH

Jonathan Freedman, in *Media Violence and Its Effect on Aggression: Assessing the Scientific Evidence*, examined most of the experimental studies conducted on violence in media and found them lacking in both consistent definitions of what constitutes aggression or violence, as well as flawed methods of research and a continuing confusion of correlation with causation. The work of Barker and Petley in their volume, *Ill Effects: The Media/Violence Debate*, along with the work of David Gauntlett in that same book, deepens the critique voiced by Freedman. One of the major flaws of these studies is their set of assumptions about human subjects. These assumptions give no room for people, children, or adults to interpret or make sense of their own actions. Meaning, though, is important. How we understand fantasy and reality, imagination and reason, aggressive play from real assault, is critical in our ability to assess risk to ourselves and to others. The media effects perspective, unfortunately, does not take meaning seriously, assuming that people are either overtly or covertly manipulated into believing and acting the way that they do simply by exposure to media images. The larger social context within which we understand images, our everyday lives, families, social groups, and so forth is almost never integrated into this type of research on media and violence.

For example, Jeffrey Goldstein argues that the absence of volition in media effects research combined with not taking seriously the social context of media consumption distorts the understanding of the role media play in the lives of children and adults. Some researchers take this lack of choice even further, arguing that the meanings we make of media violence are not significant, because our making sense of the world is only accomplished through predetermined social lenses that condition us to look at the world in a very specific way, what is often called "interpolation." This position is refuted by the research of James Tobin, who in *Good Guys Don't Wear Hats: Children's Talk about the Media* looked at how children actually understood the film medium, violent or otherwise, and pointed out the wide variety of interpretations children actually make of their experiences with media. Violent images may frighten one child and simply bore another. One cannot find a given interpretation as the "correct" one way to understand fictional violence over any other.

The real social lives of humans, our families, friends, and authority figures—that is, the larger social context—do indeed shape our responses to violent media images. The degree to which each of these variables influences behavior, and the combination of these multiple influences on behavior, has proven to be the most difficult measure for media researchers. Further complicating research models remains the distinction between fantasy violence and real violence, a differentiation especially important for children. The point here is that children have to make these distinctions in order to understand how to survive in the real world. Adults can more easily blur these distinctions if they have already established what is real and what is fantasy to begin with. Tobin's studies demonstrate that children make this distinction between fantasy and reality at a very early age.

Hence, it is not surprising that advertisers and filmmakers work hard to break these barriers down in order to cement audience identification with the product or film work at an early age. However, the fact that customers, whether children or adults, play with these boundaries, through their own critiques, jokes,

MORAL PANICS AND MEDIA FEARS

"Moral panic" was a term originally developed by Stanley Cohen in his 1972 book *Folk Devils and Moral Panics: The Creation of Mods and Rockers*. He described the organized public campaign of harassment against the emerging youth subculture of mods and rockers by the media and agents of public control, law enforcement, politicians and legislators, action groups, and the public at large. This panic over an emerging youth subculture was stimulated by converting mods and rockers into folk devils, as repositories of public anxieties over widespread social change. Erich Goode and Nachman Ben-Yehuda in *Moral Panics: The Social Construction of Deviance* as well as Barry Glassner's *The Culture of Fear: Why Americans Are Afraid of the Wrong Things* and Karen Sternheimer's *It's Not the Media: The Truth about Pop Culture's Influence on Children* extend this analysis to all types of media representations. Earlier examples of media moral panics can be seen during the 1950s with the moral campaign, organized by Dr. Fredric Wertham, a New York psychiatrist, that attacked horror comic books as contributing to juvenile delinquency. As John Springhall points out in his book, *Youth, Popular Culture and Moral Panics: Penny Gaffs to Gangsta-Rap, 1820–1996*, these patterns of social dread reflected the anxiety and fears of an emerging middle class over a corruptible working class who ignored socially "uplifting" reading in favor of "dime novels" or "penny dreadfuls." Harold Schechter, in *Savage Pastime: A Cultural History of Violent Entertainment*, describes the extreme forms of entertainment which both the early middle and working classes of pre-Victorian Europe enjoyed, making modern-day panics over television, film, and video game violence seem silly by comparison.

parodies, imitations, and other forms of meaning-making, indicates that humans are active producers often at odds with commercial producers.

MORAL PANICS AND MORAL ENTREPRENEURS

The persistence of such controversy around media effects research may be understood as a deeper crisis in how we think of children, technology, and threats in the modern world. These periodic concerns expressed as anxiety over "media violence" are given the term moral panics.

Moral panics are public campaigns that often call for censorship or express outrage at behavior or fantasies of particular lower-status social groups when those same groups are perceived as escaping the control of the dominant status group. They occur often during periods of social and technological change and may crystallize around a particular emotional issue. The early Salem witch burnings were facilitated by the panic induced by male clergy members who felt threatened by the increasing power of women in the church. Closer to our time period, concerns over comic books, pool hall attendance, heavy metal and rap music, television violence and sex, films, and a host of media activities have come under public scrutiny for their supposed corruption of morals and youth. In the 1980s, the Parents Music Resource Center went after heavy metal bands for their supposed effect on youth and the belief that such music "caused" teenage suicides. Today, it is conservative groups like Focus on the Family attacking Barbie dolls and Teletubbies or the Parents Television Council decrying acts of television violence and gore, while liberal groups attack the computer games *Manhunt* and *Grand Theft Auto* for their racial and gender stereotypes and simulated sex in hidden codes. While racists and sexist attitudes persist in our society, the degree to which media cause those attitudes has yet to be demonstrated by effects research, and media and First Amendment scholars argue that the values of an

MORAL ENTREPRENEURS AND MEDIA CONSUMPTION

Originally coined by the sociologist Howard Becker in his 1963 work, *Outsiders: Studies in the Sociology of Deviance*, moral entrepreneurs work as crusading reformers attempting to clean up what they perceive as the failure of lower-status groups. With humanitarian intents, such groups and individuals often work in a paternalist fashion to shape the behavior of those in social classes below them, usually taking on and being offended by the representations of working- or lower-class culture. Moral entrepreneurs work to mobilize social groups and the public at large against what they perceive as threats to the dominant social order, helping to define what is considered deviant behavior. The use of labeling and stereotyping often operates in constructing definitions of what is deviant. These labels are, in turn, used by moral entrepreneurs to support their actions against the offending representations. For example, by invoking moral outrage against rock music, the Parents Music Resource Center signaled to concerned parents that they shared their values and concerns. This solidarity is, in turn, cemented by creating an "out" group, while reinforcing the prejudices of the "in" group.

open society and that the attendant civil liberties enjoyed therein outweigh unproven media effects assertions.

What is interesting is that in most of the qualitative studies of children and media violence, when asked if they were affected by violent images, most children responded with the assertion that they were not affected but their younger peers were affected. Middle-class parents often voiced the same concerns—they are not affected but those lower-class folks down the block might be harmed. In other words, the panic over media and violence can be clearly viewed as a panic over status and power, with the higher-status groups—parents over children, middle class over working or lower class, whites over blacks, and so on—asserting their so-called moral authority in order to protect some supposed moral boundary of society.

The fact that these concerns over media and violence are most often promoted by advocacy groups who claim that they have children's welfare at stake, as well as media pundits, politicians looking for votes, and professional experts and organizations, indicates that the issue of media violence is one that lends itself to the work of moral entrepreneurs. Occupying a privileged position in society, such moral entrepreneurs are able to exploit their social position to assert their authority in reinforcing conventional "common-sense" folkways that appeal to many parents anxious over the behavior of their children.

"OUT OF CONTROL": FEARS OF YOUTH AND TECHNOLOGY

The third point, that parents feel their children are out of their control, is understandable given the rapid rates of technological change, the decrease in public play areas, the rise of the Internet, and the expansion of widespread social and political inequality leading to less opportunities in life for members of both the working and middle classes. According to Dr. Henry Jenkins, director of the Comparative Media Studies program at the Massachusetts Institute of Technology, the moral panic that surrounds the issues of violence and media can be traced to our fear and anxieties over adolescent behavior, a fear of new technology, and the expansion of youth culture throughout the media landscape into all areas of everyday life. In addition, the deep fear of the intermingling of the private and public spheres of everyday life is expressed not only in terms of parental fear of children being exposed to media violence, but also in images of sexuality and online predatory behavior. Given the widespread adult ignorance of technology and science, it should not be surprising that when their son or daughter knows more about the technology than they do, parents feel at a distinct disadvantage. Such competency on the part of one's children raises a host of questions about parental authority as well as ideas of childhood innocence, which is challenged as children gain more knowledge through the Internet, television, and film.

Indeed, the old Victorian myth of innocent children without greed, desire, or competency is under attack. The response by parents is often to either demonize children, to ignore them, or to idealize them as little angels, all revealing a lack of understanding of the complex reality of childhood in the modern world. But seeing technology and media violence as destroying the innocence of childhood is just as misleading as assuming that children are powerful liberators of modern technology and can easily withstand onslaughts of media violence. What is required, as Gerard Jones points out in *Killing Monsters: Why Children Need Fantasy, Super Heroes, and Make-Believe Violence*, is for children to feel safe in playing with their fantasy monsters, whether it is in a book, on television, in film, or a video game. Playing with and killing monsters in a fantasy world may be just another way to keep these monsters from becoming our everyday harsh realities.

See also Children and Effects; Government Censorship and Freedom of Speech; Media Literacy; Obscenity and Indecency; Pornography; Presidential Stagecraft and Militainment; Representations of Masculinity; Representations of Race; Representations of Women; Sensationalism, Fear Mongering, and Tabloid Media; Shock Jocks; Video Games; Women's Magazines; Youth and Media Use.

Further Reading: Anderson, Craig A., and B. J. Bushman. "The Effects of Media Violence on Society." *Science* 295 (2002): 2377–78; Anderson, Craig A., and B. J. Bushman. "Human Aggression." *Annual Review of Psychology* 53 (2002): 27–51; Bandura, Albert. *Aggression: A Social Learning Analysis.* Englewood Cliffs, NJ: Prentice-Hall, 1973; Bandura, Albert. *Social Learning Theory.* New York: General Learning Press, 1977; Barker, Martin, and Julian Petley, eds. *Ill Effects: The Media/Violence Debate.* New York: Routledge, 2001; Becker, Howard. *Outsiders: Studies in the Sociology of Deviance.* New York: Free Press, 1997; Buckingham, David. *After the Death of Childhood: Growing up in the Age of Electronic Media.* Malden, MA: Polity, 2005; Cohen, Stanley. *Folk Devils and Moral Panics: The Creation of Mods and Rockers.* London: MacGibbon and Kee, 1972; Feshbach, Seymour, and Robert D. Singer. *Television and Aggression: An Experimental Field Study.* San Francisco: Jossey Bass, 1971; Freedman, Jonathan L. *Media Violence and Its Effect on Aggression: Assessing the Scientific Evidence.* Toronto: University of Toronto Press, 2002; Gerbner, George, Larry Gross, Michael Morgan, and Nancy Signorielli. "Growing Up with Television: The Cultivation Perspective." In *Media Effects: Advances in Theory and Research,* ed. Jennings Bryant and Dolf Zillman, 17–41. Hillsdale, NJ: Lawrence Erlbaum, 1994; Glassner, Barry. *The Culture of Fear: Why Americans Are Afraid of the Wrong Things.* New York: Basic Books, 1999; Goldstein, Jeffrey H. "Does Playing Violent Video Games Cause Aggressive Behavior?" *Playing by the Rules: The Cultural Policy Challenges of Video Games Conference,* Cultural Policy Center, University of Chicago, October 27, 2001, http://culturalpolicy.uchicago.edu/conf2001/papers/goldstein.html; Goldstein, Jeffrey H. *Why We Watch: The Attractions of Violent Entertainment.* New York: Oxford University Press, 1998; Goode, Erich, and Nachman Ben-Yehuda. *Moral Panics: The Social Construction of Deviance.* New York: Blackwell Press, 1994; Gauntlett, David. "The Worrying Influence of 'Media Effects' Studies." In *Ill Effects: The Media/Violence Debate,* ed. Martin Barker and Julian Petley, 47–62. New York: Routledge, 2001; Jenkins, Henry. *Fans, Bloggers, and Gamers: Exploring Participatory Culture.* New York: New York University Press, 2006; Jones, Gerard. *Killing Monsters: Why Children Need Fantasy, Super Heroes, and Make-Believe Violence.* New York: Basic Books, 2002; Schechter, Harold. *Savage Pastime: A Cultural History of Violent Entertainment.* New York: St. Martin's Press, 2005; Springhall, John.

Youth, Popular Culture and Moral Panics: Penny Gaffs to Gangsta-Rap, 1820–1996. New York: St. Martin's Press, 1998; Sternheimer, Karen. *It's Not The Media: The Truth about Pop Culture's Influence on Children.* Boulder, CO: Westview, 2003; Tobin, Joseph. *Good Guys Don't Wear Hats: Children's Talk About the Media.* New York: Teachers College Press, 2000.

Talmadge Wright

WOMEN'S MAGAZINES

Women's magazines are among the most popular forms of print media in America, yet ever since the 1830s, when they began to succeed commercially, there has been heated debate surrounding their impact on women. Still in play today is the critique spearheaded by Betty Friedan in her groundbreaking best-seller, *The Feminine Mystique* (1963). Friedan charged that women's magazines make women miserable by telling them their only success in life lies in fulfilling their femininity. At the same time, other critics have castigated women's magazines as proto-feminist, claiming that they divert women from their true sources of satisfaction—hearth, family, home. Still others have criticized women's magazines for their many contradictions. Of these, some argue that competing visions offer women valuable life choices, while others say mixed messages ensnare women in anxiety and self-doubt. What's really going on? Do popular women's magazines harm and oppress women?

A scathing critique of women's magazines was the fulcrum on which Friedan's book turned. Friedan named the "problem that has no name," the consistent, coercive rendering of women as weak and passive, devoid of worldly ambition, and dependent upon men for both personal identity and fulfillment. And the central culprit in the creation and maintenance of this, the feminine mystique, was the popular women's magazine.

A long line of criticism has echoed Friedan. Contemporary commentators decry popular women's magazines for debilitating women, making them dependent on men (and on the magazines themselves), preventing self-realization, promoting self-denial, and creating the woman reader as little more than consumer, ornament, maid, or baby machine. These arguments remain strong across

MEN'S MAGAZINES

Do men's magazines construct *their* readers as helpless consumers of products that express their identity? Initially, all magazines were men's magazines; they presumed a male reader. Differentiation was by class, not gender, and the "gentleman's magazine" denoted a more sophisticated and cultured audience. The rise of mass-market, advertising-based magazines problematized the upper-class gentlemen. Suddenly, he seemed a fop, a dandy, and as consumerism was coded as feminine, men's magazines began to emerge as a distinct genre. In the twentieth century, anticonsumerist, working-class masculinity found outlets in hypermasculine titles like *True* or *Argosy*, while publishers rescued the gentleman's magazine by masculinizing consumption. "Girly" magazines like *Playboy* or *Penthouse* used buxom women's bodies to naturalize male consumption and avoid the taint of homosexuality. Recent men's magazines, including *Maxim, Details, FHM,* and *Stuff* attempt to fuse these class-based strategies, with depictions of rough-hewn athletic manhood next to scantily clad women and high-end consumer goods. And while some scholars suggest engaging men as self-objectified consumers reinforces traditional gender inequalities, others observe a liberatory expression of a more refined masculine sensibility.

academic disciplines, and are also articulated, in updated form, in the contemporary media itself. Naomi Wolf's best-seller, *The Beauty Myth*, for example, argues that the gaunt, youthful model supplanted the happy housewife heroine as the new arbiter of successful womanhood, taking over the work of social coercion in an effort to undo the progress feminism had accomplished.

At the same time, other critics have seen women's magazines as excessively progressive. A study by the conservative Media Research Center in the mid-1990s concluded that women's magazines are left-wing playbooks for liberal activism. Christina Hoff Sommers, writing in the *Washington Post*, accused top titles including *Redbook, Mademoiselle, Good Housekeeping*, and *Parenting* of advancing feminist "Ms.-information." Soon Danielle Crittenden's *What Our Mothers Didn't Tell Us* and Wendy Shalit's *A Return to Modesty* explicitly allied women's magazines with the feminist movement, and blamed magazines for leading women away from their true pursuit of happiness—domesticity.

A third group of critics assumes both these lines of argument are accurate, and *that* is the problem. They complain that women's magazines argue both for and against sexual freedom, careerism, financial independence, couplehood, and the thinness ideal. With so many competing ideas all under the same roof, how is a reader to avoid a sense of frantic confusion and anxiety about how to add it all up right?

"POLYVOCALITY": PSYCHIC TRAP OR LIBERATING CHOICE?

Women's magazines exhibit what media theorists call "polyvocality"—a message that contains many voices. In fact, multiple messaging is a structural hallmark of the American magazine from its rise in the early republic.

American women's magazines have always been a decidedly miscellaneous form. Even the earliest versions in the 1790s contained various types of fiction, including travelogues, short stories, poems, "observations," parables and fragments, as well as nonfiction genres from advice, to instruction, to argumentative essays, to reportage, even music. They have always been composed of multiple departments and carried the contributions of different writers as well.

Scholars have mapped the polyvocality of women's magazines into the present day, despite ever-increasing marketing sophistication over time. But opinions diverge sharply on how these multiple voices play for readers. Some say the many voices all gang up to deliver the same, wrong message (whatever that message may be). Others say they bind women in a web of opposing goals. But recently, a number of scholars have seen the many voices as competing at times—and have explored the openings and options that may arise from divergent ideas and discursive competition on the page. Recent scholarship has emphasized collisions between editorial commentary and fiction, feature articles and reader letters, and all of these and advertising.

COMPETING INTERESTS: OPENING OPTIONS
OR ZERO-SUM GAME?

In contemporary women's magazines, the competing voices are seen to spring from competing interests at the heart of the enterprise itself. One the one hand, women's magazines seek to serve the interests of their readers. On the other, modern magazines depend on advertising to provide substantial portions of operating revenues as well as profits. Thus, advertiser interests, too, must be satisfied or the magazine folds. These two sets of interests are generally viewed as battling it out in a zero-sum game: what advertisers want for women—essentially, that they remain focused on their "jobs" as wives and mothers—is the opposite of what women want for themselves; when advertisers win, women lose.

Formally, this was not always the case. For their first 100 years or so, there was limited advertising in women's magazines. They were subscription-supported and copy came from amateur writers who contributed on a voluntary basis. Until the rise of the mass-market magazine in the 1890s, advertising mainly occupied small boxes on back pages, leaving the bulk of the book to be dominated by readers, writers, and editors.

The mass-market magazine model changed all that. It worked by charging subscription prices too low to sustain production costs, let alone profits, but low enough to be affordable to huge groups of readers of modest means nationwide. The amateur contributors who once provided copy were thereafter relegated mainly to roles as readers; professional writers, hired by professional editors, with the increasing input of rising marketing departments, created most of the content. Advertisers, eager to promote burgeoning new product lines, supported it all in exchange for well-positioned access to the eyes and minds of masses of women.

The standard histories say this mass-market formula was pioneered by *Munsey's*, a general-interest magazine, in late 1893. Owner Frank Munsey had lost a fortune in the "panic of 1893," one of the nation's worst depressions, and could get no credit. He was desperate for cash. So, he lowered his subscription prices from the then-standard 35 cents a copy to 10 cents. The magazine became an immediate smash, and Munsey was able to set high advertising rates based on his unprecedented circulation. In a short time, competing titles including *Collier's*, *Century*, and the muckraking *McClure's* followed suit.

Too bad that history is wrong. In fact, the leading women's magazines of the era had used a low-price formula to grow larger earlier than all these magazines. As early as 1891, the *Woman's Home Companion* achieved circulation of 125,000, the *Delineator* topped 393,000, and the *Ladies' Home Journal*, the leader of them all, garnered a circulation of over 600,000 by dropping prices to 11 cents a copy, using advertiser support to do it.

Being at the forefront of this particular innovation may be a dubious distinction, however. The mass-market magazine model shifted the dynamics of reader content and control solidly in favor of advertisers. But is it a zero-sum game?

Critics from Friedan forward argue that advertisers demand women's domesticity since it best promotes product consumption. Rather than presenting new possibilities, magazines catering to advertiser interests emphasize existing gender norms and the traditional lifestyle of housewife and mother.

Yet recent work on women's magazines reveals that the equation was and is not that simple. Considerable tension persists between the internal impulses to set boundaries and to stretch them. Issues like paid work and working mothers have consistently seen mixed messaging, leading several scholars to conclude that these collisions ultimately expand the boundaries of acceptability of work outside the home. What's more, advertiser interests have not always lined up with patriarchal concerns. Some products sell better to women as individuals, as workers, as heroines, or other identities, rather than as wives or mothers—it depends on the product. And market competition has sometimes pushed the top titles to validate new ideas in order to distinguish themselves from rival publications in the increasingly competitive women's magazine market.

There have always been gendered limits to how far any women's magazine would go. Yet the dynamics of the form and development of the industry have not made it easy to promote any single course as right for all women.

WOMEN'S MAGAZINE MANTRAS: INDIVIDUALISM AND CONSUMERISM

Amidst the debate about the politics of American women's magazines, there are two related areas of fairly wide agreement. The first is that women's magazines tend to promote individualistic solutions rather than collective, political, or activist ones. The other is that consumption is generally presented as the best solution to most problems.

The tendency toward individualistic solutions may be a defining "attitude" of the women's magazine in contemporary times. If you are unhappy with your salary, women's magazines will provide money-saving tips—not information about how to fight wage inequality or understand the gender wage gap. If you are exhausted by the struggle to balance work and family, women's magazines will provide time-saving tips or relaxation exercises to do at lunchtime or in the supermarket—not address the "second shift" of housework and childcare or corporate resistance to viable work/life balance options for the vast majority of women and men. Women's magazines will give stay-young, stay-slim exercises and make-up tips, but will never discuss female objectification or the overwhelming importance of sexual allure in women's lives.

Some say this spin is simply consistent with the American cultural zeitgeist, with its mixture of psychologizing and can-do-ism that renders most problems a question of individual effort and outlook, of pluck and luck. Others argue that the emphasis on coping disempowers women and accommodates the status quo: it turns justifiable outrage at structural inequities into personal failings or lack of effort, depriving inequality of its mobilizing power and drowning women in guilt.

Historically, women's magazines have organized women for collective action. During the "muckraking" era in the early twentieth century, all the top titles ran intensive campaigns explicitly designed to mobilize readers for reform—both inside and outside the home. The "big six" magazines organized campaigns against adulterated foods, patent medicines, child labor, corruption in public schools, and legal rights of mothers (particularly in divorce); they advocated for child welfare legislation and to help children in inner cities. These efforts have largely been ignored by journalism history, even though women's magazine campaigns continued longer than the celebrated muckrakers did and directly organized reader action: they offered free kits, formed leagues, and fostered local lobbying groups; they circulated shopping guides and monthly consumer research reports; they formed and financed information networks and institutes. (The renowned "*Good Housekeeping* Seal of Approval," first awarded in 1905, emerged from the magazine's extensive campaign against adulterated food beginning in 1900.)

Social consciousness remains in the editorial mix of contemporary women's magazines, but such explicit social organizing is much lower on the editorial to-do list today. And the shift from social improvement to individual betterment is linked to the rise of consumerism in the 1920s. Whereas a women's magazine in the nineteenth century might have included features on pending legislation of interest to women and families, by the mid-1920s the same magazine would have been more likely to run an article on how individual mothers could enhance their own and their children's physical well-being. And most of the time, the magazine would recommend the purchase of a product to do it.

The gradual shifting of political impulses into consumer choices has led some critics to label all women's magazine content "covert advertising." In this view, contents conspire in promising to improve women's lives, but actually function to raise their anxieties—which are then assuaged by the prospect of purchasing advertised products.

More recently, however, the interplay of gender, politics, and consumption has been emphasized, portraying women's magazines in less starkly sinister terms. The 1920s may have been the age of ascendant consumerism, but it was also the dawn of women's enfranchisement, and women's magazines had to pay serious attention to both. Editorial content and especially advertising often incorporated political language and longings beginning in this era. Ad and feature copy linked consumption to greater political freedom, self-representation, "liberation" from household responsibilities, and more. These moves are seen by some as legitimating politics in women's identity, self-definition, and social role. As a result, merging of politics and product consumption may have increased women's interests in real rather than consumer politics.

Today, the appropriation of political messages by consumer culture has become a widespread phenomenon across the media. But it remains a matter of debate whether or not those maneuvers replace political actions with consumer purchases. Does the pervasive use of political ideals to promote products extinguish the political content, or raise it for audiences, repeatedly, nearly everywhere they turn in our media-saturated culture?

WOMEN'S MAGAZINE AUDIENCES

Arguments and answers both depend greatly on audiences. Every camp of the women's magazine controversy relies on certain assumptions about how women readers read. Whether you argue that women's magazines disempower readers by telling them that their greatest satisfaction lies in fulfilling their femininity; steer women 180 degrees wrong by telling them their greatest satisfaction lies in independence and careerism; or cynically trap them in schizophrenic self-doubt—any of these positions envisions a reader unable to navigate magazine form and content to satisfy her own interests and pleasures.

The issue of audience agency and creativity is itself much debated in media studies. And women, particularly audiences of so-called women's genres like soap operas, romance novels, and women's magazines, have been a special focus of concern. Unlike elite and highly educated readers, popular audiences of women are often seen as passive, suggestible dupes, unable to make what they will of a media text, to master it in their own terms.

Yet media research on audience reception repeatedly finds that all kinds of audiences actively interpret what they read, see, and hear, without any special academic or analytic training to do so. Audiences are not free agents with an unlimited range of options, of course: content sets some limits to coherent readings, and it takes intellectual and social resources to decode creatively—particularly to resist or oppose dominant or "preferred" meanings. However, audiences of all sorts have proved capable of creative and self-serving interpretation, and women have repeatedly shown themselves to be as adept as anyone at constructing their own meanings from media texts.

The elitism that underlies a good deal of scholarly commentary about women's magazine readers is somewhat ironic since women's magazines are simultaneously accused of an elite bias: they are about hegemonic straight, white, middle-class women, and exclude or marginalize racial, ethnic, sexual, and socioeconomic differences. These demographic biases have always been present in women's magazines. The earliest versions appeared when only the upper crust of American women—white and bourgeois—could afford subscriptions that cost

TIMELINE

1741—First American magazines produced by Benjamin Franklin and Andrew Bradford, in Philadelphia. Bradford's monthly survives for three issues; Franklin's, only six.

1791–92—First American women's magazine, *The Ladies Magazine and Repository of Entertaining and Instructive Knowledge*, published in Philadelphia.

1791–1830—At least 100 "ladies magazines" published across the then–United States.

1830–98—*Godey's Lady's Book* published, the magazine that would be the model of the nineteenth-century women's magazine under the 40-year editorship of Sarah Hale from 1837–77.

1883—*Ladies' Home Journal* published by Cyrus Curtis, edited by his wife, Louisa Knapp, until succeeded by Edward Bok in 1889.

1890–1905—"Golden Age of Popular Magazines": Number of U.S. magazines doubles from 3,500 to over 7,000; audiences grow dramatically.

1900–1920—Age of magazine muckraking: Lincoln Steffens, Ida Tarbell, Will Irwin, Ray Stannard Baker, and Upton Sinclair invent the craft of investigative journalism, causing a sensation and driving circulations of such magazines as *McClure's, Collier's, Cosmopolitan, Everybody's, Hampton's, The Independent, Pearson's*, and *The American Magazine* to new heights.

1923—*Time* published by Henry Luce and Briton Hadden, innovating the newsmagazine and launching Time, Inc., which by the 1960s would become the largest magazine publisher in the world.

1950s—Mass-circulation magazine advertising peaks, only to be eroded by television in the 1960s, ushering in an era of niche publication.

1970—*Essence* magazine launched, marking a new level of visibility for a history comprising at least eight African American women's titles between 1891 and 1950.

1972—*Ms.* magazine launched by Gloria Steinem and Pat Carbine, continuing an extensive tradition of U.S. women's rights press that began in 1848.

1997—*Latina* launched by Christy Haubegger, the first bilingual lifestyle magazine for Hispanic women in America.

---

nearly what a skilled tradesman would earn in a week. Moreover, only this elite group was sufficiently educated to read and contribute, and had the leisure to do so. Cheaper, mass-market women's magazines made their predecessors suddenly look literary and elite by comparison, but the outreach to a mass audience still did not embrace diversity. Today, some women of color appear in top women's titles, yet the image of women and audience of interest remain decidedly white, heterosexual, and middle class.

NEW NICHES, NEW READERS—SAME DEBATES?

American media forms have tended to develop similarly, evolving from an elite, to a popular, to a specialized stage. For women's magazines, the 1970s saw the transition from the popular to the specialized phase. Television had eroded the mass-market ad base, so advertisers and readers turned to special-interest magazines. New technologies made quality publication at smaller circulations possible, and more sophisticated marketing helped both publishers and advertisers target these new niche audiences. Finally, social changes, including both the civil rights and women's movements, gave readers a dawning awareness of their identities and clout in the public sphere, including the marketplace.

The 1970s saw the birth of the black women's magazine, *Essence*, and the feminist magazine, *Ms.*; in the 1980s, *Working Woman* and *Working Mother* appeared; the 1990s saw *Latina* and Oprah Winfrey's *O*. These and others partly redressed the hegemony of straight, white, middle-class women across the women's magazine category.

But within the new niche women's magazines, the old controversies remain. *Ms.* and *Working Woman* may have made feminists and even some lesbians visible; *Essence* and *O* may have given some voice to women of color; *Latina* may have articulated ethnicity with female agency. But, at heart, do they merely repackage the same old individualistic and consumerist solutions? If difference becomes visible by including darker shades of make-up to the recommended product lists and choice comes down to the right to wear a low-cut blouse to work, is that progress?

A wider range of cultural ideas and images—even product lines and fashion statements—could give readers materials from which to construct new understandings of themselves and others. Further, when it comes to interpretation, media scholars have shown that social context matters—a lot. Beauty copy may read differently if you're from a traditionally derided or invisible group. Consumption could have a different meaning, too, if you're from a historically disadvantaged group. Individualistic solutions may offer empowerment if you are overdue for progress because the social and political will has stalled. For most women worldwide, even that much self-reliance remains a near-radical goal.

Yet, can the potential we see in such readings truly make a difference for women? That question animates the new generation of debates about the impact of women's magazines on women's lives.

See also Advertising and Persuasion; Alternative Media in the United States; Audience Power to Resist; Body Image; Hypercommercialism; Media and Citizenship; Minority Media Ownership; Public Access Television; Public Sphere; Representations of Class; Representations of Masculinity; Representations of Race; Representations of Women; Sensationalism, Fear Mongering, and Tabloid Media; Shock Jocks.

Further Reading: Aronson, Amy Beth. *Taking Liberties: Early American Women's Magazines and Their Readers.* Westport, CT: Praeger, 2002; Friedan, Betty. *The Feminine Mystique.* New York: W. W. Norton, 1963; McCracken, Ellen. *Decoding Women's Magazines: From Mademoiselle to Ms.* London: Palgrave Macmillan, 1992; Okker, Patricia. *Our Sister Editors: Sarah J. Hale and the Tradition of Nineteenth-Century Women Editors.* Athens: University of Georgia Press, 1995; Rooks, Noliwe. *Ladies' Pages: African-American Women's Magazines and the Culture That Made Them.* New Brunswick, NJ: Rutgers University Press, 2004; Scanlon, Jennifer. *Inarticulate Longings: The Ladies' Home Journal, Gender* *and the Promises of Consumer Culture.* New York: Routledge, 1995; Walker, Nancy. *Shaping Our Mothers' World: Women's Magazines.* Jackson: University Press of Mississippi, 2000; Winship, Janice. *Inside Women's Magazines.* London: Pandora, 1988; Wolf, Naomi. *The Beauty Myth: How Images of Beauty Are Used against Women.* New York; William Morrow, 1991; Zuckerman, Mary Ellen. *A History of Popular Women's Magazines in the United States, 1792–1995.* Westport, CT: Greenwood, 1998.

Amy Aronson

WORLD CINEMA

Much of the works of filmic art known as *world cinema* are unknown to audiences in the United States. It is often said that American English-speaking viewers will not tolerate subtitles, and dubbing dialogue over the voices of actors after the film is made is not an ideal alternative. But the world's cinema provides a rich tapestry of the globe, with images of stunning landscapes, remote countries, and narratives of life recognizable as part of the human condition. Even though the vast majority of such films never find their way into American multiplexes, in can be argued that cinema is especially important to an increasingly interconnected globe, one often lacking the mutual understanding needed in a world of diverse peoples and cultures. Though U.S. feature films and summer blockbusters are exported around the globe, cinema from other parts of the world, its stars and filmmakers, also exert significant influence over international moviemaking, including Hollywood.

Films are made around the world under a variety of conditions, sometimes supported by cultural institutions and government financing, at other times suppressed through state censorship or lack of funding. Many films are international collaborations of extraordinary talent. Through the course of making films, producers and directors are required to hurdle logistical as well as creative obstacles and must overcome many financial barriers. Such necessary accommodations often move the medium forward in unexpected ways. In the face of adversity, many astounding works of art are created with little money, at times using nonprofessional crews and actors, some shot in remote, rural villages, others set in dangerous, unprotected urban neighborhoods. From the gritty streets of Mexico City, director Alejandro Inarritu turned threatening conditions to his advantage by employing young gang members to protect the equipment while he made the critically acclaimed film *Amores Perros.* Inarritu won three awards at Cannes and an Oscar nomination for the film.

Iranian director Jafar Panahi was accustomed to extreme conditions while on location from his experiences making documentaries at the battlefront during the Iran/Iraq war. His first feature film, *The White Balloon,* is the story of a seven-year-old girl Aida Mohammadkhani, determined to find a special fish for a New Year's celebration. Panahi's camera follows Aide through the tangled city streets of Teheran as she struggles to find her way. Shot in real time with many first-time crewmembers, nonprofessional actors, and a tiny budget, the film is exquisitely crafted, and mostly improvised. For his efforts Panahi's *Balloon* won the Camera D'Or at Cannes in 1995. Iranian filmmakers are legendary for their collaborative spirit, and the making of *The White Balloon* was no exception. Panahi had invaluable help from master director Abbas Kiarostami.

IRANIAN NEW WAVE CINEMA

Iranian cinema became widely known to American audiences in 1997 with the U.S. release of Mohsen Makhmalbaf's *Gabbeh*, a film that vibrates with color and a magical carpet. *Gabbeh* is a life-affirming fable about a carpet that holds the secrets and tales of lost love in rural Iran. Color becomes the visual metaphor for life, and his pallet is pulled from the sky, the fields and flowers, and transfixed into the carpets of the nomadic clan he follows.

That same year Abbas Kiarostami won the Palm D'Or at the Cannes Film Festival for *A Taste of Cherry,* the enigmatic, postmodern film with an unexpected twist that set international critics abuzz debating the film's final scenes. But well before that, Kiarostami launched the Iranian New Wave with his Koker trilogy, *Where Is My Friend's House?* (1987), *And Life Goes On* (1992), and *Through The Olive Trees* (1994). Kiarostami was well known to international filmgoers after *Close-Up* (1990), an extraordinary work that weaves a true story into a feature film. Combining the real with what is fiction is a narrative form that runs through Iranian New Wave cinema.

The early films of Mohsen Makhmalbaf are woven out of his struggle against oppression and ultimate rejection of war and violence. Drawing on his own success, he founded the Makhmalbaf Film House to support other young Iranian filmmakers. His wife Marzieh Meshkini learned to make films at the school and went on to direct *The Day I Became a Woman* (2000), a three-part film celebrating the lives of three women of different ages.

Samira, Makhmalbaf's eldest daughter, began watching her father make films when she was eight years old. He let her quit Islamic high school at the age of 15, taught her filmmaking, and helped her make two award-winning features by the time she was 21. Samira's second film, *Blackboards* (2001), follows itinerant schoolteachers who carry their blackboards on their backs as they hunt for students in villages through the mountains of Iranian Kurdistan. The young director chased the fog through the mountains of Kurdistan to get the right shots, and the result is a captivating set of vivid imagery. Working primarily with nonprofessionals, Samira Makhmalbaf incorporates the many, often deadly hazards faced by the schoolteachers into the film. The blackboards take on new roles and become visual metaphors when used to carry heavy loads and after being dismantled and used as splints for broken bones.

CINEMA AND ITS CULTURE

Films often serve as a catalyst for public dialogue about a whole range of issues, including humanitarian concerns about justice, equality and human well being in general. Indeed, part of the definition of cinema itself expands outward from the making and viewing of a movie on its own, to include the "cultural sense" made of it by audiences, writers, scholars and critics alike. One unique

JOURNEY TO *KANDAHAR*

At a time when Afghanistan was still a distant Cold War memory, vaguely remembered as a battlefield where the United States backed Mujehadeen who fought to expel Soviets forces, Iranian filmmaker Mohsen Makhmalbaf made *Kandahar*. The name and the place would become unforgettable to the English speaking West, especially the United States, after 9/11. It was certainly the only one of Makhmalbaf's 17 highly acclaimed feature films to be screened at the White House, a rarity for a subtitled art-house film. But Mohsen Makhmalbaf was not motivated by the politics when he made the film, but rather by humanitarian concerns of long historical genesis.

In 1997, 28-year-old Afghan expatriate Niloufar Pazira, contacted Makhmalbaf after she received an alarming letter from a friend who had both legs blown off by a landmine there. Makhmalbaf decided to cast Pazira as the star of a fictional film, but one based on extensive research into UN documentation, and his own clandestine visit to Afghanistan. In *Kandahar*, after deplaning from a Red Cross helicopter, Pazira dons a burkha and begins a grueling trek across the desert through minefields and Taliban-controlled territory.

Kandahar would make *Time* magazine's list of the 10 best films for 2001, win the Ecumenical Prize of the Jury at Cannes, be screened in at least 40 countries, and outperform *Moulin Rouge* when released in France and Italy. The film might have been able to exert international pressure for improved conditions in Afghanistan, but after six years of the war on terror that killed thousands of Afghan civilians, because of corruption, warlords, and the resurgence of the Taliban, the conditions depicted in Makhmalbaf's film have not improved.

---

approach to discussing international art-house films is found in a book of interviews by writer Liza Béar, who talked to many first-time directors from around the world. Such writing helps illuminate the filmmaking process and the shared partnerships that develop among actors, directors, crews, and producers.

SOUTH AFRICA

Twenty years passed between the time Shawn Slovo witnessed the events in Johannesburg in 1963 and the moment she started writing the script for *A World Apart*, an autobiographical film told from the perspective of a 13-year-old girl who tries to make sense of apartheid and the hushed, secretive world of her activist parents. The daughter of Ruth First, played by Barbara Hershey, the film depicts one of the most repressive moments in South Africa when the ANC and the Communist Party were outlawed and their members exiled. As a child, Slovo was forced to share her parent's love with their struggle for justice and equality and her mother's death in 1982 left their relationship unresolved. In this film, the writer struggled to create a work of fiction from childhood memories.

Directed by Chris Menges, *A World Apart* was shot in Zimbabwe with a cast that included many first-time actors. Menges' interest in Slovo's screenplay stemmed from his experiences with apartheid while shooting a program in

South Africa for British television. Slovo and Menges worked closely on the set shaping scenes and dialogue to foreground the politics while maintaining the power of the personal story. Menges won the Special Jury Prize for First Feature at Cannes in 1988 for *Apart*.

As might be expected, this groundbreaking film about apartheid, released while the writer was still in exile, sparked heated controversies, some more surprising than others. Some critics and audiences disparage scenes in *A World Apart* for the depiction of laughter and happiness at a dinner in the meager home of poor black Africans. They questioned whether scenes of joy and dancing should be included in stories of pain and tragedy.

CUBAN CINEMA

Cuban cinema in the latter half of the twentieth century created a repertoire of films that chronicled the changes from a colonized society to a revolutionary one. In *Memories of Underdevelopment*, Tomas Gutierrez Alea's 1968 masterpiece, film audiences see the country's transformation through the eyes of a Europeanized Cuban intellectual who ultimately decides to stay, but longs for his former decadent life.

Two years earlier, Alea's adventurous mix of satire, slapstick and farce made fun of the tyranny of bureaucratic red tape in *Death of a Bureaucrat*. When a loyal Cuban is buried with his workers card and his widow can't get her pension, the film portrays the maddening bureaucratic rules in the traditions of film comedy, from Bunuel to the satire of Billy Wilder, and comedic strategies that trace back to Buster Keaton.

In a surprising revelation in a commentary included on the DVD release of *Boogie Nights*, director Paul Anderson admits that he refers to a scene from the early Cuban revolutionary film, *I Am Cuba* (1964). This is all the more surprising because the Soviet/Cuban collaboration is widely interpreted to be a work of propaganda. The Soviets reportedly wanted to emphasize the evils of colonialization, especially the actions taken by American corporations, and some scenes are considered overstated, even cartoonish. Yet many directors (including Francis Ford Coppola and Martin Scorcese) have admired the stunning camerawork, especially impressive because of the early, heavy equipment available at the time. Ironically, *I Am Cuba* is a cult classic.

CREATIVITY

Some of the best writing on film and its art seeks to understand the creative process and the conditions and experiences that spark an idea. French director Francois Ozon incorporates the enigma of creativity into the plot of his Hitchcockian thriller, *Swimming Pool* (2003), as Ozon told Liza Béar, "creativity is not something that just happens, that falls on you from the sky, but something very concrete." Yet long-time director from France Agnes Varda, with five decades of experience, found her creative inspiration in a chance encounter, a brief emotional moment that triggered her desire to launch a film.

Directors of notable films sometimes draw on the talents and spontaneity of the actors they work with to move the story forward, and hone the dialogue. Full of passion, fantasy and an ironic twist, *Speaking Parts* (1989) is directed by Atom Egoyan, who first created memorable characters as a playwright. Egoyan and the film's driving force, actress Arsinée Khanjian who plays Lisa, are both members of the Armenian diaspora who met during the thriving Toronto theater scene of the 1980s. They reveal a collaboration that results in a rare conceptual film about the nature of human desire and its interaction with the power of the image, a process fraught with certain dangers.

Some of the best examples of world cinema demonstrate a sensibility that foregrounds the profoundly social nature of the human condition. Stories that explore the longings of the human heart and the passions that bind one to another are tied to places and their histories, demonstrating that what it means to be human is not shaped in a void. As characters move through history, they are caught within declining empires, economic dislocations, repressive governments, class conflict, dangerous urban environments, or the beauty, mystery, and danger of the natural world.

HONG KONG

It was not surprising when the transfer of Hong Kong to mainland China became the setting for a film. The troubling, unfulfilled desire depicted in *Chinese Box* (1997), a film by director Wayne Wang, stars Maggie Cheung and Jeremy Irons, and expresses the ambivalence the director felt toward the changeover. Best known for his films about San Francisco's Chinatown, Wang returned to his former homeland to give narrative and visual treatment to the historic moment. Wang and his films illustrate the movement of directors across national borders, often resulting in works of keen cultural observations and hybrid forms.

In the 1980s and 1990s the Hong Kong film movement flourished. J. Hoberman of *The Village Voice* noted that at its height, colonial Hong Kong incubated a "sensationally florid" film culture. One of its most exciting directors, Wong Kar Wai, made *Fallen Angels* (1995) and *Chungking Express* (1994), films that feature the street antics of ex-cons and create memorable portraits of honkytonk Hong Kong. When Wong Kar Wai directed his romantic mystery *In the Mood for Love* (2000), the production took an unexpected turn when his long-time cameraman could not work on the film. Having to frame his own shots in the absence of his cinematographer, Wai took his own work to another level style and filmic content.

WORLD WARS

A classic genre, the war film has been made around the world by different directors, about past wars remembered, with interpretations that invariably influence the present. They sometimes tell unexpected narratives about humanity and the quest for peace.

In 1989, French director Bertrand Tavernier's *Life and Nothing But* told a classic story of war and the social unraveling that occurs in its aftermath. Set in the year 1920, two women must wait to find the remains of their loved ones who have been listed as missing in action in World War I; only then can each attempt to create a new future. Almost a century later, another French director interprets the incredible loss that was the Great War. In *Joyeux Noel*, director and writer Christian Carion tells the story of the Christmas truce of 1914 when soldiers crossed the line into no-man's-land between the trenches in at least a dozen spots along the Western Front. For a few hours it becomes common ground as they eat, sing, smoke, and celebrate mass together. Nominated for a Golden Globe and an Oscar for Best Foreign Language Film of 2006, the film won the 2005 Audience Award at the Leeds International Film Festival. In an interesting international reference that demonstrates the shared nature of global film language, in the opening battle scenes some of the tracking shots through the trenches are styled in a similar fashion to Stanley Kubrick's 1957 film *Paths of Glory*.

In other cases, a director's personal history has been shaped by war and experiences that are brought to bear on their films. Raised in France, Karim Dridi is both an insider and outsider. Dridi's father was a Tunisia military officer when he met Dridi's mother, a French nurse, on the battlefield during the Algerian-Tunisian war. Through an intimate portrait of family life, in *Bye Bye* (1996), his second feature film, the director seeks a cultural common ground that reaffirms our shared humanity regardless of race, religion, or nationality.

AUSTRALIAN FILM

When Peter Weir brought the Australian landscape to life in the atmospheric *Picnic at Hanging Rock* (1975), it was a pivotal moment in the country's film history. The stunning landscapes of Australia's desert outback had been featured in *Walkabout*, the 1971 British production by Nicolas Roeg in which two abandoned English children encounter an Aborigine on a ritual quest, and the three unlikely companions start their odyssey across the desert. But Peter Weir was born and educated in Australia, having made short films and Australian television programs and documentaries. Two years after *Picnic*, Weir would continue to explore the ambivalent interrelationships between native Aboriginal culture, Australian landscapes, and European modernity, in the film *The Last Wave*, themes that became iconic in Australian film.

Weir's 1981 film *Gallipoli*, scripted by prominent Australian playwright David Williamson, is regarded as classic Australian cinema, and the film was instrumental in giving Mel Gibson his long run as a major international film star. Weir would go on to make movies in the United States, with the wildly popular *Witness* (1985), a thriller set in Amish country, and the less accessible, *Mosquito Coast* (1986), both staring Harrison Ford.

By 1998, Peter Weir made the self-referential satire about the excesses of media power, control, and money, in the satirical "reality" film *The Truman Show*, which demonstrated his international significance as a major media figure.

AUSTRALIAN FILM RENAISSANCE

During the mid-1970s, Australia was experiencing the heady period called the Australian Film Renaissance, and directors Jane Campion and Gillian Armstrong received their degrees from the Australian Film and Television School. They would soon add their visions to the aesthetic explorations that came to define Australian Cinema.

Gillian Armstrong gave life to the plucky young female protagonist in her 1979 film, *My Brilliant Career*. In doing so, Armstrong helped Judy Davis, the star who played the 16-year-old aspiring writer who is determined to get out of the bush, become one of Australia's most popular actors at the age of 23 and just out of drama school. Both Armstrong and Davis influenced a generation of women struggling to define themselves on their own terms. Nine years later in *High Tide*, the two reunited to tell the story of anther woman and a complex emotional struggle. This character lives in a trailer park, the back-up singer for a band in a small coastal town whose life is forever changed after a surprise meeting with the teenage daughter she abandoned at birth.

In 1992 Gillian Armstrong directed *The Last Days of Chez Nous*, a drama propelled amid the interior spaces of a Sydney household where sibling rivalry, generational conflict, and family loyalties play out in the life of a writer. Her quintessential themes elucidate the personal and social conflicts between art and life. Gillian Armstrong was awarded the Order of Australia in 2007.

Judy Davis enjoys an international reputation, and throughout her career worked in a number of countries, including the United States. She had a preference for the auteur and literary, and accepted supporting roles in such films as David Cronenberg's *Naked Lunch* (1991), and the Cohen brothers' *Barton Fink* (1991). She returned to Australian cinema and under the direction of writer/actor/producer Peter Duncan, she received the Best Australian Actress Award in 1996 for *Children of the Revolution*. The quirky, epic farce also starring Sam Neill and Geoffrey Rush was distributed in the United States in 1997, and is a rare political satire about communism, one with a singularly Australian voice and unique vision of the dark comedy of global affairs.

Best known to American moviegoers for her film *Piano*, Jane Campion helped define Australian cinema as a writer-director and then producer. With its dark, defiant female protagonist, *Piano* won the 1993 Palme D'Or at Cannes, making her the first woman ever to win the prestigious award. She also won the Oscar for Best Original Screenplay at the Academy Awards that year and was nominated for Best Director. But her list of honors before *Piano* demonstrated the filmmaker's growing significance. Her first feature film *Sweetie* (1989), won the Georges Sadoul prize in 1989 for Best Foreign Film, as well as the LA Film Critics' New Generation Award in 1990, the American Independent Spirit Award for Best Foreign Feature, and the Australian Critics' Award for Best Film, Best Director and Best Actress. Her 1990 film, *An Angel At My Table,* also enjoyed international recognition with seven different awards, including the Silver Lion at the Venice Film Festival, and prizes at the Toronto and Berlin Film Festivals.

Jane Campion went on to produce *Love Serenade*, the debut feature by Australian director Shirley Barrett that won Camera D'Or at Cannes in 1997. The film's surreal, melancholy atmosphere seems to emanate from the small town in the country's south where two sisters fall for the same big-city DJ. The film moves through the stark openness of empty, fenced yards, and these bleak spaces make the lush, fetid swamp, the setting for the film's finish all the more surprising. In this story of youthful passions and middle-aged dalliance, Barrett's characters embody the tension of the place and the actions of the sisters seem to spring from the landscape itself. Nature and its atmospheres, and the characters that come to life in its settings connect Australian films and fascinate the world.

DISTRIBUTING WORLD CINEMA

In the pre-cable, pre-video, and pre-DVD mid-1970s, a vital repertory theater circuit existed with over two hundred venues across the United States. In those years, one notable independent distributor called Kino International was founded to supply classic and foreign language art films to those venues. Kino boasted a rare collection of cinematic masterworks available for theatrical distribution. Their first collection was a library of over one hundred European and Asian art films of the 1940s, 1950s, and 1960s. As technology and media corporations continue to transform, so does the availability of international films in theatrical releases. Art-houses and 35 mm films are harder and harder to find. Sometimes classic art films are shown at public theaters and film festivals, and audiences are able to see films on the big screens for which they were originally intended. With the transition to video and DVD, by the 1980s it became difficult

---

HOLLYWOOD POACHING

While world cinema often struggles at the American box office, and while—right or wrong—American distributors often declare that Americans don't like foreign films, Hollywood frequently models its scripts off successful world cinema. Hence, for instance, 2007's Oscar winner for Best Picture and Best Director, *The Departed* (2006) is a remake of Hong Kong directors Andrew Lau Wai-Keung and Alan Mak Siu-Fai's *Infernal Affairs* (2002), numerous Japanese horror films have been remade in Hollywood, including *Dark Water* (2005), *The Ring* (2002), and *The Grudge* (2004); and even classics such as John Sturges's *The Magnificent Seven* (1960) or Sergio Leone's *A Fistful of Dollars* (2004) are remakes of, respectively, Japanese director Akira Kurosawa's *The Seven Sumurai* (1954) and *Yojimbo* (1961).

In another form of poaching, Hollywood often woos foreign directors, cinematographers, actors, and, recently, stunt choreographers with its larger budgets and increased glamour and audience. Thus, for instance, from Jet Li and Chow Yun-Fat to Mike Myers and Nicole Kidman, Peter Weir and John Woo to Alfonso Cuaron and Peter Jackson, many of "American" cinema's top talents and earners are from other countries, sometimes (as with Jackson) to the benefit of the development of local cinema, but more often at the expense of their potential contribution to that development.

---

to find video distributors interested in purchasing small art films and world cinema. Today, a few independent labels carry DVDs, such as Masters of Cinema and the Criterion Collection. Kino On Video also disseminates contemporary world cinema to communities and institutions, works that are often unavailable to the public outside of a few big cities. A few notable film classics sometimes shown in these venues are worth mentioning.

Classics

One early ode to nature is a classic of world cinema and can still be found on film, playing at some festivals. *Dersu Uzala* is set in the icy forests of eastern Siberia. The film explores the friendship that grows between a Russian surveyor and Dersu, the old hunter of the Tiaga. Akira Kurosawa, best known for his original Samurai films that proved key influences on the work of Steven Spielberg, George Lucas (whose *Star Wars* very roughly follows the plot of Kurosawa's *Hidden Fortress*), Martin Scorcese, Francis Ford Coppola, and the "spaghetti westerns" of Sergio Leone, made the film late in life. With its epic turn-of-the-century storyline and its intimate portraits, many critics consider it Kurosawa's masterwork. Released in 1975, *Dersu Uzala* was the winner of the 1976 Academy Award for Best Foreign Language Film.

One of the best and most influential portraits drawn of the enduring character type, the femme fatale was done in the 1929 German film *Pandora's Box* by G.W. Pabst. A talented young woman with a penchant for the part, Louise Brooks starred as Lulu, and her character inspired many imitators in the years that followed.

German director Fritz Lang's first talkie, *M* (1931), is a renowned classic. Peter Lorre stars as a child murderer who is tracked by police through the streets of Berlin. The city is portrayed as a gridlike, paranoid nightmare, and this early use of sound heightens the film's impact and demonstrates the enormous potential of soundtracks for enhancing the art of film.

With the death of Ingmar Bergman in 2007, the Swedish film director some critics refer to as the master filmmaker of the twentieth century, tributes to his life and art noted how influential his style and themes were to world filmmakers, including such American directors as Woody Allen. Bergman made about 50 films throughout more than 40 years, many intensely focused on the relationships between men and women and the role of God in the human psyche.

La Vie De Boheme (1992), the story of struggling artists in Paris, is a quintessential art-house film by Finnish director Aki Kaurismaki. Reminiscent of Jean-Luc Godard's filming from the 1960s, it brings the world of struggling artists, their defiance, determination and frustrations to life in actions that unfold in tiny apartments and the cafes of modern-day Paris. A coproduction with France, Italy, Sweden, and Finland, the film is based on the novel, *Scènes de la Vie de Bohème,* by Henri Murger published in the 1850s.

NEW GERMAN CINEMA

The New German Cinema that began of the early 1960s and lasted into the 1980s was based on a call to rethink the filmmaking of the time, dictated as it was by commercial demands. In 1962 a group of young German filmmakers signed the Oberhausen Manifesto, a declaration that encouraged quality art-house films. The work of Rainer Werner Fassbinder, Werner Herzog, and Win Wenders, among others, found international acclaim and returned German cinema to quality it had enjoyed during the Weimar Republic. In 1979, *The Tin Drum* became the first German film to win the Academy Award for Best Foreign Language Film. Several writers and critics have noted the similarity between Werner Herzog's surreal tale, *Aguirre, the Wrath of God* (1972) and Francis Ford Coppola's 1979 classic work of war and madness, *Apocalypse Now*.

CENSORSHIP

Global cinema has also been the subject and target of censorship. In *Beijing Bicycle*, the theft of a mountain bike sets in motion a contemporary tale of class conflict and social dislocation, yet in the new China, neither this nor the other four feature films directed by Wang Xiaoshuai was theatrically released.

Many filmmakers courageously resist the dangers posed by ideologues who would control the speech and art of others. Romanian filmmaker Lucian Pintilie was forced into exile in 1972 because he refused to submit his art to what he called the capricious demands of the system. He explained that one day the censors want one thing, the next day something else. After the fall of the Ceaucescu government, Pintilie returned to his country and directed *The Oak* (1992), a scathing social satire that portrays the process by which people acquiesce to their leader's injustices, who gradually and irreversible become accustomed to the evil that becomes banal.

Soviet director Andrei Tarkovsky's feature debut *Ivan's Childhood,* about the lost spirit of a soldier boy, slipped past the censors to win the Golden Lion for Best Film at the 1962 Venice Film Festival. What might have looked to the censors like a patriotic hymn to the Red Army was internationally acclaimed and widely understood as work of outrage against violence. Although *Ivan's Childhood* made it through the bureaucracy, Tarkovsky's subsequent films were heavily scrutinized and suppressed.

The bleak, wintry landscapes of a country retreat outside Moscow are featured in *Tema (Theme)*, a film made by Soviet director Gleb Panfilov. The film details the passions and (mis)fortunes of a famous Russian playwright, Kim Yesenin. *Tema* was shown in the United States for the first time in 1987 at the New York Film Festival. Made in 1979, *Tema* stayed on the shelf for eight years because Panfilov had refused to alter the film's content. It was finally released under Glasnost and won the Golden Bear Award at the 1987 Berlin Film Festival.

Moshen Makhmalbaf experienced the economic constraints imposed on filmmakers in Iran under the government of the Shah. Though a less direct form of censorship, it was a stifling of expression nonetheless. After the revolution he visited his grandmother's grave to tell her about the changes in Iran, from a film making industry influenced by Hollywood and motivated by the singular desire to make money, into a humanist one. That change led to the flowering of Iran new-wave cinema. Filmmakers now work under the eyes of government censors in which whole topic areas are cordoned off. Yet the stories Iranian directors tell are vivid portraits of a people and their culture, from the extremes of crowded cities to dry, desert landscapes.

Kiarostami's film, *Through the Olive Trees* (1994), has suffered a type of distribution censorship. Although Miramax contracted to distribute the film, it had an exceptionally short run in some major U.S. cities. Since then, though Miramax still has the rights to the film, it has been completely unavailable and has never released on video or DVD.

Self censorship and market censorship—adhering to the often rigid aesthetic and economic necessities needed to get films made—are equally dangerous forms of constraining speech and stifling freedom of expression. The personal and cultural interactions so important to world cinema have also been blocked by visa denials. In 2002, the United States denied Abbas Kiarostami's visa after he was invited to the New York Film Festival to show his film *Ten*, a portrait of six Iranian women. In protest, Finnish director Aki Kaurismaki refused to attend the festival even though his film *The Man Without a Past* was also being shown. Kaurismaki said, "As a private citizen of Finland, I accuse the U.S. government of violating the Geneva Convention. If international cultural exchange is prevented, what is left?" The head of the festival, Richard Pena, also stated to the press that the denial of Kiarostami's visa was "unjust, extraordinarily short-sighted and a snub to a major Muslim artist."

Although Cuban filmmakers work under the eyes of government censors, their films contain ample criticism of the socialist revolution they often lovingly depict. As some writers have observed, many Cuban artists and directors have supported censorship because they feel constructive criticism is accepted. Making their socialist society better by criticizing the bad and presenting other options is one thing, but proposing an end to the revolution, in their eyes is another. Cuban cinema has been called nationalistic, but patriotic tendencies can be traced through the films of many nations, especially those of the United States.

And as Canadian filmmaker Denys Arcand learned, censorship is not always about the failure to express a political opinion, but can also be personal, such as when an individual declines to express an emotion. This was the point the director tried to express in his film *Barbarian Invasions* (2003). In the film, he tried to repair his own past through a dialogue between a son and his father. As the director, he could make the son say that he loved his father.

CONCLUSION

By 2007, global cinema had demonstrated its enduring value and essential qualities. Three of the five films nominated for an Academy Award for best-director were foreign filmmakers ("Oscars Go Global" 2007), and many films that won Oscars included international participation. With seven nominations, including best picture, Mexican director Alejandro Gonzalez Inarritu's film *Babel* links families on three continents to a tragic event in the African desert. Brad Pitt and Australia's Cate Blanchett were the featured stars, but Mexico's

Adriana Barraza and Japan's Rinko Kikuchi both received nominations for best supporting actress.

The participation of global directors, talent, and locations comes at a significant moment in America's media culture. News reporting featuring global events and cultures diminished significantly during the last two decades of the twentieth century, making the filmic representation of the world all the more important. Films are also one of the only avenues open where people from other cultures speak in their own voices and construct their own images. In addition, world cinema is thriving at a time of declining interest in going to the movie in the United States, the once most dominant form of the American popular arts experience.

Indeed, as budgets and box-office returns continue to be the measure of success in Hollywood, critics argue that films suffer. By 2007, movie attendance in America had reached its lowest point in 10 years. Though some of that decline can be attributed to the availability of video and DVDs, the two most-cited reasons for staying home were rising ticket prices and the quality of the films (Gabler 2007). Hollywood features suffer, and lose some of their magic and imagination, when marketing departments make bottom-line demands that affect creative content. Under such conditions, going to the movies is bound to lose some of its fascination. In the hands of many global filmmakers, the inspiration and practices of making movies are decidedly varied, and usually quite distinct from commercial motivations.

See also Al-Jazeera; Bollywood and the Indian Diaspora; Cultural Imperialism and Hybridity; The DVD; Global Community Media; Hypercommercialism; Independent Cinema; Nationalism and the Media; Parachute Journalism; Representations of Race; Sensationalism, Fear Mongering, and Tabloid Media.

Further Reading: Béar, Liza. *The Making of Alternative Cinema: Volume 2, Beyond the Frame: Dialogues with World Filmmakers.* Westport, CT: Praeger Publishing, 2007; Chanan, Michael. *The Cuban Image: Cinema and Cultural Politics in Cuba.* Bloomington: Indiana University Press, 1985; Chaudhuri, Shohini. *Contemporary World Cinema: Europe, the Middle East, East Asia and South Asia.* Edinburgh: Edinburgh University Press, 2006; Ezra, Elizabeth, and Terry Rowden. *Transnational Cinema: The Film Reader.* New York: Routledge, 2006; Gabler, Neal. "The Movie Magic Is Gone: Hollywood, Which Once Captured the Nerve Center of American Life, Doesn't Matter Much Anymore." *Los Angeles Times,* February 25, 2007, at http://www.latimes.com/news/opinion/commentary/la-op-gabler25feb25,0,4482096.story; Hill, John, Pamela Church Gibson, Richard Dyer, E. Ann Kaplan, and Paul Willemen, eds. *World Cinema: Critical Approaches.* London: Oxford University Press, 2000; Hjort, Mette. *Cinema and Nation.* New York: Routledge, 2000; Hoberman, J. *Vulgar Modernism: Writing on Movies and Other Media.* Philadelphia: Temple University Press, 1991; Nichols, Peter M., ed. *The New York Times Guide to the Best 1000 Movies Ever Made.* New York: Random House, 1999; "Oscars Go Global." *The Sydney Morning Harold,* January 24, 2007, at http://www.smh.com.au/articles/2007/01/24/1169594339263.html; Zaniello, Tom. *The Cinema of Globalization: A Guide to Films about the New Economic Order.* Ithaca, NY: Cornell University Press, 2007.

Robin Andersen

YOUTH AND MEDIA USE

Communications technology has come a long way. E-mail, instant messaging, blogs, and other new features in communications technology have all revolutionized the way the world communicates on a fundamental level. But no group of people has these tools mastered more than young people. As a population, youth have traditionally been presumed to play a passive role in mass media, perceived as sponges at the mercy of media messages, and absent from the production process. Yet today's rapidly changing communications environment has been cause for some to believe the role of youth in mass media is no longer as one-sided. Has the relationship between mass media and youth really changed? And if it has, how so?

Young people have historically played an interesting, yet for the most part static role in the public policy of mass communications. The dominant tradition behind discussions of youth and media, particularly in the United States, has been that of studying "effects." For many years, the prevailing school of thought asked what the impact of media messages was on young impressionable minds. As a group primarily observed by adults and the like, youth and their relationship with media have been largely misunderstood, and for good reason: young people live in a complex, rapidly changing environment, and today's communications environment is no different.

Attempting to describe youth generations, particularly that of today, poses a great challenge. Historically, research on children or youth has more often than not considered this population in negative rather than positive terms. And when displayed in a positive light, they are too often thought of merely as "someone who is *not* taking drugs or using alcohol, is *not* engaging in unsafe sex, and is

YOUTH MEDIA

Youth media programs are on the rise, both in number and prevalence. The National Federation for Community Broadcasters holds a nationwide conference, each year in a different location. Since the late 1990s one of the key features of this conference has been the National Youth in Radio Training Project (NYRTP). The program brings young people working in radio and other media formats together for skills and leadership training, and to meet other young people producing media content. This has been just one example of the increasing presence of youth in mass media. With support from local communities, youth media programs are being developed in more than half the country. In 2005, 31 states were found to be directly served by a youth media program. Of the programs currently in existence, Youth Radio has been a leader and set a number of standards for many other aspiring programs. Today, the organization offers training in radio production, video production, music production, and web design. Youth Radio is a prime example of what youth media are doing in the United States. Yet the idea and progress is growing worldwide. Your World Your Voice is an organization that brings the many varieties of youth media programs worldwide together, allowing an open exchange of perspectives, opinions, and self-expression on a host of issues affecting young people throughout the world, from health care to artistic expression. Youth media today can be described as a movement, encouraging young people to take action and become active participants in their communities, both local and global. Not all young people are fortunate enough to have these services at their disposal. And many who do not take advantage. Yet for those who do engage in these programs, the benefits can be felt for the participants as well as their respective communities, ranging from personal levels of achievement, all the way to changes in public policy.

not participating in crime or violence" (Lerner 2004, p. 1). But youth are a multidimensional, complex, and sophisticated segment of the population, as much as any other group of people. Here, we consider how media portray youth, how this unique population selects and consumes media, their media of choice, and how more and more young people are producing media themselves.

IMAGES OF YOUTH

George Bernard Shaw once said, "Youth is a wonderful thing. What a crime to waste it on children." Media images of youth have for too long relied on the traditional effects perspective that young people are lacking in positive contribution to society. In 1995, Youth Vision held focus groups with 80 Chicago adults to explore the sources of adult hostility toward youths. Adults' attitudes cited "gangs, drugs, sex, and a general feeling that youth are out of control," that youths have no respect for adults, and that teens in groups look threatening. Most felt that media played an important role in informing these opinions. Unfortunately, media messages appeared to be distorting adult perceptions. While youths accounted for 16 percent of murder arrests and 9 percent of homicides, they accounted for 48 percent of the stories on violence as a public issue. National crime and violence stories painted the same image. In this case, the press overplayed youth violence 3 to 20 times more than what youth actual contributed to murder arrest rates (Males 1998, pp. 281–82).

Neil Howe and William Strauss are scholars of historical trends. They identify a pattern in which most Americans figure that history generally moves in straight lines. Many people blame the failures and problems of their own generation on the generations that follow them. Howe and Strauss, as well as other scholars of youth, have shown that history in this case does not repeat itself. Younger generations are overall achieving far greater success in almost all areas of life—you just wouldn't know it from most common sources of news or information. Just a few high-risk indicators illustrate the progress. The United States has enjoyed a plunge in youth crime, the speed and distance of which has no precedent since the birth of modern data. From 1993 to 1998, the rate of murders committed by youth aged 12 to 17 fell by 56 percent, and the teen murder-victimization rate fell by almost the same. Violent deaths at schools declined from a high of 55 in the 1992–93 school year to 25 in 1998–99. From 1993 to 1998, the rate for all serious violent crimes committed by youths aged 12 to 17 fell by 45 percent, and the victimization rate fell nearly as much (38 percent). With respect to education, standardized measurements show progress. Measured by the National Assessment of Educational Progress (NAEP, or "Nape"), millennial 9- to 13-year-olds are doing as well or better in math and science than any Gen Xer did at that age. Though verbal skills show less-clear trends, millennials are now writing as well as Gen Xers in the early 1980s and a bit better than Boomers in the early 1970s. Additionally, all ethnic groups are improving faster than the average for all other groups. From 1973 to 1996 white students increased by 3 scale points, blacks by 16, and Latinos by 18 (Howe and Strauss 2000, pp. 162–206).

MARGINALIZED, NOT APATHETIC

One of the biggest factors leading to the status of youth in media is that most sources of news/information are primarily guided towards adults. A study released by the Pew Research Center for the People and the Press claimed that young people read the newspaper, watch television news, and listen to news on the radio at much lower rates than their older counterparts. To many of us, this isn't so surprising. But beneath the veneer of common knowledge lies a good reason. When exposed to typical news programming, "students can be seen struggling to connect the 'political' dimensions of their everyday experiences with the official discourse of politics encountered through the media" (Buckingham 2000b, p. 203).

We must see how programs define the interests of young people, address and target their audience through the use of visual and verbal language, and finally, consider whose voices are heard within these programs and how they are sanctioned to speak. The common perception that young people are disengaged and apathetic about news, politics, and civic engagement may be no truer for young people than it is for all age groups.

RELEVANCY, LANGUAGE, AND FRAMING

When political messages are targeted at young voters, addressing the concerns and issues specific to young people and speaking the language of the youth, youth audiences are easily engaged. Young people can and do participate in politics and select news media if they can find a way to connect with it. Rather than assuming those absent from the news media audience could not care less about the political process and how it affects them, we might instead ask how media enable viewers to define their relationship with the public. Young people choose to get their political information less through the usual adult news sources, and have turned to comedy shows, Internet Web sites, and chat rooms. Despite a dramatic decline between 2000 and 2004 in traditional news sources, Kohut notes that there have been large increases for comedy TV shows (up from 9 percent to 21 percent), and the Internet (up from 13 percent to 20 percent). More than twice as many teens reported regularly learning something from comedy TV shows in 2004 than they did in 2000. One show that has a particular appeal to young people is *The Daily Show with Jon Stewart*. Fully 13 percent of 18- to 25-year-olds report watching the show regularly, compared with 6 percent of the general public. *The Daily Show* is a comic and edgy news show, leading some to feel that *The Daily Show* does not qualify as being "news/political." On the other hand, many feel that maybe our understanding of what is and is not "political/news" is not adequate for the changing face of programming today.

For instance, MTV has long been thought of as a music/entertainment TV channel. But this isn't always the case anymore. In some cases, MTV connects with CNN to host presidential political debates. These debates have purposely been set up to include a young audience and have a youthful feel to them. Debates like these result in large, young audience that is engaged and active in discussion. Even though the content here may be no different than that of traditional debates, the audience perspective is different. Youth participants at these types of youth-specific debates feel that candidates are more interested in them, as opposed to the traditional format. They are also more likely to believe that candidates are more interested in youth concerns, and that young people do have a say in government. Based on this, it may be the case that young people feel more connected to the political process when media make an attempt to speak in the language of young people. If this is true, and most news/political programming is directed towards adults, then young people's alienation from and cynicism about politics could be interpreted as a result of exclusion and disenfranchisement, rather than ignorance or immaturity.

YOUTH COMMUNICATIONS ENVIRONMENT: GRABBING THE BULL BY THE HORNS

Traditional news sources in many cases have marginalized youth from any potential audience. But youth still have an active relationship with a variety of media sources. The relationship between youth and the communications technology environment they live in has resulted in more choices, and a greater degree of relevancy among those choices.

The Kaiser Family Foundation's Generation: M study characterized young people's media environments in 1999 as "media rich." In 2004, an update on the original study saw dramatic changes, so much so that they decided to change the term to "media saturated." The study showed that in 2004, 99 percent of American youth had at least one television; 97 percent had their own VCR; 34 percent had their own digital recording device; 86 percent had their own computer; 12 percent had their own laptop; 13 percent had their own handheld Internet device; 74 percent had access to the Internet; and 49 percent had high-speed connections in their home. While many young people's homes do not reflect this "media-saturated" picture, the primary socioeconomic-related differences appear for computers, Internet connections, and Internet-based programs. This being said, previous young generations could not have foreseen such a world.

Young people are taking advantage of this new climate to great lengths. Nowhere is this seen more than with Internet usage. The Pew Internet and American Life project provides the most comprehensive data on the role of Internet use. According to the study, there are many reasons to believe that today's youth have the biggest impact on digital communication technology. Internet users aged 12 to 28 years old have embraced the online applications that enable communicative, creative, and social uses. Eighty-seven percent of 12- to 17-year-olds are actively online, the most prominent of any age group. When online, they are looking for interactive media. Sixty-six percent of online 12- to 17-year-olds have downloaded audio files; 31 percent of online teens actively download videos. In addition to simply connecting to the Internet, over half of online youth are active "content creators," as they "create a personal webpage; create a webpage for school, a friend, or an organization; share original content they created themselves online; or remix content found online into a new creation." One-third of online teens report sharing their own artwork, photos, stories, or videos with others via the Internet. It must be noted that the picture of youth and the Internet is not entirely positive. There have been a number of cases where the convenience and super-fast speed of communication allowed by the Internet have resulted in gratuitous, violent, and highly charged available content. We cannot say what percent of youth are utilizing the Internet for "bad" or for "good"—just as we cannot for adults—but young people are certainly finding many creative and reflective uses for new media in particular.

In addition to the role of the Internet in young people's active consumption and production of media, some traditional news sources are finding ways to incorporate youth as part of their audiences and content contributors. Youth media programs worldwide have been in existence for at least 20 years. These programs have been providing training to preschool students up to high-school students in field production, studio production, media analysis/critical viewing, and media distribution and evaluation in audio, video, animations, print, photography, and other media formats. However, among all the formats used, computer based multimedia (e.g., Web design, digital video/audio, etc.) make up that largest percentage (54 percent). Yet what may be most important is the type of programming youth are creating. Seventy-six to one hundred percent of the time, news and documentary programming make up the largest two categories of programs produced.

Youth media programs provide numerous benefits for youth consumers and participants. They prepare youth for a digital world, facilitate learning in academic subjects, offer healthy recreational activities, prepare youth for future careers, and strengthen their respective communities. Yet more important than any of these stated benefits, youth media programs give youth a voice, sometimes rare in an adult-run world. Youth media programs provide the training and venue for youth to provide for their own.

CONSIDERING CONTEXT

Many youth are defying the stereotypes of apathy so prevalent in much youth-related public policy. To be sure, not all young people are proactively taking control of this situation or engaging in civic life. Still, it is only when accounting for the fact that youth engage in a multifaceted, complex, and diverse world that we can begin to understand how youth appear in, consume, produce, and utilize media to continue their development as individuals, groups of citizens, and members of the global community.

See also Alternatives to Mainstream Media in the United States; Children and Effects; Digital Divide; Internet and Its Radical Potential; Media and Citizenship; News Satire; Online Publishing; Political Entertainment; User-Created Content and Audience Participation.

Further Reading: Buckingham, David. *After the Death of Childhood: Growing Up in the Age of Electronic Media.* London: Polity, 2000a; Buckingham, David. *The Making of Citizens: Young People, News, and Politics.* New York: Routledge, 2000b; Campbell, P. B., L. Hoey, and L. K. Perlman. *Sticking with my Dreams: Defining and Refining Youth Media in the 21st Century.* Groton, MA: Campbell-Kibler Associates, 2001; Fisherkeller, JoEllen. *Growing Up with Television: Everyday Learning among Young Adolescents.* Philadelphia: Temple University Press, 2002; Giroux, Henry A. *The Abandoned Generation.* New York: Palgrave Macmillan, 2003; Howe, Neil, and William Strauss. *Millennials Rising: The Next Great Generation.* New York: Vintage, 2000; Kohut, Andrew. "Cable and Internet Loom Large in Fragmented Political News Universe." *Pew Research Center for the People and the Press and the Pew Internet and American Life Project,* January 11, 2004; Krolikowski, Walter P., and Michael A. Oliker. *Images of Youth: Popular Culture as Educational Ideology.* New York: Peter Lang, 2001; Lerner, Richard M. *America's Youth in Crisis: Challenges and Options for Programs and Policies.* Thousand Oaks, CA: Sage, 1995; Lerner, Richard M. *Liberty: Thriving and Civic Engagement among America's Youth.* Thousand Oaks, CA: Sage, 2004; Males, Mike A. *Framing Youth: Ten Myths about the Next Generation.* Monroe, ME: Common Courage Press, 1998; Miles, Steven. *Youth Lifestyles in a Changing World.* Milton Keynes, UK: Open University Press, 2000; Roberts, Donald F., Foehr G. Ulla, and Victoria Rideout. *Generation M: Media in the Lives of 8-18 Year Olds.* Kaiser Family Foundation, March 2005; Williamson, Howard. *Youth and Policy: Contexts and Consequences.* Aldershot, UK: Ashgate, 1997.

Dov Zacharia Hirsch

BIBLIOGRAPHY

Abercrombie, Nicholas, and Brian Longhurst. *Audiences: A Sociological Theory of Performance and Imagination.* Thousand Oaks, CA: Sage, 1998.

Adorno, Theodor. *The Culture Industry: Selected Essays on Mass Culture,* ed. J. M. Bernstein. New York: Routledge, 1991.

Altheide, David, and Robert Snow. *Media Worlds in the Postjournalism Era.* New York: Aldine de Grutyer, 1991.

Altman, Rick. *Film/Genre.* London: BFI, 1999.

Andersen, Robin. *Consumer Culture and TV Programming.* Boulder, CO: Westview, 1995.

———. *A Century of Media, A Century of War.* New York: Peter Lang, 2006.

Andersen, Robin, and Lance Strate, eds. *Critical Studies in Media Commercialism.* New York: Oxford University Press, 2000.

Anderson, Bonnie. *News Flash: Journalism, Infotainment and the Bottom-Line Business of Broadcast News.* San Francisco: Jossey-Bass, 2004.

Anderson, Chris. "The Long Tail." *Wired* (2006). Available at http://www.wired.com/wired/archive/12.10/tail_pr.html.

Ang, Ien. *Desperately Seeking the Audience.* New York: Routledge, 1991.

———. *Living Room Wars: Rethinking Media Audiences for a Postmodern World.* New York: Routledge, 1996.

Armstrong, Jerome, and Markos Moulitsas Zuniga. *Crashing the Gate: Netroots, Grassroots, and the Rise of People-Powered Politics.* White River Junction, VT: Chelsea Green Publishing, 2006.

Atton, Chris. *Alternative Media.* Thousand Oaks, CA: Sage, 2002.

Bagdikian, Ben. *The New Media Monopoly.* Boston: Beacon Press, 2004.

Balnaves, Mark, James Donald, and Stephanie Hemelryk Donald. *The Penguin Atlas of Media and Information.* Harmondsworth: Penguin, 2001.

Banet-Weiser, Sarah, Cynthia Chris, and Anthony Freitas, eds. *Cable Visions: Television Beyond Broadcasting*. New York: New York University Press, 2007.

Barker, Martin, and Julian Petley, eds. *Ill Effects: The Media/violence Debate*. New York: Routledge, 2001.

Barker, Martin, Jane Arthurs, and Ramaswami Harindranath. *The Crash Controversy: Censorship Campaigns and Film Reception*. New York: Wallflower, 2001.

Barnouw, Erik. *Documentary: A History of the Non-Fiction Film*. New York: Oxford University Press, 1993.

———. *Tube of Plenty: The Evolution of American Television*. New York: Oxford University Press, 1975.

Barthes, Roland. *Mythologies*. New York: Hill and Wang, 1976.

Baudrillard, Jean. *In the Shadow of the Silent Majorities or, The End of the Social and Other Essays*, trans. Paul Foss, John Johnston, and Paul Patton. New York: Semiotext(e), 1983.

———. *Simulations*, trans. Paul Foss, Paul Patton, and Philip Beitchman. New York: Semiotext(e), 1983.

Bellamy, R. V., Jr., and J. R. Walker, eds. *Television and the Remote Control: Grazing on a Vast Wasteland*. New York: Guilford, 1996.

Bennett, Tony, and Janet Woollacott. *Bond and Beyond: The Political Career of a Popular Hero*. London: MacMillan, 1987.

Bennett, W. Lance. *The Politics of Illusion*, 6th ed. New York: Pearson, 2005.

Berger, Arthur Asa. *Ads, Fads, and Consumer Culture*, New York: Rowman and Littlefield, 2004.

Berger, John. *Ways Of Seeing*. New York: Penguin Books, 1974.

Bird, S. Elizabeth. *The Audience in Everyday Life: Living in a Media World*. New York: Routledge, 2003.

Blackman, Lisa, and Valerie Walkerdine. *Mass Hysteria: Critical Psychology and Media Studies*. London: Palgrave, 2001.

Bobo, Jacqueline, ed. *Black Feminist Cultural Criticism*. Malden, MA: Blackwell, 2001.

Boddy, William. *New Media and Popular Imagination: Launching Radio, Television, and Digital Media in the United States*. New York: Oxford University Press, 2004.

Bogart, Leo. *Commercial Culture: The Media System and the Public Interest*. New York: Oxford University Press, 1995.

Boorstin, Daniel. *The Image: A Guide to Pseudo Events in America*. New York: Atheneum, 1961.

Bordo, Susan. *Unbearable Weight: Feminism, Western Culture, and the Body*. Berkeley: University of California Press, 1993.

Bordwell, David, and Kristin Thompson. *Film History; an Introduction*, 2nd ed. New York: McGraw-Hill, 2004.

Bourdieu, Pierre. *Distinction: A Social Critique of the Judgement of Taste*, trans. Richard Nice. New York: Routledge and Kegan Paul, 1984.

Briggs, Asa, and Peter Burke. *A Social History of the Media: From Gutenberg to the Internet*. New York: Polity, 2002.

Brooker, Will. *Using the Force: Creativity, Community and Star Wars Fans*. New York: Continuum, 2002.

Brooks, Tim, and Earle Marsh. *The Complete Directory to Prime Time Network and Cable TV Shows 1946-Present*. New York: Ballantine, 1999.

Brunsdon, Charlotte. *Screen Tastes: Soap Operas and Satellite Dishes.* New York: Routledge, 1997.

Bryant, Jennings, and Dolf Zillman, eds. *Media Effects: Advances in Theory and Research,* Mahwah, NJ: Lawrence Erlbaum, 1994.

Buckingham, David. *After the Death of Childhood: Growing Up in the Age of Electronic Media.* New York: Polity, 2000.

———. *The Making of Citizens: Young People, News and Politics.* New York: Routledge, 2000.

———, ed. *Teaching Popular Culture: Beyond Radical Pedagogy.* London: University College of London Press, 1998.

Bud, Michael, Steve Craig, and Clay Steinman. *Consuming Environments: Television and Commercial Culture.* New Jersey: Rutgers University Press, 1999.

Byerly, Carolyn M., and Karen Ross. *Women and Media: A Critical Introduction.* Malden, MA: Blackwell, 2006.

Caldwell, John Thornton. *Televisuality: Style, Crisis, and Authority in American Television.* New Brunswick, NJ: Rutgers University Press, 1995.

Cantoni, Lorenzo, and Stefano Tardini. *Internet.* New York: Routledge, 2006.

Carey, James W. *Communication as Culture: Essays on Media and Society.* Boston: Unwin Hyman, 1990.

Carilli, Theresa, and Jane Campbell. *Women and the Media: Diverse Perspectives.* New York: University Press of America, 2005.

Carter, Cynthia, and Linda Steiner, eds. *Critical Readings: Media and Gender.* Maidenhead: Open University Press, 2004.

Caves, Richard E. *Creative Industries: Contracts Between Art and Commerce.* Cambridge, MA: Harvard University Press, 2000.

Christians, Clifford, and Michael Traber, eds. *Communication Ethics and Universal Values.* Thousand Oaks, CA: Sage Publications, 1997.

Cohen, Elliot D., ed. *News Incorporated: Corporate Media Ownership and Its Threat to Democracy.* Amherst, NY: Prometheus, 2005.

Cohen, Jeff. *Cable News Confidential: My Misadventures in Corporate Media.* New York: Polipoint Press, 2006

Cole, Ellen, and Jessica Henderson Daniel, eds. *Featuring Females: Feminist Analyses of Media.* Washington, DC: American Psychological Association, 2005.

Combs, James E., and Sara T. Combs. *Film Propaganda and American Politics: An Analysis and Filmography.* New York: Garland, 1994.

Couldry, Nick. *Media Rituals: A Critical Approach.* New York: Routledge, 2003.

Couldry, Nick, and James Curran, eds. *Contesting Media Power: Alternative Media in a Networked World.* Lanham, MD: Rowman and Littlefield, 2003.

Couldry, Nick, Sonia Livingstone, and Tim Markham. *Media Consumption and Public Engagement: Beyond the Presumption of Attention.* Basingstoke: Palgrave, 2007.

Creeber, Glen. *Serial Television: Big Drama on the Small Screen.* London: BFI, 2004.

Creedon, Pamela J., ed. *Women, Media and Sport,* Thousand Oaks, CA: Sage, 1994.

Croteau, David R., and William Hoynes. *Media/Society: Industries, Images and Audiences,* 2nd ed. Thousand Oaks, CA: Pine Forge Press, 2002.

———. *The Business of Media: Corporate Media and the Public Interest,* 2nd ed. Thousand Oaks, CA: Pine Forge Press, 2006.

Curran, James, ed. *Media Organisations in Society.* London: Arnold, 2000.

Curran, James, and Michael Gurevitch, eds. *Mass Media and Society,* 2nd ed. New York: St. Martin's Press, 1996.

Curtin, Patricia, and T. Kenn Gaither. *International Public Relations: Negotiating Culture, Identity, and Power.* Thousand Oaks, CA: Sage, 2007.

Dahlgren, Peter. *Television and the Public Sphere: Citizenship, Democracy and the Media.* Thousand Oaks, CA: Sage, 1995.

Dahlgren, Peter, and Colin Sparks, eds. *Communication and Citizenship: Journalism and the Public Sphere in the New Media Age.* New York: Routledge, 1991.

Danesi, Marcel. *Brands.* New York: Routledge, 2006.

Davis, Angela, and Neferti X. M. Tadiar, eds. *Beyond the Frame: Women of Color and Visual Representation.* New York: Palgrave MacMillan, 2005.

Davis, Richard. *Politics Online: Blogs, Chatrooms, and Discussion Groups in American Democracy.* New York: Routledge, 2005.

Dayan, Daniel, and Katz, Elihu. *Media Events: The Live Broadcasting in History.* Cambridge: Harvard University Press, 1994.

Debord, Guy. *The Society of the Spectacle,* trans. Donald Nicholson-Smith. New York: Zone, 1995.

de Burgh, Hugo. *Making Journalists: Diverse Models, Global Issues.* New York: Routledge, 2005.

Diamond, Edwin, and Stephen Bates. *The Spot: The Rise of Political Advertising on Television.* Cambridge: MIT Press, 1992.

Douglas, Susan J., and Meredith W. Michaels. *The Mommy Myth: The Idealization of Motherhood and How it Has Undermined Women.* New York: Free Press, 2004.

Downie, Leonard Jr., and Robert G. Kaiser. *The News About the News: American Journalism in Peril.* New York: Vintage, 2003.

Downing, John D. H. *Radical Media: Rebellious Communication and Social Movements.* Thousand Oaks, CA: Sage, 2001.

Downing, John D. H., and Charles Husband. *Representing Race: Racisms, Ethnicity and the Media.* Thousand Oaks, CA: Sage, 2005.

Downing, John D. H., Ali Mohammadi, and Annabelle Sreberny-Mohammadi, eds. *Questioning the Media: A Critical Introduction,* 2nd ed. Thousand Oaks, CA: Sage Publications, 1995.

Duckworth, William. *Virtual Music: How the Web Got Wired for Sound.* New York: Routledge, 2006.

duGay, Paul, ed. *Production of Culture/Cultures of Production.* Thousand Oaks, CA: Sage, 1997.

Dyer, Gillian. *Advertising as Communication.* New York: Routledge, 1982.

Ellis, John. *Visible Fictions: Cinema: Television: Video.* New York: Routledge, 1993.

———. *Seeing Things: Television in the Age of Uncertainty.* London: I. B. Tauris, 2000.

Entman, Robert M. *Projections of Power: Framing News, Public Opinion, and U.S. Foreign Policy.* Chicago: University of Chicago Press, 2003.

Ewen, Stuart. *All Consuming Images: The Politics of Style in Contemporary Culture.* New York: Basic Books, 1988.

———. *Captains of Consciousness: Advertising and the Social Roots of the Consumer Culture.* New York: McGraw-Hill, 1976.

Fishman, Mark, and Gary Cavender, eds. *Entertaining Crime: Television Reality Programs*. New York: Aldine De Gruyter, 1998.

Fiske, John. *Reading the Popular*. Boston: Unwin Hyman, 1989.

———. *Understanding Popular Culture*. Boston: Unwin Hyman, 1989.

———. *Media Matters: Race and Gender in U.S. Politics*. Minneapolis: University of Minnesota Press, 1996.

Frank, Thomas. *The Conquest of Cool: Business Culture, Counterculture, and the Rise of Hip Consumerism*. Chicago: The University of Chicago Press, 1997.

Frith, Katherine T., ed. *Undressing the Ad: Reading Culture in Advertising*. New York: Peter Lang, 1998.

Frith, Katherine T., and Barbara Mueller. *Advertising and Society: Global Issues*. New York: Peter Lang, 2003.

Gabler, Neil. *Life: The Movie: How Entertainment Conquered Reality*. New York: Vintage, 2000.

Gans, Herbert. *Deciding What's News*. New York: Pantheon, 1979.

Galician, Mary-Lou. *Sex, Love, and Romance in the Mass Media: Analysis and Criticism of Unrealistic Portrayals and Their Influence*. Mahwah, NJ: Lawrence Erlbuam, 2003.

Gauntlett, David. *Moving Experiences: Media Effects and Beyond*. Eastleigh: John Libbey, 2005.

Gillespie, Marie. *Television, Ethnicity and Cultural Change*. New York: Routledge, 1995.

Gillmor, Dan. *We the Media: Grassroots Journalism by the People, for the People*. Sebastopol, CA: O'Reilly, 2004.

Giroux, Henry A. *Disturbing Pleasures: Learning Popular Culture*. New York: Routledge, 1994.

Gitlin, Todd. *Inside Prime Time*, rev. ed. New York: Routledge, 1994.

Glynn, Kevin. *Tabloid Culture: Trash Taste, Popular Power, and the Transformation of American Television*. Durham, NC: Duke University Press, 2000.

Goldfarb, Brian. *Visual Pedagogy: Media Cultures in and beyond the Classroom*. Durham, NC: Duke University Press, 2001.

Goldman, Robert, and Stephen Papson. *Sign Wars: The Cluttered Landscape of Advertising*. New York: Guilford Press, 1996.

Goldstein, Tom. *Killing the Messenger: 100 Years of Media Criticism*. New York: Columbia University Press, 2007.

Goodman, Amy, and David Goodman. *Static: Government Liars, Media Cheerleaders, and the People Who Fight Back*. New York: Hyperion, 2006.

Gray, Herman. *Watching Race: Television and the Struggle for "Blackness."* Minneapolis: University of Minnesota Press, 2002.

Gray, Jonathan. *Watching with The Simpsons: Television, Parody, and Intertextuality*. New York: Routledge, 2006.

———. *Television Entertainment*. New York: Routledge, 2008.

Gray, Jonathan, Cornel Sandvoss, and C. Lee Harrington, eds. *Fandom: Identities and Communities in a Mediated World*. New York: New York University Press, 2007.

Gross, Larry. *Up From Invisibility: Lesbians, Gay Men, and the Media in America*. New York: Columbia University Press, 2001.

Grossberg, Lawrence, Cary Nelson, and Paula A. Treichler, eds. *Cultural Studies*. New York: Routledge, 1992.

Habermas, Jürgen. *The Structural Transformation of the Public Sphere: An Inquiry into a Category of Bourgeois Society,* trans. Thomas Burger. New York: Polity, 1989.

Hackett, Bob, and Bill Carroll. *Remaking Media: The Struggle to Democratize Public Communication.* New York: Routledge, 2006.

Hallin, Daniel. *We Keep American on Top of the World: Television, Journalism, and the Public Sphere.* New York: Routledge, 1994.

Harrington, C. Lee, and Denise D. Bielby. *Soap Fans: Pursuing Pleasure and Making Meaning in Everyday Life.* Philadelphia: Temple University Press, 1996.

Harrison, Jackie. *News.* New York: Routledge, 2005.

Hartley, John. *Understanding News.* New York: Routledge, 1982.

———. *Popular Reality: Journalism, Modernity, Popular Culture.* London: Arnold, 1996.

———. *The Uses of Television.* New York: Routledge, 1999.

———, ed. *Creative Industries.* Malden, MA: Blackwell, 2005.

Hebdige, Dick. *Subculture: The Meaning of Style.* London: Methuen, 1979.

Helford, Elyce Rae. *Fantasy Girls: Gender in the New Universe of Science Fiction and Fantasy Television.* New York: Rowman and Littlefield, 2000.

Hendershot, Heather. *Saturday Morning Censors: Television Regulation Before the V-Chip.* Durham, NC: Duke University Press, 1998.

Hentoff, Nat. *Freedom of Speech for Me But Not for Thee: How the American Left and Right Relentlessly Censor Each Other.* New York: HarperCollins, 1992.

Herman, Edward S., and Noam Chomsky. *Manufacturing Consent: The Political Economy of the Mass Media.* New York: Pantheon, 1988.

Herman, Edward S., and Robert W. McChesney. *The Global Media: The New Missionaries of Global Capitalism.* London: Cassell, 1997.

Hermes, Joke. *Reading Women's Magazines: An Analysis of Everyday Media Use.* New York: Polity, 1995.

Hertsgaard, Mark. *On Bended Knee: The Press and the Reagan Presidency.* New York: Farrar, Straus and Giroux, 1988.

Hesmondhalgh, David. *The Cultural Industries.* Thousand Oaks, CA: Sage, 2002.

Hilliard, Robert L., and Michael C. Keith. *Dirty Discourse: Sex and Indecency in Broadcasting,* 2nd ed. Malden, MA: Blackwell, 2007.

Hills, Matt. *Fan Cultures.* New York: Routledge, 2002.

Hilmes, Michele, ed. *The Television History Book.* London: BFI, 2004.

Hofrichter, Richard, ed. *Reclaiming The Environmental Debate: The Politics of Health in a Toxic Culture.* Boston: MIT Press, 2000.

Hoover, Stewart. *Religion in the Media Age.* New York: Routledge, 2006.

Hoover, Stewart, and Lynn Schofield Clark. *Practicing Religion in the Age of the Media: Explorations in Media, Religion, and Culture.* New York: Columbia University Press, 2002.

Horwitz, Robert Britt. *The Irony of Regulatory Reform: The Deregulation of American Telecommunications.* New York: Oxford University Press, 1989.

Hunt, Darnell, ed. *Channeling Blackness: Studies on Television and Race in America.* New York: Oxford University Press, 2005.

Inness, Sherrie A. *Tough Girls: Women Warriors and Wonder Women in Popular Culture.* Philadelphia: University of Pennsylvania Press, 1999.

Jacobson, Michael F., and Laurie Ann Mazur. *Marketing Madness: A Survival Guide for a Consumer Society.* Boulder. CO: Westview Press, 1995.

Jamieson, Kathleen Hall. *Dirty Politics: Deception, Distraction, and Democracy.* New York: Oxford University Press, 1992.

Jenkins, Henry. *Textual Poachers: Television Fans and Participating Culture.* New York: Routledge, 1992.

———. *Convergence Culture: Where Old and New Media Collide.* New York: New York University Press, 2006.

Jhally, Sut. *The Codes of Advertising: Fetishism and the Political Economy of Meaning in the Consumer Society.* New York: Routledge, 1987.

———. *The Spectacle of Accumulation: Essays in Culture, Media, and Politics.* New York: Peter Lang, 2006.

Jhally, Sut, and Justin Lewis. *Enlightened Racism: The Cosby Show, Audiences, and the Myth of the American Dream.* Oxford: Westview, 1992.

Jones, Gerard. *Honey, I'm Home! Sitcoms: Selling the American Dream.* New York: Grove Weidenfeld, 1992.

Jones, Jeffrey P. *Entertaining Politics: New Political Television and Civic Culture.* New York: Rowman and Littlefield, 2004.

Kearney, Mary Celeste. *Girls Make Media.* New York: Routledge, 2006.

Kellner, Douglas. *Media Culture.* New York: Routledge, 1995.

Kendall, Diana. *Framing Class: Media Representations of Wealth and Poverty in America.* New York: Rowman and Littlefield, 2005.

Kerr, Aphra. *The Business and Culture of Digital Games: Gamework and Gameplay.* Thousand Oaks, CA: Sage, 2006.

Khermouch, Gerry. "Special Report: The Best Global Brands." *Business Week Online,* http://www.Businessweek.com/magazine/content/02_31/63945098.htm

Kilbourne, Jean. *Can't Buy Me Love: How Advertising Changes the Way We Think and Feel.* New York: Touchstone, 1999.

Klein, Naomi. *No Logo.* New York: Picador, 2002.

Kline, Stephen. *Out of the Garden: Toys and Children's Culture in the Age of TV Marketing.* London: Verso, 1993.

Klinenberg, Eric. *Fighting for Air: The Battle to Control America's Media.* New York: Metropolitan Books, 2007.

Klinger, Barbara. *Beyond the Multiplex: Cinema, New Technologies, and the Home.* Berkeley: University of California Press, 2006.

Knightley, Phillip. *The First Casualty: The War Correspondent as Hero and Myth-Maker from the Crimea to Kosovo.* Baltimore: The Johns Hopkins University Press, 2002.

Kompare, Derek. *Rerun Nation: How Repeats Invented American Television.* New York: Routledge, 2005.

Kubey, Robert. *Creating Television: Conversations with the People Behind 50 Years of American TV.* Mahwah, NJ: Lawrence Erlbaum, 2004.

———, ed. *Media Literacy Around the World.* Edison, NJ: Transaction, 2001.

Kumar, Deepa. *Outside the Box: Corporate Media, Globalization and the UPS Strike.* Urbana, IL: University of Illinois Press, 2007.

Kunz, William M. *Culture Conglomerates: Consolidation in the Motion Picture and Television Industries.* Boulder, CO: Rowman and Littlefield, 2006.

LaMay, Craig L., and Everette Dennis. *Media and the Environment.* Washington D.C.: Island Press, 1991.

Lazere, Donald P., ed. *Reading and Writing for Civic Literacy: The Critical Citizen's Guide to Argumentative Rhetoric.* Paradigm Publishers, 2005.

Lessig, Lawrence. *Free Culture: The Nature and Future of Creativity.* New York: Penguin, 2005.

Leung, Linda. *Virtual Ethnicity: Race, Resistance and the World Wide Web.* Burlington, VT: Ashgate, 2005.

Levinson, Paul. *The Soft Edge: A Natural History and Future of the Information Revolution.* New York: Routledge, 1997.

Lewis, Jon, ed. *The End of Cinema As We Know It: American Film in the Nineties.* New York: New York University Press, 2001.

Lewis, Justin. *Constructing Public Opinion: How Political Elites Do What they Like and Why We Seem to Go Along with It.* New York: Routledge, 2001.

Lewis, Justin, and Toby Miller, eds. *Critical Cultural Policy: A Reader.* Malden, MA: Blackwell, 2002.

Lewis, Justin, Sanna Inthorn, and Karin Wahl-Jorgensen. *Citizens or Consumers? What the Media Tell Us About Political Participation.* Buckingham: Open University Press, 2005.

Lewis, Lisa A., ed. *The Adoring Audience: Fan Culture and Popular Media.* New York: Routledge, 1992.

Lewis, Peter M. *The Invisible Medium: Public, Commercial and Community Radio.* Basingstoke: MacMillan, 1989.

Lipsitz, George. *Time Passages: Collective Memory and American Popular Culture.* London: University of Minnesota Press, 1990.

Livingstone, Sonia. *Young People and New Media: Childhood and the Changing Media Environment.* Thousand Oaks, CA: Sage, 2002.

Livingstone, Sonia, and Peter Lunt. *Talk on Television.* New York: Routledge, 1994.

Lotz, Amanda. *Redesigning Women: Television After the Network Era.* Urbana: University of Illinois Press, 2006.

———. *The Television Will Be Revolutionized.* New York: New York University Press, 2007.

Lull, James, ed. *Culture in the Communication Age.* New York: Routledge, 2001.

Lyon, David. *Surveillance Society.* Milton Keynes: Open University Press, 2001.

MacDonald, J. Fred. *Television and the Red Menace: The Video Road to Vietnam.* New York: Praeger, 1985.

Macedo, Donaldo P., and Shirley R. Steinberg, eds. *International Handbook of Media Literacy.* New York: Peter Lang, 2007.

Marchand, Roland. *Advertising the American Dream: Making Way for Modernity 1920–1940.* Berkeley: University of California Press, 1985.

Marshall, P. David. *Celebrity and Power: Fame in Contemporary Culture.* Minneapolis: University of Minnesota Press, 1997.

Massing, Michael. *Now They Tell Us: The American Press and Iraq.* New York: New York Review of Books, 2004.

Mayer, Jeremy D. *Running on Race: Racial Politics in Presidential Campaigns, 1960–2000.* New York: Random House, 2002.

McAllister, Matthew. *The Commercialization of American Culture: New Advertising, Control, and Democracy.* Thousand Oaks, CA: Sage, 1996.

McCall, Jeffrey. *Viewer Discretion Advised: Taking Control of Mass Media Influences*. New York: Rowman and Littlefield, 2007.

McCarthy, Anna. *Ambient Television: Visual Culture and Public Space*. Durham, NC: Duke University Press, 2001.

McChesney, Robert W. *The Problem of the Media: US Communication Politics in the Twenty-First Century*. New York: Monthly Review, 2004.

McCourt, Tom. *Conflicting Communication Interests in America: the Case of National Public Radio*. Westport, CT: Praeger, 1999.

McEnteer, James. *Shooting the Truth: The Rise of American Political Documentaries*. Westport, CT: Praeger, 2006.

McLuhan, Marshall. *Essential McLuhan*, ed. Eric McLuhan and Frank Zingrone. Concord, ON: Anansi, 1995.

———. *Understanding Media: The Extensions of Man*. Cambridge: MIT Press, 1997.

McManus, John H. *Market-Driven Journalism: Let the Citizen Beware*. Thousand Oaks, CA: Sage, 1994.

McNair, Brian. *Introduction to Political Communication*. New York: Routledge, 1995.

———. *Cultural Chaos: Journalism and Power in a Globalised World*. New York: Routledge, 2006.

Means Coleman, Robin. *African American Viewers and the Black Situation Comedy: Situating Racial Humor*. New York: Garland, 2000.

Meehan, Eileen, and Ellen Riorden, eds. *Sex and Money*. Minneapolis: University of Minnesota Press, 2002.

Messaris, Paul. *Visual Persuasion: The Role of Images in Advertising*. Thousand Oaks, CA: Sage Publications, 1997.

Meyer, Philip. *The Vanishing Newspaper: Saving Journalism in the Information Age*. Columbia, MO: The University of Missouri Press, 2004.

Meyer, Thomas. *Media Democracy: How the Media Colonize Politics*. New York: Polity, 2002.

Meyrowitz, Joshua. *No Sense of Place: The Impact of Electronic Media on Social Behavior*. New York: Oxford University Press, 1985.

Miller, Mark Crispin, ed. *End of Story, Seeing Through Movies*. New York: Pantheon, 1990.

———. *Boxed In: The Culture of TV*. Evanston, IL: Northwestern University Press, 1988.

Miller, Toby, Nitin Govil, John McMurria, and Richard Maxwell.. *Global Hollywood 2*. London: BFI, 2005.

Mittell, Jason. *Genre and Television: From Cop Shows to Cartoons in American Culture*. New York: Routledge, 2004.

Moeller, Susan D. *Compassion Fatigue: How the Media Sell Disease, Famine, War and Death*. New York: Routledge, 1999.

Morley, David. *Television, Audiences and Cultural Studies*. New York: Routledge, 1992.

———. *Home Territories: Media, Mobility and Identity*. New York: Routledge, 2000.

Morreale, Joanne, ed. *Critiquing the Sitcom*. Syracuse, NY: Syracuse University Press, 2003.

Moulitsas, Markos, and Jerome Armstrong. *Crashing the Gates: Netroots, Grassroots, and the Rise of People-Powered Politics*. White River Junction, VT: Chelsea Green, 2007.

Mulvey, Laura. "Visual Pleasure and Narrative Cinema." *Screen* 16, no. 3 (1975): 6–19.

Murray, Susan, and Laurie Ouellette, eds. *Reality TV: Remaking Television Culture.* New York: New York University Press, 2004.

Myers, Kathy. *Understains: The Sense and Seduction of Advertising.* London: Comedia, 1986.

Myers, Marian. *News Accounts of Violence Against Women: Engendering Blame.* Thousand Oaks, CA: Sage, 1997.

———, ed. *Mediated Women: Representations in Popular Culture.* Cresskill, NJ: Hampton Press, 1999.

Nacos, Brigitte L. *Mass-Mediated Terrorism: The Central Role of the Media in Terrorism and Counterterrorism.* New York: Rowman and Littlefield, 2007.

Naficy, Hamid, ed. *Home, Exile, Homeland: Film, Media, and the Politics of Place.* New York: Routledge, 1999.

Nava, Mica, Andrew Blake, Iain MacRury, and Barry Richards, eds. *Buy This Book: Studies in Advertising and Consumption.* New York: Routledge, 1997.

Neale, Stephen. *Genre.* London: BFI, 1980.

Newcomb, Horace, ed. *Television: The Critical View*, 7th ed. New York: Oxford University Press, 2006.

Newhall, Beaumont. *The History of Photography.* New York: Museum of Modern Art, 1982.

Newman, James. *Videogames.* New York: Routledge, 2004.

O'Barr, William M. *Culture and the Ad: Exploring Otherness in the World of Advertising.* Boulder, CO: Westview, 1994.

Ong, Aihwa. *Flexible Citizenship: The Cultural Logics of Transnationality.* Durham, NC: Duke University Press, 1998.

Opel, Andy, and Donnalynn Pompper, eds. *Representing Resistance: Media, Civil Disobedience, and the Global Justice Movement.* Westport, CT: Praeger, 2004.

Ouellette, Laurie. *Viewers Like You? How Public TV Failed the People.* New York: Columbia University Press, 2002.

Parenti, Michael. *Inventing Reality: The Politics of the Mass Media.* New York: St. Martin's Press, 1986.

Park, David J. *Conglomerate Rock: The Music Industry's Quest to Divide Music and Conquer Wallets.* New York: Rowman and Littlefield, 2007.

Parks, Lisa, and Shanti Kumar, eds. *Planet TV: A Global Television Reader.* New York: New York University Press, 2002.

Pearson, Roberta, and Willaim Uricchio, eds. *The Many Lives of the Batman: Critical Approaches to a Superhero and His Media.* New York: Routledge, 1991.

Peters, John Durham. *Speaking into the Air: A History of the Idea of Communication.* Chicago: University of Chicago Press, 1999.

Petracca, Michael, and Madeleine Sorapure, eds. *Common Culture: Reading and Writing About American Popular Culture*, 3rd ed. New York: Prentice Hall, 2000.

Postman, Neil. *Amusing Ourselves to Death: Public Discourse in the Age of Show Business.* London: Penguin, 1986.

Potter, James W. *Media Literacy*, 3rd ed. Thousand Oaks, CA: Sage, 2005.

Preston, Ivan L. *The Tangled Web They Weave: Truth, Falsity, and Advertisers.* Madison: University of Wisconsin Press, 1994.

Quart, Alissa. *Branded: The Buying and Selling of Teenagers.* Cambridge, MA: Perseus Publishing, 2003.

Rapping, Elayne. *The Looking Glass World of Nonfiction Television.* Boston: South End Press, 1987.

Rennie, Ellie. *Community Media: A Global Introduction.* Lanham, MD: Rowman and Littlefield, 2006.

Riegert, Kristina, ed. *Politicotainment: Television's Take on the Real.* New York: Peter Lang, 2007.

Ross, Karen. *Women, Politics, Media: Uneasy Relations in Comparative Perspective.* Cresskill, NJ: Hampton Press, 2002.

Rushkoff, Douglas. *Coercion: Why We Listen to What "They" Say.* New York: Riverhead Books, 1999.

Rutter, Jason, and Jo Bryce, eds. *Understanding Digital Games.* Thousand Oaks, CA: Sage, 2006.

Sadler, Roger L. *Electronic Media Law.* Thousand Oaks, CA: Sage, 2005.

Sandvoss, Cornel. *Fans: The Mirror of Consumption.* New York: Polity, 2005.

Schatz, Thomas. *Hollywood Genres: Formulas, Filmmaking, and the Studio System.* New York: Random House, 1981.

Schechter, Harold. *Savage Pastime: A Cultural History of Violent Entertainment.* New York: St. Martin's Press, 2005.

Schiller, Dan. *How to Think About Information.* Urbana, IL: University of Illinois Press, 2006.

Schiller, Herbert I. *Culture Inc.: The Corporate Takeover of Public Expression.* New York: Oxford University Press, 1989.

———. *Mind Managers.* Boston: Beacon Press, 1973.

Schlesinger, Phillip, Rebecca E. Dobash, Russell P. Dobash, and C. K. Weaver. *Women Viewing Violence.* London: BFI, 1992.

Schudson, Michael. *Discovering the News: A Social History of American Newspapers.* New York: Basic Books, 1978.

Seib, Philip. *The Global Journalist: News and Conscience in a World of Conflict.* New York: Rowman and Littlefield, 2002.

Seiter, Ellen. *Sold Separately: Children and Parents in Consumer Culture.* New Brunswick, NJ: Rutgers University Press, 1993.

———. *Television and New Media Audiences.* Oxford: Clarendon, 1999.

———. *Internet Playground: Children's Access, Entertainment, and Mis-Education.* New York: Peter Lang, 2005.

Semonche, John E. *Censoring Sex: A Historical Journey Through American Media.* New York: Rowman and Littlefield, 2007.

Shanahan, James, and Michael Morgan. *Television and its Viewers: Cultivation Theory and Research.* Cambridge: Cambridge University Press, 1999.

Shoemaker, Pamela J., and Akiba A. Cohen. *News Around the World: Content, Practitioners, and the Public.* New York: Routledge, 2005.

Siegel, Paul. *Communication Law in America.* New York: Rowman and Littlefield, 2007.

Signorielli, Nancy, and Michael Morgan, eds. *Cultivation Analysis: New Directions in Media Effects Research.* Newbury Park, CA: Sage, 1990.

Silverblatt, Art. *Media Literacy: Keys to Interpreting Media Messages,* 2nd ed. Westport, CT: Greenwood, 2001.

Silverstone, Roger. *Television and Everyday Life.* New York: Routledge, 1994.

———. *Why Study the Media?* Thousand Oaks, CA: Sage, 1999.

———. *Media and Morality: On the Rise of the Mediapolis.* Cambridge: Polity, 2006.

Skewes, Elizabeth A. *Message Control: How News is Made on the Presidential Campaign Trail.* New York: Rowman and Littlefield, 2007.

Solomon, Norman. *War Made Easy: How Presidents and Pundits Keep Spinning Us to Death.* New York: John Wiley and Sons, 2005.

Solove, Daniel. *The Digital Person: Technology and Privacy in the Information Age.* New York: New York University Press, 2004.

Sperber, A. M. *Murrow: His Life and Times.* New York: Fordham University Press, 1998.

Spigel, Lynn, and Jan Olsson, eds. *Television After TV: Essays on a Medium in Transition.* Durham, NC: Duke University Press, 2004.

Sproule, J. Michael. *Propaganda and Democracy: The American Experience of Media and Mass Persuasion.* Cambridge: Cambridge University Press, 1997.

Starr, Paul. *The Creation of the Media: Political Origins of Modern Communications.* New York: Basic Books, 2004.

Stauber, John, and Sheldon Rampton. *Toxic Sludge Is Good for You! Lies, Damn Lies and the Public Relations Industry.* Monroe, ME: Common Courage Press, 1995.

Stephens, Mitchell. *The Rise of the Image The Fall of the Word.* New York: Oxford University Press, 1998.

Straubhaar, Joseph D. *World Television: From Global to Local.* Thousand Oaks, CA: Sage, 2007.

Street, John. *Mass Media, Politics and Democracy.* London: Palgrave, 2001.

Streeter, Thomas. *Selling the Air: A Critique of the Policy of Commercial Broadcasting in the United States.* Chicago: University of Chicago Press, 1996.

Tedford, Thomas, and Dale Herbeck. *Freedom of Speech in the United States.* State College, PA: Strata, 2005.

Thornton, Sarah. *Club Culture: Music, Media and Subcultural Capital.* New York: Polity, 1995.

Thussu, Daya Kishan. *International Communication: Continuity and Change,* 2nd ed. London: Hodder Arnold, 2006.

———, ed. *Media on the Move: Global Flow and Contra-Flow.* New York: Routledge, 2006.

Thussu, Daya Kishan, and Des Freedman, eds. *War and the Media.* Thousand Oaks, CA: Sage, 2003.

Tinic, Serra. *On Location: Canada's Television Industry in a Global Market.* Toronto: University of Toronto Press, 2005.

Tomlinson, John. *Cultural Imperialism.* Baltimore: Johns Hopkins University Press, 1991.

Tunstall, Jeremy. *The Media Were American: US Mass Media in Decline.* New York: Oxford University Press, 2007.

Turner, Graeme. *Understanding Celebrity.* Thousand Oaks, CA: Sage, 2004.

Turow, Joseph. *Media Today: An Introduction to Mass Communication.* New York: Houghton Mifflin, 2003.

Turow, Joseph. *Niche Envy: Marketing Discrimination in the Digital Age.* Cambridge: MIT Press, 2006.

Vaidhyanathan, Siva. *Copyrights and Copywrongs: The Rise of Intellectual Property and How it Threatens Creativity.* New York: New York University Press, 2001.

Valdivia, Angharad N. *Feminism, Multiculturalism, and the Media: Global Diversities.* Thousand Oaks: Sage, 1995.

van de Donk, Wim, Brian D. Loader, and Dieter Rucht, eds. *Cyberprotest: New Media, Citizens, and Social Movements.* New York: Routledge, 2004.

van Dijk, Jan A. G. M. *The Deepening Divide: Inequality in the Information Society.* Thousand Oaks, CA: Sage, 2005.

van Zoonen, Liesbet. *Entertaining the Citizen: When Politics and Popular Culture Converge.* New York: Rowman and Littlefield, 2004.

Wasko, Janet. *How Hollywood Works.* Thousand Oaks, CA: Sage Publications, 2003.

———. *Understanding Disney: The Manufacture of Fantasy.* Cambridge: Polity Press, 2001.

Webster, James G., and Patricia F. Phalen. *The Mass Audience: Rediscovering the Dominant Model.* Mahwah, NJ: Lawrence Erlbaum, 1997.

Williams, Raymond. *Television: Technology and Cultural Form.* London: Routledge Classics, 2003.

Williamson, Judith. *Decoding Advertisements: Ideology and Meaning.* London: Marion Boyars, 1978.

Wolf, Mark J. P., and Bernard Perron, eds. *The Videogame Theory Reader.* New York: Routledge, 2003.

ABOUT THE EDITORS
AND CONTRIBUTORS

Robin Andersen is Professor of Communication and Media Studies and Director of the Peace and Justice Studies Program at Fordham University. She is author of *Consumer Culture and TV Programming* and *A Century of Media, A Century of War* and coeditor of *Critical Studies in Media Commercialism*.

Jonathan Gray is Assistant Professor of Communication and Media Studies at Fordham University. He is author of *Watching with The Simpsons: Television, Parody, and Intertextuality* and *Television Entertainment*, and editor (with Cornel Sandvoss and C. Lee Harrington) of *Fandom: Identities and Communities in a Mediated World* and the quarterly journal *Popular Communication: The International Journal of Media and Culture*.

Steve Anderson is the founder of the Center For Information Awareness, a nonprofit media organization that publishes *COA News*, among other activities. Steve is also an online video producer and is currently a graduate student at the Simon Fraser School of Communication, studying participatory online media, political economy of online media, public service media, media funding models, and telecommunications policy.

Mark Andrejevic is a Research Fellow at the Centre for Critical and Cultural Studies at the University of Queensland and Associate Professor in the Department of Communication Studies at the University of Iowa. He is the author of *Reality TV: The Work of Being Watched* and *iSpy: Surveillance and Power in the Interactive Era*.

Amy Aronson is Assistant Professor of Journalism and Media Studies at Fordham University. She is the author of *Taking Liberties: Early American Women's*

Magazines and Their Readers, and an editor of the quarterly journal, *Media History*. A former editor at *Working Woman* and *Ms.*, she has also coedited a centennial edition of Gilman's *Women & Economics* and the two-volume *Encyclopedia of Men and Masculinities*, which won a Best of Reference Award from the New York Public Library in 2004.

Ivan Askwith is a graduate of MIT's Comparative Media Studies Program, an affiliated researcher with MIT's Convergence Culture Consortium, and a Creative Strategist with Brooklyn-based creative agency Big Spaceship. He is also a contributor to such publications as *Salon* and *Slate*, on topics including post-broadcast television, popular culture, and audience engagement.

Aaron Barlow teaches English at New York City College of Technology (CUNY). He is the author of *The DVD Revolution: Movies, Culture and Technology; The Rise of the Blogosphere*; and *Blogging America: The New Public Sphere*.

Jack Z. Bratich is Assistant Professor of Journalism and Media Studies at Rutgers University. He has written articles that apply autonomist social theory to such topics as audience studies, reality TV, political intellectuals, and popular secrecy. His book, *Conspiracy Panics: Popular Culture and Political Rationality*, will be published in 2008.

Lisa Brooten is an Assistant Professor at Southern Illinois University Carbondale, College of Mass Communications and Media Arts, Department of Radio-Television, and a member of the Advisory Board of SIU's Global Media Research Center. She has published on gender and media; alternative and community media; and indigenous media and social movements.

Patrick Burkart is an Assistant Professor of Communication at Texas A&M University, and coauthor of *Digital Music Wars: Ownership and Control of the Celestial Jukebox* (with Tom McCourt). He researches and teaches in the areas of telecommunications and media studies.

Jane Caputi is Professor of Women's Studies at Florida Atlantic University. She is the author of *The Age of Sex Crime; Gossips, Gorgons, and Crones: The Fates of the Earth*; and *Goddesses and Monsters: Women, Myth, Power, and Popular Culture*. She also has made an educational documentary, *The Pornography of Everyday Life* (www.berkeleymedia.com).

Kristina Chew is Assistant Professor of Classics in the Department of Modern and Classical Languages at Saint Peter's College. She writes a daily blog, Autism Vox, and is writing a book about autism education and the classics.

Mike Chopra-Gant is a Senior Lecturer in Media and Cultural Studies at London Metropolitan University, where he is also the convenor of the university's American Popular Culture research group. He has published several articles on gender, film, and television and is the author of two books, *Hollywood Genres and Postwar America* and *Cinema and History*.

Kate Coyer is a postdoctoral research fellow with the Annenberg School for Communication at the University of Pennsylvania and Central European University (CEU) in Budapest. She has been producing radio and organizing media campaigns for the past 20 years and has helped build community radio stations in the United States and Tanzania with the Prometheus Radio Project. She is coeditor of the *Handbook of Alternative Media* and the author of numerous chapters and articles.

Garry Crawford is a Senior Lecturer in Sociology at the University of Salford. His research focuses primarily on media audiences and fan cultures. In particular, he has published on sport fan culture, including the book *Consuming Sport: Sports, Fans and Culture*, and more recently, on digital gaming patterns. He is review editor for *Cultural Sociology*.

John D.H. Downing is Director of the Global Media Research Center in the College of Mass Communication and Media Arts at Southern Illinois University, Carbondale. His most recent books are *Radical Media: Rebellious Communication and Social Movements*; the *Sage Handbook of Media Studies,* of which he is editor-in-chief; and *Representing "Race,"* coauthored with Charles Husband. Previous books include *Film and Politics in the Third World*; *Questioning the Media: A Critical Introduction*; and *Internationalizing Media Theory*. He has also recently published a series of shorter studies of the global Independent Media Center movement, is editing an encyclopedia of social movement media, and is an editor of the new journal *Global Media and Communication*.

Diane Farsetta is the Senior Researcher at the Center for Media and Democracy (CMD), a nonprofit media watchdog group that focuses on the public relations industry. She heads CMD's "No Fake News" campaign and coauthored two investigative multimedia reports on video news releases, "Fake TV News" and "Still Not the News." She also contributes to WIMN's Voices, a group blog hosted by Women In Media & News, and hosts radio news and public affairs shows on Pacifica Network affiliate WORT in Madison, Wisconsin.

Katherine Frith is Associate Professor of Communication and Information at Southern Illinois University. Her books include *Advertising in Asia: Communication, Culture and Consumption*; *Undressing the Ad: Reading Culture in Advertising*; and (with Barbara Mueller) *Advertising and Societies: Global Issues*; and she has published in multiple collections and journals.

Brian Goldfarb is a digital media artist, curator, and Associate Professor of Communication at the University of California, San Diego. His research and creative production focuses on media studies and contemporary visual and digital culture. He is the author of *Visual Pedagogy: Media Cultures in and beyond the Classroom*. His current projects include *Global Tourette*, a digital documentary and transnational media exchange project.

Tom Goldstein is Director of the Mass Communications program at the University of California at Berkeley. Goldstein, the former dean of the journalism schools at Columbia University and at Berkeley, has published widely on journalism standards. His most recent book is *Journalism and Truth*.

Joshua Green is a Postdoctoral Associate in the MIT Program in Comparative Media Studies. His work examines the future of television in a digital environment, especially the interaction between new distribution platforms, television branding strategies, and changing audience practices. He has published on user-generated content; Australian national identity and the composition of the cultural public sphere; the memorialization of Australian television; television branding and scheduling strategies; and youth media use.

Robert A. Hackett is Professor of Communication at Simon Fraser University. He co-directed NewsWatch Canada, a news media monitoring project, from 1993 to 2003, and has helped to found several community-based media action and education initiatives, including Vancouver's annual Media Democracy Day. He is coeditor of *Democratizing Global Media: One World, Many Struggles* and *The Missing News: Filters and Blind Spots in Canada's Press*, and author of *News and Dissent: The Press and Politics of Peace in Canada* and (with Yuezhi Zhao) *Sustaining Democracy: Journalism and the Politics of Objectivity*.

DeeDee Halleck is Professor Emerita in the Department of Communication at the University of California at San Diego. She is the author of *Handheld Visions: The Impossible Possibilities of Community Media*, and is founder of Paper Tiger Television and co-founder of the Deep Dish Satellite Network, the first grass-roots community television network.

Margot Hardenbergh is on the faculty of the Department of Communication & Media Studies at Fordham University. She has a background producing documentaries and public affairs programming for television and published articles and book chapters on values in the news, television history, and women in journalism.

C. Lee Harrington is Professor of Sociology and Affiliate of the Women's Studies Program at Miami University. Her areas of research include television studies, sociology of culture, and audience/fan studies. She is the coauthor of *Soap Fans: Producing Pleasure and Making Meaning in Everyday Life* and the coeditor of *Popular Culture: Production and Consumption*, both with Denise D. Bielby, and is coeditor of *Fandom: Identities and Communities in a Mediated World* with Jonathan Gray and Cornel Sandvoss.

Arthur S. Hayes, an Associate Professor with Fordham University's Communication & Media Studies Department, has published in the areas of ethnic media, journalism ethics, and media law.

Heather Hendershot is Associate Professor of Media Studies at Queens College and Director of the Film Studies Certificate Program at the CUNY Graduate Center. She is the author of *Saturday Morning Censors: Television Regulation before the V-Chip* and *Shaking the World for Jesus: Media and Conservative Evangelical Culture*. Hendershot is also editor of *Nickelodeon Nation: The History, Politics and Economics of America's Only TV Channel for Kids*.

Dov Zacharia Hirsch is Executive Director of Youth Media Worldwide and Mile High Youth Media, where he manages and coordinates an organization in the

Denver metro area that provides media training to youth in digital video and audio production, sound engineering, Web design, press coverage, and various other skills. His research analyzes the democratic potential of your media production.

John Hutnyk is Professor and Academic Director of the Centre for Cultural Studies at Goldsmiths College. He is the author of several books including *The Rumour of Calcutta: Tourism, Charity and the Poverty of Representation*, *Critique of Exotica*, and *Bad Marxism: Capitalism and Cultural Studies*.

Gwenyth Jackaway is Associate Professor of Communication and Media Studies at Fordham University. She is author of *Media at War: Radio's Challenge to the Newspapers, 1924–1939*. Her research and teaching interests include freedom of speech, children and media, and media effects.

L. S. Kim is Assistant Professor of Film and Digital Media at the University of California, Santa Cruz. Her work focuses on racial discourse, postfeminism, and intertextuality. Her current book, *Maid for Television: Race, Gender, and Class on the Small Screen*, examines the intersection of race and class relations embodied in a long history of television maids as integral (rather than marginal) to the idealized American family. She is also developing writing on "New Orientalism" (theory and criticism about cross-cultural media forms, for example, the action genre, and anime) and has published on Asian American media culture.

Jeffery Klaehn's professional work has been published in a wide range of noted scholarly journals. He is the editor of several books, including *Filtering the News: Essays on Herman and Chomsky's Propaganda Model*, *Bound by Power: Intended Consequences*, *Inside the World of Comic Books*, and *Roadblocks to Equality: Women Confronting Boundaries*.

Beth Knobel is Assistant Professor of Communication and Media Studies at Fordham University. Before joining the Fordham faculty, she spent 15 years working in Russia as a journalist, most recently as Moscow Bureau Chief for CBS News. Dr. Knobel, the winner of an Emmy and several other awards, is currently working on a book about the coverage of foreign news by U.S. network television.

Deepa Kumar is Assistant Professor of Journalism and Media Studies at Rutgers University. She is author of *Outside the Box: Corporate Media, Globalization and the UPS Strike* and has published on media and gender, war, imperialism, globalization, and class.

William M. Kunz is Associate Professor in the Interdisciplinary Arts & Sciences program at the University of Washington Tacoma. He is the author of *Culture Conglomerates: Consolidation in the Motion Picture and Television Industries*.

Paul Levinson is Professor of Communication and Media Studies at Fordham University. His books include *The Soft Edge: A Natural History and Future of the Information Revolution*, *Cellphone: The Story of the World's Most Mobile Medium*, *Realspace: The Fate of Physical Presence in the Digital Age*, and *Digital McLuhan: A Guide to the Information Age*.

Justin Lewis is Professor of Journalism, Media and Cultural Studies at Cardiff University, UK. He is author of numerous books, including *Constructing Public Opinion: How Political Elites Do What They Like and Why We Seem To Go Along With It*, (with Sanna Inthorn and Karin Wahl-Jorgensen); *Citizens or Consumers: What the Media Tell Us about Political Participation*; *Shoot First and Ask Questions Later: Media Coverage of the War in Iraq* (with Sut Jhally); *Enlightened Racism: The Cosby Show, Audiences, and the Myth of the American Dream*; *Art, Culture and Enterprise: The Politics of the Cultural Industries*; and (with Toby Miller) *Critical Cultural Policy Studies*.

James Lull is Professor Emeritus of Communication Studies at San Jose State University, California. He is author of many books including *Culture-on-Demand* and *Media, Communication, Culture*. His latest work is *The Great Chain of Communication: Evolution from Dawn to Digital*, now in press.

Ernest Mathijs is Assistant Professor of Film Studies and Drama at the University of British Columbia, Canada. He has published widely on alternative and cult cinema. His most recent books are *The Cult Film Reader* (with Xavier Mendik) and *The Cinema of David Cronenberg*.

Casey McCabe is currently pursuing her master's degree in women's studies at Florida Atlantic University. She received her bachelor of arts from the University of Connecticut in women's studies and sociology.

Tom McCourt is Associate Professor of Communication and Media Studies at Fordham University. He is author of *Conflicting Communication Interests in America: The Case of National Public Radio* and (with Patrick Burkart) *Digital Music Wars: The Ownership and Control of the Celestial Jukebox*.

Carl McKinney is a Doctoral Candidate at University of California, San Diego. His research examines the intersections of persistent, virtual worlds with political and economic systems, with a particular focus on how legal regimes shape the formation of both individual and community identity.

John McMurria is currently Assistant Professor of Communication at DePaul University. In addition to his published articles in book anthologies and journals, he is coauthor, with Toby Miller, Nitin Govil, Richard Maxwell, and Ting Wang, of *Global Hollywood 2*. He is working on a critical cultural policy history of cable television in the United States.

Jason Mittell is Assistant Professor of American Studies and Film and Media Culture at Middlebury College. He is author of *Genre and Television: From Cop Shows to Cartoons in American Culture*, as well as numerous chapters and articles, and is currently writing a textbook on television and American culture, as well as a book on narrative complexity in contemporary American television.

Nancy Morris is Associate Professor in the Department of Broadcasting, Telecommunications and Mass Media at Temple University. She is author of *Puerto Rico: Culture, Politics and Identity*, and coeditor of *Media and Globalization: Why the State Matters*.

Vincent Mosco is Professor of Sociology and Canada Research Chair in Communication and Society at Queen's University. He is the author of numerous books, articles, and policy reports on the media, telecommunications, computers, and information technology. Dr. Mosco's 2004 book, *The Digital Sublime: Myth, Power, and Cyberspace*, won the 2005 Olson Award for outstanding book in the field of rhetoric and cultural studies. His most recent book, completed with Catherine McKercher, is titled *Knowledge Workers in the Information Society*. He is also working on a revised edition of his 1996 book *The Political Economy of Communication* (with Chinese-, Korean-, and Spanish-language editions).

Tamao Nakahara received her Ph.D. from the University of California at Berkeley. Her publications include "Barred Nuns: Italian Nunsploitation Films" in *Alternative Europe* and "Making Up Monsters: Set and Costume Design in Horror Films" in *Horror Zone*. She has taught at University of California at Santa Cruz, and currently produces films and works in new media in Silicon Valley.

Philip M. Napoli is Associate Professor of Communications and Media Management and Director of the Donald McGannon Communication Research Center at Fordham University. He is author of *Media Diversity and Localism: Meaning and Metrics* and *Audience Economics: Media Institutions and the Audience Marketplace*.

Mohammed el-Nawawy is Assistant Professor and Knight-Crane Chair of Communication at Queens University of Charlotte. He is author of *The Israeli-Egyptian Peace Process in the Reporting of Western Journalists* and (with Adel Iskandar) *Al-Jazeera: The Story of the Network that Is Rattling Governments and Redefining Modern Journalism* and *Al-Jazeera: How the Free Arab News Network Scooped the World and Changed the Middle East*.

J. Scott Oberacker is a doctoral candidate in the Department of Communication at the University of Massachusetts, Amherst. He has published on documentary and public television. He is currently writing a dissertation on Michael Moore, documentary film, and the politics of representation.

Laurie Ouellette is Associate Professor in the Department of Communication Studies at the University of Minnesota, Twin Cities. She is author of *Viewers Like You? How Public TV Failed the People* and (with James Hay) *Better Living through Reality TV: Television and Post-welfare Citizenship*, and editor (with Susan Murray) of *Reality TV: Remaking Television Culture*.

Carlos Pareja is an educator, activist, and video maker who has been working since 1996 around issues involving media and culture. He has produced various videos with the Paper Tiger Television collective and facilitated media literacy and video production workshops with organizations like the Educational Video Center, Hunter and Lehman Colleges, and the Museum of Television and Radio. He has presented at various grassroots media panels and community screenings and is currently developing and managing the educational and community partnership efforts at Brooklyn Community Access Television (BCAT).

W. Allison Perlman is Lecturer of Visual Studies at Penn State Erie, where she teaches film and media courses. Her current research examines the intersection between media-reform activism and twentieth-century social movements in the United States.

Victor W. Pickard is a doctoral candidate in the Institute of Communications Research at the University of Illinois, Urbana-Champaign. His research explores the intersections of media policy, politics, and democratic theory, and has been published in a number of academic journals. Currently he is writing a dissertation on postwar U.S. communications policy.

Aswin Punathambekar is Assistant Professor in the Department of Communication Studies at the University of Michigan–Ann Arbor. He has published articles on media globalization, Bollywood, and E-governance. He is coeditor of *Mapping Bollywood: Films, Cultures, and Identities in a Global World*.

Chad Raphael is Associate Professor of Communication at Santa Clara University. He is the author of *Investigated Reporting: Muckrakers, Regulators, and the Struggle over Television Documentary*, and other research on digital media, news and politics, and environmental communication.

Jean Retzinger is a lecturer in the Group Major in Mass Communication at the University of California, Berkeley. She teaches courses in media theory and popular culture and has published on food and agriculture from an environmental communication perspective.

Tissa Richards is a graduate of University of California, Berkeley, and founder of Marketing Logix, Inc. She is Consultant and Strategist of corporate branding, positioning, and marketing.

Cornel Sandvoss is Senior Lecturer and Subject Leader in Media and Cultural Studies, University of Surrey, UK. He is author of *Fans: The Mirror of Consumption* and *A Game of Two Halves: Football Fandom, Television and Globalisation*, and editor (with Jonathan Gray and C. Lee Harrington) of *Fandom: Identities and Communities in a Mediated World* and (with Alina Bernstein and Michael Real) of *Bodies of Discourse: Sports Stars, Mass Media and the Global Public*.

David Sanjek is the Director of the BMI (Broadcast Music, Inc.) Archives. In 2008, he will publish *Always on My Mind: Music, Memory and Money* and *Stories We Could Tell: Putting Words to American Popular Music*.

Avi Santo is Assistant Professor in the Department of Communications at Old Dominion University. He is the cocreator of Flow: Television and Media Culture (www.flowtv.org) and the Co-coordinating Editor of MediaCommons: A Digital Scholarly Network (http://mediacommons.futureofthebook.org). His research interests include licensing and authoring transmedia brands, cultural constructions of heroism, and Inuit media and globalization.

Matt Soar is Assistant Professor of Communication Studies at Concordia University, Montréal. His creative and scholarly work address visual culture, cultural production, representation, media literacy, graphic design, and advertising. He has just completed "Almost Architecture," a database narrative about signs and public space.

Serra Tinic is Associate Professor of Media Studies in the Department of Sociology at the University of Alberta, Canada. She has published journal articles and book chapters on media globalization, consumer culture, and transnational television. She is also the author of *On Location: Canada's Television Industry in a Global Market*.

Michael V. Tueth, S. J., Associate Professor of Communication and Media Studies at Fordham University, has written extensively on television comedy in his book, *Laughter in the Living Room: Television Comedy and the American Home Audience*, as well as in contributions to several other books and journal articles on the subject. He also provides book and film reviews for the Jesuit weekly journal of opinion, *America*.

James VanOosting is Professor of Media Theory and Director of the Institute for Narrative Studies at Fordham University. He has published four novels and six nonfiction books. Currently, he is at work on a new novel as well as a book on narrative theory.

Christopher A. Vaughan is Associate Professor of Communications at Dominican University of California. He has been a Pulitzer Prize finalist, a foreign correspondent, a historian, a journalism and media studies educator, and a founder of a Webzine. His research interests include media history, international communication, mediated memory, media literacy and criticism, and new media. A book under contract examines the construction of the Philippines and Filipinos in U.S. media during the conquest and colonization of the Philippines.

Paul Vinelli is a graduate student in the Department of Communication at the University of California, San Diego. His research interests include privacy, data aggregation, the culture of diagnosis in medical communities, and the history of the blues.

Karin Wahl-Jorgensen is a Senior Lecturer at the Cardiff School of Journalism, Media and Cultural Studies at Cardiff University. She is interested in the relationship between journalism, democracy, and citizenship, and her work has appeared in more than 20 different international, peer-reviewed journals. She is the author of *Journalists and the Public: Newsroom Culture, Letters to the Editor, and Democracy*, and *Citizens or Consumers? What the Media Tell Us about Political Participation* (with Justin Lewis and Sanna Inthorn), and editor of *Mediated Citizenship*, and (with Thomas Hanitzsch) *Handbook of Journalism Studies*.

Brenna Wolf is MA candidate in the Communication and Social Justice program at the University of Windsor. Prior to graduate school, she worked on media activism and independent media projects for the last eight years.

Talmadge Wright is Associate Professor of Sociology at Loyola University Chicago. He has researched topics as diverse as homeless social movements and urban social policy, urban design and architecture, and mass media and popular culture. He has actively written about housing, homelessness, and homeless social movements since 1987, and continues an interest in media representations of homeless people. His current work centers on the symbolic meanings game players create in playing computer games, the social formation of gender roles, and the pleasures and anxieties of virtual violence.

Bill Yousman is Assistant Professor in the Department of Communication at Central Connecticut State University. He has published work in peer-reviewed journals and anthologies on race and popular culture, media literacy, and alternative media.

INDEX